TRUE BLUES

The Politics of Conservative Party Membership

PAUL WHITELEY

PATRICK SEYD

AND

JEREMY RICHARDSON

CLARENDON PRESS · OXFORD

Oxford University Press, Walton Street, Oxford OX2 6DP
Oxford New York
Athens Auckland Bangkok Bombay
Calcutta Cape Town Dar es Salaam Delhi
Florence Hong Kong Istanbul Karachi
Kuala Lumpur Madras Madrid Melbourne
Mexico City Nairobi Paris Singapore
Taipei Tokyo Toronto
and associated companies in
Berlin Ibadan

Oxford is a trade mark of Oxford University Press

Published in the United States
by Oxford University Press Inc., New York

British Library Cataloguing in Publication Data
Data available

Library of Congress Cataloging in Publication Data
Whiteley, Paul.
True blues : the politics of Conservative Party membership / Paul
Whiteley, Patrick Seyd, and Jeremy Richardson.
Includes bibliographical references and index.
1. Conservative Party (Great Britain) I. Seyd, Patrick.
II. Richardson, J. J. (Jeremy John) III. Title.
JN1129.C7W54 1994 324.24104—dc20 94–3535
ISBN 0–19–827785–7
ISBN 0–19–827786–5 (Pbk.)

3 5 7 9 10 8 6 4

Printed in Great Britain
on acid-free paper by
Biddles Ltd., Guildford and King's Lynn

TRUE BLUES

ACKNOWLEDGEMENTS

Our researches into the Conservative party could not have been completed without the encouragement and support of a number of people whom we are pleased to acknowledge.

First, we would like to thank the Economic and Social Research Council without whose financial support (Grant No: Y304253008) this research would have been impossible. Professor Hugh Berrington was a moving force in itemizing ESRC funds for various subsidiary election-related projects, of which this was one. His initial and subsequent interest in our project has been valuable.

Additional funds were provided by the Universities of Sheffield and Warwick Research Funds, and we are grateful to the Sheffield Research committee members for their continuing support for the party membership projects based at Sheffield.

Professor Denise Lievesley of the ESRC Data Archive at the University of Essex provided invaluable advice on sampling and on other methodological aspects of this, and the earlier Labour party survey.

Keith Britto at Conservative Central Office was enthusiastic about the project throughout; he helped steer the proposal through the various party committees and secured the support of party headquarters. In addition, he assisted us in our liaisons with the agents and officers of the local Conservative Associations. He answered all our queries and requests with unceasing patience and goodwill: we hope his commitment to independent research has been reinforced by the end-product. Jeffery Speed, Director of Constituency Services at Conservative Central Office, helpfully answered all our requests. We are particularly grateful to Lord Goold and James Goodsman for their assistance in facilitating the Scottish survey.

We are grateful to the party officers in all thirty-four Constituency Associations who participated in this research project. Without their collaboration in providing the membership lists, we could not have made the initial contact with the individual party members. Above all, however, we thank the individuals who took the time and trouble to complete the questionnaires; without their commitment, all our efforts would have been in vain. Similarly, we thank the agents and party members in the Eastleigh, Manchester Hazel Grove, and Glasgow Cathcart Constituency Associations for agreeing to collaborate in the pilot interviews from which the final questionnaires emerged in much-improved form.

Paul Bissell was the project Research Officer in day-to-day charge of the survey. His efficiency and commitment ensured its completion. A very enthusiastic group of Sheffield University undergraduates assisted at all stages of the survey. It was clear at the time that they enjoyed this practical aspect of political studies (and perhaps also the opportunity to supplement their inadequate student grants!) and we hope they learned as much from the project as we enjoyed their good humour and company. They were: Emma Carrington, Matthew Carter, Tom Fyans, Greig Goodings, Sarah Holloway, Janette King, Jason Langford, Richard Lazenby, Bryn Morgan, Dermot Mullan, Steven Palfrey, Caroline Scott, Deborah Shaller, Guy Thompson, Ian Venables, Stuart Wales, and Zoe Woodward. In addition, Alan Johnson was the main coder of the questionnaires; his knowledge of the intricacies of occupational classifications must now be unsurpassed.

Among the University of Sheffield administrative staff, we would like to thank in particular Jean Johnson who was very supportive of the project and went out of her way to smooth out any financial difficulties. Jean Orme, in the Computing Services department, again inputted our data with unfailing efficiency. During the time that we have been engaged in these party membership surveys we have seen her staff drastically reduced; the pressure on her time has therefore been considerable, but she has maintained an excellent service. In our view, she is a priceless asset to the social science community at the University. Finally, Dr Hawthorne and his staff in the Academic Secretary's office provided us with extensive support at the time of the dispatch of the questionnaires, for which we are grateful.

We believe that party members have tended to be neglected by researchers in the past; it is for this reason that we have conducted studies, first, of Labour and now of Conservative party members. On a personal note, we are committed to the idea of encouraging and supporting voluntary political action by ordinary people, and in our view the political party is a key agency for encouraging this type of participation. None of the authors, however, are members of the Conservative party. This is not a book designed to defend or attack, support or oppose Conservative beliefs or policies; rather it is designed to try to understand Conservative grass-roots activism. The final acknowledgement is the most important. Transatlantic collaboration has been fun and has been greatly helped by electronic mail, but there are times when there has been a price in domestic cares; neither of the first two named authors could have succeeded in their tasks without the warm friendship and love of Sue and Ros.

Williamsburg, Sheffield, and Warwick
March 1994

CONTENTS

FIGURES

TABLES

1
Introduction and Overview

> In the course of 23 years' solid work for the party, during which I held senior office at both constituency and area level, I cannot recall any period of total demoralisation comparable to the situation we now face. The Tory party is a geriatric organisation, now in an advanced state of decline.
>
> Letter to *The Times*, 23 September 1993

The Conservative party is the governing party of modern British politics. Its electoral record surpasses all its party rivals. Whenever we determine the emergence of mass democracy in Britain, the Conservatives have been in office, either as a single party or a coalition partner, for most of the time since then. Despite this, as the quote from the party member above illustrates, the party is in serious difficulties, facing financial problems, a rebellious parliamentary party, and an apparently demoralized grass roots.

The purpose of this book is to examine this paradox of unprecedented political and electoral success sitting alongside apparent decay and decline. In the following pages we aim to examine the state of the Conservative party viewed through the eyes of the grass-roots members. We will be examining a social profile of the members, looking at their political activities and political experiences, together with their attitudes and beliefs about politics, society, and the party system. We will also examine their impact on aspects of the political system, particularly in relation to the effects of campaigning on election outcomes.

Overall, the aim is to see if the above quote actually does give a true picture of the state of the grass-roots party, viewed through the lens of a national random sample survey of the members taken in early 1992. The story is a complex one, which entails looking at incentives for participation in grass-roots party politics and at the involvement of the members within the party organization and in the wider political system. But we hope that the reader will come away with an accurate picture of the state of the party.

If we examine the period since 1883, after adult males in both county and borough constituencies had been enfranchised, we find that the Conservatives have been in government for 72 years, or 65 per cent of that time. If we take the period during which all adults have been enfranchised, then in the 65 years since the 1929 general election, the Conservatives have been incumbent some 65 per cent of the time.[1] Finally, if we consider 1950 to be the watershed for mass democracy, the first time in a general election that each elector had just one vote, then the Conservatives have been the party of government for 73 per cent of the time.

Considering its dominant position in modern British politics, it is a puzzle why the Conservative party is so understudied. Moran notes that 'the Conservative Party is the most successful mass political organisation in Britain, yet it has been neglected by scholars' (1989: 107). Historians are the exception to this generalization, since they have written numerous studies of Conservative Prime Ministers (Feiling, 1946; Blake, 1955, 1966; Middlemass and Barnes, 1969; Rhodes James, 1970; Horne, 1988, 1989; Gilbert, 1991) and also some studies of the parliamentary and extra-parliamentary parties (Blake, 1970; Lindsay and Harrington, 1974; Ramsden, 1978).

Political scientists have been much more reticent about studying the Conservative party. There has been no shortage of studies of Conservatism (Greenleaf, 1983; Harris, 1972; Eccleshall, 1990), and 'Thatcherism' in particular has generated a growth industry of academic and journalistic studies (Keegan, 1984; Riddell, 1985; Minogue and Biddis, 1987; Jenkins, 1987; Kavanagh, 1987; Gamble, 1988; Skidelsky, 1988; Young, 1989). But, with some notable exceptions (McKenzie, 1964; Harris, 1972; Gamble, 1974; Norton, 1978; Layton-Henry, 1980; Norton and Aughey, 1981; Holmes, 1985), neither recent Conservative governments, the Conservative parliamentary party, nor the extra-parliamentary party have received that much attention.

The Conservative party has one of the most successful records of recruiting individual members of any party in Western Europe in the post-1945 period (Katz and Mair, 1992). In Chapter 2, we will examine the current membership numbers in greater detail;

---

[1] Both these figures slightly underestimate Conservative dominance of British politics. Blake (1970: 281–3) includes both the second Lloyd George coalition of 1919–22 and the first Ramsay MacDonald coalition of 1931–5 as Conservative-dominated governments: our calculations exclude both.

here, the point we wish to make is that little attempt has been made to study this mass, extra-parliamentary party. This is partly a result of Conservative attitudes to its own mass membership; the party has hierarchical norms, which magnify the importance of leadership, and tend to play down the significance of the mass membership. In addition, however, the one major examination of the Conservative party since 1945 contributed greatly to the neglect of the party's grass roots by arguing that in 'an analysis of power within the party they (i.e., members of local Conservative constituency associations) are of little importance' (McKenzie, 1964: 258). That conclusion, which arose from an exhaustive analysis of the party's records, has remained the conventional wisdom in most academic work on this matter.

Yet it is the members of the 634 local Conservative constituency associations in Great Britain who select the parliamentarians who, in turn, help to determine the future direction of the party, and who choose the future party leader. In 1992 seventy-six new Conservative MPs were elected to the House of Commons; the party members in these particular constituency associations are very likely to have selected the Conservative party leader and possible Prime Minister for the first quarter of the twenty-first century.

Party members are important, however, not only as selectors; they also provide the bulk of the income which ensures the party's day-to-day maintenance and operations. We examine the question of party finance in more detail in Chapter 2, but here we note that British parties receive very limited state financial assistance. As a consequence, the Conservative party has to solicit funds from its supporters; companies have provided significant sums of money, particularly at election times, but party members' fund-raising activities should not be underestimated. In 1993 the Conservative party chairman stated that 70 per cent of the party's total income is raised by members in their local constituency associations.

Individuals who decide to subscribe to a political party play a vital part in maintaining the health of the party system. As Sir Norman Fowler, Conservative party chairman, stated in 1993: 'It is the voluntary commitment which gives a political party its strength. That means a strong party must have a large, nationwide membership' (*Hansard*, 22 June, col. 206).

Thus a political party, even one as electorally successful as the Conservatives, requires active volunteers. Party members are not only selectors and fund-raisers; they are also representative figure-heads in their local communities. The Conservative party cannot purchase the necessary staff or provide the resources to ensure a Conservative presence throughout Great Britain; therefore, the members are both the party's standard-bearers and its eyes and ears. Furthermore, these local partisans give the party a legitimacy in the community which is fundamental to electoral success.

Any political organization wanting to succeed has to be good at communicating its message to potential customers. It can be argued that the development of sophisticated communications techniques in general, and television and opinion polling in particular, renders party members largely redundant. However, party members still offer a medium through which party leaders can communicate their message to a wider public.

The Conservative party has been fortunate in having the support of most of the British press since 1945 (Seymour-Ure, 1974). Sometimes, however, the Press displays a political independence which undermines Conservative communication strategies. During the summer months of 1993, for example, John Major was heavily criticized by many of the Conservative party's traditional allies, such as the *Sun*, *The Times*, the *Daily Mail*, and the *Daily Telegraph*. It was interesting that his response to this criticism was to tour parts of Britain to meet party members, in order to communicate the party's message direct to its traditional supporters. He hoped to present an alternative message to the voters, different from the 'biased' one coming from the Press and from broadcasting. When parts of the Press are no longer so loyal to the party as in the past, then the party leaders' need for their 'ambassadors in the community' (Scarrow, 1990) will be greater.

Opinion polls are one of the key means by which party leaders measure public opinion; they are not perfect, however, since they offer only a snapshot of public opinion, and do not discriminate between 'informed' and 'uninformed' opinion. Party members offer an alternative means for measuring public opinion. They are often closer to the public than the parliamentarians, and, since party members live and work in their local communities, their views are of value. Ministers may take their views to be a better guide to 'informed' opinion—that is, the opinions of individuals who really care about a particular issue—than mass opinion polls. Furthermore, if party members provide insight into the opinions of traditional Conservative party supporters, the bedrock on which all electoral success is based, then they are performing a valuable function for the party.

Party members still provide an important means through which political leaders can communicate with and consult the public. It is often argued that they are an unrepresentative minority of the public. They are certainly a small minority of the electorate, but the common assumption that these volunteers hold 'extreme' opinions, which party leaders would do well to ignore, is not true. Evidence from the present study (see Chapter 3) reveals that party leaders are right to think of them as being a sounding-board for the opinions of Conservative party supporters in the wider electorate.

Recent developments in Conservative party politics are likely to mean that membership will become more, rather than less, important over time. The party's finances are in a parlous state. In 1993 the party had a cumulative deficit of £19 million; it had overspent by a large amount, and companies in recession were unwilling to donate as much money to the party as in the past. Furthermore, revelations in 1993 about funds from foreign businessmen, in one case apparently involving fraud, have created a sense of unease. This might persuade some company chairmen to stop donating money to the Conservative party, in order to avoid upsetting their shareholders. Possible future change in the laws regarding party funding, such as a law requiring greater disclosure of donations (Hansard Society, 1991) or one forbidding foreign-company donations, could reduce Conservative corporate income, and thus re-inforce the importance of individual party members in fund-raising.

The Conservative party has traditionally maintained a very effective national election-campaigning organization (Crewe and Harrop, 1986, 1989). If, however, some of the financial and communication resources can no longer be guaranteed in the future, then there will be a need for more local voluntary helpers in election campaigns. Furthermore, if the Conservative party is confronted at the constituency level by increasingly active Liberal Democrat and Labour party campaigners, as these parties recognize the need for greater local activism,[2] then it will have to rely more on its grass-roots activists.

[2] e.g. the Labour party's appointment of twenty-four full-time agents in 1993 to work with groups of local parties.

Party members are important for winning election campaigns. It has been the conventional wisdom for many years to argue that elections are won or lost exclusively at the national level. In the 1950s and 1960s voters tended to shift in a uniform manner throughout Britain, and it was argued that this reflected the efforts of the party professionals located in London to get across their message. By the 1990s, however, there is much greater spatial variation in voting behaviour than has been the case previously, which suggests that local effects are increasingly important (Johnston *et al.*, 1988).

Of course, certain factors unrelated to local campaigns, such as demographic changes or changes in the local economy, are clearly important in explaining these spatial variations. But the state of a party's local organization and its campaign efforts are also important. Our earlier research on Labour's electoral performance in the 1987 and 1992 general elections confirms the importance of membership and activism as factors which explain increases in the Labour vote (Seyd and Whiteley, 1992; Whiteley and Seyd, 1992). We see in Chapter 8 that the same can be said about the Conservative vote.

The Conservative party leadership recognizes the importance of party activists as election campaigners. Its own post-mortem analysis of the disastrous local election results of May 1993 suggested that lack of activism was a significant factor in explaining electoral performance,[3] and the party chairman's address to the 1993 annual party conference stressed the importance of party activists as electioneers.

Grass-roots parties are the training ground for future political leaders; it is from the ranks of party volunteers that leaders, both at the national and the local levels, are recruited. Political leadership skills will vary over time according to needs and circumstances; there is, therefore, no fixed set of requirements. However, the skills required include a clear sense of direction and vision and an abundance of energy, as well as the ability to work with others to build alliances and seek consensus. For the parliamentary leadership these skills were initially developed at the local level.

Civic life will be enhanced by ensuring a high quality of political

---

[3] Private communication to the authors from a member of the National Union Executive Committee.

leadership. One of the consequences of the removal of powers from elected local authorities, such as the creation of Urban Development Corporations and Training and Enterprise Councils and the promotion of opting-out by local schools, is that fewer incentives exist to encourage people to become elected local councillors. By reducing these incentives, the Government will affect the long-term recruitment and calibre of MPs.

Finally, party members provide a source of ideas on future policies. Of course, there are many sources for policy ideas, such as specialist advisers and consultants, think-tanks, commissions of inquiry, and pressure groups, all of which the Conservative party utilizes. But party members also provide an input which should not be ignored, and facilitate the process whereby ideas get on to the agenda of public concern.

We make no apology for re-emphasizing the claim of our earlier study of Labour party members (Seyd and Whiteley, 1992): that political parties are a vital feature of liberal democracy and that their members are of considerable importance. Parties aggregate a vast range of disparate ideas and interests into a cohesive set of political demands; they provide direction and order to government; and they ensure a greater degree of representation and political accountability.

We disagree with those who suggest that parties have less need today of their members (Bogdanor, 1993). Without a participative grass-roots membership, political parties become dominated by legislative 'notables'. Such candidate-centred parties find it more difficult to maintain their cohesion. The notables are happy to participate in the sharing of spoils, but are less willing to share the pain. Taking responsibility for tough and unpopular decisions is part of the political process; yet notables are more likely to find personal reasons for why they are unable to remain loyal to collective decisions. Responsible parties with well-developed political programmes require a participative, grass-roots membership. Governmental gridlock and paralysis are more likely with weak parties. If the party base is weakened by reducing the role and importance of party members, then the party superstructure will also be weakened. Weakening the grass roots will have disadvantageous implications for the entire political system.

Furthermore, the exercise of citizenship rights in liberal democracies involves acquiring information, understanding political problems, and participating in political action. Political parties, with their individual dues-paying members, provide one means of facilitating this citizenship. They are the most important institutional enablers outside the institutions of the State. Of course, there are other important institutional agencies, and some argue that political parties are losing their relevance in liberal democracies. Certainly the political market-place has become cluttered with a wide variety of organizations, but we disagree with the argument that parties are increasingly irrelevant. We believe that party members help keep democracy alive.

This book is written with a diverse audience in mind. First, it is written for a Conservative party audience; we hope that politically informed members at all levels of the party will take an interest in these findings about the organization to which they belong. We hope that they will not be put off by all the diagrams and tables, since we have tried hard to make the book readable for the non-specialist, even if it occasionally involves the use of advanced statistical techniques.

Secondly, it is written for an audience of professional communicators, such as journalists, pollsters, and teachers of politics. As we mentioned in the earlier study of the Labour party, the lack of a representative survey of party members has often meant that they have been stereotyped. They are thought of as being extremist, eccentric, and politically irrelevant. We believe that our findings challenge all these stereotypes. In some ways they are the unsung heroes and heroines of political life, because they help keep the party system working and democracy intact, at a time when it is under considerable strain.

Finally, it is written for an audience of political scientists who might be interested in theories of political participation, the political sociology of party organizations, electoral behaviour, and political attitudes. The responses to the questions used in the survey appear in Appendix II, to facilitate comparisons with other surveys of this type. In addition, the data are deposited in the ESRC survey archive at the University of Essex, and can be accessed by anyone who wants to do secondary analysis.[4]

In the remainder of this chapter we review in broad terms the research findings of this book.

---

[4] We would only ask that researchers send us a copy of any conference papers or published work arising from secondary analysis of the data.

A SUMMARY OF THE RESEARCH

The analysis begins in Chapter 2 by stressing the ambiguities and uncertainties surrounding the concept of membership in the Conservative party. First, no clearly defined criteria exist to define who might be eligible for membership; the barriers to entry are minimal, and this helps to explain why a large number of people have joined the Conservative party. Secondly, it is very difficult to ascertain just how many individuals do belong to the party, because all the records are kept at constituency level. Not even the party leader has an accurate estimate of the number of loyalists he can assume to be on his side; in the absence of a study like the present one, he has no way of knowing whether he is leading one million, three-quarters of a million, or half a million Conservative partisans.

We note the importance of party members for raising the funds which sustain the Conservative party as a major player in the party system. In addition to financing many of the party's activities, members act as local ambassadors to the community, as party leaders recognize, even if they pay them scant respect. They have no formal powers in policy-making and little influence over the management of finances or in party administration. There is no sense of accountability to the membership in the party.

The extent to which members play an informal role in these matters is open to dispute. One of the classic texts of British political science, Robert McKenzie's *British Political Parties* (1964), established the prevailing view that Conservative party leaders do not follow, but merely take note of, members' views. Recently, however, this view has been challenged by Richard Kelly, who argues in *Conservative Party Conferences* (1989) that members' opinions are really quite influential. We assess these conflicting points of view.

Chapter 3 provides a broad overview of the social characteristics and political views of members. Until now there have been no comprehensive national surveys of Conservative party members,[5] and therefore, we have had to rely upon either selective portraits or particular local studies. Our survey of approximately 2,500 respondents was carried out in the months before the 1992 general election, the details of which appear in Appendix I.

---

[5] In the British Election Studies of 1983 and 1987 questions about party membership were included in the surveys. Unfortunately the numbers of cases this produced were too small for comprehensive analysis.

The analysis in Chapter 3 includes an examination of the socio-economic backgrounds of members by age, class, gender, education, and income. Some comparisons are made in this chapter with Conservative voters, using data from the 1992 British Election Study (see Heath *et al.*, forthcoming). The fact that the surveys of both Conservative members and Conservative voters were conducted within a few months of each other makes the comparisons particularly appropriate. We compare their social profiles and also their attitudes on some of the major political issues of the 1990s, such as public expenditure, defence, and the role of the trade unions. In addition, we examine members' attitudes on a wider range of political issues than is contained in the British Election Study, and suggest that British Conservatism is a multi-faceted doctrine which divides into fairly distinct ideological tendencies.

Since Margaret Thatcher's departure from the party leadership there has been a constant tension between those wishing the party to adhere to her political ideals and those preferring a modified version thereof. We examine the extent to which 'Thatcherism' prevails at the party's grass roots. One particular political issue, that of European integration, is one about which Margaret Thatcher made her position absolutely clear, and we probe the differences within the party on this question. Further, we compare members' attitudes towards Margaret Thatcher and her replacement, John Major.

The Conservative party has placed considerable stress throughout its lifetime on leadership; as a consequence, its internal organizational arrangements have provided only very limited opportunities for the members to play an active part in choosing the party leader or in determining party policies. Whether these arrangements have had the members' support has never been clear, and there have been periodic attempts to increase the powers of the ordinary member. Accordingly, we examine whether members would prefer a more participative party.

Finally, in this chapter we examine the levels of activism within the party. Party members are assumed to be among the more active citizens in the community, but, as far as Conservatives are concerned, it might be more appropriate to describe many of them as the 'inactive activists'!

In Chapter 4 we examine the question of why anyone would want to join a political party in the first place. This may appear to be an easy question to address, but it has given rise to a major theoretical puzzle which has become known as the 'paradox of participation'. This is the proposition that it is irrational for individuals to join a political party in order to further any political goals which they might have, no matter how strongly they support those goals.

Before addressing this question, a preliminary exercise in mapping out the scope of participation in the Conservative party is needed, in order to clarify the concept of party membership. As we mention earlier, the notion of Conservative party membership is ambiguous, since an individual can be counted as a party member without donating any time or money to party activities. So we address this issue by probing members about the kinds of activities they undertake within the party organization.

We then go on to discuss the 'paradox of participation' as it applies to party membership, as a preliminary to developing a model which seeks to explain why individuals join a political party. We have described this model as a 'general-incentives' theory of participation (see Seyd and Whiteley, 1992), since it is based on the proposition that individuals participate in politics in response to incentives of various kinds. Some of these incentives bring private returns or benefits of the type familiar to the economist. But the model goes beyond a narrowly cast analysis of the costs and benefits of participation, to take into account the fact that individuals participate for other reasons, such as altruism and affective or emotional attachments to the party.

Thus participation is motivated by a sense of loyalty and affection for a political party which has little to do with a calculation of costs and benefits of collective action, and also by a sense of 'civic duty', a belief that individuals should be involved in politics if democracy is to work. We also suggest that individuals participate in order to achieve collective goals. These include policy objectives of various kinds, in which individuals thinks of themselves as being effective because they are part of a powerful collective organization. In other words, individuals 'think' collectively and not just 'individually', and this gives them a sense of political efficacy.

Finally, we conjecture that individuals are motivated to participate by social norms of various kinds. These are pressures to conform to the wishes of other people who are 'significant others' in their lives, or people whose opinions they listen to and respect.

After this theoretical framework is developed, we test aspects of the model using our own survey data, together with data from the British Election Study.

In Chapter 5 we examine the question of why some members become active in Conservative party politics while others remain inactive. The analysis starts by developing a measurement scale of activism, developed from a battery of questions in the survey. It turns out that there are two such scales underlying the data, one of which is referred to as an 'activism' scale, the other as a 'supporter' scale. In effect there appear to be two distinct Conservative 'parties', one made up of supporters who are largely inactive; they give money and turn up at the odd meeting, but do very little else. The second is a party of activists who attend meetings regularly, campaign at the local level, and run the local party organization.

After looking at the relationship between the social characteristics of members and their degrees of activism, the discussion goes on to test the general-incentives model of participation as applied to the exercise of explaining party activism. The results show that activism is motivated by a number of incentives. First, there are selective incentives, or private returns from political action, such as the desire to participate in politics for its own sake or the desire to build a political career. Secondly, activism is motivated by collective incentives, or the policy goals which individuals support. These policy goals are evaluated in the light of the members' sense of political efficacy; thus members who have a strong sense that they can influence the political process are more likely to translate the desire to achieve policy goals into political action than members who do not have this conviction.

A third important finding is that activism is also motivated by expressive or affective attachments to the Conservative party which have little to do with instrumental concerns such as building a political career or achieving policy goals. This finding reinforces the point that political participation cannot be understood solely in terms of the costs and benefits of political action, since these motives are not instrumental in character, but are grounded in a sense of loyalty or affection for the party.

A fourth point is that activism is also motivated by ideology, but in a manner which reverses the conventional wisdom. It is normally assumed that Conservative activists are on the right of the political spectrum; they are often described as political 'extremists'. But the evidence shows that members on the left of the ideological spectrum are more likely to be active than members on the right, once the other factors which explain participation are taken into account. Thus progressive Conservatives tend to be more active than others, although the correlation is not very strong. In this context ideology is interpreted as a private motive for participating in politics, much as religious beliefs motivate the active church-goer.

Chapter 6 focuses more closely on an analysis of Conservative party ideology. The terms 'left' and 'right' are often used in political discourse to summarize a wide range of political beliefs. Discussions of ideology are often couched in terms of a single 'left–right' dimension; this chapter shows that Conservative party ideology cannot be captured by a single dimension, but rather involves three separate dimensions or scales. There are clusters of attitudes centring around three different sets of issues, which we label 'progressivism', 'individualism', and 'traditionalism'.

Progressivism is associated particularly with the Macmillan era of Conservative party politics, although its antecedents go back to Disraeli's 'One-Nation' Toryism. Progressives stress the importance of intervention in, and regulation of, the economy, in order to sustain full employment and promote growth and to provide a safety net for the poor or weaker members of society. Individualists, by contrast, favour privatization, fiscal orthodoxy, and cuts in the welfare state as a means of promoting work incentives. Finally, traditionalists are concerned with protecting national sovereignty, opposing institutional reforms such as European integration, and with moral questions such as abortion-law reform.

The evidence suggests that modern Conservative ideology is an amalgam of all three factors; there are predominantly progressive party members, predominantly traditionalists, and also members who are strongly individualistic. But there are also members whose beliefs are a mixture of all three elements. Perhaps the most interesting finding in this chapter is that there are many more progressive Conservatives in the grass-roots party than conventional wisdom would suggest.

A common 'meta-dimension' which underlies each of these components of Conservatism is a dimension of attitudes to state intervention in the economy and in society. Thus some members favour state intervention in the economy but not in moral or social matters; others take the opposite position. The analysis shows that this pattern of attitudes partly reflects members' socio-economic status, but also their basic political values acquired in adolescence and early adulthood, which in turn reflect the attitudes prevalent in society during those formative years.

Finally in Chapter 6, we examine 'Thatcherism', and try to characterize it in terms of these general dimensions of Conservative party ideology. The discussion in this section suggests that while Mrs Thatcher had a distinctive set of ideological beliefs shared by a number of the grass-roots members, 'Thatcherism' has not significantly influenced ideological tendencies in the party. Thus there is no evidence that the party has shifted significantly to the right as a consequence of Thatcherite ideas or policies.

In Chapter 7 we examine the attitudes of party members to the Conservative party and its organization, as well as their attitudes to other parties and the relationships they have with the wider society. Activists who attend meetings tend to have a fairly favourable view of them, regarding them as efficiently run, easy to understand, and united. When asked about the content of these meetings, members indicated that they spent a considerable amount of time discussing fund-raising and organizational matters. But it was clear that members also discuss local and national politics at meetings.

When asked about their feelings towards the Conservative party organization and the party leadership, most members felt very warm and supportive of both. There was some correlation between attitudes to these institutions and levels of activism and ideological belief, but this was not very strong. In addition, members were asked various questions about their attitudes to the reform of the party organization, such as the suggestion that the leadership be elected by the entire party membership. In the latter case a majority of the members favoured the idea of electing the leader at the grass-roots level, but a plurality opposed the converse idea that Conservative Central Office should participate more fully in the selection of local candidates. However, on the question of the desirability of coalition government, an issue to do with reforming the wider political system, members were adamantly opposed.

As regards their feelings towards political opponents, not surprisingly, members were more opposed to the Labour party than to the Liberal Democrats, although they did not feel particularly warm towards either. But one surprising finding was that their strongest feelings of hostility were not reserved for the Labour party, their main opponent, but for the nationalist parties and the Greens.

On the question of their feelings towards many of the institutions of the British state, members were certainly very respectful of institutions like the monarchy, the armed forces, and the police. They have rather less respect for the House of Commons, the judiciary, and the Church of England, but they still view these institutions favourably; and finally they feel fairly neutral about the European Community, although they tend to dislike its president, Jacques Delors. Their hostility is reserved for the Trades Union Congress, and interestingly enough for the *Sun* newspaper.

A final topic in Chapter 7 is the extent to which party members are part of a community network of 'notables' or influential individuals who exercise power in the local community. This follows from the idea that the Conservatives are the 'natural' party of government, the argument being that local élites have close ties with the party, and that this automatically makes it politically influential. This is an interesting idea, but there is little evidence in support of it in the survey. Members are not very well represented on official bodies like the local magistrates' bench or on unofficial bodies like the local chamber of commerce, and are not closely linked with local networks of influential organizations. Moreover, the organizations which they do belong to, like the National Trust and the World Wildlife Fund, are quite peripheral to the institutions which exercise power.

In Chapter 8 the focus of the discussion moves from an analysis of the social and political characteristics of party members to an analysis of the effects of membership on the vote in a general election campaign. There is a lively debate in the literature on electoral behaviour about the influence of local campaigns on the vote. Many commentators see the modern election campaign as something which is fought out exclusively at the national level, largely in the media. On this view, local parties have little influence on a campaign.

The relationship between campaigning and the vote is examined, using campaign spending data at the constituency level in the 1987 and 1992 general elections. The use of local spending data as an indicator of campaign activities like canvassing and delivering leaflets is controversial, and it has not been possible to verify this measure until quite recently. But data from the British Election Study of 1987, together with information from the earlier Labour party study (Seyd and Whiteley, 1992), show that spending data are quite a good measure of local campaigning. Further evidence to support this is discussed in Chapter 8.

The analysis in this chapter also shows that local campaigning by the Conservative party is quite important in influencing the vote. The estimates from a model developed in the chapter show, for example, that if the Conservatives had increased their spending on local campaigns in the general election of 1992 by about ten percentage points, they would have obtained nearly 1.5 per cent more of the total vote than they actually received.

If an additional direct measure of canvassing is included in the model, which unfortunately can be done only for the 1987 general election, the effects of campaigning on the vote are even more marked. The estimates show that if the Conservative party had both spent and canvassed about 25 per cent more than they actually did in 1987, they would have captured an additional sixteen seats in the election. Assuming the same relationships existed in 1992, extra effort at the grass-roots level could have saved a number of seats which were lost to Labour and the Liberal Democrats.

The final section of Chapter 8 is devoted to simulating the outcome of the 1987 election using the model of the local vote developed in the chapter. Different assumptions are fed into this simulation about the extent of campaigning both for the Conservatives and for the other parties active in the election. The results are very interesting, and suggest that there is an asymmetric effect at work with regard to campaigning at the local level. That is, if the Conservative campaign is significantly worse than that of its rivals, the party will be 'punished' more in terms of loss of seats than it will be 'rewarded' by a gain in seats if the Conservative campaign is better than its rivals. The moral of this story is that the party cannot afford to let the grass roots decline, since it would face quite severe electoral consequences if it did so, particularly if the other parties sustained their local campaigns at present levels or even increased them.

The final chapter brings the strands of the discussion together, and uses the earlier findings to address both the magnitude and the causes of the decline of the grass-roots party. The estimates of the size of the decline are very approximate, because the data on membership over time are very limited. However, the estimates available suggest that the party has been losing, on average, about 64,000 members a year since 1960. Furthermore, they suggest that if nothing is done to halt this decline, the party will fall to below 100,000 members by the end of the century.

The chapter is devoted to examining the causes of the decline in the light of the general-incentives theory discussed earlier. That discussion suggested that a variety of factors account for the decline, including social and cultural changes which have weakened the incentives to participate, like the rise in female participation in the work-force, the growth of the leisure industry, and the increase in some interest groups, all of which may provide an attractive alternative to party activism.

But it is also the case that the party is to a significant extent the author of its own problems. The dramatic decline in the powers and prestige of local government has significantly weakened one of the most important selective incentives for participation, the desire to develop a career in politics. Similarly, the shift to the right in the ideological centre of gravity of the party under the leadership of Mrs Thatcher discouraged many progressive Conservatives, who, as we pointed out earlier, are more commonly found in the grass roots than conventional wisdom suggests.

Progressive 'One Nation' Conservatives have also been discouraged by changes in policy goals, such as the shift away from redistribution of income, which has brought in its wake significant increases in poverty. In addition, many grass-roots members have been disheartened by policy failures, like the severe economic recessions of 1980–1 and 1989–92. Once lost to the party, these members may be very difficult to recruit again, even if economic performance subsequently improves.

Finally, the discussion in Chapter 9 turns to an examination of the steps which the party leadership might take to try to reverse this decline in membership. These ideas all basically come down to the same point: the party leadership needs to take membership seriously, to make an effort to try to give sympathizers an incentive to join and to remove some of the disincentives to participation which have been erected over the past decade and a half. The book closes with some advice from Benjamin Disraeli, founder of the modern Conservative party, whose political genius saved the party from becoming a rump of aristocratic landowners, an outcome which looked very likely to occur in the middle of the nineteenth century. His advice is highly relevant to the modern Conservative party, even though it was given more than 125 years ago.

2

Party Members in Context

The Conservative party has been recruiting members for a very long time, and it is often claimed to have had the largest membership of any such party in a liberal democracy (Von Beyme, 1985; Katz and Mair, 1992). It has been recruiting members since the time of the great Reform Act of 1832, when local Conservative associations first began to be formed. The aim at the time was to mobilize the new middle-class voters and attract their support. Further expansions of the franchise in 1867 and 1883 provided an additional stimulus to the recruitment of Conservative supporters by local associations.

In 1867 party representatives from fifty-five cities and towns agreed to form the National Union of Conservative and Constitutional Associations (McKenzie, 1964: 150–9), thus establishing an extra-parliamentary body with the task of encouraging the formation of local Conservative associations and co-ordinating efforts to recruit members and win elections. The subsequent development and growth of individual party membership was stimulated, first, by the expansion of the franchise; second, by the Corrupt Practices Act of 1883, which required that voluntary workers undertake election campaigning which had previously been handled by paid agents and canvassers; and, third, by the proposal of the Maxwell-Fyfe Committee on Conservative party organization (1949) to ban the practice of wealthy parliamentary candidates and MPs donating large sums of money to constituency associations.

In his classic study of political parties, Maurice Duverger asks: 'How do we define a party member?', and answers that membership 'varies according to the party: each holds to a concept of membership which is peculiar to it' (1954: 61). Certainly membership of the British Conservative party is distinctive, because no one can directly join the party as such. Thus the Conservative party is not a formal, national entity (Ewing, 1987), but is, rather, a shorthand term for three separate organizations.

First, there is the National Union of Conservative and Unionist

Associations,[1] which has overall responsibility for 634 constituency associations in England, Scotland, and Wales;[2] secondly, there is Conservative Central Office, which employs the full-time professional staff engaged in running party and regional headquarters; and, thirdly, there is the Conservative parliamentary party, organized and run by the party whips' office.

The fragmentary nature of the Conservative party was confirmed in 1982 by the Court of Appeal when it was called upon to decide whether Central Office's income was liable for corporation or income tax. The court's judgment was that the Conservative party did not exist in law as an unincorporated association, and it confirmed the original legal judgment that 'the Conservative Party is a political movement with many parts (some of which are unincorporated associations) which in practice work together to a common end. The links between those parts (which are reflected at every level) are ... functional and not constitutional' (*All England Law Reports*, 1982: 60).

The court's decision meant that money coming into Conservative Central Office is held not for the benefit of the Conservative party, but for control by the party leader. The only common link in the organization, according to the Court of Appeal, is the party leader, and apart from him or her, 'the separate bodies which make up the party, cooperate with each other for political purposes but maintain separate existences for organisational purposes' (ibid.).

The absence of a written constitution to draw together the separate elements reinforces the fragmentary aspect of the Conservative party. Nevertheless, we will use the singular term throughout this book to describe all elements of the party, while recognizing that the title, in fact, refers only to the party in Parliament.

An individual intending to join the Conservative party applies to the local Conservative constituency association in the place in which he or she resides or has business connections. Only constituency associations recruit party members, by contrast with the

[1] The National Union of Conservative and Constitutional Associations was renamed the National Union of Conservative and Unionist Associations in 1885.

[2] Since 1991 the National Union has organized constituency associations in Northern Ireland, and, at the time of writing, nine have been established. The Conservative party in Scotland is an entirely separate entity with a distinct bureaucracy, but the Scottish constituency associations are affiliated to the National Union.

Labour party, where applications for individual membership have been processed at party headquarters since 1990. The recruitment of Conservative members is a local responsibility, and constituency associations jealously guard their local autonomy on this and other matters.

Thus in 1993, when the leadership of the National Union attempted to require constituency associations to adopt both a new set of model rules and a code of practice and to submit an annual return detailing their membership activities (Conservative Party, 1993*a*: 22–3), none of these proposals secured the necessary two-thirds majority at a meeting of the Central Council. This was because local representatives were suspicious that these changes would lead to centralized control of constituency activities.

Individuals become members of local constituency associations, and these associations have to be approved by the National Union's Executive Committee and pay an annual affiliation fee.[3] There is, however, no direct link between the individual member of an association and the National Union. Thus, by joining a constituency association, an individual Conservative does not become a member of the National Union. Furthermore, if an individual falls foul of the local Conservative association and is expelled by that organization, he or she has no right of appeal to any national party body; acceptance into, and dismissal from, the Conservative association is an exclusively local matter.

A further implication of this organizational structure is that local Conservative associations are under no obligation to report their membership details to the National Union, and therefore at the centre there is only scant knowledge of either the exact number of members or their social composition.

In the years immediately following the Second World War, the party claimed that membership increased dramatically from just under one million to over two and three-quarter million (McKenzie, 1964: 187). In the 1980s the Conservative party referred vaguely to a figure of one and a half million members, which by the 1990s had been reduced to one million.

Numerous attempts have been made by academics to ascertain a more accurate figure for the party membership; for example, the

---

[3] *Rules and Standing Orders of the National Union of Conservative and Unionist Associations*, Rule IIIa, 1990.

most comprehensive and detailed study of the Conservative party (McKenzie, 1964) suggested a figure of 2.25 million members in the 1960s. Blondel (1974: 89) estimated a figure of about 2.8 million at this time. The individual memberships of both of Britain's major parties peaked, however, in the mid-1950s, and have since declined. Rose (1976: 153) estimated a figure of 1.5 million by 1970, and the committee established to consider financial aid to political parties, the Houghton Committee (HMSO, 1974), estimated an average membership in each constituency association of 2,400, which would give a national membership of 1.5 million, a figure which Norton and Aughey (1981: 213) believe to be fairly accurate. In his study of party finance, Pinto-Duschinsky (1981: 154) reckoned on a figure of 1.4 million. Finally, Tether (1991), on the basis of a survey of thirty constituency associations, suggests a figure of 1 million.

In the absence of some type of national membership scheme, the only way to get an accurate picture of the size of the Conservative party membership is to conduct a representative survey of local associations. Without this, there is no way of knowing the exact number of members with any accuracy.

Our sample of constituency associations reveals evidence of a difference between the membership numbers claimed by association officers and the actual number of members calculated from the membership lists we obtained from the local associations. The differences between claimed and actual membership ranged from an overestimate of 69 per cent to an underestimate of 194 per cent! One reason for these differences arises from the ambiguities surrounding the definition of a party member, which we referred to earlier. This means that the definition of membership can differ from party to party.

What is clear is that the Conservative party wishes to recruit as many people as possible, and it does not want to create barriers to membership. One Central Office official, in discussions with the authors, likened his party's membership to that of the motoring organizations, the AA and the RAC, who recruit as many motorists as possible, and then distinguish between full and associate members. The associate members pay to protect themselves against breakdown, but then play little or no part in the associations' affairs. The Conservative party wants to attract people who are willing to pay a sum of money to support Conservative principles

TABLE 2.1. *Party Membership in the Sampled Constituency Associations*

	Stated membership	Actual membership
Region 1. Greater London		
Carshalton/Wallington	1,100	1,943
Streatham	1,200	1,341
Holborn/St Pancras	395	409
Hornchurch	1,000	710
Sutton/Cheam	1,600	2,443
Region 2: North		
Bishop Auckland	300	246
Darlington	500	538
Region 3: North-West		
Davyhulme	2,500	1,675
Crosby	1,050	826
Pendle	300	304
Region 4: Yorkshire		
Sheffield Brightside	70	70
Boothferry	2,300	1,389
Leeds North-East	1,600	2,078
Region 5: East Midlands		
Bosworth	800	796
Nottingham South	1,200	1,149
Wellingborough	250	735
Region 6: West Midlands		
Burton	1,300	1,194
Staffordshire Moorlands	480	441
Region 7: Eastern		
Harlow	1,000	897
Stevenage	1,000	942
Central Suffolk	1,400	2,177
Region 8: South-East		
Brighton Pavilion	947	612
Wealdon	3,000	2,522
Region 9: Wessex		
Wycombe	1,200	803
Southampton Itchen	2,800	2,564

TABLE 2.1. *Continued*

	Stated membership	Actual membership
Portsmouth North	2,500	2,354
Region 10: Western		
Bristol North-West	2,291	2,960
Falmouth and Camborne	1,400	1,118
Region 11: Wales		
Monmouth	1,800	1,435
Brecon and Radnor	3,000	934
Region 12: Scotland		
Caithness and Sutherland	450	557
East Angus	1,200	1,259
Falkirk West	600	718
Glasgow Cathcart	400	430
Total	40,933	40,569
Mean	1,204	1,193

or to protect themselves from socialism, but who do not want any further political involvement. They pay an insurance premium to stave off catastrophe.

The lack of a clear definition of a Conservative party member means that the party is quite vague as to what constitutes a member: individuals are expected neither to declare their attachment to a particular set of attitudes, ideals, or policies, nor to pay a minimum level of subscription.[4] A member of the Conservative party can be someone who feels very strong attachment to Conservative ideals or, on the other hand, someone whose political identification is weak.

Another aspect of this vagueness is that an individual can pay whatever subscription to the local party association that he or she

[4] *Model Rules* defines party membership in terms of support for the objectives of the local constituency association. These are listed as securing the election of Conservatives to the House of Commons, to the European Parliament, and to local government; the raising of funds locally; the maintenance of an up-to-date electoral register; and finally, to spreading 'the knowledge of Conservative principles and policy, and generally to promote the interests of the Party in the constituency' (Conservative Party, 1990: clause 2).

pleases; and, in fact, our survey shows that there were some people clearly identified as members, both in terms of the local records and in terms of their own perceptions, who paid nothing at all to the local association by way of a subscription.

Constituency association officers who assisted us in the survey claimed an average membership of 1,204; but the records show that they had an actual average membership of 1,193. Projecting these figures nationally would result in an actual individual membership of 756,000. Thus it would be reasonable to conclude that the party membership is currently about three-quarters of a million people.

There was also some disparity between the names included on constituency association local lists and the perceptions of individuals as to whether or not they belonged to the Conservative party. For example, it was clear that on occasion individuals who had donated money to the local Conservatives were included in the lists as party members. Some 2 per cent of those listed as members turned out not to be so when they were asked about this in our survey.

Overall, then, the political criteria for membership are loose, the financial investment is variable, and the organizational responsibility for the membership is decentralized.

THE RECRUITMENT OF PARTY MEMBERS

In Chapter 4 we will examine in detail the question of why anyone would want to join the Conservative party; here we pose the alternative question of why the party should want to recruit members in the first place: what are the party leadership's reasons for recruiting individuals as members?

The first answer to this question relates to election campaigns. Even though conventional academic and political wisdom over the past thirty years has been that elections are won or lost almost exclusively at the national level, primarily through the broadcasting and newsprint media, nevertheless, the party's recruitment pack produced by Central Office stresses the role of members as campaigners. It argues that members should be involved in 'an all-year-round process of communicating with the members of our local community, seeking their views and putting across our message' (Conservative Party, 1993*c*). We will consider how effective party members are in mobilizing the vote in Chapter 8; here we examine their potential effectiveness as 'ambassadors for Conservatism' in the local community.

To do the job effectively, the party leadership has to communicate its ideas to all individual members, and there has to be an organizational structure for the members to report views within their local communities back to the leadership. A recent comparative study of mass parties in Western Germany and Britain suggests that the British Conservative party has the least developed communications network of all the major parties in these countries (Scarrow, 1990).

The party places little emphasis on making its members better ambassadors by providing them with a regular newsletter or with regular training courses on communications skills. It does, however, maintain an elaborate consultative network, organized by the Conservative Political Centre (CPC), which enables all those individual members who wish it, to participate in a regular feedback process of discussion. Topics are chosen nationally for discussion, and then briefings and questions are sent out to the CPC discussion groups in the constituencies. Each CPC group produces a report, which is sent back to party headquarters, and the main findings are collated, summarized, and circulated to the party leader, the party chairman, Ministers or Shadow Party personnel, and National Union and Central Office officials. Norton and Aughey (1981: 218) suggest that at the end of the 1970s the number of groups submitting reports ranged between 500 and 600, involving between 4,500 and 6,500 participants. Evidence from our survey reveals that 1 per cent of the membership belong to a local CPC group, which would mean that around 7,500 participate in these consultative exercises. Impressive as these figures might seem, there are critics within the Conservative party, as we will see later, who argue that the party leadership takes little note of members and that the party structure affords little opportunity for their voice to be heard or taken seriously.

A second important reason for recruiting members is that they help to fund the party nationally. Every constituency association is assigned a fixed sum of money, its 'target quota', which it is expected to send to the party's central funds. These quotas are calculated on the basis of the number of Conservative voters in the constituency. According to the published results for 1991–2, constituency associations contributed £1.3 million towards the expected total quota of £2.4 million, some 54 per cent of the total (Conservative Party, 1992: 144–59).

At one end of the scale, ten constituency associations contributed almost £250,000 to central funds, and at the other end, some 105 associations contributed nothing at all. Overall, then, a majority of constituency associations failed to meet their target quotas.

In his study of party finance, Pinto-Duschinsky (1981) states that constituency quota payments accounted for one-fifth of the party's central income between 1966 and the late 1970s, and he argues that since 1945 the party's central headquarters has become dependent to a considerable extent on locally raised funds. However, if one takes into consideration all income coming from the localities to the centre, and not just the quota payments, then the importance of the fund-raising activities of local members is seen to be even greater than this figure would suggest. Rose (1976) asserts that the bulk of party funds are raised by constituency associations; for example, he argues that between 1966 and 1970 the Conservative party's income averaged £3.4 million annually, of which two-thirds came from constituency associations.

One problem in determining the amount that party members raise is that the party did not, until 1993, publish detailed financial accounts. In 1993, however, the party's funding became a matter of public debate, primarily as a consequence of a House of Commons Select Committee inquiry. At this inquiry the party chairman revealed that the sums of money raised by constituency associations to meet their annual financial quota are only the tip of a financial iceberg. Maintaining an efficient, professional party organization is expensive, and the party could not manage it solely on this income. He revealed that the party's total income in 1992 was £26 million, of which £18 million came from members' fund-raising activities in their associations.[5] According to this, some 70 per cent of the party's national income comes from fund-raising by grass-roots members in their own localities.

In addition, local parties hold extensive financial resources which remain at local level and therefore enable them to run election campaigns and engage in other political activities in a manner they

---

[5] Memorandum of Evidence from the Chairman of the Conservative Party Organization to the Home Affairs Select Committee, May 1993.

deem appropriate. For example, constituency associations employ their own agents, who may have a decisive impact on the effectiveness of the local party organization and, therefore, upon the Conservative party's electoral performance. Some 421 full-time agents were employed by the local parties in 1966; by 1980 the number had declined to 330, and by 1993 it had dropped further to 234, no doubt as a result of a declining party membership (Pinto-Duschinsky, 1981: 154).

Thus local funds play an important part, both directly and indirectly, in the Conservative party's electoral performance, a point we will develop further in Chapter 8. Recruiting members is therefore of considerable importance if the Conservative party is to maintain all the activities which it believes are necessary for the success of a major political party.

The party leadership is keen, therefore, to encourage individuals to become party members, in order to assist in electioneering and fund-raising. At the same time, there is little encouragement for individuals to join and participate directly in the policy-making process. This is largely because the structure and culture of the party affords little opportunity for such participation. Nevertheless, this does not mean that party members are entirely without influence, and we discuss the scope and limits of their influence next.

THE POLITICAL INFLUENCE OF PARTY MEMBERS

The Conservative party is not characterized by a high level of internal democracy, in the sense of individual participation by the membership in Conservative policy-making through the National Union. In the formative years of the National Union, Conservatives were recruited into constituency associations which were primarily social organizations offering opportunities for individuals to rub shoulders with the aristocracy. Ramsden states that the party structures developed after 1867 were 'artificial growths, fostered by the few to involve and socialize the many into the disciplines of party' (1978: xi). The classic, oft-repeated statement by Balfour that he would rather consult his valet than the National Union (McKenzie, 1964: 82) confirms the limited political importance of the party member. A succinct commentary on internal party democracy came from Sir Charles Marston in 1929, when he described the Conservative party as 'autocracy masquerading as a democracy' (McKenzie, 1964: 181).

A newsletter of the Charter Movement, a group of members campaigning for greater party democracy, states that: 'Central Office claims the Conservative Party is a modern democratic body but this is nonsense' (Charter Movement, 1991: 2). The same issue of *Charter News* writes of the Conservative party's 'sham claims to be democratic', and compares party management to 'an old style East European way of running politics'. Such comments as these reinforce Duverger's (1954) point that, generally, Conservative parties are pre-mass-democratic, cadre-type organizations which, with the expansion of the franchise, have needed to establish an individual membership for electoral reasons. Their members, however, have remained institutionally and culturally subordinate to the parliamentary leadership.

This thesis was confirmed by Robert McKenzie in the most comprehensive study of power within the Conservative party that has ever been undertaken; no other author, before or since, has examined all parts of the party in such meticulous detail. His overall conclusions about the relationships between the parliamentary, professional, and voluntary parts of the party are as follows:

The party in parliament has preserved its autonomy; the Central Office has continued to function in effect as the personal machine of the Leader and has fulfilled most of the Executive responsibilities of the National Union; and the latter organisation has, with varying degrees of docility, fulfilled its function as an electoral machine and a channel of communication between the parliamentary leaders and their followers in the country. (McKenzie, 1964: 180)

Power formally resides with the parliamentary party and, in particular, with the person elected as its leader. Nevertheless, the leader does not possess complete autocratic powers, since, as McKenzie points out, the incumbent 'ignores the moods and opinions of the National Union at his peril' (1964: 220). The National Union is 'a vast sounding board of Conservative opinion' (ibid.), and therefore has to be taken seriously. It has influence, but it lacks authority. On matters of policy-making, finance, and candidate selection, 'the really vital spheres of party activity' (1964: 210), committees report to the party leader and not to the National Union.

McKenzie argues that there have been very few occasions when the National Union has had 'a decisive influence' (1964: 221) on party policy; the only two he regards as significant were the pressures leading to the breakup of the coalition government in 1922 and grass-roots support for the introduction of the Trades Disputes Act in 1927.

The major forum of the National Union, its annual conference, serves 'primarily as a demonstration of party solidarity and of enthusiasm for its own leaders' (McKenzie, 1964: 189), and is more of a rally for the faithful than a deliberative assembly. McKenzie cautions, however, that although party leaders cannot be bound by conference decisions, they can be embarrassed by them. Conservative leaders lack the reliable bloc votes to sustain them at their conferences which Labour leaders possessed at the time McKenzie was writing, and therefore they have to rely on a combination of their personal authority and the traditional deference of the rank and file (1964: 198).

In his analysis of the distribution of power within the party, McKenzie argues that members 'are of little importance' (1964: 258). Down at the local grass roots, in his view, the party members' primary purpose is 'to conduct propaganda and raise funds' (1964: 244). Furthermore, he applauds their lack of importance, because he believes that the norms of parliamentary democracy require that the leaders of parliamentary parties be accountable directly to the voters and not to the party members. He feels that these 'ardent partisans' (1964: 230) hold opinions more extreme than either party leaders or party supporters, and therefore should not play a direct role in policy-making. Whether or not they are 'ardent partisans' is a question we will discuss in Chapter 6.

It is interesting to note the reaction to McKenzie's thesis at the time of its first publication. Whereas his analysis of the distribution of power within the Labour party, which he believed to be very similar to that of the Conservatives, prompted intense academic scrutiny as well as political controversy (Crossman, 1961; McKenzie, 1961; Pelling, 1961; Birch, 1964; Rose, 1976) and various comprehensively argued rebuttals (Beer, 1965; Minkin, 1978), his conclusions regarding the Conservative party prompted little debate and no rebuttal. The closest to a challenge came much later from Gamble (1974), who suggested that Conservative politics were an elaborate conciliatory process between the contradictory requirements of power and electoral support.

In Gamble's view the opinions of party activists, expressed at annual party conferences, were not irrelevant; party leaders had to win their activists' support for policies which might not fit with traditional Conservatism. The conventional wisdom, however, of academics, political journalists, and even Conservative activists was that McKenzie was basically correct in his interpretation of Conservative party politics.

The consensus seems to be that individual members have played a subordinate role in policy-making, and their only significant power has been to select parliamentary candidates. They have been involved in policy-making only on occasions when parliamentarians, involved in an intra-party dispute, have attempted to mobilize support at grass-roots level as a means of advancing their case.

One example of this was Lord Randolph Churchill's 'Tory Democracy' campaign in 1883–4, which was primarily a challenge to the party leadership of Salisbury and Northcote. Part of this challenge was a demand for a greater political role for the National Union (McKenzie, 1964: 167–73; Feuchtwanger, 1968). Another example occurred during the disputes over Conservative foreign policy in the 1930s, when the anti-appeasers mobilized as much support as they could muster within the National Union (McKenzie, 1964: 230). A third, contemporary example has occurred during the long-running debate over Britain's membership of the European Community. The Conservative MPs opposed to Britain's membership on the terms outlined in the Maastricht Treaty have been actively mobilizing support within the extra-parliamentary party.

There has been one specific campaign, however, to make the party leadership more accountable to the individual party membership, which had its origins in the grass-roots membership. In the late 1960s a group from the Greater London Young Conservatives (GLYC) produced a pamphlet, *Set the Party Free*, which was extremely critical of party organization, and described the party as 'one of the least democratic organisations in Britain outside the Freemasons' (1969: 20).

Their purpose in writing the pamphlet was 'to hasten the demise of the Tory party as a private club and its regeneration as a democratic organisation' (1969: 43). They demanded the 'fundamental democratisation of the organisation' (1969: 9), and in particular, that the powers of the National Union relative to Central

Office be strengthened. They wanted constituency associations to be reorganized along more political lines, with officers of both the National Union and Central Office to be elected, and the annual party conference to be less stage-managed by the party leadership. They succeeded in persuading the National Union to establish a committee of inquiry, the Chelmer Committee, in 1970 to ascertain 'the extent to which the Conservative Party, in all its aspects outside Parliament, might be made more democratic'; but this particular initiative generated much internal party hostility, and ultimately failed (Seyd, 1975).

The demand from the grass roots for a more democratic party has not completely disappeared. Some of the personnel from the GLYC who produced *Set the Party Free* have been actively involved in two contemporary groups campaigning for greater party democracy: the Charter Movement and the Party Reform Steering Committee.

We have already referred to the Charter Movement's critique of party democracy. A group of party members first produced their charter of demands, *A Charter to Set the Party Free,* in 1981, and since then have published a regular *Charter News.* They argued in their original charter that the party 'has been treated as the personal property of its successive leaders' for more than a century, and that now was the time for the membership 'to take possession of what is rightfully theirs'. Centralization, secrecy, and deference are the principles by which the party is governed, and as a result 'it is not democratic . . . (but) feudal'. Their ten demands included a directly elected policy committee; elected party officers responsible for party organizational and financial matters and answerable to directly elected executive bodies; that the Central Council be the governing body of the party; that the annual party conference be run by an elected committee; and that all members in constituency associations have a direct vote in the selection and reselection of parliamentary candidates.

The Party Reform Steering Committee, established in 1992, was conceived originally by members of the Charter movement as a means of attracting wider support for two specific proposals: first, that one-half the members of the National Union Executive Committee be directly elected by members of the Central Council in a postal ballot, and second, that the National Union should take over responsibility for party finances from Central Office.

The demands of both the Charter Movement and the Party Reform Steering Committee have been turned down consistently by senior personnel within the National Union and Central Office. Eric Chalker, a leading figure in the reform movement since the late 1960s, received a low vote in the ballot among National Union Executive Committee members for the chairmanship of that body in 1991. This reveals the limited support for greater party democracy which existed at that time at that level of the party organization.

Another setback to the reformers occurred when senior party officers rejected the Party Reform Steering Committee's demand for a special Central Council meeting to discuss their proposals, even though they were supported by the fifty constituency associations stipulated in the party rule book. This indicated the readiness of senior officials to basically ignore grass-roots opinion.

Nevertheless, there is some recognition in the recent Feldman Report on the voluntary party that all is not well, and of the need to be more responsive to the grass roots (Conservative Party, 1993*b*). This report recognized the need for the party to be more open, for members to have 'more say in the affairs of Central Office', and for there to be more scope for 'participation and consultation' (1993*b*: 15).

The party has responded to these concerns by expanding the number of constituency association representatives on the National Union Executive Committee. However, this is a very limited response to the demands for greater membership participation. The extent to which the bulk of the membership wants the party to provide greater scope for their participation and the extent to which they are dissatisfied with the structures of the party will be discussed more fully in Chapter 7.

We referred earlier to the uncontroversial reception given to McKenzie's thesis about the distribution of power within the Conservative party. Since publication of the first edition of his book in the mid-1950s, other academics, Conservative politicians, and political journalists have reiterated his thesis. For example, Ball describes the annual conference as 'essentially a rally of the party faithful, an occasion for the grassroots to see and hear their national leaders' (1981: 211); Ingle believes that the annual conference is a 'public relations exercise' (1987: 58); Gilmour, an ex-Cabinet Minister, regards conference proceedings as 'more of an exercise in revivalist enthusiasm than a serious discussion of issues and policies' (1971: 80); and, finally, Hugo Young (1987) writes of the annual party conference as being 'less a conference than a festival of worship'.

Recently, however, this prevailing wisdom has been challenged by Richard Kelly (1989) in *Conservative Party Conferences* and in subsequent publications (1991*a*, 1991*b*, 1992). Kelly is critical of McKenzie for judging the effectiveness of the annual Conservative party conference by the same criteria as its Labour party counterpart. He argues that the two parties are rather dissimilar, basing this conclusion on two lines of reasoning.

First, he points out that the Conservative conference is the culmination of an extensive range of functional and area conferences, the 'Conservative conference system' (1989: 184) as he describes it, which take place throughout the year and enable the party leadership to sound out activists and for them to express their opinions. Kelly points out that, in addition to the five functional conferences,[6] something in the range of sixty area and area sectional conferences take place in a year. He estimates that in 1986 at least one party conference took place somewhere in the country each week, and that this total conference system involved about 20,000 participants.

Kelly believes that observers attending the annual conference each autumn are likely to misjudge the mood of unity, thinking it to be evidence of deference and powerlessness. By contrast, he argues that the party leadership responds to its soundings of activist opinions as expressed in this conference system. What appears therefore to be a well-stage-managed and bland rally of the party faithful is actually the final stage of a process of activist participation which goes on throughout the year.

On this view, the party leadership has listened to and responded to these grass-roots pressures, and is therefore applauded for its responsiveness at the annual conference. The Press and political observers at their October seaside trip have missed the previous debates, and they observe only the final crowning ceremony.

A second point in Kelly's argument is that by concentrating on the formal aspects of intra-party democracy, such as resolutions, amendments, and votes, which prevail within the Labour party,

---

[6] Conservative Graduates, Women, Trade-Unionists, Local Councillors, and Young Conservatives.

observers ignore such informal features of debate as mood and atmosphere. He argues that the Conservative grass roots 'have considerable influence upon ministerial initiatives' because senior party leaders 'regard party activists as fairly reliable representatives of public opinion and so listen carefully to their views, as expressed during the season of Conservative party conferences' (1989: 184).

These views may not be reflected in particular resolutions, amendments, or ballots; rather, it is the tenor of the speeches and the floor's reaction to them—in other words, the 'atmosphere' of a conference debate—which plays an important part in the two-way communication of views between the leadership and the grass roots.

Kelly thus rejects the view that the Conservative party has an 'oligarchic leadership and servile membership', arguing instead that it is a 'vibrant and diverse organisation' in which 'activists are much more influential than hitherto assumed' (1989: 188). Thus intra-party democracy exists in the Conservative party, but in an 'oblique and informal way' (ibid.).

The difficulty with this interpretation is of course in testing it. It is obviously very difficult to measure such an informal mechanism of pressure as a conference 'mood', given that it is very difficult to know if the leadership actually responds to such pressures. Kelly (1991*b*) cites one example of leadership responsiveness to informal pressures, in relation to the reform of local government taxation in the mid- to late 1980s. The party leadership responded to criticisms of the rating revaluation exercise in Scotland in 1985, and subsequently abandoned the original four-year implementation programme for the poll-tax in 1987.

Moreover, its decision to provide local councils with central government grants to alleviate the worst effects of the local tax and grant reforms in 1989 was prompted by pressure. He argues that the party's policies in this area emerged not as the result of hostile motions or ballots, but as a consequence of informal pressures by party activists.

Kelly does not, however, discuss the possibility that the mood of the voters prompted these shifts in policy, rather than the attitudes of the party members. There is some evidence from Conservative conferences that activists were in favour of the community charge, yet the party leadership abandoned the policy once it became apparent that the majority of voters were opposed. Furthermore, there are other instances where the apparent moods of a party conference—for example, on capital punishment, coloured immigration, or membership of the European Community—have been ignored.

McKenzie made clear that no Conservative party leader could afford to entirely ignore the grass roots. Clearly their views, as expressed through the various forums of the National Union, are one factor to be taken into consideration by the party leadership when deciding policies and strategies. Nevertheless, McKenzie argued that the combined power of history, cultural expectations, and practice ensures that members' powers are very limited. Kelly has ensured that commentators are now aware of the wide range of conferences, not just the annual conference and the Central Council, which exist for members to express their opinions. However, he overstates the case for party democracy within the Conservative party.

The distribution of political power within British parties is highly complex, and is dependent upon a range of factors which can vary over time. Claims made that the Labour party is a democratic organization in which individual members can, through the annual party conference, determine party policy are wide of the mark. Nevertheless, as Minkin's (1978, 1992) studies of both the Labour party conference and the trade-union connection reveal, the role of extra-parliamentary institutions is of prime importance in determining both the party's policies and its political strategies. In the Conservative party, however, the extra-parliamentary wing plays no role of comparable significance.

The traditional culture of the Conservative party emphasizes leadership; the party is the personal vehicle of the person selected, or elected since 1965, to lead it. This was the Court of Appeal's judgment in the tax case referred to earlier. Hierarchy, respect for, and deference to leaders have been the prevailing values of Conservatism. So long as the party leader continues to maintain electoral success, he or she will receive political loyalty. There is none of the sense of participation and egalitarianism which has prevailed in the Labour party. Formal authority is vested in the Conservative leader by the parliamentarians; that person then has the power to make appointments in the parliamentary party and the party bureaucracy, and their responsibility and accountability is to the leader.

The party has no constitution which might accord other institutions any formal powers. There is certainly no document which stipulates the powers of members in the area of policy-making. No statements are made by party leaders which legitimate members in a policy-making role, as compared with statements such as 'In the Labour party, policy is made by the members' (Labour Party, 1983). Intra-party politics is complex and variable within the Labour party, and the members' role in policy-making has been reduced since 1983; none the less, their formal and informal powers produce a form of intra-party politics very different from that of the Conservative party.

However, Kelly's argument that observers have paid little attention to the Conservative 'conference system', the wide range of area and functional conferences, is valid. The opportunity to express opinions in these venues is considerable, and they provide party leaders with the opportunity to 'test the party waters'. No politician would be foolish enough not to use these conferences to listen to the opinions of those attending.

Kelly's argument that changes are occurring in both society and the Conservative party which increase the likelihood of membership involvement is also convincing. Long-term structural and socio-economic changes—in particular, shifting patterns of authority, the recruitment of a new generation of young professional Conservative members, a declining deference to authority in society, and, finally, a political programme which encourages citizens' empowerment, both in the market-place and in society generally—will all have an impact on internal party affairs.

Furthermore, recent events within the party, such as the removal of Mrs Thatcher from leadership by the parliamentary party, the revelations about party funding, and the poor election campaigns of 1987 and 1992, have prompted pressures for greater grass-roots involvement.

The Conservative conference system, however, does not provide an opportunity for party members to directly elect a body which represents them, in the way that Labour's National Executive Committee represents the grass-roots membership, independent of the parliamentary leadership. Moreover, the decisions taken within the Conservative conference system have no formal authority of any sort, to the extent that there is no formal record of the decisions taken which might then feed into the parliamentary party. This means that there is only the vaguest sense of platform accountability during conference debates. Many observers believe that platform personnel are more concerned to enhance their individual careers by successfully managing the conference representatives than in representing and being accountable to those on the floor.

Admittedly, the party leadership has no control over the initial agendas of the conference system. For example, constituency associations can submit as many resolutions as they please to the annual conference, giving them the opportunity to 'let off steam'. However, there is strict control of the agenda for debate at the annual conference, in which the leadership plays a key role, and there is no accountability to the conference for the decisions taken over the scheduling of debates.

One way to address this debate about the power of party members *vis-à-vis* the leadership is to ask the members what they think about their influence on the party and on policy-making. We will examine attitudes to this issue more fully later, but for now it is interesting to note some of the responses to questions in the survey. Some 55 per cent of members agree or strongly agree with the proposition that 'People like me can have a real influence on politics if they are prepared to get involved' (25 per cent disagree or strongly disagree); and 33 per cent disagree or strongly disagree with the proposition that 'The party leadership doesn't pay a lot of attention to the views of ordinary party members' (43 per cent agree or strongly agree). Finally, 74 per cent agree or strongly agree with the statement 'When Conservative party members work together they can really change Britain' (8 per cent disagree or strongly disagree).

While opinions on this issue are far from unanimous, these statements none the less support the proposition that many members feel quite influential. Thus it would be quite wrong to argue that in general they feel powerless and unable to influence the party leadership and Conservative party politics. In other words, members' own perceptions of their role in politics are inconsistent with the McKenzie thesis, and rather more consistent with the Kelly thesis.

We will return to a discussion of this evidence in a later chapter, but for the moment it would be fair to conclude that the original McKenzie thesis probably exaggerates the power of the leadership *vis-à-vis* the members, and overstates the weakness of the grass-roots membership. On the other hand, the party has no procedures formalizing the accountability of the party leadership to the members, and there are enough members who are sceptical about the responsiveness of the leadership to suggest that Kelly rather overstates the opposite case. Members may not be as weak as McKenzie suggests, but nor are they as influential as Kelly suggests.

RESEARCH ON PARTY MEMBERS

We have emphasized up to this point the limited amount of research which exists on Conservative party politics. As one author has commented, 'The Conservative Party is one of the least studied political organisations in Britain' (Bulpitt, 1991). Furthermore, those studies of the Conservative party that do exist tend to concentrate upon histories of Conservative governments and biographies of Conservative leaders, which reflects, in part, the non-Conservative political disposition of most British political scientists.

There is also a view that little of value will be learned from a study of Conservative intra-party politics. Bulpitt believes that the relationship between leaders and followers in the Conservative party is 'a huge subject and probably a dreary one' (1991: 10) best left to sociologists and psychologists!

The dearth of empirical studies of the party means that we possess little accurate information about the numbers, motivations, social composition, or attitudes of the party members. The same limiting factors apply, as mentioned before, in attempting to obtain such information: namely, the initial expense of conducting a national, representative survey and the difficulties faced when all party records are lodged with over 600 constituency associations.

Inevitably, therefore, studies of the party's grass roots tend to be based either upon surveys of particular constituency associations, selective participant observation of particular groups of Conservatives, or surveys of particular groups within constituency associations. Examples of the latter would include Blondel (1973: 99), who suggests that business and professional men predominate in local associations, and McKenzie, who refers to members as 'ardent partisans' and 'scorpions in the constituency associations' (1964: 230, 633).

One of the very few attempts to examine the nature of constituency association leaders was a study of constituency chairmen carried out in 1969 (Butler and Pinto-Duschinsky, 1980). The conclusions were that local party officers were mainly male business executives or proprietors. The difficulty with this survey, however, as the authors admit, is that the information was based upon interviews with Conservative area agents in England and Wales, rather than with the chairmen themselves. Thus it relies on the interpretations of other people, rather than on those of the members of the group being studied.

Another interesting study, by Bealey, Blondel, and McCann (1965), was part of a wider examination of the Newcastle-under-Lyme constituency, and included the local Conservative association. Their conclusions were that the typical Conservative party member is in a high occupational status group, does not belong to a trade union, is an Anglican, was educated beyond the age of 15, is more likely to be female, is aged between 50 and 59, and reads either the *Daily Mail* or the *Daily Express*.

Bealey and his colleagues asked Conservatives for their opinions on three issues: crime and punishment, national service, and immigration, and on the basis of their responses concluded that the members were essentially moderates. Published almost thirty years ago, this was one of a few studies of grass-roots politics. Nevertheless, it has the obvious limitation of lacking representativeness. It is impossible to say how typical the Newcastle-under-Lyme Conservatives are in relation to the national membership.

An alternative approach, which tries to meet this objection, is to observe Conservatives in a wider setting. Morris (1991) writes 'about the people who make up the Conservative Party', and does this by talking to party members at all levels and in all parts of the country. He suggests that individuals are motivated to become members primarily because of their social backgrounds, but a conformist instinct or a dislike of state intervention will also encourage a party commitment. He states that at the grass-roots level the party is run by the retired, who convey an overwhelming ethos of amateurishness, and that the main focus of their activities is fund-raising. Again, this type of study has its value in providing a flavour of Conservative politics, but there is still the problem of representativeness.

One author who has attempted to overcome these limitations is

Richard Rose (1976), who examined all the resolutions submitted by local associations to the five annual party conferences held between 1955 and 1960. His conclusions were that non-partisanship and apathy prevailed among Conservative ranks; furthermore, he asserts that there was no relationship between partisanship on policy views and the 'safeness' of a Conservative seat. He concluded that constituency activists were not extremists, and furthermore that many of them were not even strongly partisan.

A similar study of conference resolutions submitted between 1945 and 1973 (Wilson, 1977) concluded that there was little apparent ideological consistency among the sentiments expressed.

Apart from these two studies of conference resolutions, there have been no national surveys of constituency opinions, with the exception of the present study and the British candidate study, which includes a survey of 601 Conservative party members involved in the selection of parliamentary candidates in twenty-six constituencies (Norris and Lovenduski, 1992).

In the next chapter we provide an overview of the findings of the survey of Conservative party members carried out for the present study. The methodological details of the survey can be found in Appendix I, but, briefly, it involved selecting a random sample of Conservative party members in Great Britain, so as to obtain a representative picture of the grass roots of the party as a whole.

3

Who Are the Members?

In this chapter we will provide an overview of the social and political characteristics of the grass-roots Conservative party membership. This begins with an examination of Conservative members' socio-economic backgrounds, and continues with a discussion of their attitudes to certain key political issues. We will also compare the party members with Conservative voters, to see what similarities and differences exist between the two groups. Our survey of party members and the 1992 British Election Study were conducted within a few months of each other, so comparisons of Conservative voters and party members are particularly accurate. In the final section of the chapter we examine their contacts with the party organization, their rates of activism, and the extent to which they vote in general elections.

A SOCIO-ECONOMIC PROFILE OF THE MEMBERS

The typical Conservative party member is retired, comes from a middle-class occupational background, is an owner-occupier, and possesses few educational qualifications. Men and women belong to the party in roughly equal numbers.

The age profile of the membership is skewed very markedly towards the elderly, the average age of the members being 62. Almost one-half of the membership is aged 66 or over, while only 5 per cent are under the age of 35. This is a very striking profile, and suggests that unless the Conservative party renews itself by recruiting many more younger members in the near future, it could face a very drastic decline in grass-roots membership over the next decade. On the assumption that the average life expectancy of a party member is 75 years, the party stands to lose more than 40 per cent of its membership over the next decade.

The task of recruiting additional young members is of course made harder by the reluctance of young people to become involved

TABLE 3.1. *Socio-economic Characteristics of the Party Membership: Gender, Age, and Education* (percentages)

Gender (N = 2405)	
Male	51
Female	49
Age (N = 2424)	
25 and under	1
26–35	4
36–45	11
46–55	17
56–65	24
66 and over	43
Type of school last attended (N = 2429)	
Primary/Elementary	13
Secondary Modern/Technical/Scottish Secondary	26
Grammar/Scottish Senior Secondary	28
Comprehensive/Scottish Comprehensive	3
Direct grant/Grant-Aided	1
Private fee-paying/Scottish independent	23
Other	5
Age at end of full-time education (N = 2412)	
16 and under	55
17–18	25
19 and over	19

Note: Figures in this table, and all subsequent tables, have been rounded, and therefore may not total 100.

in politics (Parry *et al.*, 1992: 153–5); but it is clear at the present time that, despite the enormous electoral success of the Conservative party, it has failed to attract the Conservatively-inclined among the more politically aware and interested youth.

In the 1950s the Young Conservatives was a buoyant organization with a membership of around 100,000. At that time it was renowned for its social activities, which helped to recruit young people into the party (Layton-Henry, 1973). Now, however, the Young Conservatives lacks both social and political appeal. Neither the National Association of Conservative Graduates nor the Conservative Collegiate Forum, two Conservative groups organizing among youth in higher education, have succeeded in recruiting large numbers. In addition, the Federation of Conservative Students has been disbanded because its attitudes and behaviour became embarrassing to the party leadership.

Among Young Conservatives there is today an active and vociferous group of Thatcherites, critical of the Conservative government, whose prominence may be damaging attempts to recruit young people into the party. In fact, in recent years the party leadership has experienced difficulties with its youth organizations similar to those of the Labour party leadership.

Because of their age, the majority of party members have not participated in the growth which has occurred in higher education since the 1960s. Over one-half (55 per cent) left school at the age of 16 or under. Not surprisingly, therefore, the typical party member lacks many of the formal educational qualifications which are common among the middle class today: almost one-third (31 per cent) have no educational qualifications at all, and only 12 per cent possess a university degree. Conservatives are often suspicious of modern educational trends and critical of current educational standards, and this may be, in part, because their world is far removed from that of today's schools, colleges, and universities.

In many of the studies of the Conservative party élite great emphasis is placed upon the importance of private education (see Butler and Pinto-Duschinsky, 1980). Public schools have always been important in Conservative politics; their values tend to be traditional, their former pupils are more likely to be Conservative voters, and they train future Conservative élites.[1]

The number of Conservative MPs educated at private, fee-paying schools has always been high (Blondel, 1963; Guttsman, 1963; Mellors, 1978; Moran, 1985); yet their selectors, the local constituency association members, have been largely educated at state schools. One in eight of the party members completed their education at a state primary or elementary school, one in five at a secondary modern school, and a further one in four at a grammar school. So, in fact, the great majority of party members have been educated in state schools, and only about one-quarter went to private schools.

[1] According to the 1992 British Election Study, 11.5% of the electorate went to private schools, and of these some 52% were Conservative voters, compared with 41% who were Conservatives in the electorate as a whole.

TABLE 3.2. *Socio-economic Characteristics of the Party Membership: Work Sector, Class, Housing Tenure, Share Ownership, and Income* (percentages)

Type of work organization of sector (N = 2082)

Private company/firm	60
Nationalized industry	5
Local authority	14
Health authority/hospital	7
Central government/Civil Service	6
Other	10

Socio-economic occupational classification (N = 2095)

Salariat	55
Routine non-manual	18
Petty bourgeoisie	13
Foreman and technician	6
Working class	8

Type of housing tenure (N = 2419)

Own property	91
Rented from council	3
Rented privately	3
Rented from housing association	1
Living with family/friends	1

Share Ownership (N = 2416)

Yes	70
No	30

Household income (£ p.a.) (N = 2295)

Under £5,000	8
£5,000–£10,000	18
£10,000–£15,000	19
£15,000–£20,000	15
£20,000–£30,000	19
£30,000–£40,000	10
£40,000–£50,000	5
£50,000 and over	8

Given the age profile of the membership, it is not surprising that only a minority (29 per cent) were in full-time work. Among those still working or previously employed, a clear majority (60 per cent) earned their living in the private sector, and some 31 per cent worked in the public sector of the economy. Of the latter, teachers were the only large distinct occupational group among the members. It is often assumed that the Conservative party is over-whelmingly a businessman's party. In fact, while the traditional local businessman who owns his company and employs a labour force is represented within its ranks, the party's membership is much more varied in terms of occupational backgrounds.

The Conservative party is overwhelmingly a middle-class party. If we use the occupational classification adopted in the British Election Study (Heath *et al.*, 1991), fewer than 10 per cent are traditional manual workers, among whom farm-workers are the largest group. A further 6 per cent are foremen and technicians. Working-class Conservatism has been an important contributory factor in the party's electoral dominance, but it is weak at the grass roots.

Over half (55 per cent) of the members are in the salariat, which includes a very broad span of occupations; teachers are the largest single group, followed closely by financial-service workers, such as accountants, underwriters, brokers, and tax specialists. The tradi-tional professions of law and medicine are less well represented; judges, barristers, solicitors, consultants, doctors, and dentists make up only a small part of the membership. There are, in fact, more nurses than consultants or doctors among the membership. Mar-keting and public-relations executives are also a significant group among the salariat, and so are those in administrative positions in either central or local government.

Julian Critchley (1985) has suggested that the grass-roots Con-servative party has become dominated by estate agents; but while that may have occurred in his Aldershot constituency, they have only a very small presence, constituting 1 per cent of the salariat, among the membership at large.

Just under one-fifth of the members are routine, non-manual workers, most of whom are clerks, cashiers, typists, secretaries, and receptionists. Finally, a further 13 per cent are categorized as petty bourgeois, of whom 98 per cent are self-employed; in this group proprietors of small businesses predominate (24 per cent). There are fewer farmers than might be expected, considering the Conservative party's historic attachment to British agriculture; in fact, there are more farm-workers than farmers in the membership. The historic links between farming and the Conservative party have always been close; so also have the links with the building and brewing industries, though only a small number of members are builders or publicans, constituting 5 and 3 per cent respectively of this category.

The language of class politics is very often downplayed by Conservatives; they regard class categories as divisive and unreal. Margaret Thatcher described class as a 'Communist concept'. Nevertheless, when members were asked whether they thought of themselves as belonging to any particular social class, almost two-thirds (62 per cent) responded positively, and of these, three-quarters described themselves as being middle-class, and about 19 per cent as working-class.

About 80 per cent agreed that their families belonged to a social class when they were young, and 40 per cent of these described this as 'working class'. Thus many members think of themselves as being upwardly mobile, having moved from the working class in their youth to the middle class at the present time. Whether upwardly mobile individuals are more likely to join the Conservative party or whether membership of the Conservative party affirms an individual's sense of upward mobility is hard to say, but certainly members have a clear sense of upward mobility.

Just as members' work experiences have been in the private sector of the economy, so also their living experiences have been in the private sector of the property market. Nine of every ten owned their own property, and only 3 per cent rented accommodation from the local council. Only a very small number (4 per cent) had benefited from the Conservative government's 'right to buy' legislation, and purchased rented council property. This was mainly because the vast majority of Conservative members have been owner-occupiers for many years.

Further evidence of members' practical experience of the private property market is revealed by the fact that almost three-quarters (70 per cent) own stocks and shares. Members may not have been in a position to benefit directly from the Government's sale of council houses because so few lived in such properties, but they participated in the Government's privatization of public

TABLE 3.3. *Socio-economic Characteristics of the Party Membership: Religion and Ethnicity* (percentages)

Religion (N = 2435)	
Non-believer	11
Protestant (Church of England/Scotland)	70
Nonconformist (Methodist, Baptist, United Reform Church)	7
Roman Catholic	7
Christian, but no denomination	4
Jew	1
Muslim	1
Other	1
Ethnic Origin (N = 2375)	
White	99
Asian	1

utilities: 72 per cent bought shares in the newly privatized industries. For the majority of members this was not, however, their first experience of 'popular capitalism', since 62 per cent owned shares prior to the privatization programme. Nevertheless, an additional 10 per cent of members were attracted to investing in stocks and shares.

A large share-owning membership suggests a reasonable household income. However, with such a large number of elderly and retired persons, it is not surprising that more than a quarter have household incomes below £10,000 per year. At the other end of the scale, however, just under a quarter have a household income above £30,000 per year, with almost one in ten of the members receiving more than £50,000 each year. There is no evidence of a bunching of members into distinct groups of rich and poor. Only a small number are either very rich or very poor; there is a relatively even spread of household incomes among the majority, with the median income being in the £15,000–20,000 range.

If, in the past, the Church of England has been described as the 'Conservative party at prayer', then today's Conservative party can be described as the 'political wing of the Church of England'. Thus it is not a party of atheists and agnostics; only 11 per cent of members reject any identification with a religion. Among religious believers, seven in every ten belong to the Church of England or

TABLE 3.4. *Newspaper Readership* (percentages; N = 2417)

No daily newspaper	11
Daily Express	14
Daily Mail	17
Daily Telegraph	28
The Times	6
Other daily papers (*Sun, Daily Mirror, Independent, Financial Times, Today*)	8
Other combinations of daily papers (e.g. *Daily Telegraph* with *Daily Mail*)	16

to the equivalent church in Scotland. Less than 10 per cent are Roman Catholic, and only 1 per cent are Jewish.

In the 1980s the party attempted to recruit people from ethnic minorities, particularly from the Asian community. These efforts, however, have made little impact on the overall composition of the membership, which remains overwhelmingly white.

Finally, the Conservatism of the members is reflected in their newspaper-reading habits. Most read either the quality *Daily Telegraph* (28 per cent) or one of the two middle-brow mass dailies, the *Daily Mail* (17 per cent) or the *Daily Express* (14 per cent). Neither of the two Murdoch-owned, Conservative-supporting daily newspapers, *The Times* and the *Sun*, are read by significant numbers of members.

In the light of these results it is interesting to examine how socially representative the members are of Conservative voters in general. In Table 3.5 we compare some of the social characteristics of members and voters, the information on the latter taken from the British Election Study of 1992.

Conservative members and voters are strikingly similar in their patterns of both home ownership and household income. With few exceptions they are home-owners, and both groups have an average household income of between £15,000 and £20,000 per annum. They are also very similar in their educational upbringing; over one-half of members and nearly two-thirds of Conservative voters left school at the age of 16 or earlier. Thus neither Conservative members nor Conservative voters are highly educated; fewer than one in five remained in full-time education beyond the

TABLE 3.5. *Social Characteristics of Conservative Party Members and Voters* (percentages)

	Members (N = 2467)	Voters (N = 2779)
Gender		
Male	51	45
Female	49	55
Age		
25 and under	1	9
26–35	4	20
36–45	11	18
46–55	17	18
56–65	24	14
66 and over	43	21
Social Class		
Salariat	55	38
Routine non-manual	18	24
Petty bourgeoisie	13	12
Foreman and Technician	6	5
Working class	8	22
Housing tenure		
Own property	91	86
Rented from council	3	7
Other rented	5	7
Age at end of full-time education		
16 and under	55	64
17–18	25	19
19 and over	19	14
Household income (£ p.a.)		
Under £10,000	26	25
£10,000–£15,000	19	14
£15,000–£20,000	15	16
£20,000 and over	42	44

age of 19. There are only slightly more graduates among party members (12 per cent) than among voters (8 per cent).

Major differences do occur between the two groups, however, in age and class profiles. Almost one-half of Conservative voters are under the age of 45, but fewer than one in five of the members are in this age-group. There are nine times more Conservative voters under the age of 25 than there are party members. Eight in every ten party members are aged 46 and above, a much higher proportion than among the voters. Among those aged 66 and above, there are twice as many Conservative members as there are voters.

There is also a marked disparity in the class background of the two groups. Much of the Conservative party's electoral support comes from the middle class, in particular from the salariat and those in routine, non-manual jobs. Without the electoral support of the working class, however, the Conservative party would never have been so electorally successful (McKenzie and Silver, 1968). In the 1992 general election almost one-quarter of the party's voters were manual workers, but few from among this group were party members. Almost three times as many Conservative voters as members are working-class in terms of their occupational status.

At the other end of the occupational scale, a greater proportion of Conservative members than voters are from the salariat. Routine, non-manual workers are under-represented within the Conservative party as compared to the numbers who voted Conservative in 1992. Only among the petty-bourgeoisie and the labour 'aristocracy' of foremen and technicians are there similar proportions of party members and Conservative voters.

We should not be surprised at this social imbalance between members and voters. The working class is under-represented in all aspects of British political life (Parry *et al.*, 1992: 124–35). Even the Labour party, whose origins and purpose were to represent working-class interests in Parliament, has fewer manual-worker members than middle-class members (Seyd and Whiteley, 1992). There are very few organizations in which working-class people predominate at both top and bottom; the majority of trade unions and some sporting, recreational, and leisure organizations are the limit of working-class participation.

Does it matter if the party's membership is so much older and more middle-class than its voters? It might not if the image the party communicates to this electorate strikes a positive chord. If, however, the language the membership uses, the issues it debates, and the policies it concerns itself with are not those of the voters, then the party leadership's task of electoral mobilization will be made more difficult. If party members are to serve as 'ambassadors in the community', then they need to be sensitive to local opinions; otherwise their role in helping to communicate the party leadership's views to the voters, and vice versa, will be impaired.

If the messages being conveyed to the voters by the members are those of an increasingly elderly, middle-class group of people, then the party leadership's task is that much greater, since it has to appeal to two distinct constituencies; the problem is that the members and voters may have few shared concerns. However, the party leadership's task of catering to a broad electoral constituency is made easier by the party norms and procedures which restrict the role of the party member in policy deliberations. The limited formal role that the party membership is given in internal party affairs enables the leadership to concentrate upon the wider constituency without too much pressure from within.

Nevertheless, as we pointed out in Chapter 1, the party member has a formal role in candidate selection, and therefore plays a significant part in determining the future direction of the party. Furthermore, as we saw in Chapter 2, Kelly (1989) has argued that the activists, defined in terms of those who attend party conferences, have a significant role in influencing party policy, even if this is seldom exercised by formal votes. We question whether that role is as significant as he suggests; nevertheless, the number and range of party conferences does allow activists the opportunity to voice their opinions in a multitude of forums. These channels of influence from the grass-roots party require the leadership to maintain a careful strategy of consultation and negotiation if it is not to face damaging internal dissension.

We examine the members' attitudes in more detail in Chapter 6, in a discussion of the ideological beliefs of the grass-roots party, but here a preliminary outline of their opinions is given.

THE POLITICAL ATTITUDES OF PARTY MEMBERS

When members were asked whether the Conservative party should stick by its principles, even at the expense of the loss of an election, an overwhelming 81 per cent agreed. This suggests that down at the grass roots there exists a party which is very keen to retain its ideological distinctiveness, and is unwilling to make electoral compromises. But the precise nature of these principles is not easy to ascertain, since the Conservative party is often reticent about defining them. Many leading party members deny the existence of Conservative ideological beliefs, arguing instead that Conservatism is essentially a pragmatic political philosophy (Gilmour, 1977).

Others claim that because the Conservative party has dominated twentieth-century electoral politics, it has become a governing party, with the result that Conservatism is no more than a pragmatic response to the particular requirements of office at any particular moment of time (Bulpitt, 1986; Norton, 1992: 33). Other theorists, however, suggest certain underlying Conservative 'themes': for example, commitments to inequality, private property, and the traditional family.

Often this discussion of Conservative principles is conducted in abstractions, in terms of general values and principles, rather than specific political attitudes. We ascertained members' opinions by asking them a large number of attitude questions covering a wide range of contemporary political issues, the detailed discussion of which is in Chapter 6. We suggest, as already indicated, that British Conservatism divides into three broad ideological tendencies: traditionalism, individualism, and progressivism.

Conservative traditionalists are wary of social and political change; so, for example, they are less sympathetic towards the emancipation of women, the availability of abortion, and the easing of divorce laws. They approve of both authority and discipline; they favour punishment to deter crime and the maintenance of capital punishment for murder. They are patriots who are proud of Britain's past and believe that its institutions, such as the monarchy and the House of Lords, should be maintained. They believe that British institutions should not be undermined by the European Community; nor should British culture be subordinated to a mix of cultures within a multi-ethnic society.

We select here some of the traditionalist indicators in our survey in order to illustrate these beliefs. Almost three-quarters (70 per cent) of the membership believe that a Conservative government should encourage repatriation of immigrants, and two-thirds (69 per cent) think that the death penalty should be reintroduced

TABLE 3.6. *Members' Attitudes to Traditionalist Issues* (percentages)

	(a)	(b)	(c)	(d)	(e)
Agree	70	69	60	33	47
Disagree	19	24	27	48	43
Neither	12	7	13	19	10

Notes: Party members were asked to respond on a five-point scale ('strongly agree', 'agree', 'neither', 'disagree', 'strongly disagree') to the following statements:

(a) 'A future Conservative government should encourage the repatriation of immigrants.'

(b) 'The death penalty should be reintroduced for murder.'

(c) 'Divorce has become too easy these days, and the divorce laws should be tightened up.'

(d) 'A future Conservative government should make abortions more difficult to obtain.'

(e) 'All shops should be allowed to open on Sundays.'

The 'strongly agree' and the 'agree' and the 'strongly disagree' and 'disagree' have been combined.

as a punishment for murder. A majority (60 per cent) believe that the divorce laws should be made more rigorous in order to discourage the rising trend of divorces; a minority (43 per cent) oppose the opening of all shops on Sundays, and a smaller minority (33 per cent) want access to abortion to be made more difficult.

Progressive Conservatives accept political and social change as being necessary for the preservation of the traditional fabric of society, in particular the maintenance of private property and social hierarchy. To do this, they believe that a strategy of timely concessions to pressures for reform is often necessary; so, for example, many Conservatives argued in 1943 that the recommendations of the Beveridge Committee should be accepted because, in the words of Douglas Hogg, 'if you do not give the people social reform they are going to give you social revolution' (Addison, 1977: 232).

Progressives argued for a post-war political settlement based upon government intervention and Keynesian macro-economic management of the economy and a universal health service paid for by taxing the better-off. Today progressives emphasize the State's responsibility for the alleviation of poverty, for bringing about a limited redistribution of income and wealth, and for

TABLE 3.7. *Members' Attitudes to Progressive Issues* (percentages)

	(a)	(b)
Agree	74	27
Disagree	13	52
Neither	12	21

Notes:
(a) 'Unemployment benefit should ensure people a reasonable standard of living.'
(b) 'Income and wealth should be redistributed towards ordinary working people.'

	(c)	(d)
Should	81	64
Should not	11	22
Doesn't matter	8	13

Notes: Party members were asked to respond on a five-point scale ('definitely should', 'should', 'doesn't matter', 'should not', 'definitely should not') to the statements that the Government should/should not:
(c) 'spend more money to get rid of poverty'.
(d) 'give workers more say in the places where they work'.
The 'definitely should' and 'should' and the 'definitely should not' and 'should not' have been combined.

regulating and managing economic resources in the community's interests.

Almost three-quarters (74 per cent) of the membership believe that unemployment benefit should be at levels which ensure a reasonable standard of living for the unemployed, and an even larger majority (81 per cent) think that the Government should spend more money to relieve poverty. Almost two-thirds (64 per cent) believe that workers should be given more say in their places of work. However, the majority of members do not believe that it is the Government's responsibility to redistribute income and wealth to ordinary people; progressives are among the minority (27 per cent) on this issue.

Finally, individualists are closely identified with the ideals of *laissez-faire*. They believe that government intervention in the economy should be reduced, since it is only by stimulating market

TABLE 3.8. *Members' Attitudes to Individualist Issues* (percentages)

	(a)	(b)	(c)
Should	64	65	60
Should not	16	23	27
Doesn't matter	20	12	13

Notes: The Government should/should not:
 (a) 'encourage private education'.
 (b) 'introduce stricter laws to regulate the trade unions'.
 (c) 'cut income tax'.

	(d)	(e)
Agree	55	37
Disagree	28	51
Neither	17	12

Notes:
 (d) 'A future Conservative government should privatize British Coal.'
 (e) 'A future Conservative government should not privatize British Rail.'

forces that the economy will work efficiently. They also view the welfare state with hostility, believing that it undermines individual enterprise and creates a dependency culture. Individualistic conservatism is well represented among Conservative grass roots on some issues. Around two-thirds of the members want to encourage private education, to further restrict trade unions, and to cut income tax. They also want to extend the privatization programme to include British Coal and British Rail.

Later, in Chapter 6, we extend this analysis of the three Conservative ideological tendencies, and show that traditionalism is not as cohesive as individualism or progressivism. This confirms the point that Conservatism is a multi-faceted doctrine which does not precisely subdivide into neatly defined categories.

Before we conclude this initial discussion of grass-roots political opinions, however, there are two specific topics which should be addressed. First of these is the subject of Britain's membership of the European Community, which cuts across some traditional Conservative political loyalties. Deep divisions on this subject

TABLE 3.9. *Members' Attitudes to the European Community*
(percentages)

	(a)	(b)	(c)	(d)	(e)
Agree	68	67	53	57	22
Disagree	22	16	31	31	63
Neither	10	17	16	12	16

Notes:

(a) 'Britain's national sovereignty is being lost to Europe.'

(b) 'Britain should stay in the European Exchange Rate Mechanism.'

(c) 'Conservatives should resist further moves to integrate the European Community.'

(d) 'A future Conservative government should not agree to a single European currency.'

(e) 'A Conservative government should aim to make Britain part of a federal Europe.'

emerged among Conservative MPs over the issue of Britain's ratification of the Maastricht Treaty, and it is interesting to see how far these divisions extended to the party's grass roots.

Second, even though Margaret Thatcher was removed from the party leadership in November 1990, her legacy after fifteen years as party leader inevitably remained, and it is pertinent to ascertain the extent to which 'Thatcherism' prevails at the grass roots.

CONSERVATIVES AND THE EUROPEAN COMMUNITY

Party members were asked to respond to five indicators of their attitudes to the European Community (EC). First, they were asked whether they believed that, as a result of Britain's membership of the EC, its national sovereignty was diminishing, and over two-thirds (68 per cent) agreed that it was. Their opinions about this development were examined by asking them if Britain should remain within the European Exchange Rate Mechanism, which included the pound at the time of the survey, and two-thirds (67 per cent) of them agreed. This aspect of the loss of sovereignty was not opposed by the majority.

Members did not want to extend the powers of the EC further, however. Thus a majority (53 per cent) did not wish to see further

European integration; nor did they support the creation of a single European currency (57 per cent). However, on both integration in general and with regard to a European currency in particular, there is a significant pro-European sentiment among about one-third of the membership. The strongest test of support for European integration was provided by a question which asked members if they felt that Britain should become part of a European federal state; only about one in five (22 per cent) agreed with this idea.

It is clear that support for Britain's membership of the EC is there in the grass-roots party, and this influenced debates prior to the ratification of the Maastricht Treaty. It is of course possible that the campaign against ratification of the treaty by a hard core of Conservative MPs has modified that grass-roots support to some extent, and it may be that the majority who oppose further EC integration will have grown. Nevertheless, the fact that somewhere between one-fifth and one-third of the members are ardent Europeanists makes the task of party management difficult on this issue.

On the issue of further European integration, Margaret Thatcher has made clear her opposition to aspects of the Maastricht Treaty and to any further progress on this issue. But since losing the party leadership, her influence has been considerably reduced. It is interesting, however, to examine the extent to which she remains popular among grass-roots party members, since this provides an index of the influence she might have over future policies. We turn to this next.

MARGARET THATCHER'S POLITICAL LEGACY

Speaking to an American audience after her removal as party leader, Margaret Thatcher claimed that 'Thatcherism will live. It will live long after Thatcher has died' (*Guardian*, 22 April 1992). However, an examination of grass-roots opinions shows that support for Thatcherite principles is mixed among the membership.

Members favour privatization, but they are sceptical of some of the benefits claimed for this process. For example, a majority believe that both British Coal and British Rail should be privatized, but they also believe that the privatization programme has merely replaced public with private monopolies, and that the consumer needs protection from the free market.

TABLE 3.10. *Members' Attitudes to 'Thatcherite' Policies* (percentages)

	(a)	(b)	(c)
Agree	57	56	61
Disagree	25	25	24
Neither	18	19	15

Notes:
   (a) 'The consumer needs much stronger protection from the effects of the free market.'
   (b) 'Privatization of public enterprises has resulted in private monopoly rather than public monopoly.'
   (c) 'The welfare state undermines individual self-reliance and enterprise.'

	(d)	(e)	(f)	(g)
Should	81	51	80	60
Should not	11	33	13	31
Doesn't matter	8	16	7	9

Notes: The Government should/should not:
   (d) 'spend more money to get rid of poverty'.
   (e) 'encourage the growth of private medicine'.
   (f) 'put more money into the NHS'.
   (g) 'reduce government spending generally'.

Members' responses to questions concerning welfare also reveal a mix that is not consistently Thatcherite. Over one-half believe that the welfare state undermines individual self-reliance, and in line with such sentiments, almost two-thirds (64 per cent) support private education. A rather larger number (68 per cent) think that the introduction of market forces has improved the quality of services in the National Health system. On the other hand, only a bare majority (51 per cent) believe that private medicine should be encouraged, while eight in every ten members believe that the government should spend more money to remedy poverty and put more money into the National Health Service.

Many members, of course, are elderly, and are faced directly with problems of ill health and in some cases, poverty. Thus their personal circumstances may lead them to a modification of their Thatcherite principles. We examine Thatcherism in greater detail in Chapter 6, but here we suggest that the Conservative party has not really been converted to Thatcherism. There is support for some distinctively Thatcherite policies, but Conservatives in general are more progressive than many Thatcherites might wish to admit.

MEMBERS' OPINIONS ON INTERNAL PARTY MATTERS

Within the Conservative party great emphasis has always been placed on the qualities of the leadership, because the leaders have been accorded such great power: for example, power to appoint the Chairman of Conservative Central Office and the Shadow Cabinet when the party is in opposition. Considerable deference is displayed within the party towards leaders, unless they are electoral liabilities, and then they are ruthlessly removed from office. However, there have always been demands for greater party democracy, extending back to Randolph Churchill's 'Tory-Democracy' campaign of the early 1880s (Feuchtwanger, 1968).

In the 1970s a group of Young Conservatives in the Greater London region spearheaded a demand for greater party democracy (Seyd, 1975), and some of the same personnel involved in that movement are engaged in a similar campaign today to make the party more democratic. The Charter Movement is demanding that senior party officers be elected, that the main National Union committees be composed of elected party activists, and that the party's financial accounts be fully published.

In view of the importance attached to leaders in the party, it is interesting to examine the attitudes of party members to their leaders. We asked members to describe in their own words the qualities which they thought were necessary for party leadership; they ranked honesty as the most important, followed closely by firmness and conviction. These qualities dominated others such as the ability to get on well with people, the ability to communicate, intelligence, compassion, common sense, patriotism, vision, statesmanship, diplomacy, and principled commitment.

Our survey was conducted fourteen months after John Major was elected as party leader, at a time when his ranking among the general public was at its lowest point since he became Prime Minister. What did members think of him in comparison with Margaret Thatcher? When asked to express their feelings about various

TABLE 3.11. *Members' Ratings of the Conservative Leadership*
(out of 100 percentages)

	0–20	21–50	51–80	80+	Mean
John Major	0	6	52	42	80
Margaret Thatcher	1	10	45	44	78
Norman Lamont	2	34	59	5	59
Chris Patten	1	24	66	9	64
Norman Tebbit	1	21	59	19	67
Douglas Hurd	1	14	68	17	70
Kenneth Baker	3	34	58	5	59
Kenneth Clarke	3	28	62	7	61
William Waldegrave	2	29	63	6	61
Edward Heath	17	57	24	3	41
Lynda Chalker	2	32	62	4	59
Geoffrey Howe	6	42	48	4	53
Nigel Lawson	9	53	36	2	47
Teresa Gorman	5	54	39	2	51
Malcolm Rifkind	3	40	55	3	56
Michael Heseltine	3	22	64	12	64
Virginia Bottomley	1	20	72	7	64
David Hunt	4	43	49	4	55
Ian Lang	3	44	49	4	55
Michael Forsyth	5	51	40	4	52
Edwina Currie	5	31	57	7	57

senior party personnel on a scale ranging from zero to one hundred, members gave John Major a slightly higher ranking than his predecessor (a mean score of 80 compared with 78). The negative and positive feelings towards them both can be ascertained by comparing the scores of 50 or below and the scores of 80 and above; John Major is less disliked, but Margaret Thatcher evokes slightly more enthusiasm.

What is clear is that members are far less enamoured of most of Thatcher's critics. Ex-Conservative Prime Ministers might be expected to generate a reservoir of good will at the grass roots, but Edward Heath evokes considerable dislike. If dislike is measured by the percentage of members who return a score from 0 to 20, then Heath attracts greater hostility than Paddy Ashdown; members have no time for party disloyalty. It would appear likely, therefore, that Thatcher's ranking will drop as a consequence of her criticisms of the Conservative government led by her successor.[2]

Two of Thatcher's senior Ministers who resigned from office in protest at her style of premiership, Nigel Lawson and Geoffrey Howe, rank low in members' estimations. However, another of Thatcher's critics, Michael Heseltine, who had resigned much earlier from her Cabinet and had stood in the first ballot of the 1990 leadership election, ranked higher than many of her other Cabinet colleagues, although not as high as Norman Tebbit.

In the second ballot to elect a party leader, after Margaret Thatcher had withdrawn, Douglas Hurd came in a poor third, and one commentator argues that his campaign never really took off because he was too gentlemanly (Norton, 1993: 57). Nevertheless, Hurd has qualities which are clearly appreciated by members who ranked him third after Major and Thatcher.

We referred earlier to the demands of the Charter Movement for a more democratic party. There would appear to be support for more membership participation and a downgrading of the dominance of the parliamentary party among the Tory grass roots; for example, one-half expressed agreement with the view that the party leader should be elected by all party members. Some sense of the frustration felt by members that the leadership does not take enough note of them is revealed by the fact that a plurality (43 per cent) believe that 'The party leadership doesn't pay a lot of attention to the views of ordinary party members'.

Many members distrust Conservative party headquarters, a fact which we encountered in the course of organizing the survey; this distrust was confirmed in relation to the question of selecting parliamentary candidates; a plurality (41 per cent) rejected the idea that Conservative Central Office 'should have a more influential role in the selection of parliamentary candidates'.

Recently, the Conservative party's failure to select the most appropriate candidate for a particular constituency, particularly in by-elections, has attracted unfavourable press comment, and unflattering comparisons have been made with the Labour party

---

[2] A follow-up survey of this group of Conservative party members in 1994 will reveal whether this has been the case.

TABLE 3.12. *Members' Attitudes to the Party Leadership and Conservative Central Office* (percentages)

	(a)	(b)	(c)
Agree	50	43	31
Disagree	35	33	41
Neither	15	24	28

Notes:

(a) 'The Conservative party leader should be elected by a system of one party member, one vote.'

(b) 'The party leadership doesn't pay a lot of attention to the views of ordinary party members.'

(c) 'Conservative Central Office should have a more influential role in the selection of parliamentary candidates.'

in this regard. Labour's organizational reforms of the late 1980s gave its headquarters more control over candidate selection, particularly for by-elections. Therefore, there has been some pressure to increase the power of Conservative Central Office over candidate selection. However, as the responses show, such a move would encounter a lot of grass-roots opposition.

Finally, in this chapter, we compare and contrast the attitudes of party members and Conservative voters. It is widely assumed that the party membership is unrepresentative of its voters, and this may be one of the reasons why the Conservative party organizational structure limits the powers of the membership. It is interesting to examine the accuracy of this picture of the membership. We will concentrate our attention at this stage on some of the issues central to British Conservatism: namely, inequality, individual self-reliance, nationalism, and anti-trade unionism.

THE POLITICAL ATTITUDES OF PARTY MEMBERS AND VOTERS

We saw earlier that party members and voters have quite distinct demographic profiles; party members are older and more middle-class than voters. This could cause the party leadership problems if its more active supporters were to hold opinions which were not shared by voters. The party leadership might be forced into responding to conflicting pressures from within the party and from the wider electorate. The Labour party faced this dilemma in the early 1980s when its active members were pursuing policy goals, such as extending public ownership, abandoning nuclear-defence commitments, and withdrawing from the European Community, which were not the opinions of the majority of Labour voters. Does the Conservative party face a similar problem?

The membership survey and the British Election Study were conducted within three months of each other, thus enabling a useful comparison of attitudes to be drawn. On a wide range of policy matters covering government expenditure, public and private service provision, income distribution, the trade unions, defence, and penal affairs, it is apparent that there are no major differences of opinion between members and voters, only differences in the level of intensity with which the opinions are held.

For example, whereas over two-thirds (69 per cent) of members wish the death penalty to be reintroduced, a mere plurality (49 per cent) of Conservative voters share that opinion. On the other hand, whereas party members are evenly divided on the question of whether to increase defence expenditure, Conservative voters are much firmer in their view that defence expenditure should not be reduced; two-thirds of voters, compared with one-half of members, disagree with the idea that defence spending should be reduced.

On the question of trade unions, however, members are more likely than voters to want further legal restrictions. On other matters, members and voters share similar views. They are both strongly of the opinion that government expenditure should be increased in order to reduce poverty and to improve the quality of the National Health Service. In addition, they share a strong view that unemployment is not the fault of the individual.

In a final section of this chapter we examine the political experiences of party members within the party organization, which throw light on their level of contacts with the party. In addition, we examine the extent to which members are actively involved in party politics at the grass-roots level.

THE POLITICAL EXPERIENCES OF MEMBERS

Members' 'political experiences' refer to the scope and duration of their contacts with the Conservative party, including things like

TABLE 3.13. A Comparison of the Political Attitudes of Party Members and Conservative Voters (percentages)

	(a)		(b)		(c)		(g)	
	Members	Voters	Members	Voters	Members	Voters	Members	Voters
Should	46	28	81	89	51	43	64	69
Should not	50	67	11	8	33	35	22	21
Doesn't matter	5	5	8	3	16	22	13	10

	(d)		(e)		(f)	
	Members	Voters	Members	Voters	Members	Voters
Should	80	87	65	52	16	6
Should not	13	8	23	25	64	81
Doesn't matter	22	7	6	12	20	13

Notes: The Government should/should not:
(a) 'spend less on defence'.
(b) 'spend more money to get rid of poverty'.
(c) 'encourage the growth of private medicine'.
(d) 'put more money into the NHS'.
(e) 'introduce stricter laws to regulate the Trade Unions'.
(f) 'get rid of private education' (voters)/'(Not) encourage private education' (members).
(g) 'Give workers more say in the places where they work'.

TABLE 3.13. *Continued*

	(h)		(i)		(j)		(k)	
	Members	Voters	Members	Voters	Members	Voters	Members	Voters
Agree	27	28	24	30	69	49	6	6
Disagree	53	50	52	48	24	35	79	81
Neither	21	22	25	22	7	17	15	13

Notes:

(h) 'Income and wealth should be redistributed towards ordinary working people.'

(i) 'The Government should give more aid to poorer countries' (voters)/'The Government should give more aid to Africa and Asia' (members).

(j) 'The death penalty should be reintroduced for murder' (voters)/'The Government should bring back the death penalty' (members).

(k) 'When somebody is unemployed, it is usually their fault.'

TABLE 3.14. *Political Experiences and Political Contacts between Members and the Conservative Party* (percentages)

Years' membership in the party	
Up to 5 years	19
5–10 years	15
10–15 years	12
15–20 years	10
20–25 years	9
25+ years	35
Was membership uninterrupted?	
Yes	91
No	9
Strength of attachment to the party	
Very strong	28
Fairly strong	49
Not very strong	17
Not at all strong	6
Contact with party activists in previous year	
Not at all	23
Rarely (once or twice)	30
Occasionally (three to five times)	21
Frequently (more than five times)	26

the length of time they have been members, the strength of their attachments to the party, and their contacts with the party organization. Data on these matters are set out in Table 3.14.

In view of the age profile of the membership, it is perhaps not surprising that some 35 per cent have been party members for more than a quarter of a century. Moreover, the great majority of these have been members continuously, without interruption during this period. So the party has a large number of loyal members who have been attached to it for many years. At the same time, however, some 19 per cent of members joined within the last five years, and approximately 45 per cent have joined since 1979, the year which brought Mrs Thatcher to power. So it is clear that the party does not have a problem in recruiting new members, although as we have seen, it does have a problem in recruiting young members.

TABLE 3.15. *Rates of Activism within the Party Organization*
(percentages)

Attendance at a party meeting in previous year	
Not at all	68
Rarely (once or twice)	14
Occasionally (three to five times)	7
Frequently (more than five times)	11
How active members consider themselves to be	
Very active	5
Fairly active	12
Not very active	35
Not active	48
Amount of time devoted to party activities in the average month	
None	77.8
Up to 5 hours	14.4
5–10 hours	4.1
10–20 hours	2.0
20–30 hours	0.7
30–40 hours	0.4
40+ hours	0.6
How active members are compared with five years ago	
More active	8
Less active	25
About the same	58
Not a member five years ago	10

Some 77 per cent of members are very or fairly strongly attached to the party, but more than 50 per cent have little or no contact with the party organization in the sense of meeting other Conservative activists. Thus a relatively large number of party members are isolated from the day-to-day activities of the party organization. Just over one-quarter of the members have frequent contact with party activists. Given this, it is perhaps not surprising that, as we see in Table 3.15, more than two-thirds of the members did not attend a meeting in the year prior to the survey, and only about one in ten attend meetings frequently.

In order to probe the levels of activism within the party, members were asked: 'How active do you consider yourself to be in the Conservative Party?' As the responses in Table 3.15 indicate, only

5 per cent of members considered themselves to be very active, and 12 per cent thought that they were fairly active. We probe this issue in much more detail in Chapter 5, but these responses suggest that somewhere between 15 and 20 per cent of party members think of themselves as being active. If, however, we take a more precise, but not particularly demanding, definition of activism, to include anyone who devotes at least some time to party activities in the average month, then the third section of Table 3.15 shows that around 22 per cent of the members are active in this sense.

We suggested in the previous chapter that the total membership of the party at the time of the survey must have been just over 750,000, which implies an active membership of about 165,000 (that is, 22 per cent of this figure). The question about time spent on party activities in the average month was also used in our earlier survey of Labour party members, and that survey suggested that the Labour party had about 147,000 active members in 1989 (Seyd and Whiteley, 1992: 88). Thus, although the Conservatives have a significantly larger overall membership, they have only marginally more activists than Labour.

However, another question, which was also used in the earlier survey, has disturbing implications for both the major parties in British politics. This is a question about members' perceptions of their rates of activism over time. Some 25 per cent of the members thought that they were less active, and only 8 per cent thought that they were more active, than five years previously. In the case of the Labour party, we interpreted the answers to the same question as evidence of a 'de-energizing' of the grass-roots party over time.[3]

If we subtract the percentage who are more active from the percentage who are less active, some 17 per cent of Conservatives have become 'de-energized' over a five-year period, in comparison with 23 per cent of Labour party members. The fact that a smaller proportion of Conservatives have become less active than Labour members is small comfort to the party, however, since, as we pointed out in Chapter 2, the Conservative party has a smaller proportion of activists to begin with. In one respect, the figures for the Conservatives are worse than those for Labour, since more than three times as many Conservatives have become less active

---

[3] In the Labour survey, some 43% of respondents stated that they were less active, and 20% stated that they were more active compared with five years previously (Seyd and Whiteley, 1992: 89).

TABLE 3.16. *Voting Behaviour and Party Membership* (percentages)

Did they vote in the 1987 election?	
Yes	98
No	2
Party voted for in 1987	
Conservative	98
Labour	0.2
Alliance	2
Have they always voted for the same party?	
Yes	81
No	18
Party previously voted for if not the same (N = 525)	
Did not vote	6
Conservative	16
Labour	33
Alliance	28
Labour and Alliance	10
Other	7

than have become more active, a significantly larger ratio than for Labour.

These figures suggest that both parties have been experiencing a serious and continuing 'de-energizing' process in their grass roots. Of course, this process cannot be fully examined with only a cross-section survey of the type used here, but ongoing research is probing this question in much greater detail, since it represents an intriguing and possibly serious problem for British parliamentary democracy.[4] We examine this question more fully in Chapter 9.

The final table in this chapter examines the voting behaviour of party members. Some 98 per cent of the members claimed to have voted in the general election of 1987, a significantly higher percentage than claimed this among respondents to the British Election Study survey of that year. In that survey, 86 per cent of respondents claimed that they had voted in the election (Heath *et al.*, 1991: 165).

[4] The ESRC is currently funding panel surveys of both Labour and Conservative party members, which are being conducted by the present authors. Since panels involve interviewing the same respondents on more than one occasion, they are able to probe the dynamics of membership over time in a way which is not possible with cross-section surveys.

The authors of the 1987 election study volume point out that respondents in election study surveys have consistently reported much higher levels of turn-out than the official results. But research using official turn-out records appears to show that much of the difference between the reported and the official figures can be explained by limitations of the Electoral Register and by a tendency for non-voters selected in the election study sample not to respond to the survey (Swaddle and Heath, 1989). Thus the tendency for individuals to exaggerate their electoral participation appears to be relatively small.

If we apply the same reasoning to the present survey, then it means that we can be fairly confident that at least 95 per cent of party members voted in the election, which attests in part to the efficiency of the local Conservative associations on election day. Considering that so many of the members are elderly and therefore less mobile than the electorate as a whole, the local constituency associations clearly did a thorough job of helping their members to get to the polls on election day.

Not surprisingly, the vast majority of members voted Conservative in that election, although interestingly enough, just under 2 per cent voted for the Alliance parties, and six respondents, or 0.2 per cent of the sample, voted Labour! Thus members are a valuable electoral resource for the local constituency parties.

Turning to the question of whether the members always vote for the same party, some 18 per cent had at one time or another voted for a different party. Of these, the largest group were former Labour voters (33 per cent), closely followed by former Alliance voters (28 per cent), which mostly means to ex-Liberal voters. Party members who voted for another party tended to be disproportionately working-class, most of them former Labour voters; they also tended to be middle-aged. Elderly Conservatives were very likely to have been Conservative voters all their lives, since only 13 per cent of them had ever voted for another party.

This concludes our overview of the social and political characteristics of Conservative party members. We now move to a more specific examination of their experiences, activities, and attitudes in the next few chapters. We begin with a discussion of the motives that members had for deciding to join the Conservative party in the first place.

4

Joining the Conservative Party

Having examined a profile of the social-background characteristics and attitudes of the Conservative party members in the survey,
we are now in a position to examine the question of why people
join the Conservative party. Though the principle focus of this
chapter is explaining the recruitment of party members, we will
also examine the mechanics of joining and the experiences which
individuals had in becoming party members. This throws considerable light on the effectiveness of the party organization at the local
level in recruiting new members.

We begin with a discussion of what it means to the average
respondent in the survey to be a party member. This is a necessary
preliminary because there is a real ambiguity about the meaning
of party membership, since, as we pointed out in Chapter 2, the
status of the member is not very well defined. This leads into a discussion of how individual respondents went about becoming party
members and the different routes to party membership which exist.

Following that, we focus on the key issue of why people join the
party in the first place. In examining motives for joining, we utilize
the general-incentives model of political participation, which was
originally developed to explain why individuals joined the Labour
party (see Seyd and Whiteley, 1992). The present chapter uses an
extended and developed version of this model.

THE MEANING OF CONSERVATIVE PARTY MEMBERSHIP

As we have seen, the Conservative party is unusual by comparison
with other British political parties, in that party membership is
rather ill-defined. There is no minimum subscription, and *Model
Rules* defines party membership in rather vague terms, as requiring that individuals give generalized support to the policy objectives and candidates of the party. Thus it is hard to distinguish
precisely between party members and party supporters.

The discussion of Chapter 3 showed that the great majority of party members are not involved in the day-to-day activities of the party. Only a small minority go to party meetings, and many have little or no contact with party activists, and consider themselves to be inactive. Thus, for many members there is a real question as to what membership of the Conservative party actually means.

A battery of questions was included in the survey designed to elicit information about the political activities of the members. These questions are examined more fully in Chapter 5, but they throw considerable light on the meaning that members attach to their own role in the Conservative party. The activities listed were chosen to be representative of the full range of political activities undertaken by party members. They are arranged in increasing order of costliness, from a comparatively low-cost activity like putting up an election poster to a very high-cost activity like running for elected office. Of course, perceptions of the costs of these activities vary among respondents, but generally the earlier items are less costly in terms of time and effort than the later items.

If we examine the range of activities in Table 4.1, it is interesting to note that only in one case do a majority of respondents occasionally or frequently undertake that activity, and that is donating money to the party. This finding confirms the evidence presented in Chapter 3 that grass-roots Conservatives are not very active politically.

The second most popular activity is displaying election posters in a window, but even this low-cost activity is engaged in frequently by only 18 per cent of the respondents. In face-to-face interviews carried out for the pilot survey for this project, it became apparent that many Conservatives were reluctant to advertise their politics to outsiders. This was partly due to a conviction that politics is a private matter, not to be discussed with strangers, and partly due to a fear that in some places advertising their allegiance would bring social ostracism. This may explain why a majority of members are reluctant to display posters. It may also explain why the Conservatives lagged well behind the other parties in the number of election posters they distributed during the 1992 general election campaign (Denver and Hands, 1992).

Relatively few Conservatives said that they had delivered leaflets during an election campaign, and even fewer said that they had canvassed voters on behalf of the party. We suggested earlier that

TABLE 4.1. *Political Activities Undertaken by Members* (percentages)

Question: We would like to ask you about political activities you may have taken part in during the last FIVE years.

Activity	How often have you done this?			
	Not at all	Rarely	Occasionally	Frequently
Displayed an election poster in a window	51	8	23	18
Signed a petition supported by the party	53	14	26	8
Donated money to Conservative party funds	16	12	45	28
Delivered party leaflets during an election	63	4	13	20
Attended a party meeting	53	13	19	15
Helped at a Conservative party function (e.g., a jumble sale)	58	9	17	16
Canvassed voters on behalf of the party	77	6	9	9
Stood for office within the party organization	89	2	4	5
Stood for elective office in a local government or national parliamentary election	94	1	2	3

the total membership of the party at the time of the survey must have been around 750,000; thus, if about 18 per cent of the members frequently or occasionally canvass during elections, that would imply that a group of about 135,000 Conservative party members canvassed during the 1992 general election campaign. This is rather less than the 170,000 members who canvassed for the Labour party during that election.[1]

[1] This assumes that Labour had about 300,000 members at the time of the election, and that they were as active in canvassing as the 57% who said that they canvassed frequently or occasionally for the party at the time of the 1989 survey (Seyd and Whiteley, 1992: 234).

At the high-cost end of the activism scale, some 9 per cent of members stood for office inside the party organization, and about 5 per cent occasionally or frequently stood for office in a local or national election. These are the really active members who keep the party organization running at the local level on a day-to-day basis. It may be recalled from Chapter 3 that the activists varied from between 15 and 20 per cent of the members, using a subjective scale of measurement. Alternatively, they represented about 22 per cent of the members, using the criterion that they did at least some party work in the average month.

In evaluating the costs of activism, it is also important to consider the rewards. Thus, although standing for office is a high-cost activity, it may bring rewards if it also leads to nomination for a winnable council seat, for example. This in turn would bring direct financial rewards.

Overall, the results in Table 4.1 indicate that for most party members, membership means donating money to the party on a regular basis, and little else. For the most part they do not get involved in campaigning, canvassing, or attending meetings. In that respect they do not differ very much from individuals who are not members but who strongly identify with the party.

Given this, it is interesting to probe a little deeper into the activity of giving money to the party, and this is done in Table 4.2, which contains information about individual contributions to the party and attitudes that members have to donating money.

The first column of Table 4.2 contains information on the distribution of subscription payments to the party at the time of the survey. It can be seen that some 2 per cent of party members gave nothing at all to the party by way of subscription, although the mean subscription was just over £12, and the median was £10. At the other end of the scale, an affluent 1 per cent of the members gave more than £100, the highest single subscription payment being £270.

However, subscription payments are a relatively poor guide to the amount of money contributed to the party by members. The Conservative party at the local level undertakes a lot of fund-raising, and members appear to give additional money to the party over and above the basic subscription. When this is taken into account, the mean contribution to the party was just over £66, with some 13 per cent of the members giving more than £100.

TABLE 4.2. *Indicators Relating to Donating Money to the Party*

Range of contributions	Membership subscription (£)	Total contribution (£)	Total should contribute (£)
None	2	9	3
£1–£10	40	12	14
£10–£20	40	21	24
£20–£30	12	22	24
£30–£50	2	11	8
£50–£100	3	13	16
£100+	1	13	12

Question: Generally speaking, do you think that the annual membership contribution to the party made by a member like yourself is too little, too much, or about right?

Too little	19
Too much	1
About right	80

However, in this case the mean is distorted by the presence of large donors. The median contribution to the party was £20, which gives a much better picture of the average contribution of the typical member. This figure shows that the average member gives about two-thirds as much again to the party over and above the basic subscription.

The third column in Table 4.2 shows the amount that members thought they ought to give by way of contributions to the party. In this case the mean was about £44, which suggests that some of the large donors feel that they are actually giving too much![2] The median figure for an appropriate donation was the same as the actual median contribution of £20. Taken in conjunction with the figures in Table 4.2, which show that 80 per cent of the members think that their contribution to the party is about right, the data suggest that the party has already tapped much of the potential for donations of money from its members.

[2] Some 23% of donors who gave more than £100 thought that they should give less. At the other end of the scale some 72% of those who gave nothing thought that they should give more!

To summarize, for most respondents in the survey, being a party member is a private activity which they do not like to advertise by, for example, putting up posters during an election. For them, membership of the party principally means giving money, and not much else. They are, on the whole, generous in their donations, so much so that a few of the large donors actually think that they should contribute less to the party. In the light of this discussion, the next section considers alternative pathways to party membership, or the routes taken by members when they joined in the first place.

PATHWAYS TO PARTY MEMBERSHIP

An important aspect of understanding why people join the Conservative party is to examine the actual mechanics of how they came to join in the first place. In particular, it is interesting to know how many of the members were 'self-starters'—that is, took the initiative to join on their own—and how many were 'recruits', who joined as a result of initiatives from other members or the party organization. Table 4.3 contains information about these alternatives.

The data in Table 4.3 show that the Conservative party recruits most of its members by approaching them to join. But when 'self-starters' approach the party, they have no difficulty in making contact. It appears that local Conservative parties are well organized and orientated towards recruiting new members. However, as the third part of Table 4.3 indicates, most of the people who were approached about joining already had contacts with the party through family or social links, which obviously makes the task of recruiting them easier.

Since Conservative membership appears to have been declining steadily over the years, it might be thought that the party's 'outreach' activities are not very effective, and that it should develop new methods of recruiting members, as the Labour party is currently doing. It may be that the party is too reliant on social contacts for replenishing its ageing membership.

The question in the third part of Table 4.3 asked respondents to indicate if they had become members as a result of various types of contacts. They were asked to choose as many options as they felt applied to them when joining, so a particular respondent could, for example, say that he or she had become a member as a result

TABLE 4.3. *Experiences of Recruitment* (percentages)

Question: Thinking back to the time you first joined the Conservative party, did you approach the party to apply for membership, or did they approach you?

I approached the local party	33
The local party approached me	51
Don't remember	16

Question: If you approached the local party, did you find it easy or difficult to make contact with them?

Very easy	45
Easy	49
Difficult	5
Very difficult	1
	(N = 997)

Question: Did you become a member of the Conservative party as a result of:

Doorstep canvass	12
Social contacts	23
Conservative club	8
Work contacts	2
Family contacts	22
Party political broadcast	1
Constituency association 'book scheme'	1
Combination of the above	20
None of these	7
Others	5

of both social contacts and a doorstep canvass. As a result, some 20 per cent gave combinations of options when they replied.

When this 20 per cent is disaggregated into subgroups, about half of them are accounted for by three combinations of alternatives; some 3 per cent of the respondents said that they were recruited through social contacts and a Conservative club, 5 per cent through social and family contacts, and a further 2 per cent through a combination of all three. Clearly, social and family contacts are very important for recruitment into the Conservative party.

TABLE 4.4. *Sources of Recruitment by Years when Members Joined*
(percentages; N = 1780)

Years joined	Recruited by:			
	Canvassing and PPBs	Social networks	Family contacts	Work contacts
Pre-war	3	32	64	0
1940s	8	48	43	1
1950s	8	48	41	3
1960s	15	53	30	3
1970s	25	52	20	2
1980s	26	55	16	3
1990s	21	64	15	1

A more detailed analysis of the third part of Table 4.3 reveals that interesting changes have taken place in the pattern of recruitment over time. This throws important light on the issue of how the Conservative party renews itself as time goes by. A breakdown of patterns of recruitment by decades when members were first recruited appears in Table 4.4. This table includes the percentages of members recruited via canvassing and party political broadcasts, social contacts, work contacts, and family networks.

It can be seen from Table 4.4 that family contacts played a very important role in recruitment for members who joined before the Second World War. But the importance of family has declined significantly over time, just as the importance of social contacts has increased. It is also the case that canvassing and party political broadcasts have come to play an increasingly important role in recruitment from the late 1960s onwards. Thus recruitment has increasingly come to rely on the party organization or social networks which link up with the party organization.

Overall, Table 4.3 appears to suggest that individuals join the party because they have social links with it or because they have been persuaded to do so by other members or in the course of election campaigns. This interpretation is problematic, however, since many people have social links with the party organization who do not end up becoming party members. Similarly, many people are canvassed by the party during an election campaign who do not end up joining. Any adequate account of why people join the party must explain why some people who have social links with the party or who are canvassed end up joining, while many others with the same type of links do not join.

A theoretical explanation of why people join the party has to go beyond describing their social, family, or political contacts with the party, and examine individual motives for joining. Only in this way is it possible to explain why some people with those types of contacts join, while others do not.

Accordingly, to explain why some people join the party, we use the general-incentives theoretical framework. This model of political participation is grounded in the assumption that people join a political party or become active once they have joined in response to different kinds of incentives. Some of these are private incentives of the type familiar to the economist—that is, incentives based upon private returns from political participation. Others are more collective in character, and are based upon the idea that members get involved in order to pursue policy goals which, as they see it, will make citizens overall better off.

There are also incentives rooted in expressive attachments, altruistic concerns, and social norms, all of which are non-instrumental motives for joining the party. A non-instrumental motive for joining is a motive which is unrelated to any private or collective returns that participation might bring. These motives may derive from a sense of loyalty and attachment to the Conservative party or a sense of duty that the citizen should participate in politics. In addition, some individuals join the party because they have been persuaded to do so by someone close to them, and this is another type of non-instrumental motive for joining.

Since the general-incentives model can be used to explain why individuals join the party in the first place and why some of them become active once they have joined, it is the basis of the discussion in this and the subsequent chapter on party activism. In the next section we spell out in detail the theoretical framework.

GENERAL INCENTIVES AND POLITICAL PARTICIPATION

The notion that individuals get involved in politics in response to incentives of various kinds seems fairly obvious and straightforward. However, there are logical problems associated with this idea, so much so that it has not really been used generally to explain political participation of the orthodox kind.[3] For example, the most recent and comprehensive work on political participation in Britain, by Parry, Moyser, and Day (1992), explains participation in terms of individual and group resources and values, rather than as the response of individuals to incentives of various kinds. The model utilized by these authors derives from a long-established tradition of work on political participation in the United States (see Verba and Nie, 1972; Verba *et al.*, 1978; Barnes and Kaase, 1979).

Interestingly enough, research on incentives for political action has concentrated primarily on 'unorthodox' political participation, which involves activities such as protest behaviour, rioting, and political rebellion (Muller, 1979; Muller and Opp, 1986; Finkel *et al.*, 1989; Opp, 1990; Muller *et al.*, 1991).

The logical problem associated with the idea that individuals get involved in politics in response to incentives applies specifically to collective incentives: that is, those associated with the achievement of group objectives, such as the policy goals adopted by a political party. The problem has become known as the 'paradox of participation', a term first introduced by Mancur Olson (1965), in an influential book.

To understand the problem, it is necessary to recognize that Olson used the rational-choice tradition of the economist. Such theory postulates that individuals make decisions solely on the basis of the costs and benefits associated with the different courses of action open to them. The paradox of participation is that rational, self-interested individuals do not generally participate in any activity which aims to achieve collective goals. This is because such goals are examples of collective goods.

A collective good has two properties: jointness of supply and the impossibility of exclusion (see Samuelson, 1954). Jointness of supply means that one person's consumption of the good does not

---

[3] A distinction is made in the political science literature between 'orthodox' and 'unorthodox' forms of participation. The former refer to the standard methods of influencing the government and policy-making by such activities as voting, signing petitions, joining interest groups, and political parties. The latter refers to protest activities like marching and organizing boycotts which are legal in most democratic societies, but are not recognized by many people as being conventional methods for influencing the government. Unorthodox participation can also refer to illegal activities such as rioting and, in the extreme, terrorism and guerrilla warfare. See Marsh, 1977.

reduce the amount available to anyone else. An example of this would be national defence, since once the Government has provided defence, a newly arrived member of the society immediately starts to consume the good, and this consumption does not reduce the supply available to everyone else. This is in sharp contrast to a private good like, say, apples, in which one person's consumption reduces the amount available to everyone else.

The impossibility-of-exclusion aspect of collective goods means that individuals cannot be prevented from consuming the good once it has been provided, even if they did not contribute to its provision in the first place. Thus the newly arrived member of a society mentioned above immediately begins to consume the benefits of defence spending, even though he or she did not contribute to its provision initially.

The great problem with collective goods is that it is very difficult to get people to contribute voluntarily to their provision when they can free-ride on the efforts of others. If one does not pay the price of apples, one goes without; but if one does not pay the cost of defence, one still gets the benefits of the security which it brings. This is why governments often finance collective goods by compulsory taxation.

The relevance of this point to the question of political participation derives from the fact that the 'products' of a voluntary organization like a political party are collective goods, an insight due to Olson. Thus the policies promoted by a political party affect everyone when they are implemented, regardless of whether or not an individual participated in politics in order to promote these policies in the first place.

Given that fact, the rational actor who is contemplating joining a party because she favours its policies is faced with the following choices. If she joins the party, she incurs the costs of doing so, but does not materially increase the chances that the party will get elected so that it will be in a position to implement the policies. On the other hand, if she does not join, and the party succeeds in getting elected, she will enjoy the benefits of the policies without having to bear the costs of achieving them.

Thus she can avoid the costs and get the benefits if the party is elected, and avoid the costs while getting no benefits if it fails to be elected. Either way, greater returns can be obtained by not joining the political party. Thus it is not rational to participate in politics for the purpose of promoting collective policy goals.

This paradox provides a theoretical explanation of the extensive survey evidence which shows that high-cost types of political participation like party activism attract only relatively small numbers of individuals, something which appears to be true in a wide variety of political systems (see Verba *et al.*, 1978: 57–62). The evidence from the 1984 survey of political participation in Britain referred to earlier, for example, suggested that just under 7.5 per cent of the electorate were party members (Parry *et al.*, 1992: 113), and even fewer were party activists.

The Olson model would explain this low figure in terms of the limited incentives for participation that parties can offer, and argue that in any case these incentives are not based on collective goods or policy objectives. Other theories of groups are unable to explain this important finding; for example, Truman (1951) argues that groups are ubiquitous in politics, but he has no explanation as to why so few people are actively involved in such groups, by comparison with the size of the electorate as a whole.[4]

The limited incentives for involvement were referred to by Olson as 'selective incentives', or inducements to participate which are unrelated to the collective goods that the organization was set up to provide. These selective incentives are private goods in the sense that anyone who does not contribute will not receive them. In his book he illustrates such incentives in the case of trade unions (Olson, 1965: 73). Trade unions provide selective incentives, like legal advice and insurance, which are available only to members, and which provide an inducement to join. By contrast, the collective goods supplied by trade unions, such as improvements in wages and conditions of service, are of course available to non-union members, which produces a free-rider problem.

Thus, any incentive-based theory of why people join a political party has to deal with the paradox of participation. In the subsequent discussion we set out a general-incentives theory of political participation which addresses this issue and at the same time

---

[4] Truman makes a distinction between a potential and an actual group, suggesting that potential group members are mobilized to become active if their interests are threatened by another active group. By this logic, many are inactive because their interests are not threatened in this way. The problem with this explanation is that it does not deal with the problem of collective action—the incentive that individuals have to free-ride on the efforts of others, even when they want to pursue group interests; for someone whose interests are threatened still has an incentive not to get involved. Secondly, it does not explain why any groups should be active in the first place.

explains why many people who join the Conservative party do so in order to promote the policy goals of the party, something which is inconsistent with the Olson model.

The essence of the theory is that, in order to explain political participation, we need to consider a wider array of incentives than narrowly defined individual incentives. Thus the Olson model, while plausible and insightful, is too narrowly focused to give an adequate account of why people should join a political party. However, in making this point, we are not ignoring the central insight of Olson's theory, which is the idea that individuals become politically active in response to incentives of various kinds.

We referred to selective incentives above, and these may be important for understanding why some people join the Conservative party. Selective incentives in this context are of three types: process, outcome, and ideological incentives.

'Process incentives' refer to motives for participating which derive from the process of participation itself. Different writers have referred to a number of different motives which might be counted under this heading. Tullock (1971) has written of the 'entertainment' value of being involved in revolution; Opp (1990) writes about the 'catharsis' value of involvement in political protest. For some people, the political process is interesting and stimulating in itself, regardless of outcomes or goals. Party membership is a way of meeting like-minded and interesting people, and for some this is motive enough for getting involved.

'Selective-outcome incentives' refer to motives concerned with achieving certain goals in the political process, but goals which are private rather than collective. A potential member might harbour ambitions to become a local councillor, for example, or the local mayor, or even to be elected to the House of Commons. Others may want nomination from the Conservative party to be a school governor or a local magistrate. Yet others might be interested in the business connections that party membership can bring, particularly in areas where the party is strong in local government. There are many motives which come under this heading, but they all share the common characteristic of providing private rather than collective returns from participation, since they are not available to non-members.

A third type of motivation is ideology, the explanation for this being rooted in the so-called law of curvilinear disparity (see May,

1973; Kitschelt, 1989). This is the proposition that rank-and-file members of a political party are likely to be more radical than the party leadership or the voters. Thus there is a curvilinear relationship between ideological radicalism and the position of the individual within the organizational hierarchy of a party. In the case of the Conservative party this would mean that the members were to the right of both the voters and the leadership.

This is an interesting idea, but it needs more explanation. In the context of the present model, we would explain it in terms of process motives for involvement. Thus ideological radicalism would motivate individuals to join the party because it allows them to interact with like-minded people and give expression to deeply held beliefs. Their involvement is prompted by motives similar to those of the active church-goer: membership of a church allows religious people to give expression to their beliefs, as well as to become part of a congregation.

It can be seen that a number of incentives exist to promote political participation, which are independent of the collective incentives which create the paradox of participation. However, these selective incentives are really applicable only to a potential member of the party who intends to become active. For those people who regard their party membership as a private matter, not to be discussed or shared with other people, it is difficult to see how they can be motivated to join by selective incentives of the type we have discussed. This is an important point, since as we mentioned earlier, many Conservatives do regard party membership as a private matter.

It is possible to explain why somebody would wish to join the party while remaining inactive, in pursuit of collective goals of the type which involve the paradox of participation, even in a narrowly cast rational-choice model. The key to understanding this is the relationship between costs and benefits of party membership. What matters in a rational-choice model is the individual's perceptions of those costs and benefits.

Thus a rational individual may perceive that his or her own contribution to the collective good is negligible, but collective action will still be rational for that person if they also see the costs as being negligible as well. In other words, it is the perceived difference between costs and benefits which matters, not some 'objectively' defined measure of the benefits alone.

This has a further implication: namely, that when perceptions of both benefits and costs are small, it is not rational to calculate them precisely. The exercise of assessing costs and benefits is itself costly, and does not warrant the return when those costs are trivial. Thus it is rational to operate with a threshold below which one does not assess the precise costs and benefits of collective action in making a decision to participate (see Barry, 1970; and Niemi, 1976). In this situation, becoming a member without having selective incentives makes sense, provided one believes that one is making a non-zero contribution to the collective good.

However, the general-incentives framework goes beyond a narrowly cast rational-choice model of collective action to consider a wider set of factors motivating individuals to participate. It includes 'solidaristic' motives for involvement, or motives based on collective as opposed to individualistic thinking. Any adequate theoretical account of collective action needs to consider situations in which the individual 'thinks' collectively, or at the level of the organization, rather than just at the level of the individual. We conjecture that individuals think of the group welfare, as well as their own welfare, when making a decision to participate. The most obvious example of such group thinking occurs in the family, where the relevant question is very often not 'What is best for me?', but rather 'What is best for all of us?'

If this idea is applied to explaining membership in a political party, then it implies that one reason why some individuals join is because they believe that the Conservative party collectively makes a difference to outcomes. They still undertake a calculus of costs and benefits, but it is focused at the level of the party as a whole, not just at their own level. If they reach the conclusion that the party as a whole can make an important difference to the lives of people with whom they identify, then they will join. The corollary of this is that if they conclude that the party cannot make a difference, then they will not join.

Collective incentives are motivated by collective goods, or the policy goals of the Conservative party. Thus individuals who think in these terms believe that the party will defend the nation, increase prosperity, promote the interests of people like themselves, and generally implement policies which will improve Britain. Whether they join the party or not depends on whether they see it collectively as a vehicle for achieving those goals.

Clearly, such motives are subject to the 'free-rider' problem, in that individuals may be tempted to let other people do the work to advance such policy goals. In a purely individualistic world in which people do not think in solidaristic terms at all, virtually nobody would participate for this reason. But if our conjecture is true, then individuals will participate because they feel that they are part of an effective group.[5]

'Collective' incentives for joining the party can be of two kinds: positive and negative. Individuals will participate not only because they want to promote particular policy goals, but also because they oppose other people's collective goals. On the one hand, they may be motivated to get involved because they support some aspect of Conservative party policy; on the other, they may participate because they oppose some aspect of the policies of a Labour government. Positive incentives involve promoting what are seen as collective goods, whereas negative incentives involve opposing what are seen as collective bads.

Muller and his associates have introduced the idea of a 'unity principle': that is, a norm that all members of the group should contribute to collective action if the collective good is to be provided (Muller and Opp, 1986, 1987; Finkel *et al.*, 1989). They describe this norm as 'calculating Kantianism'. When faced with the possibility of free-riding on the efforts of others, group members ask themselves the question 'What if everyone did that?'; and since the answer is that the collective good would not be provided if everyone tried to free-ride, they choose to participate.

The basic idea behind this reasoning is that individuals can be motivated to participate by altruism. They may be conscious of the paradox of participation, and they may even discount collective thinking of the type discussed above. But they participate anyway, out of a sense of duty or a moral imperative. This is an aspect of the 'civic culture', a set of norms and beliefs about the political system and the role of the citizen in it (see Almond and Verba, 1963). It provides a further motive for joining the party which must be considered within the framework of general-incentives theory.

Very often, altruistic concerns will be expressed in terms of

---

[5] It is important to point out that this represents a departure from the rational-choice framework. In that framework all action is individualistic, and the idea of collective thinking has no meaning.

idealistic goals, such as the desire to 'build a better Nation' or because of a general belief in 'Conservative principles'. Such general
motives may of course have policy implications, but a moral imperative is the driving force behind the decision to participate, not
the specific policy goal.

Another set of factors which explain participation within the
general-incentives framework are motives based on emotional or
affective attachments to the Conservative party. These motives lie
outside the standard cost–benefit model of decision-making, with
its emphasis on cognitive calculations. Such motives have long
been discussed in the literature on party identification, since the
early theorists saw partisanship as an affective orientation towards
a significant social or political group in the individual's environment (Campbell *et al.*, 1960); they have also been discussed in
relation to economic voting (Conover and Feldman, 1986) and in
the US literature on presidential voting (Marcus, 1988). A formal
theory of expressive voting has been developed which postulates
that voters are motivated by a desire to express support for one
candidate or policy outcome over another, independently of
whether or not their vote influences outcomes (Brennan and
Buchanan, 1984; Carter and Guerette, 1992).

Accordingly, we reason that some people will be motivated to
join by an expressive attachment to the Conservative party which
has little to do with the benefits they might receive from membership, either at the individual or the collective levels. Such motives
for joining are grounded in a sense of loyalty and affection for the
party which is unrelated to cognitive calculations of the costs and
benefits of membership.

Finally, social norms constitute a fifth set of motives for joining
the party. These too lie outside the scope of a narrow rational-
choice model of participation. A key feature of such norms is that
they are enforced by other people, who express approval or dis-
approval of the behaviour of the individual concerned (see Elster,
1989: 97–151). Thus party members motivated by social norms
are responding to the perceived opinions of 'significant others',
individuals whose opinions they respect and value. Social norms
have been used to explain voting behaviour (Riker and Ordeshook,
1968), and constitute a different factor in explaining why some
people should become members of the party.

Applying this to membership of the Conservative party, if an individual is raised in a family which has an active tradition of involvement in the party, then those norms of participation will very likely be passed on and influence their behaviour. Just as there is evidence to suggest that partisan attachments are handed down from generation to generation, albeit in an attenuated form (Butler and Stokes, 1974), so it seems likely that the same will be true of party membership and party activism.

Overall, then, the general-incentives theory of political participation postulates that five distinct factors are at work in explaining why people join a political party or become active once they have joined. These are selective and collective incentives, altruism, affective or expressive motives, and social norms.

In the light of this analysis, we can go on to examine various predictions based on this analytical framework, which in turn can be tested by survey data.

APPLYING GENERAL-INCENTIVES THEORY

We have suggested that the five factors discussed in general-incentives theory will play an important role in explaining both why individuals join the party and why they become active once they have joined. If these factors are important in explaining why some people join the party while others do not, then we should observe clear differences between party members and supporters who are not members.

If we compare Conservative members and Conservative supporters or identifiers in the electorate, then we would expect the former to be more highly motivated than the latter in relation to each of the five factors. Thus members should be more in favour of Conservative policies; they should be more emotionally attached to the party, more motivated by process, outcome, and ideological incentives, and feel a greater sense of duty to participate; and finally, they should be more influenced to participate by people who are close to them.

Unfortunately we do not have the data to test all these possibilities, since that would require a survey of Conservative voters which contained the same questions as the survey of party members. However, limited comparisons can be made between the members in the survey and Conservative identifiers included in the 1992

British Election Study.[6] The comparisons are limited, since the election study was not designed to test incentive theories of political participation. However, in Table 4.5 we compare the responses of party members and Conservative identifiers to a set of questions which relate to general-incentives theory.

The first section of Table 4.5 relates to expressive or affective attachments to the Conservative party. It is fairly clear that members are more strongly attached to the party than identifiers; some 33 per cent of members are very strongly attached, compared with only 19 per cent of identifiers. So the evidence is consistent with the proposition that expressive attachments motivate individuals to join the party. Of course, with a cross-section survey of this type there is always ambiguity about the causal sequence at work— that is, whether expressive attachments motivate participation or the other way round. But our theoretical argument is that membership is motivated by various incentives, and thus the expressive attachment to the party should occur prior to participation. The reverse possibility leaves the motives for joining the party unclear; nor does it explain why members should become more attached to the party as a result of joining, when so many of them have little contact with it as members. Thus it seems plausible that expressive attachments lead to joining the party, rather than the other way round.

Collective incentives are measured by policy goals, and in this case we compare party members with Conservative identifiers in the election study on eight separate issue indicators. If collective incentives motivate individuals to join the party, then members' policy preferences should be closer to those of the Conservative government than is true of identifiers. So, in order to judge this, we need to evaluate the policy preferences of the Conservatives in office.

To consider each policy indicator in turn, eliminating poverty has not been a high priority of the Conservative government, so we would expect to see members giving this a lesser priority than identifiers. There are no significant references to poverty in the 1992 Conservative manifesto, despite the fact that poverty grew

---

[6] A Conservative identifier is someone who replied 'Conservative' in response to the question in the election study which asked: 'Generally speaking, do you think of yourself as Conservative, Labour, Liberal Democrat (IF SCOTLAND: Nationalist/IF WALES: Plaid Cymru), or what?'

TABLE 4.5. *A Comparison of Party Members and Conservative Identifiers in Relation to Incentives for Joining the Party* (percentages)

Expressive attachments
Question. Would you call yourself a very strong Conservative, not very strong, or not at all strong?

	Members (N = 2466)	Identifiers (N = 702)
Very strong	33	19
Fairly strong	50	53
Not very strong	14	28
Not at all strong	4	NA

Collective incentives
Question: Please indicate whether you think that the Government should or should not do the following things, or doesn't it matter either way?

	(percentages saying definitely or probably should)	
	Members	Identifiers
Get rid of poverty	80	87
Encourage private medicine	52	42
Put more money into the NHS	79	87
Introduce stricter laws to regulate trade unions	67	51
Give workers more say in the places where they work	64	71
Spend less on defence	44	28
Redistribute income and wealth	25	32
Give more aid to poorer countries	23	30

Efficacy

People like me can have a real influence on politics if they are prepared to get involved (members)	55 (agree/strongly agree)
	24 (disagree/strongly disagree)
People like me have no say in what the Government does (identifiers)	33 (agree/strongly agree)
	43 (disagree/strongly disagree)

T ABLE 4.5. *Continued*

Selective-outcome incentives

A person like me could do a good job of being a local Conservative councillor (members)	28 (agree/strongly agree)
	48 (disagree/strongly disagree)
I feel I could do as good a job as an MP or councillor as most other people (identifiers)	23 (agree/strongly agree)
	48 (disagree/strongly disagree)

Selective-process incentives

Question: Did the person vote in the previous election?

	Members	Identifiers
Yes	98	88
No	2	12
Percentage who voted Conservative in the previous election	98	91

---

rapidly during the Thatcher years. The number of households with incomes below 50 per cent of the average increased from 9.4 per cent in 1979 to 19.4 per cent in 1987, the last year for which statistics are available (see Bradshaw, 1992).

Assessing the Government's priorities in the field of health care is also quite complex. For example, both the Government and its critics can be right about the debate over health 'cuts'. There is no doubt that public expenditure on health has increased in real terms, suggesting that the Government has recognized the political importance of the NHS. However, these real increases have often not met increased demand due to both population changes and real increases in the costs of medical treatment. It is fair to say, however, that the Government has been anxious to reduce the rate of growth in health expenditure funded by the State (and has had some successes), to increase the efficiency with which existing resources are used, and to increase the number and range of charges for health. In all, this has encouraged the growth of private health care (Wistow, 1992).

In the sphere of industrial relations, the main aim of government policy has been, in Crouch's words, to '(a) reduce the scope of regulations designed to protect labour and (b) increase the scope of regulations controlling trade union behaviour' (1990: 322). On this view, workers' rights have been significantly reduced during the last decade, except in relation to the rights of trade-union members in such matters as the closed shop, strike ballots, and trade-union elections and financing. Minimum-wage legislation and a number of benefits have been eliminated, and the Government has opposed the Social Chapter, or the European Community charter on workers' rights. So, it would be fair to say that the Government opposes giving workers more rights in the work-place. In addition, it has passed a series of Industrial Relations Acts, all of which have restricted the rights of trade unions.

Defence policy has presented the Conservative government with a difficult dilemma. The general concern to maintain a strong defence force has to be matched against the need to manage the public expenditure problem. In the early years of the Thatcher government, defence expenditure rose quite steeply. However, as Hogwood reminds us, 'The post-1979 rise should be seen in the context of the 1977 NATO agreement, accepted by the Labour Government, that defence expenditure should rise in real terms by 3% per year for the period 1979 to 1984' (Hogwood, 1992: 44). As he notes, once that commitment had been met, the Treasury has managed to secure real reductions in defence expenditure since 1987, including the 1993 expenditure round. Thus, if policy priorities are measured by expenditure, then for the past six years, defence appears to have been a declining priority for the Conservative government.

In relation to the redistribution of income and wealth, government policies have consistently worked in favour of increasing inequality over time. Johnson points out that income tax, which is progressive, fell from 33 per cent of total taxation in 1978 to 26.5 per cent in 1989 (1991: 141–3). During the same period, VAT, which is a regressive tax, rose from 9.1 to 16.9 per cent of taxation. Thus tax policy has clearly served to increase inequality. Overall, the share of national income going to the top 10 per cent of the population increased from 18.1 per cent in 1979 to 22.7 per cent in 1989; at the other end of the scale, the share going to the bottom 10 per cent fell from 4.6 to 4.1 per cent (Johnson, 1991: 313).

Finally, another aspect of attitudes to inequality relates to foreign aid. This has been a consistently low priority of the Government, falling from 2.2 per cent of public expenditure in 1978 to 0.95 per cent in 1989. Generally, the Conservative government is reluctant to give foreign aid priority, on the grounds that it creates dependency.

If collective incentives motivate party membership, we would expect to see consistent differences between members and identifiers in relation to these issues: members should be less supportive of measures to eliminate poverty, less in favour of health spending and more in favour of private medicine, more in favour of stricter laws to regulate unions and less in favour of workers' rights, more in favour of defence spending, less in favour of reducing inequality, and finally, less in favour of giving foreign aid.

The evidence in Table 4.5 supports these conclusions in each policy area except that of defence spending. It may be recalled that defence spending rose initially and then fell under the Conservative government, so arguably this is an ambiguous case anyway. Apart from this, members' policy preferences are clearly closer to those of the Conservative government than are those of identifiers. These findings are consistent with the proposition that agreement with the policy goals of the Conservative government motivates individuals to join the party.

A sense of personal efficacy is an important aspect of political participation, and we would expect that members should feel a greater sense of efficacy than supporters who are not members. The relationship between personal efficacy and collective incentives for joining the party are analysed more fully in Chapter 5, but for the moment we can see that the evidence in Table 4.5 is consistent with this expectation.

Unfortunately the wording of the efficacy indicators in the two surveys was rather different, and this may very well have influenced the answers. But notwithstanding this fact, members are more likely to think that they can influence politics than identifiers. The most appropriate comparison in this case is between the 55 per cent of members who believe that they can influence politics and the 43 per cent of identifiers who disagree with the proposition that they have no say in what government does.

Selective-outcome incentives are measured by two slightly different indicators in the two surveys, both being measures of political ambition, or a feeling that the respondent could do well as an elected representative. As we shall see in Chapter 5, this is particularly important for explaining why some party members become active in politics, but it also appears to differentiate members from supporters. Differences are not large, but it is clearly the case that members are more likely to express political ambitions than identifiers.

Finally, in Table 4.5, we examine voting behaviour as a rough guide to process incentives, or the desire to be involved in politics for its own sake. This is a very approximate measure of process incentives, since voting behaviour involves other considerations as well as the desire to participate in politics. However, the evidence shows that members are both more likely to vote and more likely to vote Conservative than identifiers. In so far as voting is a measure of process incentives, members are more motivated by such considerations than non-members.

Overall, these comparisons between members and non-members show that responses are consistent with the predictions of general-incentives theory. Of course, a specially designed survey of Conservative identifiers in the voting population is needed to fully examine this question, but such comparisons as can be made between members and supporters in the electorate as a whole affirms this conclusion.

Comparing the responses of members and non-members is one way to test incentive theory. Another way is to ask members why they joined the party in the first place, and then to examine the answers to see if they can be classified according to the various categories of the theory. An open-ended question was included in the survey which asked: 'What was your MOST important reason for joining the Conservative party?' In some ways this might be regarded as a better measure of motives for joining the party than any other, since it does not restrict responses to pre-defined categories; respondents can write in anything they like. For this reason it provides important information on motives for joining.

In Table 4.6 it can be seen that motives for joining the party fell quite easily into the five categories of incentives theory; only about 5 per cent of motives for joining cannot be classified according to these categories. To give meaning to these categories, we illustrate them with examples of individual responses from the survey.

The first category in Table 4.6 relates to altruistic motives for joining the party. This is illustrated by the comments of a 38-year-old female teacher who wrote: 'If we do not contribute towards society—we have no right to criticize others who devote themselves

TABLE 4.6. *The Most Important Reason for Joining the Conservative Party* (percentages; N = 2467)

Question: What was your MOST important reason for joining the Conservative party?

Altruistic motives

To promote freedom		2.5
To promote the interests of the nation		3.3
To help the party financially		1.9
	Total	7.7

Collective positive incentives

To support free enterprise or capitalism		3.4
To support Thatcherism		3.3
To achieve economic prosperity		2.2
Because of general Conservative policies		8.4
Because of specific national policy concerns		1.4
Because of specific local policy concerns		1.5
	Total	20.2

Collective negative incentives

To oppose the Labour party or trade unions		11.5
To oppose other parties		3.7
To oppose the local council		0.2
	Total	15.4

Expressive attachments

An attachment to Conservative principles		10.5
Belief in the Conservative party leadership		1.0
Generalized loyalty to the party		10.5
	Total	22.0

Selective-outcome incentives

For career reasons		1.0
In order to become a councillor		0.4
	Total	1.4

Selective-process incentives

For social reasons		11.4
To work in elections		1.5
To support the local MP		1.5
	Total	14.4

TABLE 4.6. *Continued*

Social norms		
Through the influence of parents		8.3
Through the influence of a spouse or children		2.2
Through the influence of friends or colleagues		1.1
Persuaded by a canvasser		2.0
	Total	13.6
Unclassified		5.3

to the service of the community.' A 37-year-old maintenance engineer put it in the following terms: 'I wanted to feel I was helping in some way, other than putting a cross down on election days.'

Collective positive incentives concern the policy goals of the Conservative party, and as a means of motivating membership, such goals can be quite varied. One 75-year-old former school caretaker said that he joined because 'The Conservative party keeps prices down'. Another retired member, a former electrical contractor, explained his motives for joining in the following terms: 'They try to control immigration—the country cannot cope with all those immigrants.'

Aversion to other parties, particularly the Labour party, played a prominent role in the minds of some members who were motivated by collective negative incentives. One 39-year-old dentist explained that he wanted to join 'to support a party that would break down the all-consuming "welfare state" mentality that has been generated in this country by years of socialist thinking'. A 35-year-old retired secretary put this in stronger terms, saying that she was motivated to join by 'loathing and disgust at the Socialists who are the party of envy and spite'.

Respondents who had expressive or affective attachments to the Conservative party tended to explain their motives for joining in rather general terms. A 49-year-old builder saw joining the party as 'A committed act to back up my feelings'. A 55-year-old staff nurse cited the fact that she 'approved of Conservative philosophy, i.e. the maximum freedom of the individual within the law'.

Individuals who cited selective incentives for participation tended to be much more specific. One 68-year-old former executive explained that he joined the party in order 'to become a school governor'. A 51-year-old fireman said that he joined 'to enable my name to go forward for selection to my local Parish Council'. Both replies were examples of selective-outcome incentives.

A number of respondents cited process incentives for joining the party. One 23-year-old fund-raising agent explained: 'I had just helped in a General Election in which our MP had been defeated, and was so worked up that I wanted to get more involved.' Simplest of all, a 68-year-old former secretary stated: 'I joined in order to make contact with fellow Conservatives locally.'

Finally, those who joined as a result of social norms were mainly influenced by their families and friends. One 52-year-old secretary said that she joined because 'It was expected of me when I married and moved to a village, as I was known to be a Conservative voter'. Similarly, a 25-year-old radiographer explained that she had become a member because she was 'talked into it by a friend who was already a Conservative member'.

These quotes provide illustrations of different motives for joining the party which the members shared. The results in Table 4.6 show that most members were motivated to join the party by expressive attachments. Thus expressive motives, which include responses indicating a generalized support for Conservative principles and a broad loyalty to the party, were cited by approximately 22 per cent of the respondents. By contrast, selective-outcome and process incentives were cited by only about 16 per cent.

It appears that collective incentives are more important than selective incentives, with some 20 per cent of respondents citing collective positive incentives and some 15 per cent citing collective negative incentives for participating. As regards the latter, the Labour party and the trade-union movement have been an important source of new members for the Conservative party!

It is perhaps not surprising that expressive motives for participation should predominate in a party in which most members are not active. Since inactive members are not responding to selective incentives, and collective incentives are subject to the paradox of participation, we might expect expressive motives for joining to be more important than other motives in the minds of most members.

However, policy considerations or collective incentives are also important reasons for joining. This supports the conjecture that many members think 'collectively' in terms of the effectiveness of the Conservative party as a whole, when making a decision to join. In an individualistic world in which potential members considered only their own impact on policy goals, few if any members would attach importance to collective incentives. Thus the paradox of participation is essentially overcome, because members think in terms of the importance of the party, not just in terms of their own contribution to outcomes.

Another interesting feature of Table 4.6 is that social norms are quite significant in promoting membership of the Conservative party. Some 14 per cent of the members joined because of the influence of other people such as their parents or friends. Interestingly enough, a significant 2 per cent of the members joined as a result of canvassing, which again illustrates the importance of the local party organization.

CONCLUSIONS

In conclusion, individuals join the Conservative party in response to incentives of various kinds. They may be helped in making the decision to join by existing members of the party organization, since the latter plays an important role in membership recruitment. When they have joined, most see membership purely in terms of giving money to the party, rather than attending meetings, campaigning, or advertising their membership by putting up posters. On the whole they give generously to the party, to the point that some of the more affluent donors appear to resent slightly the amount that they give.

As we have seen, most party members are inactive. But there is an active group of members, which varies from between 15 and 22 per cent, depending on how political activism is measured. Since the activists are the people who keep the party organization running, provide the candidates, and do much of the work at the grass-roots level during elections, they are a particularly important group. In the next chapter we examine this group, paying particular attention to the question of why they are active, when most of their fellow members are not.

5

Explaining Party Activism

The theoretical framework which was developed in Chapter 4 to explain why individuals joined the party can also be used to explain why some of these become active once they have joined. Again, the idea is that incentives of various kinds induce the party member to become more actively involved in politics. Since these incentives have a different impact on different people, this explains why some are active and some are not.

The first stage in trying to explain political activism is to try to understand precisely what is meant by activism, and how it varies according to different social characteristics of the grass-roots party members. Accordingly, the analysis in this chapter is divided into four sections. We begin by examining the nature of party activism within the Conservative party; accounts of party politics which make crude distinctions between active and inactive members are too simplistic, since activism refers to a range of different phenomena. So the first section is devoted to examining this issue in detail.

This is followed by a second section which examines the relationship between party activism and social-background variables. It is of interest to know the extent to which political activism in the Conservative party is influenced by age, social class, gender, and other social characteristics of grass-roots members. In this section we look at such variables primarily as correlates of activism, and take up the question of their causal influence on activism later on.

The basic premise of the model introduced in Chapter 4 is that activism is directly explained by incentives of different kinds, and the third section models the causal relationship between incentives and activism. The aim of this section is to test the general-incentives model as it applies to our sample of party members.

Finally, in the fourth section, we examine the relationship between the incentive measures and the social characteristics of members, to see how incentives are influenced by social background. This section also goes on to discuss the extent to which social-background characteristics influence activism indirectly via the incentive measures.

MEASURING PARTY ACTIVISM

We have suggested that party activism is not a dichotomous variable whereby it is possible to categorize members as either active or inactive. Rather, it involves a continuum of political activities; at one end of the scale, members who are very inactive will merely pay their dues, vote Conservative, and possibly identify strongly with the party, but do nothing else. At the other end of the scale, there are the 'full-time' activists who are office-holders within the organization, elected representatives on the local council, attendees at all important party meetings, and prominent participants in local campaigns or elections.

Between these two extremes are 'sporadic interventionists' (Dowse and Hughes, 1977), who may get involved at election times, but are generally inactive otherwise. Some of these may attend the odd party meeting or be interested in a particular aspect of party work such as fund-raising, without getting involved in other types of activity; others may become involved on the fringes of the party via social and business networks linked to the party, and confine their activities to representing it on outside bodies as school governors or members of a health authority.

The political activities set out in Table 4.1 in the previous chapter do not constitute an exhaustive list of all possible types of political activities, but they do encompass most of the important aspects of party work. This includes election-related activities such as delivering leaflets and canvassing, fund-raising, participating in political campaigns, and representing the party on internal and external bodies. Thus the list covers all the most important activities undertaken by the party at the local level.

As mentioned earlier, the political activities listed in Table 4.1 are arranged in rough order of increasing costliness; that is, more effort is required as one moves down the table. Not surprisingly, this produces a pattern of declining participation, although the pattern is not uniform.

The responses to the different measures in this table can be aggregated into an overall scale of activism by giving each member a score depending on how he or she responds to the questions.

This is particularly useful for purposes of analysing the correlates of activism, as well as for examining the influence of the various incentive measures on activism. However, before this can be done, it is necessary to determine if the responses actually do aggregate into a single overall scale. This is considered next.

We can see if there is a single underlying activism scale among Conservative party members by means of a factor analysis. Factor analysis is a statistical technique which enables us to examine whether or not there are underlying 'structures' to the political activities listed in Table 4.1. If, for example, members who stood for office within the party organization were also found to be very likely to canvass at election times, to give money to the party, and to regularly attend party meetings, then these three indicators would be highly correlated, or 'loaded', on a single underlying activism factor. On the other hand, if the active canvassers differed from those who attended meetings, who in turn differed from the people who gave money to the party, then no such factor would be present, and there would be little structure to the data; rather, there would be several factors. Thus factor analysis determines whether or not the indicators in Table 4.1 provide a good overall measure of activism.

The factor loadings or correlations listed in Table 5.1 suggest that there are two independent factors underlying the responses in Table 4.1. The first factor, which is easily the more important of the two, explains nearly 50 per cent of the variance in the data, and loads strongly on relatively high-cost measures of participation. Thus individuals who canvass quite a lot also attend meetings, deliver leaflets, and help at party functions. It also appears that elected representatives within the party organization and in local government tend to be highly involved in these activities as well. For this reason, this factor is labelled the 'Activist' scale.

The second factor, which is independent of the first, relates principally to low-cost political activities like donating money to the party, signing petitions, and displaying election posters. Individuals who do these things tend not to canvass during elections or to get involved in the party organization, although some of them attend meetings or on occasion help out at party functions. Accordingly, this second factor is labelled the 'Supporter' scale.

These results provide confirmation of the idea that two rather distinct grass-roots Conservative 'parties' exist. One is a party of

TABLE 5.1. *Factor Analysis of Political Activity Items*

Activities	Factors	
	Activist scale	Supporter scale
Canvassed voters on behalf of the party	81	
Stood for office within the party organization	78	
Attended a party meeting	74	41
Delivered party leaflets during an election	72	
Helped at a Conservative party function (e.g., a jumble sale)	70	40
Stood for elective office in a local government or national parliamentary election	70	
Signed a petition supported by the party		79
Displayed an election poster in a window		68
Donated money to Conservative party funds		64
Eigenvalue	4.36	1.17
Percent of variance explained	48.5	13.0

Note: The table contains the varimax rotated factor loadings which exceed 0.40 in value, multiplied by 100 for ease of interpretation. The initial factor scores were obtained by means of a principal components analysis of the items in Table 4.1, using pairwise deletion of missing data and Kaiser's criterion for factor extraction. The latter extracts all principal components with eigenvalues ≥ 1.

activists who are involved in campaigning, attending meetings, and running elections; the second is a party of supporters who do not get involved in these activities at all, but do get involved in fairly low-cost things like signing petitions and giving money to the party.

The factor scores for the activism and supporter scales were calculated, and these will be used in later analysis.[1] However, they

[1] If the standardized variables are regressed on the activism factor, we get a set of regression coefficients known as factor score coefficients. These scores, together with the individual responses to the questions, can be used to calculate an activism score for each respondent.

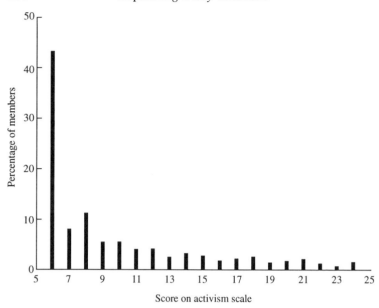

F I G. 5.1 The activist distribution

are rather hard to interpret if one merely wants to examine overall rates of activism, so in Figures 5.1 and 5.2 we have summed the
individual scores of each respondent on the two scales for purposes of comparison.[2]

It is apparent from Figure 5.1 that the distribution of activism
within the Conservative party is very skewed to the inactive end
of the spectrum. This is a confirmation of the evidence in Table
4.1, and shows that in terms of these indicators more than 40 per
cent of party members are totally inactive. On the other hand, the
distribution of low-cost measures relating to the supporter scale is

---

[2] Six variables make up the activism scale in Fig. 5.1. Thus, if a particular respondent never stands for office either in the party or outside, they score 1 for each
of those variables; if they rarely help at a party function, they score 2 for that
variable; if they occasionally deliver leaflets, they score 3 for that variable; and
finally, if they frequently canvass and attend meetings, they score 4 for each of
those variables. Thus their total score on the activism scale is 15. This method of
calculating an overall activism score for each respondent is simple but inefficient,
since it does not take into account the fact that the variables are not all equally
important determinants of activism and need to be weighted according to their
importance. Such weighting is done in the case of the factor scores, and so all the
analysis apart from that relating to figs. 5.1 and 5.2 use the factor scores.

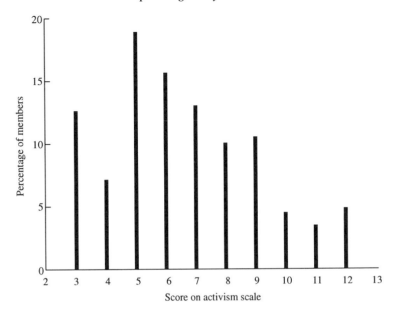

Fig. 5.2 The supporter distribution

much less skewed, with only just over 12 per cent of members being in the totally inactive category. Thus the two scales differ significantly from each other. In the light of these findings, we consider the relationship between activism and social-background characteristics next.

THE CORRELATES OF ACTIVISM

To facilitate comparisons, the activism scale was recoded into four categories.[3] The relationship between the activism scale and various social-background characteristics is shown in Table 5.2. Relationships can be interpreted by comparing rates of activism for all

---

[3] The standard deviation of the activist scale provides an 'average' measure of dispersion of the scores, and can be used to categorize the scale. Thus those with values of up to one standard deviation higher than the minimum activism score were described as 'not at all active'; those with values up to one standard deviation above this category were described as 'not very active'; those with values up to one standard deviation above that were described as 'fairly active'; and those with values above that were described as being 'very active'.

TABLE 5.2. *The Relationship between Activism and Social Characteristics* (percentages)

	Not at all active	Not very active	Fairly active	Very active
All respondents	46	30	13	11
Age				
18–25	49	13	22	17
26–45	43	31	13	13
46–65	42	31	14	12
66+	49	30	12	9
Class				
Salariat	41	32	14	13
Routine non-manual	47	29	15	10
Petty bourgeoisie	45	33	9	13
Foreman and technician	46	40	12	3
Working class	53	24	12	11
Gender				
Male	48	29	12	12
Female	44	32	15	11
Income				
Under £10,000	49	28	14	10
£10,000–£30,000	46	30	12	12
£30,000+	42	33	14	11
Graduate				
Yes	40	30	13	17
No	46	30	13	11

respondents, which appear first, with those for various subgroups, which appear lower down in the table.

The relationship between activism and age is shown in the first section of the table, and it can be seen that younger members are significantly more active than older members. Members in the age-group 18–25 years are nearly twice as likely to be in the very active group as compared with members overall. Secondly, retired members are slightly less active than members in general, although in this case the effects are rather modest.

The second section of Table 5.2 shows the relationship between activism and social class, and it appears that members of the salariat and petty bourgeoisie groups are more active than members of the working class, although the differences are not great. Interestingly enough, although it appears that workers are less active than the middle class, they are more likely to be active than foremen and technicians. Party members in this group are very under-represented in the very active category.

The next two sections of Table 5.2 show activity rates among men and women and activity rates by household income, and it appears that there are no significant correlations between these variables; thus men are no more active than women, and affluent members are no more active than poorer members. However, the last section shows that graduates are more likely to be active than non-graduates, although again the correlation is not very strong.

A lot of research on political participation suggests that educated people are more likely to be politically active than the uneducated (Verba *et al.*, 1978; Parry *et al.*, 1992). This is because they have more resources and a greater sense of political efficacy, or a subjective feeling of political competence. This also appears to be the case for Conservative party members.

However, we must be slightly cautious in interpreting these findings. Mrs Thatcher was a very 'strong' leader, and set the ideological tone of the party for over a decade. There is at least the possibility that those on the left, the so-called 'wets', decided to become less active, or indeed to leave the party, over this relatively long period of time. Mrs Thatcher's own phrase 'not one of us' may have had broader effects than just within the Government. With a new party leader this picture may have changed.

The really notable finding in Table 5.2 is that the young are significantly more active than the middle-aged and old. As we saw in an earlier chapter, the Conservative membership is, on average, rather old by comparison with Conservative voters, and only about 1 per cent of party members are under the age of 25. It is clear that the scarcity of young members in the party is one of the reasons why the distribution of activism in Figure 5.1 is so skewed towards the inactive end of the spectrum. If the party were able to recruit more young members, it would significantly increase the amount of grass-roots activity.

Table 5.3 examines the relationship between ideology and activism. In the academic literature this relationship has been discussed

TABLE 5.3. *The Relationship between Ideology and Activism*
(percentages)

	Not at all active	Not very active	Fairly active	Very active
All respondents	46	30	13	11
Ideology in the party				
Left	53	30	9	8
Centre-left	46	32	13	9
Centre	53	30	10	7
Centre-right	40	31	16	14
Right	42	31	13	14
Ideology in Britain				
Left	46	31	15	8
Centre-left	45	35	15	5
Centre	51	31	11	8
Centre-right	45	31	14	10
Right	42	29	14	15

extensively, and is formalized in terms of the law of curvilinear disparity (May, 1973; Kitschelt, 1989), mentioned in Chapter 4. It will be recalled that this is the proposition that political activists in a party are more likely to be radical than the party leadership on the one hand and the party voters on the other.

This pattern of attitudes produces a curvilinear relationship between ideological radicalism and the position of a member within the party organization. In this case it would imply that Conservative party activists are to the right of both inactive members and the party leadership, making them more radical than inactive members. Later, in Chapter 6, we show that the left–right scale used in Table 5.3 correlates with 'Thatcherite' ideological tendencies. Thus the evidence appears to indicate that activists were more 'Thatcherite' in their ideological beliefs than inactive party members.

Research on the Labour party found that party activists were to the left of inactive members, and this was explained in terms of incentive theory (Seyd and Whiteley, 1992: 101). On this view, activism is motivated by ideological incentives, because it allows radicals to give expression to strongly held beliefs. Thus ideology provides a process incentive to participate in politics.

In Table 5.3 we examine the relationship between ideology and activism using two scales in the survey. Respondents were asked to locate themselves along a nine-point left–right scale in relation to the Conservative party and then in relation to British politics.[4] For ease of comparison the nine-point scales have been recoded.[5]

There is clear evidence in the table that members who think of themselves as being on the right or centre-right are significantly more active than members who think of themselves as being on the left or centre-left. In the case of the left–right scale for the party, some 27 per cent of people on the right were very or fairly active, compared with only 17 per cent of people on the left. Similarly, 53 per cent of leftists were not active at all, compared with only 42 per cent of rightists. A similar pattern exists in the second part of Table 5.3, although it is not quite so marked as in the first part. Thus there is support for the curvilinear-disparity thesis.

In the next section we go on to examine the determinants of activism, in terms of the general-incentives model.

EXPLAINING PARTY ACTIVISM

The general-incentives model of participation was set out in Chapter 4, and is grounded in the assumption that participation occurs in response to different kinds of incentives. The model takes into account the paradox of participation, or the proposition that rational actors will not participate; but it goes beyond a narrowly cast economic analysis of incentives to include emotional attachments to the party, moral concerns, and social norms, variables which lie outside the standard cost–benefit approach to decision-making.

Our model is based on a rational-choice analysis of participation. The simplest version of such a model applied to the analysis of political activism includes the following variables:

---

[4] The full wording of the questions can be seen in Appendix II, questions 30 and 30a. These scales provide useful summary measures of ideological beliefs, and are significantly related to attitudes to a wide variety of issues in contemporary British politics, as can be seen from the discussion in Ch. 6.

[5] Respondents coding 1 or 2 are described as 'left'; 3 or 4 as 'centre-left'; 5 as 'centre'; 6 or 7 as 'centre-right'; and 8 or 9 as 'right'.

$$A_i = (p_i)(B) - C_i \qquad (1)$$

where A_i is the level of activism of individual i; p_i is the probability that i's participation will bring about the collective good or policy goals of the party; B represents the collective benefits or public goods resulting from the implementation of a party programme; C_i represents the costs to i of contributing to the collective good.

The origin of the paradox of participation is the fact that p_i appears vanishingly small in most situations, since the individual is unlikely to make any significant contribution to winning an election or changing national policy outcomes. Thus, as long as costs are non-zero, activism appears to be irrational.

In political science there have been a number of approaches to dealing with this paradox as it arises in the model. The first appeals to threshold arguments, suggesting that individuals will not calculate the costs and benefits of collective action when these are very small (Barry, 1970; Niemi, 1976). It is an approach which applies to the calculus of voting, and it may also explain why some individuals join a political party with the intention of remaining inactive. But it cannot explain party activism, since this is generally a very high-cost activity.

A second approach focuses on the game-theoretic characteristics of collective action. Hardin (1971) first pointed out that the collective-action problem was really an N-person prisoner's-dilemma game. Since then, a developing literature suggests that co-operation can be obtained in the prisoner's dilemma and the collective good provided two conditions are met: first, participants should not discount the future too much, since myopia sharply reduces the pay-offs from co-operative action; secondly, the game should be repeated over time, since the dominant strategy in the one-shot game is always non-cooperation (Taylor, 1976; Axelrod, 1984).

Unfortunately these ideas do not apply readily to explaining party activism. While it is true that party activism involves a re-peat game (that is, members interact over many years), and many party members have a long-term perspective on politics, game-theoretic solutions to the problem of co-operation are not particularly relevant. One such solution, for example, discussed by Axelrod (1984) is described as a 'tit-for-tat' strategy; it involves players retaliating against non-cooperation by other players with the same kind of behaviour themselves. Axelrod found that this was a very good way of inducing co-operation between players in collective-action problems.

However, applied to the problem of participation, this would imply that party activists could induce other party members to become active by 'dropping out' themselves or becoming inactive in retaliation for their lack of active support. It is difficult to see why such a threat would motivate such members to become involved, particularly if they reason that their own participation is unlikely to make any difference to outcomes.

A third approach to the collective-action problem is to argue that altruistic concerns play an important role in the calculus of participation, which is something we discussed in Chapter 4. Mueller (1989: 362), for example, suggests that voters take into account the welfare of other voters in deciding if they should participate in an election, and this ultimately explains why they vote. He describes this as a 'Jekyll and Hyde' view of human nature, with part of the motivation for voting being selfish and part altruistic.

The suggestion is that if individuals take into account the welfare of other people, this provides an additional incentive to vote. Margolis (1982) develops a similar argument that a 'fair shares' principle operates in the calculus of voting, whereby participation is motivated by a mixture of selfish and altruistic goals traded off at the margin in decision-making.

This is interesting, but it is theoretically incoherent. In a rational-choice model it is easy to see why individuals would pursue their own interests. But it is not at all easy to see why they would pursue anyone else's interests. In other words, if the basic assumption of the model is that human behaviour is motivated by self-interest, why should anyone care about the welfare of other people?

However, it is possible that the paradox of participation does not apply to party activism, since in many cases the probability that an individual can influence the provision of the collective good, p_i, is not negligible. Activists can be influential in obtaining public goods, something which is not generally true for other types of collective action such as protesting in the streets or trying to overthrow the Government. Party activists may not be unique in this, since some interest-group activists may also have an objective basis for a sense of political efficacy as well. But we also think that party activists have advantages, particularly in comparison with individuals involved in unorthodox types of political action, such as protest marches and demonstrations.

There are two reasons for suggesting why this is the case. First, as members of the 'middle-level élite', party activists have direct access to policy-makers within the organizational structure of their political party. Panebianco (1988: 22–3), for example, argues that while the relationship between leaders and members in mass parties is one of unequal power, it is none the less reciprocal, with grass-roots members controlling organizational resources, which makes them valuable to the leadership.

In Chapter 2 we discussed the research by Kelly (1989) which suggests that Conservative party members can be quite influential in shaping the policies and opinions of the political leadership, although this influence is rarely exercised by formal voting at party conferences (see also Norton and Aughey, 1981). Kelly may exaggerate the influence of activists in some respects, but, as we suggested in Chapter 2, Conservative activists probably have a lot more influence than the conventional wisdom, argued by writers like McKenzie (1964), would acknowledge.

A second point about grass-roots influence is that much collective action in the form of policy-making takes place at the local rather than the national level. In the language of the economist, the public goods sought by activists at this level are not necessarily all that 'lumpy'; that is, it does not require a large amount of political resources to provide them. For example, inducing the local council to make road improvements might involve lobbying by only a handful of party members. This makes p_i in our model non-zero in many cases, so that the active contribution of a few individuals can play a decisive role in their provision.

Party activists can influence local policy outcomes either by lobbying local elected representatives or by becoming elected representatives themselves. This argument will apply with particular force in localities where the Conservative party controls the local council. As a consequence, this provides an objective basis for party members' sense of subjective efficacy.[6]

[6] Table 2.1 showed that the average constituency party consists of about 1,200 members. As Table 3.15 shows, some 4% of these members devote more than ten hours of their time to party matters in the average month. Thus, in the average constituency party, some fifty people might be described as 'dedicated' activists. Given this relatively small number, each of these individuals has a reasonable basis for concluding that he or she can be influential within the local party and in local politics.

This means that many activists can be rational in participating even in a narrowly defined model like that represented by equation 1. However, our general-incentives model of participation takes into account a wider variety of factors in explaining activism. It is set out as follows:

$$A_i = (p_i)(B) - C_i + S(O_i) + S(P_i) + I_i + Al_i + S_i + E_i \qquad (2)$$

where A_i is individual i's level of activism; p_i is i's perception of the probability that his or her participation will bring about the collective good; B represents the collective goods or benefits; C_i is i's perception of the costs of activism; $S(O_i)$ represents selective-outcome incentives for activism; $S(P_i)$, selective-process incentives for activism; I_i, ideological incentives for activism; Al_i, is i's altruistic motives for participation; S_i, is i's perceptions of social norms as motives for activism; and E_i, is i's expressive or affective motives for participation.

This extended model of political activism contains the five classes of variables which were discussed in Chapter 4. First, there are selective incentives, or private returns from collective action, of a type not subject to the paradox of participation; secondly, there are collective incentives which relate to the policy objectives of the party, and these are again weighted by a measure of individual efficacy; thirdly, there are altruistic concerns which are rooted in a sense of obligation and duty, rather than in a calculus of costs and benefits; fourthly, there are social norms or motives for involvement based on a desire to conform to the opinions of other people; and finally, there are expressive motives for participation, based on affective or emotional feelings, which again are not governed by a cost–benefit calculus of the outcomes.

An alternative specification of the model incorporates the idea introduced by Muller and his associates, that a type of 'collective rationality' will influence the decision to participate in politics. They define this as a perception of the probability that the group as a whole will succeed, suggesting that this will interact with personal efficacy to determine the likelihood of participation in political action (Finkel *et al.*, 1989: 888). This idea can be incorporated into the model of activism as follows:

$$A_i = (p_i)(p_g)(B) - C_i + S(O_i) + S(P_i) + I_i + Al_i + S_i + E_i \qquad (3)$$

where p_g is i's perception of the probability that the group—that is, the party as a whole—is successful in obtaining the collective goods.

In this specification, personal perceptions and the perceptions of group efficacy interact multiplicatively, thus reinforcing each other in their impact on activism.

The various measures in the activism models were operationalized from a series of indicators in the survey of Conservative party members, and these will be described next.

The activism scale, A_i. This consists of the factor scores from the activism factor of Table 5.1. As we observed earlier, this relates to relatively high-cost activities, and as such is a good measure of the political participation of party members.

The value of the collective good, B. This was an additive measure, based on a battery of nine questions taken from the British Election Study (Heath *et al.*, 1985) which asked respondents to indicate if they thought that the Government should or should not implement various policy objectives. The policy items were: 'encourage private education', 'spend more money to get rid of poverty', 'encourage the growth of private medicine', 'put more money into the National Health Service', 'reduce government spending generally', 'introduce stricter laws to regulate trade unions', 'give workers more say in the places where they work', 'spend less on defence', and 'cut income tax'.

Responses on a five-point scale ('definitely should', 'probably should', 'doesn't matter', 'probably should not', 'definitely should not') were aggregated so that the highest scores went to those individuals taking a position on that issue which most closely accorded with that of the Conservative party. Thus individuals who most closely agree with general Conservative party views on these issues should have the greatest incentive to seek the implementation of those policies.[7]

---

[7] These indicators were discussed in relation to Table 4.5. Thus individuals who thought that the Government should definitely encourage private education and private medicine, should reduce government spending, introduce stricter regulations on trade unions, and cut income tax scored 5 for each response. Individuals who thought that the Government should definitely not spend more money on poverty or the NHS, should not give workers more say in the work-place, and should not spend less on defence also scored 5 for each response. Individuals with the opposite profile of responses scored 1 for each response. Not all statements precisely accord (or conflict) with Conservative party policies, but these codings are broadly in line with party positions on these issues.

Probability of personal influence, p_i. This was derived from a set of indicators constructed using the same nine items referred to with regard to Table 5.1 (see question 46 of Appendix II). In this case respondents were asked to indicate the extent to which they felt that they could personally influence politics by participating in these various activities. Possible responses designed to measure the extent of perceptions of personal influence were: 'a large extent', 'some extent', 'small extent', 'not at all' (scoring 4 to 1 respectively). A factor analysis of these items revealed a factor structure almost identical with that of Table 5.1, with the first factor loading on the same six items as in that table. Accordingly, this factor is labelled a 'personal influence' factor, and the factor scores are used to measure political efficacy. The scores were transformed into a probability scale which varies from zero to one. Highest scores went to those who perceived themselves to have most influence.

Probability of group influence, p_g. An additive Likert scale ('strongly agree', 'agree', 'neither', 'disagree', 'strongly disagree') was used, consisting of three indicators: 'When Conservative party members work together, they can really change Britain'; 'The local Conservative party has really made a difference to the way in which our community has developed'; and 'The party leadership doesn't pay a lot of attention to the views of ordinary party members'. Highest scores went to those strongly agreeing with the first two statements and strongly disagreeing with the third. Again, this was transformed into a probability scale.

Costs of activism, C_i. An additive Likert scale with three indicators was used: 'Attending party meetings can be pretty tiring after a hard day's work'; 'Party activity often takes time away from one's family'; and 'Working for the party can be pretty boring at times'. Highest scores went to those strongly agreeing with these statements.

Selective-outcome incentives, $S(O_i)$. These were determined using an additive Likert scale of two indicators, which measured ambitions for political advancement in the party: 'A person like me could do a good job of being a local Conservative councillor'; and 'The Conservative party would be more successful if more people like me were elected to Parliament'. Highest scores went to those who strongly agreed with the statements.

Selective-process incentives, $S(P_i)$. An additive Likert scale of three indicators was used: 'The only way to be really educated about politics is to be a party activist'; 'Being an active party member is a good way to meet interesting people'; 'Getting involved in party activities during an election can be fun'. Highest scores went to those who strongly agreed with these statements.

Ideological incentives, I_i. The respondents assigned themselves a score on a nine-point left–right scale in response to the following question: 'In Conservative party politics people often talk about "the Left" and "the Right". Compared with other Conservative party members, where would you place your views on this scale below?' The most left-wing respondents scored lowest.

Altruistic motives, A_i. This consists of three Likert-scaled items designed to measure a sense of civic obligation to get involved in politics: 'Every citizen should get involved in politics if democracy is to work properly'; 'If a citizen is dissatisfied with the policies of the government, he or she has a duty to do something about it'; 'For the Conservative party to have a reasonable chance of success, every party member must contribute as much as they can'. Highest scores went to those respondents who strongly agreed with these statements.

Social norms, N_i. Respondents were asked to 'think about those people whose opinions are especially important to you, for example, your spouse, friends or colleagues. Consider the person whose opinions you most respect. Would you say that they agree or disagree with the following statements?' This was followed by three Likert-scaled items: 'On the whole members of the local Conservative Association are respected figures in the local community'; 'Many Conservative party activists are extremists'; 'People can have a real influence on politics if they are prepared to get involved'. Highest scores went to respondents who strongly agreed with the first and third statements and strongly disagreed with the second.

Expressive evaluations, E_i. Respondents were asked: 'Would you call yourself a very strong Conservative, fairly strong, not very

TABLE 5.4. *The Correlations between the Determinants of Activism and the Activism Variable*

	Activism scale
Collective-benefits index	0.11*
Probability of personal influence	0.35*
Probability of group influence	0.05*
Index of costs of participation	−0.03
Outcome-incentives index	0.31*
Process-incentives index	0.27*
Social-norms index	0.07*
Altruism index	0.13*
Left–right ideology scale for the party	0.03
Expressive index	0.22*

* denotes coefficient statistically significant at the $p < 0.05$ level or above.

strong, or not at all strong?' The highest score along a four-point scale went to respondents who felt that they were very strong Conservative supporters.

The correlations between the activism scale and these various indices appear in Table 5.4.[8] The strongest correlation is between the activism scale and the index of personal influence. Thus, not surprisingly, members who feel fairly influential in politics are likely to be more active than those who feel powerless. There is also a much weaker, but significant, correlation between activism and perceptions of group influence. Thus it appears that a sense of personal efficacy is a much stronger correlate of activism than a sense of group efficacy.

The second highest correlation is between activism and the outcome-incentives index. This means that there is a strong tendency for activists to harbour political ambitions for elective office.

[8] The correlation coefficient measures the strength of the association between two variables, or the extent to which they vary together. A perfect positive correlation—e.g., the correlation of a variable with itself—has a value of +1.0. A zero correlation denotes that there is no association at all between the variables, and a correlation of –1.0 indicates a perfect inverse association (i.e., high scores of one variable are associated with low scores of another). The statistical significance of the correlations is referred to in the table. When a correlation is significant, it means that there is a very small probability (less than 1 in 20) that it is due to the chance characteristics of the sample, and so approximately the same correlation would exist in data from a survey of all Conservative party members.

Some of the earliest research into constituency party politics in Britain, by Holt and Turner (1968), stressed the importance of political ambition in motivating activism, and this is confirmed by these results. Since those ambitious for office have to serve an 'apprenticeship' within the party organization, it is not surprising that such individuals are active.

The third highest correlation is between activism and the process-incentives index. Clearly many activists enjoy politics for its own sake, and enjoy meeting like-minded people and participating in election campaigns. This correlation is slightly higher than the correlation between activism and expressive evaluations, which are measured by the members' strengths of attachment to the Conservative party; not surprisingly, strongly attached members are more active than weakly attached members.

The correlation between activism and the collective-benefits index is modest but statistically significant. This means that members who take policy positions favouring private medicine and private education and who favour cuts in taxes and stricter trade-union laws are more active than those who oppose these ideas. What is particularly interesting, however, is that the correlation is not at all strong; it would be an exaggeration to say that policy preferences strongly motivate activism.

Finally, two of the correlations are non-significant: the correlation between activism and perceptions of costs and that between activism and the left–right ideology scale. Thus, on the face of it, there appears to be no correlation at all between these variables in the population of all Conservative party members.

The correlations are interesting and suggestive, but since they take the variables only two at a time, they can give a misleading picture. We need to examine the relationship, for example, between outcome incentives and activism, controlling for all other variables in the model. This is done in the multiple regression models in Table 5.5.[9]

[9] The coefficients in the multiple regression models in Table 5.5 are standardized coefficients, which means that they can be interpreted in the same way as the correlation coefficients. However, each coefficient measures the relationship between that variable and activism, controlling for the influence of other variables in the model. Thus, e.g., the coefficient of the outcome-incentives variable in model B of Table 5.5 is less (0.22) than the correlation coefficient for the same variable in Table 5.4 (0.31), because of double-counting for the latter; e.g., some of the relationship between activism and outcome incentives, as measured by the correlation coefficient, is really due to process incentives, expressive evaluations, perceptions of benefits, etc.

TABLE 5.5. *The Effects of Incentives, Expressive Evaluations, Social Norms, Ideology, and Altruism on Activism*

Predictor variable	Model		
	A	B	C
Collective benefits times personal influence $(p_i)(B)$	0.34** (16.0)	0.23** (9.8)	——
Collective benefits times personal times group influence $(p_i)(p_g)(B)$	——	——	0.18** (7.5)
Perceived costs (C)	−0.04 (1.8)	−0.05* (2.3)	−0.04* (2.0)
Outcome incentives $(S(O))$	——	0.22** (10.1)	0.24** (10.8)
Process incentives $(S(P))$	——	0.18** (7.7)	0.18** (7.6)
Social norms (N)	——	−0.04 (1.7)	−0.05* (2.1)
Altruism (A)	——	−0.05* (2.1)	−0.05* (2.2)
Ideology scale (I)	——	−0.09** (3.9)	−0.09** (3.8)
Expressive index (E)	——	0.12** (4.8)	0.13** (5.4)
R^2	0.12	0.21	0.20
F statistic	130.5	63.3	57.3

* denotes statistically significant at the $p < 0.05$ level, ** at the $p < 0.01$ level.

The three models in Table 5.5 test the equations 1–3 above. The table includes standardized regression coefficients and t statistics in parentheses.[10] Model A is the simple cost–benefit specification (eqn. 1) in which the collective-benefits index is weighted by the probability-of-personal-influence variable. The results show that

[10] The t statistic is a measure of the statistical significance of a coefficient. We are using sample data to try to make inferences about the population of all Conservative party members, but our sample will very likely differ from the population, due to random chance in the process of selecting the sample. The t statistic protects the researcher from making false inferences about a population using such sample information. A significant t statistic means that a finding evident in the sample will also be present in the population.

the benefits measure has a highly significant impact on activism, an impact which is more than eight times larger than that of perceived costs. Overall, the percentage of variance (R^2) explained is not high, but it is acceptable for this type of data.[11] In this model, the benefits variable is highly significant, but the costs variable is only significant at the 0.10 level.[12] We can conclude from this model that perceptions of both benefits and costs influence activism, but the latter much less than the former.

Model B tests equation 2 above, and it is clear that several other variables have a significant impact on activism besides perceptions of costs and benefits. Both these variables are significant predictors in this more general model, with the costs variable being more significant than it is in model A. In addition, the goodness of fit of model B is considerably greater than that of model A.

Both the outcome and process indices have a highly significant and positive impact on activism; thus members who enjoy politics for its own sake and are politically ambitious are more active than those who do not enjoy politics or who are not ambitious for elected office.

The ideology scale is also a significant predictor of activism in model B. Interestingly enough, the sign of this correlation is negative, which indicates that left-wingers are marginally more active than right-wingers. This is clearly inconsistent with the curvilinear disparity thesis, since it implies that activists are to the left of nonactivists.

This multivariate finding is particularly interesting, since it casts doubt on the relationship between activism and ideology observed in Table 5.3. It suggests that the bivariate relationship is spurious,

---

[11] The R^2 coefficient measures the extent to which the independent variables can predict activism. Typically, with individual-level survey data of this type, the goodness of fit of models is not very high, and this is true for a number of reasons. Individuals are idiosyncratic, and differ from each other in a host of ways which often cannot be measured; our indicators are in any case imperfect measures of underlying theoretical constructs; there may be errors in the measurements, as, e.g., when an individual misunderstands a question; finally, there may be variables which are omitted from the models, which might be relevant for predicting activism. Regression models applied to this kind of data are able to explain variations in the dependent variable, but are seldom able to predict its behaviour with any certainty.

[12] Thus the probability of mistakenly concluding that there is a significant relationship between these variables in the population of all party members is just under 0.10; i.e., there is a one in ten chance of being wrong if we assert this.

or is caused by an interaction between ideology and other variables which are not properly controlled in that table. We show in Chapter 6 that grass-roots activists are much less right-wing or Thatcherite than conventional wisdom suggests, and this explains this finding. The view that Conservative activists are all right-wing extremists is not supported by the evidence.

Expressive evaluations have an independent impact on activism in model B, which is also an interesting finding, since it indicates that political activism cannot be understood purely in terms of a narrowly defined cost–benefit model. This is an important point, and it is worth discussing it in some detail.

In a narrowly defined cost–benefit model, selective incentives would be significant predictors of activism, since they are unaffected by the paradox of participation and are not altruistic in nature. Such a model would predict that process and outcome incentives significantly influence activism, as would ideology, since we have interpreted this in process terms; thus ideologues get private satisfaction from being active.

We have also suggested that activists in the Conservative party are rational in having a sense of personal efficacy, since they exert influence over the party leadership, which in turn affects the provision of collective goods. Thus the collective-benefits measure should also significantly influence activism, since p_i is non-zero.

However, in a narrow cost–benefit model, expressive evaluations should not be significant predictors of activism because they are not measures of selective or collective incentives. The incentives to 'free-ride' on the efforts of other people are the same for members who are strongly attached to the party as they are for members who are weakly attached. In addition, a sense of attachment to the party has no impact on whether or not members can influence the provision of collective goods. Thus the expressive evaluations are unrelated to the outcomes of political action, which would make them non-significant in a purely rational-choice model. The fact that they are significant implies that a narrowly cast rational-choice model is inadequate to the task of explaining political activism.

The same point could be made about the altruism variable, which has a weak but significant impact on activism. However, in this case the sign of the variable is the opposite of what would be expected. Thus individuals who feel that it is the duty of the citizen to participate are likely to be less active than individuals who believe the opposite. As mentioned above, the altruism scale is made up of three different indicators. Further analysis shows that the observed negative relationship derives from the fact that activists are inclined to disagree with the proposition that 'Every citizen should get involved in politics if democracy is to work properly'. This fact may well be a feature of Conservative party beliefs, deriving ultimately from an élitist view of politics.

Finally, the social-norms scale has no significant influence on activism, which means that pressure from other people appears to have little influence on members' decisions to be active. Overall then, while activism may not be explained solely by instrumental cost–benefit considerations, it is none the less true that most of the factors which explain activism are variables of this type.

Model C tests the multiplicative interaction between group and personal efficacy found in equation 3. This is not such a good fit as model B, since the interaction between these variables weakens their overall effect. Accordingly, the latter model provides a better explanation of activism.

If the social-background variables referred to in Table 5.2 are included in the models, none of the variables are significant predictors of activism, which implies that the incentives variables do a reasonably good job of modelling activism. However, since it is possible that social-background characteristics influence activism indirectly via the predictor variables in Table 5.5, we must examine their influence on the predictor variables in the activism models. We investigate this next.

SOCIAL BACKGROUNDS AND THE DETERMINANTS OF
ACTIVISM

Table 5.2 confirmed the fact that social-background characteristics were relatively weak predictors of activism, with the possible exception of age. However, if social backgrounds significantly influence the various incentive measures, this would mean that they influence activism indirectly. For example, if age, sex, and social class significantly influence outcome incentives, which are a strong predictor of activism, then these variables will also influence activism via the outcome-incentives variable. This possibility is investigated by regressing the significant predictor variables in the

TABLE 5.6. *The Influence of Social Backgrounds on the Predictors of Activism*

	$(p_i)(B)$	Costs	Outcome	Process	Ideology	Expressive
Class	−0.08**	−0.02	−0.07**	−0.04	0.01	−0.07**
	(2.8)	(0.03)	(2.7)	(1.6)	(0.4)	(2.6)
Age	−0.08**	−0.04	−0.15**	0.08**	0.17**	0.15**
	(3.0)	(1.3)	(5.6)	(2.9)	(6.1)	(5.2)
Sex	−0.03	0.02	−0.17**	0.08**	0.00	0.01
	(1.0)	(0.7)	(6.7)	(3.3)	(0.1)	(0.3)
Graduate	0.02	0.05	0.07**	−0.06**	−0.09**	−0.01
	(0.6)	(1.8)	(2.6)	(2.3)	(3.5)	(0.2)
Income	0.02	0.10	0.01	−0.13**	−0.07**	0.03
	(0.8)	(3.4)	(0.4)	(4.6)	(2.6)	(1.0)
R^2	0.02	0.02	0.07	0.05	0.06	0.03
F statistic	5.2	5.8	23.1	15.2	17.9	7.6

* denotes statistically significant at the $p < 0.05$ level, ** at the $p < 0.01$ level.

incentives models on age, sex, income, social class, and graduate status. The results of this exercise appear in Table 5.6.

None of the models in Table 5.6 are particularly good fits, which implies that social-background characteristics are not very good predictors of incentives for participation. However, there are a number of interesting findings in the table, which indicate that social characteristics do influence the incentive variables to some extent.

To examine each social-background variable in turn, clearly social class influences the collective-benefits variable weighted by personal efficacy; in addition, it influences outcome and expressive incentives. The signs on these coefficients indicate that the salariat feels more influential and is more ambitious than the working class, which accords with standard interpretations of political efficacy; individuals with more resources are more likely to be involved in politics.

Age has a significant influence on all the incentive variables except perception of costs. Older party members feel less politically influential, and are less ambitious and more right-wing than younger members. However, they are more motivated by process and expressive incentives than young people. In other words, they are more attached to the Conservative party, and are more likely to enjoy politics for its own sake than the young or middle-aged. Gender influences both outcome and process incentives for participation. Thus women are less politically ambitious than men, but they are more likely to enjoy politics for its own sake.

Graduate status influences outcome, process, and ideological incentives. Thus graduates are more politically ambitious, and are distinctly more left-wing than non-graduates. In addition, they are rather less likely to enjoy politics for its own sake than other types of members. Thus they appear to be more instrumental than non-graduates.

Finally, income influences process incentives and ideology. Like graduates, affluent members are more likely to be left-wing than poor members, and they are less likely to enjoy politics for its own sake than members in general.

These findings make it possible to infer indirect relationships between the social characteristics of members and activism. Middle-class, highly educated party members with relatively high incomes are more likely to be active because of their greater sense of personal efficacy and greater desire to achieve elective office in politics. However, the same people are likely to be deterred by the fact that they do not particularly enjoy politics for its own sake. This group tends to be on the left of the party in ideological terms, and, as we observed in Table 5.3, this makes them more active.

Gender influences activism, in that women are less politically ambitious and more likely to enjoy politics for its own sake than men. In effect, they are more likely to be involved in the party for social reasons than for reasons having to do with getting elected and making policy. Finally, older people are less ambitious, feel less influential, and are more right-wing than younger members. But they are also more strongly attached to the party and more likely to enjoy politics for its own sake than the young, which makes them marginally more likely to be active for these reasons. However, the former effects outweigh the latter, which explains the finding in Table 5.2 that age inhibits activism.

Overall, we can see that political activism is influenced by political incentives of various kinds. Interestingly enough, most of these incentives are of an instrumental nature—individuals get measurable rewards from activism. They do not become active out of a sense of moral duty or because they are persuaded to do so by other people. Rather, they do it primarily for private and collective returns of various kinds. The exception is that expressive attachments to the party also motivate activism independently. Thus activism cannot be understood solely in terms of a narrow calculus of rewards and costs. Emotional ties to the party also play an important role.

In the next chapter we turn to an examination of political ideology in the Conservative party, paying particular attention to the issue of how Thatcherite the grass-roots party has become.

6

Political Ideology and Party Members

In this chapter we examine the beliefs or attitude structures among the grass-roots Conservative party members, with the aim of addressing the question 'What is contemporary Conservative ideology?' In addressing this question, the focus is not on Conservatism as a set of philosophical ideas which might be logically analysed or compared and contrasted with other belief systems, but rather Conservatism as a set of attitudes and beliefs in the minds of grass-roots party members.

The approach taken is to see if there is a small set of organizing principles which govern the attitudes of party members to a wide variety of issues in contemporary British politics. It focuses on the extent to which political attitudes are interrelated, or, in the words of one influential writer, ideologically 'constrained' (Converse, 1964). If attitudes to issues are closely related to a small number of overarching organizing principles, this implies that ideology will play a very important role in grass-roots discussions of policies and politics; debates which touch on any one of the salient issues in the belief structure will have implications for a mass of other issues, and as a consequence are likely to be intense and controversial.

On the other hand, if there are no such organizing principles, each issue will tend to be considered in isolation from the rest, with few implications for other debates within the party. In this event, it is likely that differences of opinion will not be controversial and intense. Thus the existence of belief structures at the grass-roots level has important implications for party politics and policy-making.

The discussion in this chapter begins with an examination of the literature on Conservatism seen as a structure of beliefs, which leads into the introduction of a theoretical framework for classifying contemporary British Conservatism. This framework is then tested in a section which draws on a wide variety of issue questions in the survey relating to controversial issues facing the Conservative party and contemporary British politics. In a subsequent section the correlates of ideological beliefs at the grass-roots level are examined, which involves looking at the relationship between attitude structures and social-background characteristics of grass-roots members This leads into a discussion of the causal relationships between attitudes and social characteristics.

A final section examines the relationship between Thatcherism and contemporary Conservative ideology. Thatcherism is a topic which has attracted a lot of attention among students of British politics and contemporary society (Skidelsky, 1988; Jessop *et al.*, 1988; Holmes, 1989; Riddell, 1989). So it is interesting to see if it has come to dominate the Conservative party at the grass-roots level, following the long period of Mrs Thatcher's leadership.

We begin with an examination of different perspectives on Conservative party ideology, before setting out a framework for analysing ideological beliefs within the grass-roots party.

A FRAMEWORK FOR ANALYSING CONSERVATISM

The task of defining Conservatism as an operational ideology is made difficult by the fact that prominent party members have often tended to deny that it has any explicit form. Margaret Thatcher was a Conservative rarity in her readiness to identify Conservatism in unambiguous ideological terms. The general absence of clearly defined principles arguably results in a Conservative party made up more of tendencies than well-defined factions, implying that intra-party alignments fluctuate over time and are often temporary in character. Rose (1964) identifies four such tendencies within the party; he describes them as 'reaction', 'defence of the status quo', 'amelioration', and 'reform'.

Other authors have characterized Conservatism in terms of factions, or well-defined groups; for example, Greenleaf (1983) uses the terms 'Tory paternalists' and 'libertarians'; Gamble (1974) describes factions such as the 'right progressives', 'the new right', and 'diehards', and Norton and Aughey (1981) distinguish between 'Whigs' and 'Tories', a typology elaborated by Crewe and Searing (1988).

The classification of ideological tendencies within the Conservative party developed by Norton and Aughey provides a useful framework for analysis. They divide 'Whigs' and 'Tories' into a number of subgroups; they subdivide the former into 'neo-liberal' and 'corporate' Whigs, and the latter into 'pessimistic', 'paternalistic', 'progressive', and 'combative' Tories.

In their view, Whigs are concerned principally with the most efficient means of producing wealth in society. They emphasize the importance of economic organization and, in particular, maintaining the creative dynamic of capitalism. They believe that private property and inequality are essential for economic progress. Corporate Whigs believe that government should play an important role in ensuring the stability and equilibrium of free-market capitalism. Thus they see government intervention as a creative factor in economic expansion. Government intervention to help rationalize and promote efficiency and achieve economies of scale is, on this view, an essential feature of modern capitalism. For them 'corporatist' policies like incomes policies and tripartite consultation between government, industry, and labour are to be welcomed. On this view, measures to ensure that labour and capital co-operate are vital.

By contrast, neo-liberal Whigs are free-marketeers, who believe in limited government and a *laissez-faire* approach to the economy. Their priorities are those of the small businessman, although by the mid-1970s these ideas had become something of a prevailing wisdom in many large corporations as well. Thus neo-liberals eschew incomes policies, favour deregulation, and emphasize the importance of incentives for promoting prosperity.

On the other side, Tories are primarily concerned with what they see as the moral and social well-being of the community. This involves preserving harmony, stability, and order in society. To achieve this, they believe that government needs to take an active role in reconciling conflicting interests. Among Tories, the 'pessimists' fear the consequences of change, since this puts traditional moral and social values at risk, but on the other hand they tend to view change with a certain sense of detachment, because they believe it to be inevitable. By contrast, 'combative' Tories share this distrust of change, but are more likely to fight it. Unlike pessimists, they engage in moral crusades to maintain law and order, to restore discipline in both the home and schools, and to establish selective social benefits. 'Combative' Tories unashamedly embrace what they see as the values of the middle class, values which revolve around thrift, property, accumulation of wealth, and self-advancement.

'Paternalistic' Tories are concerned with the condition of the people, and have a clear sense of duty and service to the community; but they expect this to be reciprocated by deference towards authority and an acceptance of hierarchical structures in society. Finally, 'progressive' Tories have more updated attitudes than paternalists, and have adapted to the modern world. For them the State has a positive role to play in ensuring a fair distribution of wealth and in helping to preserve the sense of one nation.

While providing a rich framework for understanding ideological tendencies within the Conservative party, Norton and Aughey's analysis is not, however, without flaws. First, it tends to confound ideas and styles; there is, perhaps, a fairly clear ideological distinction between Whigs and Tories, but the distinction between 'pessimistic' and 'paternalistic' Tories seems to be principally a matter of style, reflecting different individual temperaments and approaches to politics, rather than any fundamental differences of ideas.

Secondly, the categories overlap to a significant extent, something hard to avoid given that they are defined in terms of general values and principles rather than specific issue positions. For example, while attitudes to capital punishment may well distinguish progressive Tories from Tory traditionalists, it is not clear if support for, say, incomes policies distinguishes progressive Tories from corporate Whigs. Norton and Aughey believe that support for incomes policies is a distinctively corporate Whig position, but it seems likely that progressive Tories would also support such 'corporatist' approaches to economic management.

Given the inherent ambiguities of a typology of general values, we adopt a different approach. This involves classifying ideological tendencies within the party in terms of the predicted attitudes of different hypothesized ideological groupings. This approach makes it much easier to test the validity of such a classification of attitudes. Thus, we adapt and modify Norton and Aughey's typology, but, unlike them, try to analyse grass-roots ideology in terms of attitudes to contemporary political issues.

Research on political ideology viewed as a belief structure has focused principally on voters. Thus Himmelweit and colleagues (1981) showed in their panel surveys that voter attitudes were structured into two 'supra-families' of issues. These families of issues relate, first, to economic policy, attitudes to public ownership, and education; and secondly, to law and order and social issues.

In their analysis of electoral behaviour, Heath, Jowell, and Curtice (1985: 107) suggested that voters' 'general ideologies' were more influential in determining voting behaviour than attitudes to specific issues. Similarly, Rose and McAllister (1990) found that attitudes to economic issues clustered together among the electorate, and had a strong influence on voting behaviour.

Research on the ideological beliefs of party members has been more limited. But Seyd and Whiteley (1992) showed that the beliefs of grass-roots Labour party members are structured around a small number of basic principles, relating to public ownership, localism, and attitudes to political reform.

Up to this point, there has been no equivalent research on Conservative party members, although Norton has provided an a priori classification of ideological groupings within the back-bench party in the House of Commons (1990). But this has not, as yet, been validated by direct measures of back-bench attitudes.

Our reading of contemporary accounts of Conservative party ideology suggests that ideological divisions within the party fall into three broad categories: traditionalism, individualism, and progressivism. These divisions have largely grown out of the experiences of the Conservative party both in government and opposition since its growth into a mass party in the latter half of the nineteenth century (Blake, 1970).

Traditionalism is perhaps the oldest ideological tendency within the party, being rooted in the values of the land-owning aristocracy. It stresses patriotism and authority, but often opposes social and political changes such as the emancipation of women, racial integration, the legalization of abortion, and easier divorce. In echoing Joe Chamberlain's 'Social Imperialism' (Jay, 1981), it tends to oppose Britain's closer involvement in Europe, and is covertly, if not occasionally overtly, racist. Traditionalists are also strong supporters of the idea of social 'discipline' and law and order; they strongly favour capital punishment and emphasize the importance of punishment as a means of dealing with crime. Another feature of traditionalism is support for existing political institutions; traditionalists tend to oppose constitutional changes in society, preferring to retain old forms of government in the belief that the longevity of institutions gives them particular legitimacy. They are strongly attached to the monarchy and to institutions like the House of Lords, and would oppose constitutional changes like the introduction of a Bill of Rights.

Turning next to individualism, this has its origins in nineteenth-century Cobdenite market liberalism, which emerged within the Liberal party, but migrated to the Tories after the Liberal split over Irish home rule in 1885 (see Marquand, 1988: 125–7). Individualism is preoccupied with *petit-bourgeois* concerns over private property and the interests of the small businessman. It supports the ideal of *laissez-faire* and reduced government intervention in the economy. The most enthusiastic supporters of the Conservative government's privatization programmes can be found among this group.

Individualists believe that the welfare state undermines self-reliance and enterprise, and that the Government should cut taxes and de-regulate business. They also tend to oppose extensions of the welfare state, fearing that this will promote idleness, and they are inclined to blame the victim when it comes to explaining the origins of poverty or unemployment.

Finally, progressive Conservatism also has a long pedigree, being originally associated with Disraeli's 'One Nation' Toryism (see Blake, 1970: 124). It was revived and revitalized, however, by the post-war election defeat of the Conservatives and the perception arising from that defeat that the party needed to modernize itself. Progressive thought flourished first in opposition, and then influenced Conservative thinking in government as the party adapted to the changes introduced by the post-war Labour government. These ideas were most closely associated with R. A. Butler (1971). Progressives accept and support the Beveridge welfare state and Keynesian methods of macro-economic management. They were eclipsed to some extent by the rise of Mrs Thatcher, but an articulate progressive position continued to be expressed in the party by MPs like Ian Gilmour (1983).

Progressivism stresses the importance of a social safety net to deal with poverty, in addition to a limited redistribution of income and wealth. It espouses a paternalistic commitment to caring for all members of the community, and favours government intervention in the economy to regulate markets in the interests of both consumers and producers.

In the light of this discussion, we turn next to the task of measuring the three components of contemporary Conservative ideology.

MEASURING THE COMPONENTS OF CONSERVATISM

The three broad dimensions of contemporary Conservative ideology—traditionalism, individualism, and progressivism—are operationalized in terms of a variety of issue indicators, as set out in Table 6.1. The classification in this table is made on the basis of a priori judgements about the components of Conservative ideology, but these are subsequently subjected to a confirmatory factor analysis to test the validity of the classification scheme.

The indicators in Table 6.1 are all Likert statements or close variants of such statements, and measure ideological beliefs in terms of attitudes to various controversial issues within both the Conservative party and British politics. In addition, there are the two left–right scales referred to in Chapter 3, which have been successfully used to identify ideological variations within the electorate in a variety of democratic systems (see Barnes and Kaase, 1979).

The indicators of traditionalism focus on national sovereignty, issues of constitutional reform, moral issues to do with abortion and divorce, capital punishment, and attitudes to defence spending. As they appear in this table the statements are worded so that traditionalists will tend to agree with them.[1] Thus traditionalists will resist further European integration; they will oppose constitutional reforms like a Bill of Rights, support the repatriation of immigrants, deplore social changes leading to easier divorce and abortion, and oppose cuts in defence spending. In addition, they will be strongly in favour of the reintroduction of capital punishment.

By contrast, the indicators of progressivism focus primarily on domestic welfare issues such as government spending on poverty and the National Health Service, the redistribution of income and wealth, unemployment compensation, and the regulation of markets

---

[1] Several statements in the questionnaire are worded in such a way that traditionalists are likely to disagree with them. These appear with (not) or (doesn't) in the table, to indicate this fact. Thus, as they appear in the tables, traditionalists will agree with them. The same approach is taken for indicators of individualism and progressivism.

TABLE 6.1. *Indicators of Ideological Groupings in the Conservative Party*

Traditionalism

A future Conservative government should encourage repatriation of immigrants.

All shops should (not) be allowed to open on Sundays.

A future Conservative government should make abortions more difficult to obtain.

The death penalty should be reintroduced for murder.

Conservatives should resist further moves to integrate the European Community.

There is no need for a Bill of Rights in this country.

The reduction in East–West tensions (doesn't) mean(s) that Britain can make significant cut-backs in defence spending.

Divorce has become too easy these days, and the divorce laws should be tightened up.

The Government should (not) give more aid to poor countries.

Child benefit should be abolished.

Progressivism

The Conservative party should adjust its policies to capture the middle ground of politics.

The next Conservative government should establish a prices and incomes policy as a means of controlling inflation.

Income and wealth should be redistributed towards ordinary working people.

The consumer needs much stronger protection from the effects of the free market.

Unemployment benefit should ensure people a reasonable standard of living.

Britain's present electoral system should be replaced by a system of proportional representation.

The Government should spend more money to get rid of poverty.

The Government should put more money into the National Health Service.

The Government should give workers more say in the places where they work.

The public enterprises privatized by the Conservative government should be subject to stricter regulation.

TABLE 6.1. *Continued*

Individualism

A future Conservative government should privatize British Coal.

High income tax makes people less willing to work hard.

Introducing market forces into the National Health Service means that the quality of our health will improve.

The welfare state undermines individual self-reliance and enterprise.

Schools should (not) be encouraged to opt out of Local Education Authority control.

Government should encourage private education.

Government should encourage the growth of private medicine.

The Government should reduce government spending generally.

The Government should introduce stricter laws to regulate the trade unions.

The Government should cut income tax.

General

In Conservative party politics people often talk about the 'left' and the 'right'. Compared with other Conservative party members, where would you place your views on this scale below?

And where would you place your views in relation to British politics as a whole (not just the Conservative party)?

---

and industries. In addition, there is a general indicator of support for a centrist electoral strategy for the Conservative party. Again, the statements in Table 6.1 are worded in such a way that progressives would be expected to agree with them.

The indicators of individualism focus principally on privatization, fiscal orthodoxy, the regulation of trade unions, and criticism of the welfare state. Individualists favour the privatization of the coal industry, the introduction of market mechanisms into the National Health Service, reduced government spending in general, and cuts in income tax; they tend also to agree with the proposition that the welfare state undermines individual self-reliance and enterprise. Finally, they are opposed to trade unions, seeing them as monopolistic, rent-seeking organizations.

Table 6.2 contains a confirmatory factor analysis derived from the thirty-two indicators of Table 6.1. The analysis produced a total of four significant orthogonal, or independent, factors, using

TABLE 6.2. *A Confirmatory Factor Analysis of Attitude Indicators*

Attitude Indicator	Factors			
	I	II	III	IV
Spend more on poverty	0.66			
Protect consumers from free markets	0.60			
Introduce a prices and incomes policy	0.59			
Spend more on the NHS	0.59			
Make unemployment benefit reasonable	0.57			
Redistribute income and wealth	0.53			
Capture middle ground of politics	0.53			
Give workers more say in work-place	0.51			
Regulate privatized industries	0.50			
Introduce proportional representation	0.41			
Encourage private education		0.69		
Encourage private medicine		0.67		
Markets in the NHS improve the service		0.57		
Privatize British Coal		0.55		
Introduce stricter trade-union laws		0.49		
Left–right scale for Conservatives		−0.46	−0.50	
Left–right scale for British politics		−0.45		
Cut income tax		0.43		
Reintroduce the death penalty			0.67	
Encourage repatriation of immigrants			0.62	
Resist further European integration			0.55	
Give more foreign aid			−0.52	
Abolish child benefit			0.46	
Make abortion more difficult				0.76
Make divorce more difficult				0.70
Allow all shops to open on Sundays				−0.59
Eigenvalues	3.82	3.15	1.70	1.58
Variance explained	14.7	12.1	6.5	6.1

Note: Factors: I = progressivism, II = individualism, III = general traditionalism, IV = moral traditionalism.

the criterion that a factor have an eigenvalue greater than 1.5.[2] The rotated factor matrix from this exercise appears in Table 6.2, which includes all loadings or correlations between factors and indicators greater than ± 0.40.

The four factors explain about 39 per cent of the variance in the issue indicators, which suggests that while attitudes are structured among Conservative party members, the degree of structuring is not very high. This point is reinforced by the fact that six of the thirty-two indicators do not load significantly on the factors, and thus are unrelated to the dimensions identified by the factor structure.[3]

The first factor in Table 6.2, which explains 14.7 per cent of the variance, is clearly a progressive factor, since it includes all ten of the indicators of progressivism. Thus Conservatives who support public spending on poverty are also likely to be in favour of the regulation of markets, the redistribution of income and wealth, incomes policy, and the provision of adequate unemployment benefits. They are also likely to favour giving workers more say in the work-place.

The second factor is unambiguously an individualism factor, since six of the indicators of individualism load highly on it. However, it is rather narrower than the indicators of individualism listed in Table 6.1, excluding the indicators of attitudes to welfare and to reductions in government spending. All the measures of privatization, with the exception of the opting-out of schools, load significantly on this factor. Thus respondents favouring privatization of the coal industry also favour private education, private medicine, and the introduction of market mechanisms into the National Health Service. The two left–right scales load highly on it

[2] Table 6.2 contains rotated factor loadings from a principal-components analysis of the indicators, with pairwise deletion of missing values. The requirement that a factor should have an eigenvalue of 1.5 is more stringent than the standard Kaiser's criterion, which requires an eigenvalue of only 1.0. Kaiser's criterion, though widely used, is rather undemanding, since it represents the variance which is likely to be explained by an 'average' variable (see Harman, 1967).

[3] Two of the non-significant indicators relate to traditionalism: 'There is no need for a Bill of Rights in this country' and 'The reduction in East–West tensions doesn't mean that Britain can make significant cut-backs in defence spending'; and four of them relate to individualism: 'High income tax makes people less willing to work hard', 'The welfare state undermines individual self-reliance and enterprise', 'Schools should not be encouraged to opt out of local education authority control', and 'The Government should reduce government spending generally'. Since the individualism factor contains indicators of tax cuts and private education, then really only two of the latter measures do not appear in the factor structure.

also, both with negative signs. This indicates that left-wing Conservatives, as measured by these scales, are likely to disagree with privatization and tax cuts.

The third factor is clearly a traditionalism factor, since it loads significantly on attitudes to immigration, the death penalty, and opposition to further European integration. Interestingly enough, the left–right scale for the Conservative party also loads highly on this factor as well as on the individualism factor. Again, the negative sign of this loading suggests that liberal Conservatives oppose the death penalty and further restrictions on immigration, and tend to favour European integration.

An important feature of the traditionalism indicators, however, is that the measures of moral traditionalism load on a separate factor from those of general traditionalism. Moral traditionalism refers to attitudes to abortion, divorce, and Sunday trading. This suggests that traditionalism, as operationalized by these indicators, is more heterogeneous than progressivism or individualism. Factors III and IV are independent of each other, which implies that respondents who favour the death penalty or the repatriation of immigrants do not necessarily favour restrictions on abortion or divorce.

Overall, the factor analysis, which uses a wide variety of issue indicators, confirms the existence of the dimensions of progressivism, individualism, and traditionalism in contemporary Conservative party ideology. But the results also show that traditionalist attitudes are rather more fragmented than can be captured in a single dimension. Moreover, the left–right scale applied to the Conservative party appears to provide an excellent summary measure of important components of both individualism and traditionalism.

Table 6.3 shows the distribution of opinions on the twenty-six issue indicators which make up the factor structure. There are several interesting features of this table. First, it seems clear that grass-roots Conservatives are more progressive than conventional wisdom would suggest. Thus majorities of members favour pursuing policies designed to 'capture the middle ground of politics'; they strongly favour making unemployment benefit adequate to support a reasonable standard of living. In addition, they strongly favour protecting consumers from the free market and regulating industries which have been privatized. Equally, majorities favour spending more money on the Health Service and on reducing

TABLE 6.3. *The Distribution of Opinions on the Indicators in the Factor Structure* (percentages)

Indicator	Strongly agree	Agree	Neither	Disagree	Strongly disagree
Progressivism					
Protect consumers from free markets	13	44	18	22	3
Introduce prices and incomes policy	12	31	12	32	14
Make unemployment benefit reasonable	14	60	13	11	2
Redistribute income and wealth	5	22	21	41	11
Capture the middle ground of politics	16	54	14	14	2
Regulate privatized industries	25	48	13	13	1
Introduce proportional representation	5	18	12	42	22

	Definitely should	Probably should	Doesn't matter	Probably should not	Definitely should not
Spend more on poverty	29	52	8	9	2
Spend more on the NHS	31	49	7	11	2
Give workers more say in the work-place	16	48	13	18	4

	Strongly agree	Agree	Neither	Disagree	Strongly disagree
Individualism					
Introduce markets in the NHS to improve the service	15	53	15	14	3
Privatize British Coal	11	43	17	22	6

T ABLE 6.3. *Continued*

Indicator	Definitely should	Probably should	Doesn't matter	Probably should not	Definitely should not
Encourage private education	28	36	20	12	3
Encourage private medicine	17	35	16	26	7
Introduce stricter trade-union laws	27	38	12	20	3
Cut income tax	20	40	13	22	4

	Strongly agree	Agree	Neither	Disagree	Strongly disagree
Traditionalism					
General					
Reintroduce the death penalty	36	33	7	17	7
Encourage repatriation of immigrants	32	38	12	15	4
Resist further European integration	19	34	16	28	3
Give more foreign aid to poor countries	2	21	25	41	11
Abolish child benefit	7	13	12	53	15
Moral					
Make abortion more difficult	12	21	19	35	13
Make divorce more difficult	18	42	13	23	4
Allow all shops to open on Sundays	16	31	10	23	20

poverty and giving workers greater say in the work-place. Only two of the progressive indicators are opposed by majorities; these are the indicators of redistribution of income and wealth and electoral reform. Thus some 52 per cent of respondents oppose the former, 64 per cent the latter.

It is particularly interesting to note that incomes policy, the keystone of the Heath administration's macro-economic policy after 1972, is favoured by some 43 per cent of respondents, only marginally fewer than the number who oppose it. This is true despite the fact that the Thatcher administration strongly opposed such 'corporatist' approaches to macro-economic management.

If there is evidence in Table 6.3 that many grass-roots Conservatives have progressive views, there is also clear evidence that many support individualism in the form of privatization and tax cuts. Majorities favour privatization of coal, introducing market mechanisms into the National Health Service, and encouraging private education and private medicine. However, roughly one-quarter of respondents oppose these privatization programmes, and so market solutions to economic problems are not without their critics within the grass-roots party. A similar point could be made about cuts in income tax; some 60 per cent of party members favour cuts in income tax, but slightly more than one-third are either opposed or indifferent to such cuts. So it would not be true to say that opinions on these issues are uniform within the party.

The distribution of opinions on indicators of the two traditionalism factors are more divided. There is strong support for the repatriation of immigrants and the death penalty, significant support for resisting further European integration, but much less support for restricting abortion, and little support for abolishing child benefit. Equally, most favour no restrictions on Sunday trading.

Overall, these results suggest that the Conservative grass-roots party members tend to be progressive, individualistic, and to some extent traditionalist. On the one hand, they tend to be rather chauvinist, anti-immigrant, and anti-trade union, as well as being in favour of market solutions to economic problems; but on the other, they are also concerned about protecting consumers from the free market, regulating privatized industries, and ensuring that children and the unemployed get adequate financial support.

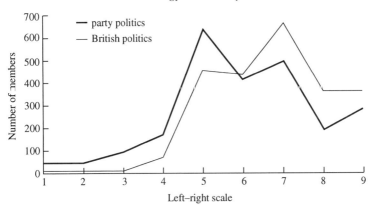

F IG. 6.1 The left–right ideology scales and party members

Moreover, their political instincts are to 'capture the middle ground' of politics.

Further insight into the ideological beliefs of grass-roots Tories can be obtained from Figure 6.1, which shows the distribution of opinions on the two left–right scales in the survey. It will be recalled that both scales were related to the individualism factor, and that the Conservative party scale was related to the traditionalism factor as well.

It is clear from the distribution of opinions on these scales that most Conservatives think of themselves as being on the centre-right both within the Conservative party and within British politics as a whole. The mean scores on the two scales were 6.0 and 6.7 for the party and British politics respectively, suggesting that Conservatives think of themselves as being more centrist in relation to the party than in relation to British politics.

What is interesting, however, is that some 41 per cent of members placed themselves in the left to centre categories (1 to 5) on the party scale, which, given the results of the factor analysis, implies that they tend towards the anti-traditionalist and anti-individualist ends of the spectrum. By contrast, only 20 per cent place themselves in the right-wing categories (8 and 9) on the scale. Thus grass-roots Conservatives are not the extreme right-wing reactionaries they are often portrayed as being. The party contains a significant number of liberal Conservatives.

In the next section we examine some of the correlates of ideological beliefs among the grass-roots party members.

CORRELATES OF IDEOLOGY

In the light of this evidence, it is interesting to examine the relationship between the social-background characteristics of party members and their attitudes to the issues which make up the ideological structure. To simplify things, we will examine these relationships for one issue indicator taken from each of the four factors in Table 6.2. In each case the indicator with the highest factor loading will be used to represent that factor.

Table 6.4 examines the relationship between the social characteristics of party members and their attitudes to spending money on poverty, the strongest indicator of progressivism. The table should be read by comparing the first row, which contains responses for all members in the survey, with rows further down, which contain responses for various subgroups.

It can be seen that Conservatives tend to be very supportive of government spending on poverty, and that the variations within subgroups of party members in their attitudes to this issue are not large. Thus, routine non-manual workers and the petty-bourgeoisie, such as the self-employed and small shopkeepers and foremen and technicians, tend to be marginally more in favour of spending than the white-collar members of the salariat or working-class Conservatives, but differences between these groups are not large. The only differences which really stand out clearly in Table 6.4 are between young Conservatives and the rest and between non-religious and religious.[4] In both cases the former are much less supportive of spending on poverty than the latter. The relationship between age and attitudes must be interpreted with care, however, since, as we have already seen, the sample of young party members is very small, and in this table is based on only twenty-three cases. Thus, sampling variation might account for some of this pattern, although even when that is taken into account, there is still a significant relationship between age and attitudes to spending

[4] Religiosity is derived from the answers to question 41 of Appendix II. Any respondent who answered yes to this question, whether Christian or non-Christian, was categorized as being religious.

TABLE 6.4. *The Relationship between Attitudes to Spending more on Poverty and Social Characteristics* (percentages)

Statement: The Government should spend more money to get rid of poverty.

	Definitely or probably should	Doesn't matter	Definitely or probably should not
All respondents	81	8	11
Class			
Salariat	79	9	12
Routine non-manual	83	8	9
Petty bourgeoisie	81	6	13
Foreman and Technician	82	9	8
Working class	77	12	11
Age			
18–25	61	13	26
26–45	81	8	12
46–65	83	7	10
66+	79	9	12
Gender			
Male	77	10	13
Female	83	7	10
Income			
Under £10,000	80	9	11
£10,000–£30,000	79	8	12
£30,000+	82	8	10
Graduate			
Yes	73	11	17
No	82	8	10
Religiosity			
Religious beliefs	82	8	10
No religious beliefs	69	10	21

on poverty.[5] Other interesting differences in attitudes to poverty exist: between women and men and between graduates and non-graduates, the former being more supportive of spending to alleviate poverty than the latter in each case. Since attitudes to poverty are closely related to other indicators of progressivism, we can infer that a similar pattern of responses will exist in the case of attitudes to spending on the National Health Service, consumer protection, unemployment benefits, and the other items which make up the progressive factor of Table 6.2.

Table 6.5 examines the relationships between social characteristics and attitudes to private medicine, the best indicator of the individualism factor. Overall, Conservatives are more supportive of private medicine than opposed, but patterns of opinion are more divided by comparison with the issue of poverty. In this case there is rather more variation within the subgroups than there was in regard to poverty. One clear difference exists between the salariat and petty-bourgeoisie on the one hand and the working class on the other; the former are much more in favour of private medicine than the latter. Some 39 per cent of working-class Conservatives are opposed to private medicine, a marked difference from the 30 per cent of the salariat who hold this view.

Other subgroups which are more supportive of private medicine include young Conservatives, males, the affluent, and graduates. By contrast, females, the poor, and non-graduates are less supportive of private medicine. By contrast with Table 6.4, there appears to be little difference between religious and non-religious on this issue. Again, similar patterns exist for the other indicators of individualism, such as attitudes to tax cuts and the introduction of stricter laws for trade unions.

Table 6.6 examines the relationship between attitudes to the death penalty and social characteristics, this being an excellent indicator of traditionalism. Generally, Conservatives are very supportive of the reintroduction of capital punishment for murder, but again there are some interesting differences across subgroups. Working-class Conservatives are much more supportive than the middle class; the old are more supportive than the middle-aged or

---

[5] The chi-squared statistic calculated from the relationship between age and attitudes to spending on poverty is 11.15, which demonstrates that there is a statistically significant relationship between these two variables ($p < 0.10$), even when sampling variation is taken into account.

TABLE 6.5. *The Relationship between Attitudes to Encouraging Private Medicine and Social Characteristics* (percentages)

Statement: The Government should encourage the growth of private medicine.

	Definitely or probably should	Doesn't matter	Definitely or probably should not
All respondents	51	16	33
Class			
Salariat	53	16	30
Routine non-manual	45	19	36
Petty bourgeoisie	59	13	28
Foreman and Technician	49	11	40
Working class	47	14	39
Age			
18–25	74	26	—
26–45	53	19	28
46–65	51	13	35
66+	52	17	31
Gender			
Male	55	16	30
Female	49	16	35
Income			
Under £10,000	48	17	35
£10,000–£30,000	49	17	34
£30,000+	61	13	26
Graduate			
Yes	55	16	30
No	51	16	33
Religiosity			
Religious beliefs	52	16	32
No religious beliefs	50	18	32

TABLE 6.6. *The Relationship between Attitudes to Reintroducing the Death Penalty and Social Characteristics* (percentages)

Statement: The death penalty should be reintroduced for murder.

	Strongly agree or agree	Neither agree nor disagree	Strongly disagree or disagree
All respondents	69	7	24
Class			
Salariat	65	8	27
Routine non-manual	70	5	25
Petty bourgeoisie	68	6	26
Foreman and Technician	83	6	12
Working class	83	6	11
Age			
18–25	70	—	30
26–45	65	5	30
46–65	66	7	27
66+	73	8	19
Gender			
Male	72	7	21
Female	66	8	26
Income			
Under £10,000	77	7	16
£10,000–£30,000	70	7	23
£30,000+	62	6	32
Graduate			
Yes	53	10	38
No	72	7	21
Religiosity			
Religious beliefs	69	7	24
No religious beliefs	72	8	21

the young; the poor are more supportive than the affluent; the highly educated are much less supportive than the rest; and finally, religious people are less supportive than non-religious. Similar responses will be found in the case of attitudes to immigrants and European integration.

Finally, in Table 6.7 we examine the relationship between attitudes to abortion, the most salient indicator of moral traditionalism, and social characteristics. Generally, Conservatives are not in favour of restrictions on abortion, although foremen and technicians, the retired, women, and the poor are more in favour than their counterparts. There is a marked tendency for the retired and the poor to be opposed to abortion. Finally, those who are religious are very much more likely to favour restrictions on abortion than are non-religious. Similar points could be made about attitudes to divorce and Sunday trading.

The results in Tables 6.4–6.7 are interesting, but since the relationships are bivariate, it is impossible to say which of them are influenced by interactions with other variables. To separate out the individual effects, we use a multiple regression model. Table 6.8 shows data from regression models which predict respondent scores on the four factors identified in Table 6.2,[6] from the six social characteristics referred to in Tables 6.4–6.7.

The results in Table 6.8 indicate that while social-background variables are not strong predictors of ideological variations within the Conservative party, three of these variables fairly consistently influence ideology: income, age, and religiosity.[7]

In the case of income, affluent Conservatives tend to be individualistic and anti-progressive, but also anti-traditionalist. Generally,

---

[6] The dependent variables in these models are the factor scores extracted from the analysis. These are generated from the following expression: $f_{ij} = \sum w_{jk} x_{ik}$. That is, for respondent i, the score for the jth factor is estimated from that person's response to variable x_k. In other words, the factor scores are weighted sums of responses to the variables which load highly on that particular factor.

[7] Note that the age and income variables are not categorized in these models as they were in Tables 6.4–6.7, in order to maximize the variance in the independent variables. A low score on any one of the ideology variables means that a particular respondent scores highly on that attribute—e.g., is very progressive or very individualistic, etc. Thus high-income earners are not very progressive, which means that they have high scores on the progressive factor, which in turn produces a positive coefficient of 0.12; similarly, high-income earners tend to be rather individualistic, which means that they have a low score on the individualism factor, and this produces a negative coefficient of −0.15.

TABLE 6.7. *The Relationship between Attitudes to Restrictions on Abortion and Social Characteristics* (percentages)

Statement: A future Conservative government should make abortions more difficult to obtain.

	Strongly agree or agree	Neither agree nor disagree	Strongly disagree or disagree
All respondents	33	19	48
Class			
Salariat	30	22	47
Routine non-manual	35	15	50
Petty bourgeoisie	27	18	55
Foreman and Technician	39	15	46
Working class	32	18	50
Age			
18–25	22	9	70
26–45	20	15	64
46–65	29	18	54
66+	42	22	37
Gender			
Male	31	24	45
Female	36	15	49
Income			
Under £10,000	45	18	38
£10,000–£30,000	31	20	49
£30,000+	28	18	55
Graduate			
Yes	28	18	53
No	33	19	48
Religiosity			
Religious beliefs	35	19	46
No religious beliefs	20	16	64

TABLE 6.8. *Social Backgrounds as Predictors of Ideology*

Predictor	Progressivism	Individualism	Traditionalism (general)	Traditionalism (moral)
Income	0.12**	−0.13**	0.23**	0.09**
	(4.0)	(4.8)	(8.8)	(3.1)
Age	−0.01	−0.14**	−0.13**	−0.20**
	(0.4)	(4.7)	(4.8)	(7.0)
Religiosity	−0.11**	0.03*	0.08**	−0.13**
	(4.1)	(1.0)	(3.0)	(4.9)
Graduate	0.11**	0.02	0.16**	0.00
	(3.9)	(0.6)	(6.0)	(0.0)
Gender	−0.04	0.04	0.02	−0.11**
	(1.4)	(1.6)	(0.9)	(4.0)
Class	−0.02	0.05	−0.08**	0.00
	(1.8)	(0.6)	(2.8)	(0.1)
R^2	0.06	0.05	0.17	0.10
F statistic	14.1	6.6	45.1	24.6

* significant at the $p < 0.05$ level, ** significant at the $p < 0.01$ level.

they tend to be economic and moral 'de-regulators', preferring private-market solutions to economic problems and individual choice in matters of abortion and divorce.

By contrast, elderly Conservatives are likely to be qualified individualists as well as traditionalists, although there is no evidence that they are anti-progressive. Thus they support privatization programmes, but do not object to tighter regulations on industry, and support greater consumer protection. Alongside this goes a strong preference for capital punishment, opposition to European integration, and support for the repatriation of immigrants.

Religious Conservatives tend to be more progressive than non-religious Conservatives; in addition, they tend to be anti-individualists, anti-traditionalists in a general sense, but rather traditionalist in a moral sense. Thus they are less inclined to support the death penalty, but more inclined to support restrictions on abortion.

Graduates are rather like affluent Conservatives, in that they tend to be anti-progressive and anti-traditionalist in a general sense, but there is no evidence that they tend to be more individualistic or more morally traditionalist than other Conservatives.

Finally, the remaining social characteristics each influence only one of the four components of Tory ideology. Thus women are more morally traditionalist, but not more or less progressive, individualistic, or generally traditionalist; working-class Conservatives tend to be more generally traditionalist, strongly favouring capital punishment, for example, but do not differ in other respects.

In the light of these findings, we consider the factors which might explain these ideological differences next.

EXPLAINING IDEOLOGICAL VARIATIONS WITHIN THE CONSERVATIVE PARTY

Political ideology is a complex phenomenon which cannot be explained simply by social characteristics. But an individual's social background influences his or her outlook on life, because these characteristics produce different life experiences. For example, the affluent have a different perspective from the poor, because affluence brings with it a different set of experiences from that of poverty. For this reason, it is interesting to examine the links between such characteristics and political ideology.

The general-incentives model introduced in an earlier chapter suggests that participation by party members is motivated by a combination of self-interest and altruism. A similar point can be made about the ideological beliefs of party members; individuals come to believe the things they do partly because to do so serves their interests as they see them, but also because they believe that wider social interests are served by those ideas.

In this discussion, three broad components of Conservative ideology were identified: progressivism, individualism, and traditionalism. A common underlying dimension to each of these factors is the amount of state or government intervention in the economy or society which the individual supports. As we have seen, progressives favour a lot of state intervention in the form of government spending, regulation, and redistribution. By contrast, individualists favour government withdrawal from economic intervention, preferring the State to tax less and regulate less. Similarly, while traditionalists are not in favour of economic regulation, they favour

Issues	Favour state intervention	Oppose state intervention
Economic issues	Progressives	Individualists
Social and moral issues	Traditionalists	

FIG. 6.2 A classification of Conservative party ideology

moral and social regulation. Resisting European integration, repatriating immigrants, and restricting abortion imply a strong interventionist state, which aims to enforce a particular vision of the social order. These distinctions are clarified in Figure 6.2.

In Figure 6.2, progressives appear in the quadrant favouring economic intervention, individualists in the quadrant opposing this. Thus if Conservative ideology were simply a matter of attitudes to state intervention in the economy, then party members would be distributed along a single progressive–individualist dimension. However, there are the traditionalists, who are principally concerned with moral and social regulation and who may be indifferent or divided on matters of economic intervention. This adds an extra dimension to Conservative ideology, captured by the lower quadrants in the diagram.

The labels in the different quadrants of Figure 6.2 are of course general indicators of ideological beliefs, not precisely defined distinctions. It is possible, for example, that some individualists, along with some progressives, will be found in the fourth quadrant favouring both economic and social deregulation. Moreover, there may be significant overlaps between the different quadrants in relation to specific issues. But this diagram provides a useful way of thinking about contemporary Conservative party ideology.

In the light of these distinctions, it is possible to examine the relationship between self-interest and ideological beliefs. The relationship is likely to work in the following way: individuals who have the resources and power to care for themselves and their families are likely to oppose government regulation and intervention in the economy. This is true for two reasons: first, education and affluence give them the abilities and resources to provide for themselves without relying on the State; secondly, state intervention brings with it the burden of additional taxation, and the affluent bear what they are likely to feel is a disproportionate share of this burden.

Consequently, affluent Conservatives are likely to be less progressive, more individualistic, and possibly less traditionalist if they extend their aversion to state regulation to moral and social questions. This is because these ideological positions imply less state intervention in the lives of the individual. The same point could be made about graduates, many of whom are also fairly affluent. Thus affluent Conservatives and graduates are likely to be economic and possibly moral 'de-regulators'.

Elderly Conservatives, particularly the retired, are not at all likely to be affluent; as we observed earlier some 24 per cent of all respondents had household incomes of under £10,000 per year, but some 38 per cent of the over-65 age-group were in this income category. Unlike affluent Conservatives, the elderly are not anti-progressive, but they do tend to be traditionalists who favour strong state action to support their views.

On the other hand, the elderly also appear to be strong individualists, a fact that seems to be inconsistent with a preference for state intervention. However, a close examination of the items making up the individualism scale shows that the elderly differ significantly from other Conservatives on only one of the measures which make up this scale. They are more likely to favour stricter laws for trade unions, the one item in the individualism scale which calls for greater government intervention in the economy.[8] In general, then, the elderly tend to be economic and moral regulators by comparison with other Conservatives.

However, ideological beliefs within the Conservative party cannot be explained solely by self-interest. Another factor which relates

---

[8] Some 75% of retired Conservatives favour stricter laws to regulate trade unions, compared with 60% of Conservatives who are not retired.

particularly to the link between ideology and age is suggested by Inglehart (1990) in his study of political values in advanced industrial societies. His work is best known for the suggestion that a new dimension of political conflict has become increasingly important in industrial democracies over time: a conflict between what he terms 'Materialist' and 'Post-Materialist' values. The former concern economic well-being and physical security of the individual; the latter, issues regarding self-expression, participation, and the quality of life.

It is an extensive and complex thesis with many implications, but from our point of view one of the theoretical propositions which underpin the analysis is most relevant. This is the proposition that 'one's basic values reflect the conditions that prevailed during one's pre-adult years' (Inglehart, 1990: 68). In other words, basic values or ideological beliefs are broadly defined in pre-adult years, and subsequently they tend to remain fairly stable, even in the face of considerable individual and social change. Inglehart presents a considerable amount of evidence collected over a period of years to support this idea.

This has clear implications for the relationship between age and ideology, since it suggests that different age-cohorts will tend to have attitudes which reflect the social views prevailing when they were in their pre-adult years. Thus the elderly, whose pre-adult experiences were acquired at a time when abortion was illegal, divorce socially frowned on, and capital punishment legal, and when the 'permissive society' did not yet exist, are likely to have more traditional values than the young and middle-aged.

This may also explain in part why young Conservatives in the survey appear to be less progressive and more individualistic than middle-aged Conservatives. In the case of the young, their formative political experiences were acquired entirely during the Thatcherite period. We discuss Thatcherism below, suggesting that it was individualistic, traditionalist, and anti-progressive; thus, if this socialization hypothesis has validity, it would imply that young Conservatives would tend to reflect Thatcherite beliefs, because these ideas were dominant in the party during their pre-adult years. By contrast, middle-aged Conservatives, whose pre-adult experiences were acquired in the Macmillan or early Heath period, are likely to be a lot more progressive, reflecting the dominant ideological tendencies within the party at that time.

TABLE 6.9. *Attitudes to Spending on Poverty and Restrictions on Abortion by Religious Affiliation* (percentages)

	'Spend more on poverty'		
Religious affiliation	Definitely or probably should	Doesn't matter	Definitely or probably should not
No affiliation	69	10	21
Roman Catholic	79	11	11
Church of England	82	8	10
Church of Scotland	79	9	12
Other Christian	82	5	12
Non-Christian	89	3	8
	'Restrict abortion'		
	Strongly agree or agree	Neither agree nor disagree	Strongly disagree or disagree
No affiliation	20	16	64
Roman Catholic	66	12	22
Church of England	31	20	49
Church of Scotland	38	20	42
Other Christian	35	22	42
Non-Christian	33	10	56

If self-interest and pre-adult socialization are influential factors, then altruism is also likely to play a role in an individual's ideological perspective. This can be seen in the case of religiosity. Religious Conservatives are more progressive, less individualistic, less generally traditionalist, and more morally traditionalist than other Conservatives. This pattern can be observed in more detail in Table 6.9, in which attitudes to spending on poverty, the most significant indicator of progressivism, and abortion, the best indicator of moral traditionalism, are categorized by religious affiliation.

In Table 6.9 all party members with a religious affiliation are more in favour of government spending on poverty than those who have no such affiliation. Interestingly enough, the strongest supporters of spending to alleviate poverty are those affiliated with non-Christian groups, such as Jews, Hindus, Muslims, and Sikhs. But members of the Church of England, who make up 62 per cent of the sample, are significantly more in favour of such spending than the non-affiliated. By contrast, religious respondents are all more likely to favour restrictions on abortion when compared with the non-affiliated, although clearly Roman Catholics stand out in this regard.

Overall, social-background characteristics do not have a strong influence on ideology. This is not surprising, since ideology is a complex phenomenon, influenced by many factors. But social characteristics do influence the ideological beliefs of Conservatives, and the pattern of influences is consistent with motives which are both self-interested as well as altruistic in character.

In the light of this analysis, the next section examines Thatcherism as a distinctive set of ideas within Conservative ideology.

THATCHERISM AND CONSERVATISM

Mrs Thatcher was leader of the Conservative party for more than fifteen years. The distinctive feature of her premiership was that, in the words of Kavanagh, 'She dismissed what she regarded as woolly talk about consensus politics' (1990: 201), and went on to preside over a significant shift to the right in the policy goals of the Conservative party. The consensus politics of 'Butskellism' came to an end during her leadership. She was also a distinctively ideological Conservative, eschewing pragmatism and compromise in favour of principles and conflict.

'Butskellism' was based on the proposition that, rhetoric aside, there were no really fundamental differences between the two major parties in British politics (Beer, 1965; Mackintosh, 1982; Gamble, 1990). The basic argument was that fundamental policy differences between the parties had disappeared, following a convergence around the principles of Keynesian macro-economic management and the Beveridge welfare state, after the Second World War. Thus Samuel Beer writes: '(T)he ideological gap between the parties narrowed as Labour's retreat and the Conservatives' advance left the two parties occupying the common ground of the Welfare state and the Managed Economy. Along with this decline in ideology, class antagonism, as compared with the inter-war period, also greatly subsided' (Beer, 1965: 386).

Thatcherism has given rise to a burgeoning literature, the main theme of which has been to try to explain why Mrs Thatcher was successful, despite breaking so clearly with the consensus politics of the post-war era (Skidelsky, 1988; Holmes, 1989; Riddell, 1989).

One interesting interpretation of her success, by Crewe and Searing, argued that 'Mrs Thatcher made her way in the Con-servative party by joining together components from two familiar perspectives: liberal Whiggery and traditional Toryism' (1988: 378). Crewe and Searing's analysis of Tory élite opinion and mass elec-toral opinion on the eve of her election as party leader suggested that this combination of ideological beliefs attracted only a minority of both Conservative MPs and voters. Thus, they suggest, her strategy was not to adapt Conservative party ideology to the beliefs of the electorate, but rather to 'educate' both the Conservative party and the voters and to adjust their values and beliefs in favour of this ideological mix. Thus political re-education was required to change the consensus.

Analyses of British public opinion both by Crewe and Searing and by the team conducting the British Election Study (see Heath *et al.*, 1991) have shown that with the possible exception of the issue of nationalization, the British public remain stubbornly re-luctant to adopt Thatcherite beliefs. If the electorate remained largely unmoved by Thatcherism, an interesting question concerns the effect that it had on the Conservative party. In an analysis of the attitudes and composition of the parliamentary Conservative party, Norton (1990, 1992) has suggested that Mrs Thatcher did not succeed in creating a parliamentary party in her own image. However, up until the present survey, this question has not been addressed for the Conservative party as a whole.

To assess the impact of Thatcherism on the Conservative party, it is necessary to clarify its meaning in terms of wider Conservative party ideology. There is a fair degree of consensus about the ideological characteristics of Thatcherism, though much less con-sensus about its achievements. Peter Riddell provides a summary description of Mrs Thatcher's approach to politics, which fairly represents the range of views about the meaning of Thatcherism. He writes:

Her approach has revolved around a number of themes—a belief in Britain's greatness and the assertion of national interests, a prejudice against the public sector (at any rate in economic and industrial affairs), a backing for the police and the authorities in fighting terrorism and upholding law and order, a strong dislike of trade unions, a general commitment to the virtues of sound money, a preference for wealth creators over civil servants and commentators, and a support for the rights of the individuals to make their own provision for education and health. (Riddell, 1989: 4)

In a similar vein, Jenkins sees part of Mrs Thatcher's appeal as a championing of the taxpayers, particularly the skilled working class, against what she saw as overbearing organizations such as the Treasury, the trade unions, and local-government landlords (Jenkins, 1989). In this respect he believes that Thatcherism is an echo of the radical Toryism of Joseph Chamberlain.

In terms of the four factors of progressivism, individualism, general traditionalism, and moral traditionalism discussed earlier, Thatcherism represented a clear shift away from progressive ideas towards individualism and traditionalism. With regard to individualism, it favoured privatization, de-regulation, tax cuts, and free-market solutions to economic problems. But it also represented a shift towards traditionalism, exemplified by Mrs Thatcher's support for capital punishment in free votes on this issue in the Commons, her vocal opposition to European integration, and her attitudes to restrictions on immigration and abortion.

Given this, if Mrs Thatcher succeeded in radicalizing the Conservative party, we should expect to see significant majorities of grass-roots members opposing most of the progressive indicators and favouring the individualism and traditionalism indicators. Thus they should oppose spending more money on poverty or the unemployed; they should favour privatization and cuts in income tax, and be opposed to further European integration. Finally, they should favour restrictions on abortion and a tightening-up of the divorce laws.

It is readily apparent from Table 6.3 that in many respects the grass-roots Conservative party is rather anti-Thatcherite. On the one hand, there is significant support for distinctive Thatcherite policies such as privatization, capital punishment, and opposition to further European integration. But, on the other hand, as we have seen, grass-roots Conservatives favour 'capturing the middle ground of politics'; they support welfare for the poor and unemployed and the regulation of markets, and many support incomes policy, which is anathema to dyed-in-the-wool Thatcherites.

Moreover, while it is true that members support the privatization programmes, they also want the newly privatized industries to be closely regulated, in order to safeguard the interests of consumers. Again, while they support stricter laws to regulate trade unions, a majority supports the idea of giving workers more say in the work-place.

Perhaps most significantly, as we saw in Figure 6.1, some 41 per cent of party members think of themselves as being on the centre-left of the ideological spectrum within the party, and only just over 20 per cent think of themselves as being on the right.

On the question of whether or not Mrs Thatcher shifted grass-roots ideology to the right, we cannot be certain of the answer in the absence of data on grass-roots beliefs prior to Mrs Thatcher's premiership. However, it would be an exaggeration to suggest that the pro-Thatcherite attitudes in the survey, such as opposition to immigration and further European integration and support for capital punishment, are the result of a programme of 're-educating' the Conservative party.

The reason for this comes from two types of evidence: first, evidence from voting surveys which pre-date the Thatcher period; second, evidence from a survey of Conservative party conference delegates carried out in 1979, at the start of Mrs Thatcher's premiership. Both show strong support for capital punishment and restrictions on immigration into Britain.

The voting evidence shows that both Conservative and non-Conservative voters were pro-capital punishment and anti-immigrant long before Mrs Thatcher became party leader. Butler and Stokes (1974: 461, 465) report that 71 per cent of the electorate wanted to retain the death penalty, and 83 per cent thought that too many immigrants had been let into Britain, in their first survey of the British electorate, conducted in 1963. The same point could be made about opposition to European integration; scepticism about the benefits of European integration among voters has been a long-running feature of British politics (ibid.: 464).

The 1979 survey of Conservative party conference delegates was part of the European middle-level élites study, a set of surveys of party members carried out throughout the European Community (see Reif *et al.*, 1980). The British part of the study included a survey of Conservative party conference delegates. As such, the respondents were not representative of Conservative party members as a whole, but they were representative of the élite of the activists—that is, those who attended the annual conference. Some 59 per cent of them agreed or strongly agreed that 'The voluntary repatriation of immigrants should be supported by the allocation of government grants'; and some 82 per cent agreed or strongly agreed that 'Capital punishment should be reintroduced in Britain for certain types of murder'.

Thus, in so far as this evidence is a guide to the opinions of party members at the time, the results suggest that Thatcherism merely aligned itself with pre-existing attitudes within the Conservative party, rather than a force which shifted opinions in a new direction.

CONCLUSIONS

In conclusion, ideological divisions within the Conservative party can be classified in terms of three broad classes of factors: progressivism, traditionalism, and individualism. Each of these aspects of ideology is influenced by the social status, age, and religious affiliations of the grass-roots members. Each factor can be regarded as an indicator of an underlying attitude to the role of the State in the lives of the citizens. Affluent, high-status Conservatives tend to be against government intervention in either the economy or society. By contrast, elderly Conservatives, many of whom are on low incomes, tend to favour state intervention both in the economy and in matters of morality and social conduct. Religious Conservatives also tend to favour government intervention.

These relationships can be explained by a combination of self-interested and altruistic motives, together with pre-adult political experiences. The latter produces a relationship between ideology and age which is independent of any other social characteristics.

The results appear to confirm the hypothesis that Thatcherism as a doctrine appears to have done little to 're-educate' the Conservative party, by transforming it into a more strongly traditionalist and individualistic organization. In this respect, the experience of the Conservative party is similar to that of the electorate as a whole, who appear largely untouched by these ideas. Of course, there are many traditionalists and individualists within the grass-roots party, but that appears to have been true for many years, long before Mrs Thatcher became leader.

In addition, there is a lot of support for 'One Nation' Tory policies like incomes policy, regulation of markets, and social-welfare spending. Chauvinism aside, many grass-roots Conservatives are quite progressive in their attitudes to many of the contemporary issues of British politics. Certainly, they are more progressive than conventional wisdom suggests.

In this chapter we have focused on the attitudes and ideological beliefs of members in relation to society and politics. In the next chapter, we narrow the focus somewhat to examine how members see the Conservative party itself, paying particular attention to the question of whether or not they feel that they can influence party policies and the policy-making process within the party.

7

Perceptions of the Party and Society

In Chapter 2 we referred to the fact that party membership is a variable concept, and depends upon the traditions and political culture of the party under consideration. As far as the Labour party is concerned, individual membership has always necessitated a personal commitment to declared principles and a fixed financial arrangement, and it also implies a participative involvement in party affairs.

In fact, the levels of personal commitment and participation in the Labour party vary widely (Seyd and Whiteley, 1992); nevertheless, barriers to entry into the party have always existed, because membership has been seen as a distinct, unique phenomenon. Faced, however, in the 1990s with a decline in membership, the Labour party leadership has begun to remove barriers to entry as it attempts to recruit more individuals who do not necessarily possess either the principled commitment or the desire to participate which was assumed to be a prerequisite for joining the party in the past.

By contrast, the Conservative party has always sought to create as few barriers to entry as possible; thus it requires no individual commitment to specific ideals nor the annual payment of a minimum subscription. Instead, it welcomes into its ranks as many as possible, the majority of whom will do no more than contribute money.

We referred in Chapter 2 to the Central Office official who distinguished between 'full' and 'associate' members. As we have seen in Chapters 3 and 5, the majority of the members are 'associates' in this sense. Two-thirds of the members had not attended a party meeting in the previous twelve months, and just one in five had attended either 'occasionally' or 'frequently'.

We suggested earlier that for many people Conservative party membership can best be seen as an insurance premium; in this

TABLE 7.1. *Attendance at Party Meetings* (percentages)

Question: Thinking back over the LAST TWELVE MONTHS, how often have you attended a LOCAL (e.g., ward or constituency) Conservative party meeting?

Not at all	68
Rarely (once or twice)	14
Occasionally (three to five times)	7
Frequently (more than five times)	11

case, payment of a sum of money to insure against socialism. It is not surprising, therefore, that few attend party meetings; paying an insurance premium ensures that others will provide the necessary cover. However, it might also be argued that few attend party meetings because they are so unattractive to the average member.

Accordingly, we asked those members who did attend a party meeting in the last year what they thought of them. Of course, we recognize that this is a group of people who are more likely to regard meetings favourably; nevertheless, their responses are a good guide to the attitudes of informed party members to the institutions of the party itself.

ATTITUDES TO PARTY MEETINGS

Overall, members reveal a very positive attitude towards meetings. Few would appear to dislike them, or attend merely out of a sense of duty. The overwhelming majority believe that meetings are interesting, efficiently run, easy to understand, and united. They also regard meetings as neither modern nor old-fashioned. While four in every ten believe that meetings are neither distinctively left- or right-wing, a majority perceive them to be clearly right-wing; almost no one feels that a local party meeting reflects the left-wing sentiments that exist within the party.

The relationship between ideology and meeting attendance can be clarified a little by examining the distribution of the respondents along the left–right ideology scale for the party introduced earlier. What is noticeable is that those who identify themselves as being on the left are less likely to attend party meetings, by

TABLE 7.2. *Members' Perceptions of Conservative Party Meetings*
(percentages)

Members who thought meeting was very or fairly:

Interesting	81
Friendly	81
Efficiently run	84
United	79
Easy to understand	82
Modern	40
Left-wing	1
Boring	9
Unfriendly	10
Badly run	9
Divided	10
Hard to understand	5
Old-fashioned	24
Right-wing	57

neither:

Interesting nor boring	10
Friendly nor unfriendly	9
Efficiently nor badly run	7
United nor divided	11
Easy nor hard to understand	12
Modern nor old-fashioned	37
Left- nor right-wing	42

Note: Approximately 27 per cent of members responded to this set of
questions.

TABLE 7.3. *Members' Attendance at Party Meetings by Ideological
Predisposition* (percentages; N = 2378)

	Left	Centre-left	Centre	Centre-right	Right
All respondents	3	10	26	39	22
Meeting attendance:					
Not at all	4	11	28	37	20
Rarely	2	8	24	42	24
Occasionally	5	8	21	39	27
Frequently	1	10	17	47	25

TABLE 7.4. *Attitudes towards Party Meetings* (percentages)

	Very interesting	Fairly interesting	Neither	Fairly boring	Very boring
All respondents	31	49	10	7	2
Local office-holders	35	50	6	8	1
Non-office-holders	30	49	11	7	3
Not at all active	31	44	13	9	3
Not very active	30	51	10	8	1
Fairly active	29	51	11	6	3
Very active	35	47	8	7	3

comparison with those identifying themselves as on the right. Almost three-quarters of frequent attenders are from the party's right wing. It is possible that the right-wing culture which members perceive as dominating party meetings discourages left-wing members from attending meetings more frequently.

Those who attend party meetings, therefore, even if they do so only once or twice a year, have few negative responses to their experiences, which suggests that attendance is not influenced by any organizational features; members are not deterred from attending meetings by the perception that they are boring or unfriendly or badly run. Rather, it would seem that the culture of party membership is essentially non-participative.

There are only very slight differences in attitudes towards party meetings between the very active and the inactive, or between local association office-holders and the ordinary, rank-and-file members. Both the very active and the office-holders are slightly more enthusiastic about meetings, but the fact that these differences are so slight suggests no great dislike of the organizational aspects of local party activity among the inactive rank and filers.

From the subgroup of about one-third of members who had attended a local party meeting in the previous twelve months, it was possible to ascertain how they spent their time at these meetings. The complaint is often heard that members at party meetings are forced to devote too much of their time to the question of fund-raising and organizational matters rather than to more general political issues. When asked to say what proportion of the time at their last local meeting was devoted to internal party organizational

TABLE 7.5. *Distribution of Time at Local Party Meetings*
(percentages; average N = 688)

Topic	Time spent			
	None	Some	Most	All
Internal party organization	14	63	20	3
Fund-raising	10	67	20	3
Local politics	11	70	17	2
National politics	15	69	13	3

TABLE 7.6. *Issues Discussed at Local Party Meetings*

Issue	Percentage of local meetings at which issue was discussed
Local government	17
The economy	14
Health	10
Education	10
Law and order	10
Housing	7
Taxation	7
Defence	3
Other	3

matters, fund-raising, local politics, and national politics, members confirmed that at least some of the time was spent on all these topics. However, it appears that more time was spent on organizational matters and fund-raising than on local or national political issues.

During the time spent discussing local or national political issues, members were most likely to have discussed local government, the economy, health, law and order, and education. What exact issues were discussed under the heading 'local government' is unclear; whether it was the performance or particular policies of the local authority in which the member lived or the Conservative government's structural and financial reforms of local government would have required more detailed and probing questions.

We have seen that members have a positive attitude towards local party meetings. This raises the question of their attitudes to the party in general and the party leadership. We examine this next.

ATTITUDES TOWARDS THE PARTY AND ITS LEADERS

Members were asked to evaluate both the Conservative party and its leader, John Major, with scores assigned on a 100-point scale ranging from zero to 100. A high score meant that members felt 'warm and sympathetic' towards them, and a low score meant that members felt 'cold and unsympathetic'. The mean score both for the party and for John Major was 80, indicating a high degree of warmth towards the party organization and the leader. Members ranked only the Queen (mean score 86) and the armed forces (82) higher. The mean score for Margaret Thatcher was also high, at 78, indicating that a considerable reservoir of affection exists among the ordinary members for the former leader.

Interestingly, Conservatives rank their leader higher than did Labour members in the earlier survey (Major 80: Kinnock 73), but the position was reversed with their respective political parties (Labour party 84: Conservative party 80) (Seyd and Whiteley, 1992: 153 and 170). This reinforces the point that Conservatives place a greater stress on leadership than does Labour.

Attitudes towards both the party in general and present and past party leaders vary with social-background characteristics, political dispositions, and level of activism of the members. Thus, while few class differences existed in attitudes, affluent Conservatives were less likely to feel affection for the party and for Margaret Thatcher than poor Conservatives; similarly, the old are more affectionate towards the leaders and the party than the young, women more than men and finally non-graduates more than graduates.

The relationships between activism, ideology, and attitudes to leaders and the party are also interesting. Not surprisingly, active members are favourably inclined to all three by comparison with inactive members. But the strongest effects in Table 7.7 relate to ideology; left-wing members are considerably cooler towards them by comparison with right-wing members. Margaret Thatcher's popularity among her own grass roots was high, particularly among

TABLE 7.7. *Attitudes towards the Conservative Party and its Leadership*

	Mean thermometer scores		
	Conservative Party	John Major	Margaret Thatcher
All respondents	80	80	78
Class			
Salariat	80	80	78
Routine non-manual	84	83	80
Petty bourgeoisie	80	79	80
Foreman and technician	82	82	79
Working class	80	80	77
Income			
Under £10,000	84	83	82
£10,000–£30,000	80	80	78
£30,000+	79	80	77
Age			
18–25	81	78	78
26–45	79	76	76
46–65	79	79	78
66+	84	84	81
Gender			
Male	79	79	77
Female	83	82	80
Graduate			
Yes	77	77	74
No	81	81	80
Activists			
Not at all active	79	80	77
Not very active	82	81	80
Fairly active	83	83	80
Very active	84	82	81
Left/right placement			
Left	68	72	62
Centre-left	74	76	69
Centre	79	80	76
Centre-right	82	81	80
Right	87	85	87
Average N = 2404			

right-wing activists, where it verged on the ecstatic, but it tailed off quite markedly among the inactive and the more left-inclined. The gap between the left and the right in their attitudes to Mrs Thatcher is particularly wide at 25 points.

The gap between the left and the right in attitudes to John Major was 13 points. At the time of our survey, Major had been leader for eighteen months, time enough to distance himself from his political mentor, Margaret Thatcher, and yet he was still regarded with some misgivings on the left of the party. Not surprisingly, those on the right of the party and the very active were much more enthusiastic in their evaluations of their former party leader than their less active and left-wing colleagues.

We referred in Chapter 2 to the dissatisfaction expressed by some members with the lack of internal party democracy. Both the Charter Movement and the Party Reform Steering Committee believe that individual members should play a more important role in the party's affairs. Whether this is a view shared by party members in general is a particularly interesting question.

We asked members if they thought that the party leadership paid much attention to their views, and they were fairly evenly divided in their answers; however, a simple majority (43 per cent) believed that their views were of little importance to the leadership. Not surprisingly, activists were more likely to believe that the party leadership listens to their views than inactive members; and those on the left were much less confident that their views were considered than those on the right. The latter responses probably reflect the fact that the right has been dominant in the leadership of the party since the election of Mrs Thatcher.

With regard to various social-background variables, working-class members feel more alienated from the leadership than middle-class members, the poor more alienated than the rich, the young than the old, and finally, non-graduates than graduates.

Until 1965 the Conservative party leader 'emerged' from among the parliamentarians by a process of consultation and evolution, described by one senior Conservative, Iain Macleod, as the politics of 'the magic circle'. Edward Heath was the first Conservative leader to be elected by his parliamentary colleagues, and both Margaret Thatcher and John Major have also been elected in a similar fashion. By contrast, Labour and Liberal Democrat leaders are elected in a manner which directly involves party members.

TABLE 7.8. *Views on the Responsiveness of the Leader* (percentages)

Statement: The party leadership doesn't pay a lot of attention to the views of ordinary party members.

	Strongly agree	Agree	Neither agree nor disagree	Disagree	Strongly disagree
All respondents	7	36	25	30	2
Class					
Salariat	6	35	25	32	2
Routine non-manual	6	35	24	34	2
Petty bourgeoisie	7	36	25	30	3
Foreman and technician	6	40	22	29	4
Working class	11	29	30	28	3
Income					
Under £10,000	9	39	21	29	3
£10,000–£30,000	6	36	24	33	2
£30,000+	6	33	28	31	2
Age					
18–25	0	36	50	14	0
26–45	10	25	27	34	4
46–65	6	37	23	31	2
66+	6	38	23	31	2
Gender					
Male	7	36	24	31	3
Female	7	35	24	32	2
Graduate					
Yes	7	29	31	31	3
No	7	37	23	32	2
Activism					
Not at all active	7	38	29	25	2
Not very active	6	35	24	34	2
Fairly active	6	35	19	38	2
Very active	8	31	14	42	6
Left/right placement					
Left	11	40	24	23	3
Centre-left	9	36	27	27	1
Centre	7	34	29	28	2
Centre-right	4	37	24	34	2
Right	8	35	17	35	5
N = 2327					

Liberal Democrats elect their leader in a simple one member, one vote ballot, and Labour ballot their individual members, whose vote then comprises 33 per cent of the leadership electoral college.

We asked Conservatives whether they would like to elect their leader in a ballot of all party members, a radical proposal which not even the Charter Movement has suggested. Interestingly enough, a majority (51 per cent) agreed with this suggestion, and would like the power to elect the party leader to be given to all members.

Perhaps the parliamentarians' failure to confirm Margaret Thatcher as party leader in 1990 rankled with many members, and influenced their response to the question about electing the leader; nevertheless, the fact that a majority want the system to be changed suggests opposition to a hierarchical party structure in which parliamentarians dominate and members are subordinate.

In Chapter 2, we referred to Kelly's view that the Conservative party is becoming more difficult to manage, and that party leaders have to take more notice of grass-roots opinions because of a new intake of young, educated professionals who are more knowledgeable on political affairs and less deferential to authority. The evidence from members' responses to this particular question does not support this idea, however.

There is clear evidence to suggest that middle-class, affluent, and educated members are less likely than working-class, poor, and uneducated members to support the mass election of the leader. For example, some 45 per cent of the salariat agree or strongly agree that the leader should be elected by all the members, by comparison with 63 per cent of the working class. Similarly, 64 per cent of the low-income members agree or strongly agree with this, by comparison with 43 per cent of the affluent members. Finally, 47 per cent of the young have these opinions, compared with 54 per cent of the retired.

Furthermore, *contra* Kelly's suggestion, professionals are more likely to disagree with this idea than working-class Conservatives. Thus some 40 per cent of the professionals are against the idea, compared with only 25 per cent of the working class; 43 per cent of the affluent oppose it, compared with 26 per cent of the poor. Finally, a surprising 39 per cent of the young oppose it, by comparison with 33 per cent of the retired.

Not surprisingly, activists are not so keen to see the powers of

TABLE 7.9. *Attitudes to Electing the Party Leader* (percentages)

Statement: The Conservative party leader should be elected by a system of one party member, one vote.

	Strongly agree	Agree	Neither agree nor disagree	Disagree	Strongly disagree
All respondents	11	40	15	29	6
Class					
Salariat	10	35	16	32	8
Routine non-manual	9	44	13	28	5
Petty bourgeoisie	12	40	14	27	6
Foreman and technician	11	44	13	30	3
Working class	17	46	13	23	2
Income					
Under £10,000	16	48	11	23	3
£10,000–£30,000	9	38	17	30	6
£30,000+	10	33	13	34	9
Age					
18–25	17	30	13	22	17
26–45	12	38	18	25	8
46–65	11	36	14	33	7
66+	11	43	14	28	5
Gender					
Male	12	36	16	29	7
Female	10	42	13	30	5
Graduate					
Yes	7	27	18	36	11
No	12	41	15	27	5
Activism					
Not at all active	11	40	15	29	6
Not very active	11	42	16	27	4
Fairly active	11	34	14	35	6
Very active	10	32	10	35	14
Left/right placement					
Left	19	20	24	22	15
Centre-left	9	30	18	34	8
Centre	8	40	17	30	15
Centre-right	9	39	13	36	5
Right	17	45	11	19	7
N = 2362					

electing the party leader given to all members. Presumably, they feel that the present procedures for electing a party leader, which necessitate sounding out opinion among constituency association members, are adequate enough, since their opinions are canvassed in this process in any case.

It might be thought that those on the left of the party would expect their chances of electing a party leader closer to their views to be greater if all members were given a vote. However, compared with only 49 per cent on the left, some 62 per cent of members on the right of the party 'strongly agree' or 'agree' with this proposal. At the other end of the scale, 15 per cent of those on the left 'strongly disagree' with the idea, compared with only 7 per cent on the right. It may be that left-wing members are concerned about the influence of right-wing populism on the election of the leadership.

One significant power that party members possess, which ensures that they are not entirely subordinate in internal party relationships, is the selection of candidates for parliamentary elections. Local Conservative associations have traditionally jealously guarded their rights in this matter, and have resisted attempts by Central Office to interfere (Ranney, 1965).

Nevertheless, in recent by-elections the Conservative party has been criticized for its choice of inappropriate candidates, and there have been suggestions that greater central control is necessary in order that the party recruit the best standard-bearer in these significant tests of public opinion. The lack of parliamentary candidates who are female or from ethnic minorities has prompted some to argue the case for restricting local party autonomy and extending Central Office powers in the selection process (Norris and Lovenduski, 1992).

Members were asked whether Central Office should play a more influential role in the selection of parliamentary candidates. One-third agreed that Central Office powers should be greater, but a plurality (41 per cent) did not want greater Central Office intervention. Thus members may be conscious of their role in this important aspect of party life, but there is nothing like overwhelming support for complete constituency autonomy.

If attitudes to this question are categorized by social-background variables, working-class members are marginally more likely to favour centralization. However, the poor feel more strongly about

TABLE 7.10. *Views on the Role of Conservative Central Office in Candidate Selection* (percentages)

Statement: Conservative Central Office should have a more influential role in the selection of parliamentary candidates.

	Strongly agree	Agree	Neither agree nor disagree	Disagree	Strongly disagree
All respondents	6	26	28	35	6
Class					
Salariat	5	22	30	37	6
Routine non-manual	4	28	27	34	7
Petty bourgeoisie	8	23	26	35	7
Foreman and technician	10	31	20	36	3
Working class	5	29	27	34	5
Income					
Under £10,000	10	33	23	31	4
£10,000–£30,000	5	24	27	38	6
£30,000+	6	22	31	25	6
Age					
18–25	4	0	39	48	9
26–45	3	18	36	34	10
46–65	5	23	27	39	6
66+	9	31	25	32	4
Gender					
Male	6	23	29	36	6
Female	6	28	26	35	5
Graduate					
Yes	4	16	35	38	8
No	7	26	27	35	6
Activism					
Not at all active	7	27	30	32	4
Not very active	6	26	29	34	5
Fairly active	5	26	24	40	6
Very active	7	16	15	46	16
Left/right placement					
Left	6	13	33	37	9
Centre-left	2	12	29	47	11
Centre	5	23	31	37	4
Centre-right	3	26	29	37	5
Right	15	34	18	26	7

N = 2372

this than the rich, with 43 per cent of them in favour, compared with only 28 per cent of the rich. Again, the old are markedly more in favour than the young, and non-graduates more than graduates. Interestingly enough, women members appear to be no more in favour of this than men. Thus the argument for increasing Central Office's powers over candidate selection, as a means of increasing the number of female MPs, is not a point of view shared by women members.

Not surprisingly, those who are very active are much more likely to oppose Central Office intervention in candidate selection than the inactive. The very active are four times more likely to strongly disagree with this idea than the totally inactive. The activists clearly enjoy this local power, and do not want it diminished.

On some of the previous issues we have examined, the activists and those on the right of the party have shared similar opinions, but on this question they differ markedly. Those on the very right of the party are more likely to favour greater Central Office intervention in the candidate selection process; perhaps they are confident that after the leadership of Mrs Thatcher and now John Major, the party has a right-wing bureaucracy sympathetic to their beliefs.

One final yardstick by which members judge the party is the extent to which they think that it should be guided by principles as opposed to pursuing pragmatism in politics. Accordingly, members were asked if they thought that the party should stick to principles, even if this should lose it an election. The results of this appear in Table 7.11.

It can be seen that a clear majority of members are in favour of sticking to principles, even if this means losing an election. Class differences on this indicator are negligible, but there is a slight tendency for affluent Conservatives to be more pragmatic than the poor. Age, on the other hand, appears to have a significant influence on pragmatism, with the young and middle-aged being more pragmatic than the old and retired. Finally, gender has no influence on pragmatism, but graduates are more likely to be pragmatic than non-graduates.

Interestingly enough, there are no significant differences between activists and inactive members in this regard, but there are differences between left-wing and right-wing members. Members on the left are much more electorally pragmatic than members

TABLE 7.11. *Views on Party Sticking to Principles* (percentages)

Statement: The Conservative party should always stick by its principles even if this should lose it an election.

	Strongly agree	Agree	Neither agree nor disagree	Disagree	Strongly disagree
All respondents	23	58	9	9	1
Class					
Salariat	22	59	9	10	1
Routine non-manual	20	62	9	8	1
Petty bourgeoisie	25	54	8	12	3
Foreman and					
technician	23	59	8	8	2
Working class	28	54	9	8	1
Income					
Under £10,000	29	58	6	6	0
£10,000–£30,000	22	60	9	8	1
£30,000+	21	54	9	13	3
Age					
18–25	26	30	13	26	4
26–45	21	51	13	13	3
46–65	21	58	8	11	2
66+	26	60	7	6	1
Gender					
Male	23	56	9	11	2
Female	24	60	8	8	1
Graduate					
Yes	19	54	13	14	2
No	23	59	8	9	1
Activism					
Not at all active	22	59	9	8	1
Not very active	23	58	7	10	2
Fairly active	25	54	10	9	2
Very active	28	55	7	10	1
Left/right placement					
Left	16	47	14	18	5
Centre-left	15	63	12	8	1
Centre	18	60	11	10	1
Centre-right	22	60	7	10	1
Right	38	50	4	7	1
N = 2407					

on the right, who are very strongly inclined to stick to principles regardless of the electoral consequences.

Apart from internal party-political issues, the question of relationships between the Conservatives and other parties is of greater significance now that the electoral hegemony of Britain's two major parties has declined. Since the 1960s the strength of party identification among the voters has dropped; in the past thirty years the number of 'very strong' Conservative identifiers has declined significantly (Heath *et al.*, 1991: 14). Despite the record of electoral success over the past decade and a half, this weakening of attachments makes the Conservative vote more and more vulnerable to opposition parties.

While the Conservative party has been in power, it has not had to address the question of coalition government in Britain or consider possible electoral alliances with other parties. However, if the erosion of party identification continues, and electoral volatility produces minority governments in the future, this is an issue which the party will have to confront at some stage. Thus it is interesting to know the attitudes of party members to coalition politics in Britain.

ATTITUDES TO COALITION POLITICS AND OTHER PARTIES

It is clear from the responses to the survey that Conservatives dislike the idea of coalition government; more than three-quarters (79 per cent) regard it with hostility. But there are interesting differences between members in the intensity of their feelings about this question. Working-class members are slightly more sympathetic to coalition government than middle-class members; the poor are more sympathetic than the affluent, the old than the young, and graduates than non-graduates. Relationships are not strong, but interesting variations in opinions exist none the less.

Notwithstanding the hostility to coalition government, it might be necessary for the Conservative party in future to consider alliances with other parties in Britain's current electoral uncertainties. In view of this, it is interesting to examine what the members think of their electoral rivals.

Table 7.13 contains information about the attitudes of members

TABLE 7.12. *Views on Coalition Government* (percentages)

Statement: Coalition governments are the best form of government for Britain.

	Strongly agree	Agree	Neither agree nor disagree	Disagree	Strongly disagree
All respondents	2	8	11	53	26
Class					
Salariat	1	6	11	50	32
Routine non-manual	2	6	12	57	23
Petty bourgeoisie	2	6	7	57	28
Foreman and technician	3	10	6	62	19
Working class	3	11	9	50	27
Income					
Under £10,000	4	10	11	56	18
£10,000–£30,000	1	7	9	54	29
£30,000+	1	5	11	49	33
Age					
18–25	0	4	17	30	48
26–45	1	4	14	47	35
46–65	2	6	10	53	30
66+	3	10	9	56	22
Gender					
Male	2	7	10	50	31
Female	2	8	10	56	24
Graduate					
Yes	2	8	10	53	27
No	0	4	9	52	34
Activism					
Not at all active	3	9	13	56	19
Not very active	2	8	9	50	31
Fairly active	1	5	8	53	32
Very active	0	3	3	49	44
Left/right placement					
Left	3	16	20	42	20
Centre-left	1	10	14	54	21
Centre	3	9	11	52	24
Centre-right	1	6	8	56	30
Right	3	7	8	49	33

N = 2413

TABLE 7.13. *Intensity of Feelings about Political Opponents*
(percentages)

	0–25	26–50	51–75	76–100	Mean
Labour party	49	45	7	0	27
Liberal Democrats	32	51	16	1	37
Scottish National party	68	27	4	0	19
Green party	70	25	5	1	20
Plaid Cymru	82	16	1	0	21
Neil Kinnock	67	30	3	0	21
Paddy Ashdown	32	47	19	2	39

to the different parties and the other major party leaders. We use the same thermometer scale here, ranging from zero to 100, referred to earlier. It can be seen that, as far as other parties are concerned, members feel the greatest warmth towards the Liberal Democrats. However, it is important to remember that a score of 50 on this scale denotes neutral feelings, so the mean score for the Liberal Democrats of 37 does not imply a great deal of sympathy and warmth towards them, merely that they are disliked less than Labour or the other parties.

Another interesting feature of this table is the fact that the members are more hostile to nationalist parties and the Greens than they are to their main rival, the Labour party. The very low score for Plaid Cymru is particularly noticeable. The intensity of feelings about the different parties is also highlighted by the percentage of scores below 25. Some 82 per cent of members score the Welsh nationalist, and 68 per cent the Scottish nationalist party in this range, which implies that they strongly dislike them. It has often been argued that the Conservative party is a kind of English national party, so it is perhaps not surprising that the members are most opposed to rival nationalist movements within the British state.

The hostility of feeling towards the Greens is also quite pronounced; while less than half score Labour in the lowest quarter of the scale, some 70 per cent do this for the Greens. This is perhaps harder to explain than the feelings about nationalist parties, particularly since the Greens share some of the same values as Conservatives about conserving the countryside. But there is no question but that their hostility is quite strong.

A third feature of Table 7.13 relates to the scores of the major rival party leaders, then Neil Kinnock and Paddy Ashdown. Not surprisingly, Neil Kinnock scores significantly lower than Paddy Ashdown, but it is also interesting that he did worse than his party in the evaluations. By contrast, Paddy Ashdown did slightly better than his party. This probably reflects the kind of coverage that both leaders have received in the Press. At the time of the survey, Neil Kinnock had been under almost continuous attack in the Conservative press for some months. By contrast, Paddy Ashdown had received a much more favourable, though not uncritical, press coverage.

One interesting implication of these scores for the future relates to the perceived difference between Conservatives and the Liberal Democrats. For Conservatives, the difference between the mean scores for their own party and the Liberal Democrats was 43. For Labour party members in the earlier survey, the difference between the mean scores for their own party and the Liberal Democrats was 54 (Seyd and Whiteley, 1992: 246). This suggests that it might be easier to convince Conservatives of the need to co-operate with the Liberal Democrats, if the need arises, than it would be to convince Labour party members.

In the next section of this chapter, we turn to two particular aspects of behaviour, traditionalism and social deference, which, some argue, help to explain the Conservative party's long-term dominance in British politics.

CONSERVATIVE TRADITIONALISM AND DEFERENCE

Parkin (1967) has argued that the Conservative party's electoral hegemony in the twentieth century is a result, in part, of its close identification with Britain's traditional institutions. The Conservative party interacts easily and naturally with the monarchy, the judiciary, the Civil Service, the BBC, the Church of England, the financial institutions within the City of London, and business organizations. Trade unions are one of the few institutions which are not part of a Conservative establishment.

One of the most distinctive features of Margaret Thatcher's

TABLE 7.14. *Mean Popularity Scores for Various Institutions, Individuals, and Organizations*

	Mean score
The Queen	86
The armed forces	83
Prince Charles	75
Doctors	75
The police	73
House of Commons	68
House of Lords	62
Judges	61
Teachers	60
The CBI	60
Church of England	59
BBC	59
ITV	59
The Stock Exchange	59
Lawyers	55
European Community	51
Social workers	47
Prince Edward	46
Jacques Delors	31
The TUC	26
Sun newspaper	19

period as Conservative leader, however, was her antipathy towards many of these traditional institutions and her view that some of the 'establishment' professions required far-reaching reforms. Thus, while Conservatives may have been closely identified with traditionalism in the past, this may no longer be a feature of grassroots attitudes.

It can be seen from Table 7.14, which shows the mean scores for various institutions, that party members are certainly respectful of some of the traditional institutions, such as the monarchy, the armed forces, and the police. The Queen scores higher in their esteem than any other person or institution listed in the survey, including both the Conservative party and John Major. Clearly, however, their support for the monarchy tends to be closely identified with the person of the Queen, since Prince Charles scores lower, and they appear to feel rather cold towards Prince Edward. The latter scores lower than any other person who is not identified with the party, with the exception of Jacques Delors, who is himself a particular object of Conservative dislike.

Neither House of Parliament attracted the level of support accorded to the monarchy, the armed forces, or the police; in particular, the House of Lords scored lower than the House of Commons, suggesting that party members are less attached to aristocratic and more to meritocratic principles. Perhaps their Lordships' attempts over the last decade to modify and amend some of the Conservative government's proposals have not endeared them to the grass roots.

At the other end of the popularity scale, the Trades Union Congress, not surprisingly, attracts some hostility, but the lowest score of any institution in the list goes to the *Sun* newspaper. This is surprising, given the newspaper's strong support for the Conservatives over the last few elections. In fact, only about 3 per cent of the members are regular *Sun* readers,[1] and this is probably because most grass-roots members intensely dislike it.

At Conservative party conferences, speakers often voice suspicions that the broadcasting authorities, in particular the BBC, employ too many socialists who go out of their way to undermine government policies. Both the BBC and ITV are less popular institutions than those already referred to; nevertheless, members display no differences in their attitudes to the two broadcasting organizations. Each is given the same score as that other institutional irritant of recent Conservative governments, the Church of England. God and Mammon score equally well among Conservatives, the Stock Exchange and the Confederation of British Industry being placed alongside the established Church!

The Conservative party would expect to number those from the traditional professions, such as medicine and law, among their keenest supporters. During Margaret Thatcher's premiership, however, many of the professions were subjected to hostile criticisms and reform proposals aimed at eradicating perceived incompetence and restrictive practices were introduced. It is interesting, therefore, to see how party members view the professions.

---

[1] See the responses to the question on newspaper readership in Appendix II, question 45.

Doctors are highly regarded, but judges and lawyers attract less support. In fact, judges score equally with teachers, and lawyers come lower in members' estimation. Teachers have experienced very specific criticisms from Conservative governments in recent years, and therefore their near parity with judges is somewhat surprising. It is important to remember, however, that teachers comprise a very significant element of the party's membership. If teachers do not attract the level of opprobrium which might have been expected, then social workers are clearly an unappreciated group of professionals.

It has been argued (McKenzie and Silver, 1968; Jessop, 1974; Kavanagh, 1976) that along with a keen sense of traditionalism, Conservatives are also deferential in their attitudes and behaviour. The party has aristocratic origins and a leadership which in the past has been part of the rich social élite. It also has hierarchical values which attract people who believe in élite rule. One consequence of this is that social deference sustains the political preferences of many working-class Conservative voters, a point originally made by McKenzie and Silver (1968).

Both Jessop (1974) and Kavanagh (1976) warn, however, that deference is a complicated concept which is often used in a very loose manner. Both authors suggest the need to distinguish between political and social deference in analysing political behaviour. In particular, they caution that McKenzie and Silver's analysis of the deferential behaviour of working-class Conservatives needs to be treated with scepticism, because their evidence is based upon a very limited and restricted sample.

If, however, Conservative voters are meant to be socially deferential, then one would expect this to be apparent among the party members. We attempted to ascertain the extent of deference by asking members whether they agreed or disagreed with the statement 'It is best to leave government to people from the upper class'.

A large majority of Conservatives disagree with the statement; in this sense, therefore, they do not defer to people from an élite class background. We have referred earlier to Kelly's thesis that the young, qualified professional is less likely to defer to hierarchical traditions and values than the older, less-qualified members of the party. Looking at the relationship between social-background characteristics and deference, there is weak support for this view.

There is a slight tendency for the old, working-class, and poor members to favour government by the upper class by comparison with young, middle-class, and affluent members. For example, some 14 per cent of poor Conservatives agree or strongly agree with this statement, compared with only 9 per cent of affluent Conservatives. But relationships are not very strong.

One relationship in Table 7.15 which is striking is that between the left–right scale and deference. Some 20 per cent of members on the right agree or strongly agree with government by the upper class, compared with only 6 per cent of members on the left. At the other end of the scale, some 91 per cent of those on the left disagree or strongly disagree, compared with only 67 per cent on the right. Thus deference to aristocratic rule in the Conservative party is clearly related to political ideology.

We began this discussion by citing Parkin's (1967) thesis that the Conservative party was closely identified with many of Britain's traditional institutions, which might be expected to produce deference in both the electorate and among party members. A closely related argument, put forward by Gamble (1974), is that the Conservative party is the party of the State—that is, that Conservatives occupy positions of power and influence in state institutions either at local or national levels, which makes them the 'natural' party of government. This idea may play an important role in explaining the electoral success of the party.

The survey makes it possible to test one important aspect of this idea, the notion that party members are closely involved in leadership positions within the community. This is the idea that they are local 'notables', and gain electoral success, in part, because of this identification with leadership in the minds of the public. This is considered next, in the final section of this chapter.

CONSERVATIVES AS LOCAL 'NOTABLES'

If Conservatives are local notables, making up a significant proportion of the political élite which governs at the community level in Britain, then we would expect to observe this in the survey. There are two ways of examining this issue; one is to look at the number of Conservatives who occupy positions of power in the local community, such as local councillors, Justices of the Peace,

TABLE 7.15. *Deference among Members* (percentages)

Statement: It is best to leave government to people from the upper class.

	Strongly agree	Agree	Neither agree nor disagree	Disagree	Strongly disagree
All respondents	3	7	11	50	29
Class					
Salariat	2	6	12	49	32
Routine non-manual	1	6	10	57	25
Petty bourgeoisie	3	9	11	44	33
Foreman and technician	5	8	12	53	23
Working class	5	10	10	47	29
Income					
Under £10,000	4	10	13	53	20
£10,000–£30,000	2	6	11	50	31
£30,000+	2	7	9	48	34
Age					
18–25	0	13	9	30	48
26–45	0	4	4	40	52
46–65	2	5	9	52	32
66+	4	10	16	52	19
Gender					
Male	2	8	12	46	33
Female	3	6	11	54	26
Graduate					
Yes	2	7	11	52	28
No	2	4	10	46	39
Activism					
Not at all active	2	8	11	52	27
Not very active	3	8	12	50	28
Fairly active	3	6	11	51	31
Very active	3	5	8	45	38
Left/right placement					
Left	5	1	3	36	55
Centre-left	3	3	6	44	44
Centre	1	3	10	53	34
Centre-right	2	8	13	54	24
Right	6	14	14	44	23

N = 2413

TABLE 7.16. *Members as 'Notables' in the Community* (N = 2467)

	Yes	No
	(percentages)	
Are you currently a local Conservative councillor?	2	98
Are you currently a magistrate/JP?	1	99
Are you currently on any official bodies (e.g., school governor/Scottish school-board member, member of a health authority, Scottish community council)?	7	93

Number of members who are:

School governors	103
Health Authority members	5
Social Security Appeals Tribunal members	4
Special Constables	2
Medical Research Council members	2
Urban Development Corporation members	2
Transport Users' Consultative Committee members	1
Family Health Services Committee members	1
Disability Appeals Tribunal members members	1
Parent–Teachers' Association	1

Special Constables, and members of official bodies like health authorities and community councils. The second is to determine the extent to which Conservatives are members of 'networks of influence', which might exist in the community. If Conservatives are very likely to be members of the local chamber of commerce, the Women's Institute, or the Rotarians, they are likely to exercise influence, representing Conservative ideas within these important community organizations.

Table 7.16 contains information about the extent to which party members are local notables in the community. It is important to recognize that only a minority of members would be notables in the sense of office-holders, even if they were all very active. But what is interesting about Table 7.16 is how few members hold these positions; only 1 per cent are magistrates, and only 7 per cent are representatives on official bodies. Of course, a small percentage of the membership does add up to a significant number

TABLE 7.17. *Membership of Groups* (percentages)

National Trust	27
World Wildlife Trust	12
British Legion	8
Consumers' Association	7
RSPCA	6
NSPCC/RSPCC	6
Women's Institute	6
Christian Aid	5
Age Concern	5
Red Cross	4
OXFAM	3
Chamber of commerce	3
Rotarians	3
National Viewers' and Listeners' Association	1
SPUC	1
Chamber of Trade	1

of people; for example, the 1 per cent of members who are magistrates constitutes 7,500 individuals. Thus the data support the idea that the Conservative party is influential at the local level, but it does not support the proposition that Conservative party members are typically influential participants in their local communities.

Of course, it could be argued that representation on official bodies may be a poor guide to influence in the community. If members are strongly represented in bodies like the chamber of commerce, the Women's Institute, or the Rotarians, they are arguably just as likely to exercise influence on the local community as they are as members of an official body. However, in Table 7.17 it can be seen that few Conservatives are members of such organizations.

The most significant finding in this table is that the great bulk of party members are really only interested in two types of organization; one is the National Trust, and the second is animal welfare organizations of various kinds. Thus 12 per cent of Conservatives are members of the World Wildlife Trust, and only 3 per cent are members of the chamber of commerce.

To pursue the question of how integrated or networked members are into local communities, Table 7.18 lists the percentage of respondents who are members of additional national or local

TABLE 7.18. *Number of Additional National or Local Groups of which Respondents are Members*

Number of national groups	Members (%)	Number of local groups	Members (%)
None	71	None	81
One	17	One	13
Two	7	Two	4
Three	3	Three	1
Four	1	Four	1
Five or more	1	Five or more	1

TABLE 7.19. *Time Spent on Voluntary Work in the Average Month* (percentages)

None	75
Up to 5 hours	10
5–10 hours	6
10–20 hours	4
More than 20 hours	5

organizations, apart from those mentioned in Table 7.17. It can be seen that some 71 per cent are not members of any other national organizations, and 81 per cent are not members of any other local organizations. The question defined organizations very generally, so this might be expected to include any cultural, social, or political organizations. The evidence in this table does not suggest that members are closely involved in networks of influence.

Finally, to examine the broadest possible measure of participation in the local community, members were asked how much time they devoted to voluntary activities in the average month. This, of course, would include any type of voluntary work, from charity work to social activities, most of which are not political in any meaningful sense of the word.

It can be seen from Table 7.19 that 75 per cent of members undertake no voluntary work at all. Of the remainder, some 10 per cent are involved for up to five hours, and some 15 per cent for more than five hours per month. It is hard to make the case from these data that party members are very heavily involved in community activities, making the Conservative party in some sense the party of the State and society.

Overall, the evidence in Tables 7.16–7.19 suggests that while some Conservatives are active in the community, most are not very involved at all. Few are local notables, in the sense of serving on official bodies, and while a number are members of national and local organizations, these are mostly non-political, like the National Trust or the RSPCA. These organizations are really quite peripheral to the institutions which exercise state power.

The conclusion is that if the Conservative party is in some sense the party of the State, the political activities of its members, outside the party organization, do not appear to have much influence on state institutions. From this evidence, Conservative party members do not look at all like members of a local or national power élite, even if a few of them do exercise power in local or national politics.

This concludes our discussion of members' images of the parties and society and their roles in the wider political system. In the next chapter we change the focus of the discussion from the members to an examination of their effects on election campaigns at the constituency level.

8

Local Campaigning and the Conservative Vote

The Conservative party has traditionally enjoyed the reputation of having the most formidable election machine of any party in British politics. Robert McKenzie's (1964) description of local Conservative party organizations in their heyday of the 1950s captures this point very well. In his description of the local party organization, McKenzie mentions the 'block system' and the 'canvasser corps', the former being a group of households in a ward or polling district, which are looked after on a regular basis by the latter, a group of active party members. He describes the activities of these volunteers as follows:

Ideally the block should be looked after by the same party workers both between and during elections. Their functions are to distribute party literature: to spread verbal propaganda; to deliver invitations to meetings and social functions; to collect information for the association's 'Marked Register', to enrol members in the Association; to recruit active workers and helpers of all kinds; to act as 'intelligence officers'; to undertake election work during campaigns for both parliamentary and local government elections. (McKenzie, 1964: 255)

Thus the Conservative party, at that time, placed great emphasis on local party organization, and this was the basis of its formidable reputation.

Oddly enough, this emphasis on local campaigning currently fits very badly with contemporary conventional wisdom concerning the nature of the modern election campaign. Many journalists and academics see the modern campaign as being largely fought out on national television by the respective national party organizations and leaderships. For many, the campaign is seen as being basically a clash between the respective party leaders.

According to this view, the local campaign is largely irrelevant to the election outcome. For example, in the most recent Nuffield election study, Butler and Kavanagh ask 'Does the local campaign matter?', and then go on to conclude that 'it is hard to locate evidence of great benefits being reaped by the increasingly sophisticated and computerised local campaigning' (Butler and Kavanagh, 1992: 245).

However, those who believe that local parties play little or no role in mobilizing the electorate during general elections face a paradox: if this is true, why do the parties, particularly the Conservative party, place such an emphasis on maintaining well-organized and active local branches? Why bother with local constituency campaign organizations if they have no effect on the outcome of a general election?

The scepticism about the importance of local parties in mobilizing the vote in Britain stands in marked contrast to the findings of American research into the effects of local campaigns on electoral behaviour in the United States. Researchers have been investigating this question since the 1950s, and the evidence shows clearly that local campaigns have a significant impact on the turn-out in state and federal elections (Cutright and Rossi, 1958; Cutright, 1963; Kramer, 1970; Crotty, 1971; Herrnson, 1986; Frendreis *et al.*, 1990) and on the share of the vote obtained by the Democratic and Republican parties in national elections (Katz and Eldersveld, 1961; Patterson and Caldeira, 1984; Huckfeldt and Sprague, 1992).

To be fair, a few American studies suggest that campaigning either has no effect or has ambiguous effects (see Pomper *et al.*, 1980; Gibson and Smith, 1984). But the great bulk of the research supports the proposition that local campaigns by party members influence the vote. By contrast with this rich tradition of work, the research into campaign effects in Britain is much more limited.

The discussion in this chapter is divided into four sections; first, we review the evidence of the effects of local campaigns on the vote in Britain, which leads into a discussion of the methodological approach needed to examine this issue using census data, together with information on campaign spending by the political parties at the constituency level. This is followed by an analysis of the effects of campaigning on the Conservative share of the vote in the 1992 general election, which takes into account a number of factors that also influence the vote; part of this exercise involves examining the impact of the other major party campaigns on the Conservative vote.

Finally, in a fourth section, we apply models designed to simulate the outcome of the 1987 election, using varying assumptions about local campaigning by the political parties. The aim here is to examine the effects of different levels of campaigning on the outcome of the election.

THE EFFECTS OF CAMPAIGNING ON ELECTIONS IN BRITAIN

The literature on the effects of local campaigns on electoral mobilization in Britain is limited, but this topic has received more attention in the last couple of years than previously. There are two types of evidence to support the proposition that campaigning by local party members influences the vote; one is indirect, the other direct. We review each of these in turn.

The relationship between campaigning and the vote can be deduced from several types of indirect evidence. First, there are election results, which show that there is a relationship between marginality, or the 'winnability' of a seat, and turn-out in general elections in Britain. Denver and Hands (1974, 1985) have shown that turn-out was significantly higher in marginal constituencies by comparison with safe seats in the general elections from 1955 to 1979; moreover, this effect appeared to have grown stronger over time.

This relationship can be explained in two alternative ways. One explanation is that voters are more likely to cast their votes in marginal constituencies, since, in terms of the model of Chapter 6, the probability that an individual can influence the outcome, p_i, is higher in such constituencies. Unfortunately for this explanation, Margolis (1982: 82–95) has shown that this probability is still very small, even in such marginal constituencies; so it is hard to justify this kind of reasoning, though it may influence some people.

The second type of explanation of the effect appears more plausible; it derives from the fact that the major parties campaign more extensively in marginal seats compared with safe seats, since they believe that they have a better chance of winning those seats if they do. This heightened campaigning tends to mobilize the electors to turn out and vote.

A second type of indirect evidence in favour of local campaign effects derives from the analysis of constituency voting, particularly the work of Miller (1977). Miller showed that 'ecological', or group, effects strongly influenced voting behaviour at the constituency level in Britain over a period of half a century. He focused particularly on the relationship between class and voting, and showed that working-class people were much more likely to vote Conservative in constituencies containing many middle-class people than they were in constituencies lacking such concentrations of middle-class voters. This phenomenon continues to be an important influence on electoral behaviour today (see Harrop *et al.*, 1992).

The precise causes of these ecological effects are not known, although the most common explanation of them is couched in terms of neighbourhood influence (Berelson *et al.*, 1954; Butler and Stokes, 1974). Thus working-class people in constituencies where they come into greater contact with middle-class Conservative neighbours on a day-to-day basis are likely to be more Conservative because of the pressures to conform to a dominant local norm.

However, it seems plausible that these ecological effects may be due in part to local election campaigns. If, for example, the Conservative party is very active in strong middle-class constituencies, and other parties much less so, then local campaigns in those constituencies would favour the Conservatives. This in turn would tend to make working-class voters in these constituencies more Conservative. By contrast, working-class voters would be more likely to vote Labour in very working-class constituencies, since in that case Labour would be the dominant local party. Harrop, Heath, and Openshaw (1992) found weak support for this idea, although their evidence on local party activity was limited to looking at canvassing during only one election.

A third type of indirect evidence of the importance of local election activity comes from data on spending by parties at the constituency level during general election campaigns. Spending data can be used as a surrogate measure of local campaigning (see Johnston, 1987; Johnston *et al.*, 1989; Johnston and Pattie, 1993).

Unlike national spending, local campaign spending is tightly regulated in Britain. In 1992 the maximum spending allowed was £4,330 per constituency, plus an additional 4.9 pence per elector in county constituencies and an additional 3.7 pence per elector in borough constituencies (HMSO, 1993). On the legal definition, local spending includes the expenses of printing leaflets, advertising in local newspapers, telecommunications such as phone canvassing, the cost of hiring rooms and holding public meetings, fees paid to agents and sub-agents, and a variety of other things.

The average spending by the Conservatives in 1992 was £5,776 per constituency, slightly more than the £5,051 spent by Labour, and significantly more than the £3,168 spent by the Liberal Democrats. Altogether, the Conservatives spent an average of 79 per cent of the legal maximum on local campaigns in 1992, Labour 71 per cent, and the Liberal Democrats 43 per cent.[1] Thus there was considerable variation in local spending during the 1992 general election campaign.

However, the use of spending data as a measure of local campaigning is controversial. Butler and Kavanagh describe 'the creative accounting which is universally acknowledged to occur in expense returns' (1992: 244). Similarly, Gordon and Whiteley (1980) criticized their use on the grounds that much important campaign work such as canvassing is not measured by spending data. But recent evidence suggests that spending data actually provide quite a good measure of local campaigning by political parties (Pattie *et al.*, 1994). This research shows that spending data appear to correlate rather well with information on the extent of local canvassing obtained from the British Election Study and with data on local campaigning collected by Seyd and Whiteley (1992) in the survey of Labour party members. Spending is probably not a good guide to the precise amount of campaigning which goes on in a constituency during an election, but it is a good guide to relative campaign activity across all constituencies.

To clarify this point, if we could precisely measure the total amount of campaign work done by local party members, the relationship between this figure and local spending would not be very close; there would be quite large variations between constituencies in the amount of money spent and the amount of campaigning done. However, if the deviations from the 'true' picture are essentially random across all constituencies, spending data would still be quite useful as an indicator of campaigning, as long as constituency parties which did a lot of election work also tended to spend more money than parties which did very little.

Thus, as a relative measure of the amount of campaigning, spending data can be quite good, even if there are large random deviations from such a relationship across all constituencies. Only

---

[1] The average maximum legal spending in constituencies in 1992 was £7,244. All spending data in this section are taken from *Election Expenses* (HMSO, 1993).

if there were a systematic tendency for some parties to put in a lot of voluntary campaign work, but not to spend much money, would this relationship not exist, and this appears not to occur to any great extent.

None the less, campaign spending data are only 'proxy' measures of actual campaigning, and as such are subject to measurement error.[2] Also the range of the spending variables is restricted, and this will tend to bias the estimates of the effects. However, faced with the alternatives of estimating the effects either directly from a restricted sample of thirty-four constituencies (see below) or indirectly from spending data for all constituencies in Britain, the latter is the preferable option.

Turning next to direct evidence of a relationship between party activity and the vote in Britain, this has been quite limited until recently. Part of the scepticism about the importance of local campaigns may well have come from Robert McKenzie's study of British political parties referred to earlier. In this study, McKenzie concluded that there was no relationship between the size of the party membership and the size of the Labour vote in a small sample of constituencies in Lancashire and Cheshire (1964: 544). He interpreted this to mean that local party membership had no significant influence on the vote.

However, it appears that McKenzie misinterpreted his own evidence. Had he calculated the correlation between the vote and membership, as opposed to just looking at the raw data, he would have found this correlation to be quite high ($r = +0.54$). Since Seyd and Whiteley (1992: 95) show that the average Labour party member is fairly active in election campaigns, the size of the local party membership appears to be a good measure of local campaigning. This suggests that McKenzie's data actually support the conclusion that a large local party membership can mobilize the vote, at least in the case of the Labour party. Other case-studies of the effects of campaigning in local elections further support this inference (Pimlott, 1972, 1973; Bochel and Denver, 1972).

Seyd and Whiteley's (1992) evidence is based on a survey of Labour party members in 480 constituencies throughout Great Britain. They obtained a total sample of 5,071 respondents, which

---

[2] In particular, there is an errors in variables problem associated with the use of such measures (see Pindyck and Rubinfeld, 1991: 160).

produced an average of just under eleven party members per constituency. They used three items in a battery of questions about party activism to construct an aggregate scale of the total amount of campaigning by Labour party members in each of the constituencies in the sample. The questions used to build this scale are also used in the present survey (see question 19 of Appendix II). Respondents were asked if they had undertaken a variety of activities over the previous five-year period. The activities directly related to election campaigning were 'displaying a poster', 'delivering leaflets', and 'canvassing'. When these items were aggregated into an overall scale, they turned out to be very significant predictors of the Labour vote in the 1987 general election, in the presence of controls for various other factors which also influenced the vote. This strongly supports the proposition that local campaigning boosts the vote. Subsequent work showed that similar campaign effects occurred in the 1992 election (Whiteley and Seyd, 1992).

However, their findings are controversial, perhaps in part because they challenge the conventional wisdom that national campaigning dominates electoral politics in Britain. Their results have been criticized on the grounds that the constituency samples are too small for valid conclusions to be reached (see Denver and Hands, 1993). However, further research in a subsequent paper which addressed the methodological problems of working with small samples, sustained the original conclusions (Whiteley and Seyd, 1994). Thus local campaigning stimulates the vote, at least in the case of the Labour party.

Another sceptical view of local campaign effects comes from Butler and Kavanagh's work, which was referred to earlier. They argue that Conservative party resources and organization have traditionally been seen as superior to those of their rivals, and consequently that this should have produced a more favourable result for the Conservatives in the key marginal constituencies in the 1992 general election (1992: 245). In fact, as they point out, Labour achieved a higher swing in these constituencies in the 1992 election than it did in other types of constituencies. Butler and Kavanagh interpret this as being evidence against the importance of local campaigns.

The problem with their idea is that evidence exists which suggests that the Conservative election campaign in the key marginal constituencies in 1992 may well have been inferior to those of rival parties, particularly that of the Labour party (Denver and Hands, 1992). We have already made the point in Chapter 4 that the Conservatives have only marginally more activists than Labour, despite a much larger overall membership. That fact, together with Denver and Hands's findings that Labour and the Liberal Democrats appeared to be much more effective at concentrating campaign resources in key marginal seats than the Conservatives, suggests that the Conservative campaign might have been at a disadvantage in these seats in 1992.[3]

This weakness in marginal constituencies may, in part, be a consequence of the traditional autonomy of local Conservative associations, who jealously protect their independence from Conservative Central Office. One result of this is that Central Office finds it difficult to move volunteers between constituencies when they are planning campaign strategy.

In addition to looking at marginal seats, Denver and Hands provide further evidence of direct campaign effects (1992, 1993). They conducted surveys of local party election agents, and found strong correlations between the intensity of a party's local campaign, as reported by the agents, and the share of the vote it obtained in the 1992 election (Denver and Hands, 1992: 543). However, some of their results are puzzling, since they find positive campaign effects for Labour and the Liberal Democrats and negative effects for the Conservatives. As they point out, this means that for the Conservatives, 'stronger campaigns produced a worse result' (Denver and Hands, 1993: 11).

One explanation for these odd results might be the fact, noted above, that the Conservatives found it hard to target marginal seats in the 1992 campaign. Thus, if their biggest campaign efforts were mounted in their own safest seats, where there was little scope for increasing the Conservative vote, this might explain why campaigning had a perverse effect. However, in view of the results described below, which show positive campaign effects for the Conservatives, this appears to be unlikely.

The most likely reason for their odd findings is that there are

[3] Denver and Hands (1992) show that the correlation between an index of local party campaign activity and marginality in the 1987 election was +0.42 for Labour, +0.57 for the Liberal Democrats, and −0.01 for the Conservatives. This means that both Labour and the Liberal Democrats focused resources in their campaigns on marginal seats, whereas the Conservatives did not.

problems associated with surveying local election agents in order to try to get information about the strength of local campaigns. Unfortunately for researchers, local agents have an incentive to exaggerate the amount of activity going on in their areas. We pointed out in Chapter 2 that there is a gap between the membership of local Conservative parties claimed by constituency association officers and the actual membership on the ground. Just as agents are not necessarily reliable sources of information about the extent of local membership, they are not necessarily reliable sources of information about the scope of local campaigning either.[4] If agents systematically exaggerate the amount of campaigning at the local level and, in addition, this tendency was more marked in marginal constituencies, where the job of the full-time agent is less secure than in safe Conservative seats, this could produce the perverse effects. By exaggerating the amount of campaigning done at the local level in marginal seats, agents give the impression that campaigning reduces the Conservative vote, since the marginal constituencies had bigger swings towards Labour. Whatever the validity of this argument, there is a clear problem in relying on the reports of agents to assess local campaigns.

To summarize the discussion so far, the bulk of the US research and a growing British literature suggest that election campaigns by local party organizations influence the vote in a general election. Though some of the British evidence for this is indirect, a growing body of evidence shows direct positive effects. In the next section we examine the use of spending data to investigate the relationship between campaigning and the vote in a general election.

THE METHODOLOGY OF MODELLING THE INFLUENCE OF LOCAL CAMPAIGNS ON THE VOTE

The best way to test the influence of local Conservative association campaigns on the outcome of the election would be to repeat the same methodological approach used in the earlier study of the

---

[4] It may of course be argued that this problem should affect all parties equally, but there are grounds for thinking that it might affect Conservatives more than others. Unlike Labour and the Liberal Democrats, the Conservatives have many full-time agents who are employees of local parties. Unlike agents in the other parties, their livelihood depends on giving a good impression of their effectiveness.

Labour party (Seyd and Whiteley, 1992). Thus a large survey in many constituencies would make it possible to identify individual constituency samples and assess variations in campaigning and the vote across constituencies by means of these samples. Unfortunately, the survey of the Conservative party could not, for lack of resources, replicate this design.

Instead, as we point out in Appendix I, the survey employed a two-stage design, with the first stage consisting of a 5 per cent random sample of the constituencies in Great Britain.[5] This meant that there were only thirty-four constituencies in the study, which is quite adequate for the first stage of a study of individual members but inadequate for an aggregate study of constituency associations. Accordingly, we use constituency voting and campaign spending data, together with controls for the social characteristics of constituencies, to model relationships.[6]

While the small number of constituencies used in the study may be inadequate for a full analysis of the relationship between campaigning and the vote, the data are none the less useful for validating the spending data as an indicator of local campaigning. If campaign spending is a useful measure of constituency activity, then there should be a relationship between direct indicators of such activity obtained from the survey and measures of spending.

The relationship between Conservative spending on the campaign, expressed as a percentage of the maximum, and the size of the membership of the Conservative party, expressed as a percentage of the total electorate, for the thirty-four constituencies in the study appears in Figure 8.1.[7] The figure confirms the earlier point that while spending is not precisely related to party membership, nevertheless there is a clear tendency for large parties to spend more than small parties. The correlation between the membership data for the sample of constituencies and campaign

[5] The fact that the Conservatives have no centralized database of party members and that records are held at the constituency level motivated this approach. It meant that we had to approach each of the constituency Conservative associations individually to get permission to access their records, an exercise which took a considerable amount of time and precluded sampling a larger number of constituencies.

[6] Census information used in this chapter is taken from Crewe and Fox, 1984.

[7] The total membership is expressed as a percentage of the electorate in order to correct for differences in the size of constituencies, which themselves cause differences in the size of the local membership.

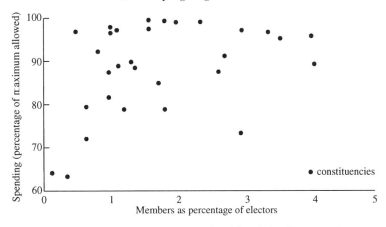

FIG. 8.1 Campaign spending and membership of the Conservative party

spending is +0.41, which indicates a highly significant, though moderate, relationship between these variables.

One interesting feature of this figure is that the variation in the size of the membership is much greater for those parties spending over 90 per cent of the maximum than for those spending between 60 and 90 per cent. This produces a curvilinear relationship between spending and membership. An alternative way of putting this is to say that small parties are quite likely to spend less than the maximum, but when a party has a membership above about 2 per cent of the electorate, it may spend the maximum, or alternatively it may spend well below the maximum.

A curvilinear relationship of this type can best be modelled by expressing the variables in logarithmic form.[8] This has the effect of making the relationship much more linear, which produces a higher correlation between the variables. The correlation between the logarithm of the spending variable and the logarithm of the membership variable is +0.60, significantly higher than the correlation between the untransformed variables.

---

[8] Readers will recall that the logarithm of a number is the power by which the base (commonly 10) has to be raised to give that number. Thus the logarithm to the base 10 of the number 100 is 2, since 10^2 equals 100. The logarithms used in this chapter are natural, or Naperian, logs, which have a base e, an irrational number approximately equal to 2.71828.

Similarly, the correlation between the untransformed spending variable and the Conservative percentage share of the vote in 1992 is +0.56, whereas the correlation between the logarithms of these variables is +0.61. This suggests that logarithmic versions of the models should be examined in subsequent analysis.

We observed in Chapter 5 that most members of the Conservative party are rather inactive, which raises questions about the validity of using membership figures to measure campaign activity at the local level. However, the correlation between the logarithm of membership and the logarithm of an aggregate activism scale derived from the survey is very strong, at +0.82, which indicates that membership is a reasonably good indicator of activism.[9] The reason for this is that the proportion of members who are active in a local party does not vary greatly across constituencies, so that total membership is a good guide to the total amount of campaign activity undertaken at the local level.

While the sample of thirty-four constituencies is too small to do any direct analysis of the relationship between party membership and the Conservative share of the vote, these results suggest that campaign spending, expressed as a percentage of the maximum allowable spending, is a fairly good measure of the size of the membership and the amount of campaigning undertaken by a local party. The high correlations with these variables in our sample support this assertion. Since spending data are available for all constituencies in Great Britain, such data can be used as a surrogate measure of campaigning. This approach has the added advantage of taking into account the campaign efforts of the other parties, since spending data are available for them as well.

It is also the case that for the 1987 general election it is possible to complement the campaign spending data for a group of constituencies with a more direct measure of campaigning obtained

---

[9] The activism index is the same as that used in the Labour study discussed earlier. Thus three of the indicators from question 19 (see Appendix II)—'displaying a poster', 'delivering leaflets', and 'canvassing'—were used to build the scale. An activism score was calculated for each respondent in the sample, so that a particular respondent scored 0 if he or she did not do the activity at all, 1 if he or she did it rarely, 2 if he or she did it occasionally, and 3 if he or she did it frequently. The activism scores were then summed for all respondents for the three items. Since the total sample consisted of 2,467 individuals, this gives an average constituency sample of just under seventy-three people in each of the thirty-four constituencies. The activism score for each constituency is then the sum of the scores for all the members divided by the total electorate in that constituency.

TABLE 8.1. *The Relationship between Campaign Spending and Canvassing in the 1987 Election* (row percentages; N = 250)

Campaign spending	Voters reporting being canvassed		
	Under 15%	15–35%	Over 35%
Low	70	23	7
Medium	42	34	28
High	23	32	45
Number of constituencies	96	76	78

from the British Election Study of that year (Heath *et al.*, 1991). In that study, which involved interviewing electors in 250 constituencies, respondents were asked if they had been canvassed by a political party during the course of the election campaign. The study consisted of 3,826 respondents, which gives an average of just over fifteen respondents per constituency (ibid.: 230–2).

The percentage of voters in each of the 250 constituencies who reported being canvassed by the Conservative party during the election campaign can be calculated from these subsamples. This information can then be used, along with campaign spending data, to evaluate the relationship between local campaigning and the vote. The relationship between the canvassing variable and the campaign spending variable is examined in Table 8.1, which gives an indication of how strongly these two measures of campaigning are associated with each other.

The figures in Table 8.1 are row percentages, and it can be seen that campaign spending is strongly associated with the amount of canvassing done by the local Conservative associations.[10] Some 70 per cent of constituency parties which spent a relatively low amount on the campaign did relatively little canvassing. At the other end of the scale, some 45 per cent of constituencies which spent a large amount on the campaign did a lot of canvassing.[11] This reinforces

[10] In Tables 8.1–8.4 low spending is defined as spending less than 75%, medium spending 75–90%, and high spending more than 90% of the maximum allowed.

[11] The correlation between the percentage of the maximum spent on the campaign and the percentage of electors canvassed by the Conservative party in 1987 was +0.43. The equivalent correlation for Labour was +0.49, and for the Liberal Democrats +0.47.

TABLE 8.2. *The Relationship between Conservative Campaign Spending and the Conservative Share of the Vote in 1992* (row percentages; N = 632)

Campaign spending	Conservative share of the vote			
	Under 20%	20–40%	40–60%	Over 60%
Low	39	51	9	1
Medium	6	28	59	6
High	2	22	70	5
Number of constituencies	70	190	342	30

the conclusion that spending data are a reasonably good guide to local campaigning at the constituency level.

In the light of this discussion we next examine the relationship between spending and the vote.

THE INFLUENCE OF CAMPAIGNING ON THE CONSERVATIVE VOTE

In this section the relationship between campaign spending and the vote in all 633 constituencies in Great Britain will be examined for the 1987 and 1992 general elections. The spending data are a surrogate measure of the campaigning undertaken by local constituency parties. To get a preliminary picture of the relationships, it is useful to look at some tables.

Table 8.2 contains information on the relationship between campaign spending and the Conservative share of the vote in 1992. These variables have been recoded into categories, and the figures in each cell of the table are row percentages. It can be seen that some 90 per cent of the Conservative constituency parties which spent a low amount on the campaign obtained less than 40 per cent of the vote in 1992.

At the other end of the scale, some 75 per cent of the parties which spent a high amount on the campaign obtained more than 40 per cent of the vote. Most of these high-spending constituencies

TABLE 8.3. *The Relationship between Conservative Campaign Spending and the Labour Share of the Vote in 1992* (row percentages; N = 632)

Campaign spending	Labour share of the vote			
	Under 20%	20–40%	40–60%	Over 60%
Low	1	6	51	41
Medium	19	39	38	4
High	32	34	33	1
Number of constituencies	143	183	241	65

had a Conservative share of between 40 and 60 per cent of the votes cast, suggesting that most campaigning went on in marginal or near-marginal seats. Overall, then, there is a clear positive relationship between spending and the size of the Conservative vote.

In Table 8.3 we examine the relationship between campaign spending by the Conservatives and the size of the Labour vote. Not surprisingly, this is nearly a mirror image of Table 8.2. Thus some 41 per cent of low-spending Conservative parties were found in constituencies where the Labour vote exceeded 60 per cent of the votes cast. At the other end of the scale, some 32 per cent of high-spending parties were in constituencies in which Labour obtained less than 20 per cent of the votes cast. Thus the Conservatives tended to spend a limited amount in safe Labour seats and a lot in marginal seats and, to a lesser extent, safe Conservative seats.

The fourth table examines the relationship between Conservative spending and the size of the vote captured by the Liberal Democrats. In this case the relationships are somewhat weaker, because there were few constituencies in which the Liberal Democrats captured more than 40 per cent of the vote. But it is interesting to note that 91 per cent of local Conservative associations which spent a low amount were in constituencies where the Liberal Democrats obtained less than 20 per cent of the vote; whereas 35 per cent of the high-spending parties were in constituencies in which the Liberal Democrats captured between 20 and 40 per cent of the vote. Thus the Conservatives tended to spend more in seats

TABLE 8.4. *The Relationship between Conservative Campaign Spending and the Liberal Democrat Share of the Vote in 1992* (row percentages; N = 632)

Campaign spending	Liberal Democrat share of the vote			
	Under 20%	20–40%	40–60%	Over 60%
Low	91	7	2	0
Medium	75	24	1	0
High	58	35	7	0
Number of constituencies	437	166	29	0

where the Liberal Democrats did well than they did in seats where the Liberal Democrats did badly.

The findings in Tables 8.2–8.4 are encouraging to those who believe that campaigning influences the vote, but they are not decisive evidence in favour of this proposition. This is because there are no controls in these tables for other variables which might account for the relationships. For example, if the local Conservative campaigns only really had an impact in constituencies containing many middle-class voters who were inclined to support the Tories anyway, then a control for the class composition of constituencies would eliminate the relationships observed in Table 8.2. In other words, if we were to separate out constituencies which had low concentrations of middle-class voters, they would show no relationships between campaign spending and the vote if local concentrations of middle-class voters accounted for the relationship in the first place.

To get an accurate picture of relationships, it is necessary to control for a number of confounding variables. This is done by means of multivariate regression models of the relationship between campaign spending and the Conservative share of the vote. There are three types of controls used in these models.

The first, and most obvious, type of control is for the impact of the local campaigns by the other political parties. The Conservatives may spend close to the maximum in a given constituency, but this may have a weak effect on the vote if the other parties are spending close to the maximum as well. By the same token, the Conservatives may spend rather less than the maximum in a locality, but this may have a strong impact if the other parties are spending much less than the maximum. Thus the competitive situation in a constituency is likely to have a strong effect on the influence of the local campaign on the vote. Accordingly, the percentages of the maximum spent by Labour, the Liberal Democrats, and any nationalist parties are included in the model.

A second type of control is for the social characteristics of the constituencies in which the local party operates. The point has already been made that very middle-class constituencies are likely to be much more receptive to Conservative party campaigning than other types of constituencies. This factor is controlled for by including the percentage of the work-force who are in professional or managerial occupations. Another such control is the percentage of owner-occupiers in a constituency. Housing tenure has influenced voting behaviour over a long period in British politics, with the Conservatives generally doing better in constituencies with a high proportion of owner-occupiers (see Heath *et al.*, 1991: 106). A further control for the social characteristics of constituencies relates to the distinction between urban and rural constituencies. The Conservatives have always had an advantage in rural areas, with the possible exception of some of the constituencies on the Celtic fringe. If opposition parties are weak in such areas, this will tend to increase the impact of the Conservative campaign on the electorate. With this in mind, the percentage of the work-force employed in agriculture is included as an additional control, in order to measure the extent to which a constituency is rural in character.

The third type of controls, for the political characteristics of constituencies, is of four types. First, there is a control for the effects of Conservative incumbency on the vote. Traditionally, the 'personal vote', or the vote which attaches to a well-known incumbent, is not thought to be very significant in British elections. In discussing the 1992 general election, Butler and Kavanagh argue that the personal vote had no impact on the outcome of the election (1992: 340). However, Cain, Ferejohn, and Fiorina (1986) suggest that an incumbent MP can build up a significant personal vote at the constituency level, and this may very well make a local campaign more effective. Thus a variable which signifies whether the seat was held by a Conservative at the start of the campaign is also included in the model.

A second control of this type is for the marginality of the seat.[12] The relationship between marginality and turn-out has already been referred to above, and in this case the focus of interest is on the effects of marginality on the Conservative campaign. If the Conservatives are incumbent, but only marginally ahead of a rival party in the popular vote, this should mobilize the local party to work particularly hard to try to retain the seat. It is also the case that Conservative Central Office tries to target marginal seats for particular attention during the campaign, even if, as we saw earlier, it may not be all that successful in doing so. Thus in marginal seats in which Conservatives are incumbent, or in which they came a close second, local campaigns are likely to be much more intensive than in other types of seats. Therefore marginality is included as a control.

A third type of political control relates to by-elections during the life of a particular Parliament. In constituencies in which a by-election took place, this may very well have led to the loss of a Conservative seat.[13] Even if this did not happen, a by-election will have altered the 'normal' political alignment of the voters, and this influences the context within which a local campaign takes place. Accordingly, a control for a by-election during the period 1987–92 is included in the model.

Finally, a fourth political control relates to the influence of the national economy on the local political situation. The British Election Study shows that the unemployed were significantly more likely to support Labour in the 1987 election, by comparison with the employed (Heath *et al.*, 1991: 162). Moreover, some 40 per cent of the electorate thought that unemployment was the most important issue facing the country in March 1992, just prior to the general election (see Gallup Polls, 1992). This easily outdistanced other issues in terms of its saliency. Thus the Conservatives were likely to face an electoral disadvantage in constituencies with a

---

[12] This is measured by the absolute difference between the Conservative share of the vote and the share of the second party when the Conservatives were incumbent and the absolute difference between the Conservative share of the vote and the vote for the winning party when they were not.

[13] There were twenty-three by-elections between the 1987 and 1992 general elections, of which the Conservatives lost seven (*The Times*, 12 Mar. 1992).

TABLE 8.5. *The Relationship between Campaign Spending and the Conservative Vote in 1992, Controlling for other Variables* (N = 633)

Predictor variables	A	B	C	D[†]
Conservative spending	0.66**	0.20**	0.21**	0.09**
Labour spending	——	−0.13**	−0.14**	−0.04**
Liberal Democrat spending	——	−0.13**	−0.13**	−0.04**
Nationalist spending	——	0.21**	0.22**	−0.02*
Professionals and managers (%)	——	0.29**	0.29**	——
Unemployed in 1992 (%)	——	−0.11**	−0.13**	——
Conservative incumbency	——	0.39**	0.39**	——
Work-force in agriculture (%)	——	0.01	——	——
By-election 1987–92	——	−0.03	——	——
Marginality of seat	——	0.01	——	——
Owner-occupiers (%)	——	0.04	——	——
Conservative vote in 1987	——	——	——	0.92**
R^2	0.46	0.83	0.83	0.94

† All variables in model D are in logarithms.
* denotes significant at the $p < 0.05$ level, ** at the $p < 0.01$ level.

high level of unemployment. Unemployment expressed as a percentage of the electorate is included as an additional control.[14]

Multiple regression models of the influence of campaign activism on the vote, together with the various controls, appear in Table 8.5. The table contains standardized regression coefficients, which can be interpreted in the same way as in Table 5.5. Model A examines the bivariate relationship between Conservative campaign spending and the vote, and this is quite strong. This is the regression equivalent to the results in Table 8.2, and provides a bench-mark against which to judge the other models. The goodness of fit, as measured by the R^2 coefficient, shows that spending is a reasonably good predictor of the vote.

Model B in Table 8.5 includes all the control variables referred to earlier, and it can be seen that Conservative spending remains a highly significant predictor of the vote, even though the magnitude

[14] Data on unemployment by parliamentary constituencies was taken from the *Employment Gazette*, table 2.10 for June 1987 (HMSO, 1987) and table 2.9 for April 1992 (HMSO, 1992).

of the effect is reduced by comparison with model A. It is interesting to note that Labour spending and Liberal Democrat spending are also statistically significant negative predictors of the Conservative vote, each having about the same effect. Clearly, spending by the main rival parties reduces the Conservative vote. The overall goodness of fit of this model is high, with an R^2 of 0.83.

One interesting finding is that spending by nationalist parties—that is, the Scottish nationalists and Plaid Cymru—is a significant positive predictor of the Conservative vote. Thus in seats where the nationalists put up candidates, campaigning by these parties appears to have helped the Conservatives. The magnitude of the nationalist effect is about the same as the magnitude of the Conservative spending variable. This may be partly because in Scotland and Wales, Labour is the leading party, and nationalist campaigning cuts into the Labour vote, rather than the Conservative vote, in these constituencies.

With regard to the social-background variables, the extent to which the constituency is middle-class, as measured by the percentage of the work-force in professional and managerial occupations, has a significant positive impact on the vote. But once this is taken into account, the percentage of owner-occupiers has no significant effect. The extent to which the constituency is rural, as measured by the percentage of agricultural workers, has no additional influence on the Conservative vote either, once the other variables are taken into account.

Two of the political control variables are significant predictors; these are Conservative incumbency, which, not surprisingly, had a highly significant positive effect on the vote, and unemployment, which significantly reduced the Conservative vote. By contrast, a by-election in the period 1987–92 and the marginality of the seat had no additional effect on the vote.

Model C in Table 8.5 is the most parsimonious version; that is, the non-significant variables in model B are excluded. The goodness of fit of model C is the same as that of model B, and the magnitudes of the effects are very similar. Thus the most important predictor of the Conservative share of the vote is the incumbency variable, followed by the percentage of professionals and managers. Conservative spending has about the same impact as nationalist spending, although the latter is of course confined to seats fought by the nationalist parties. Finally, spending by Labour and the Liberal Democrats has about the same impact as the rate of unemployment in reducing the Conservative vote in a constituency. It may be recalled that in Figure 8.1 the relationship between Conservative spending and local membership was non-linear, so that a logarithmic version of the model provided a much better fit than a linear model. This idea is applied in model D, which is a multiplicative model in which the logarithm of the Conservative vote is modelled as a function of the logarithm of the spending variables, together with a single control variable.[15] In substantive terms, this model means that the effects of campaigning get stronger, the more the parties campaign.

The control variable in this case acts as a composite control for all factors which might influence the Conservative vote other than campaign spending. This version has the best fit of all, with 94 per cent of the variance explained. It is noteworthy that the spending variables all remain significant predictors of the vote in this model.

However, it is very likely that the influence of campaigning on the vote is understated in the model. This understatement comes about because the control variable, the Conservative share of the vote in 1987, may be accounting for some of the variance which actually should be explained by local campaigning. This is because the size of the 1987 Conservative vote is itself, in part, explained by local campaigning. Thus parties which campaigned heavily in 1992 were also quite likely to have campaigned a lot in 1987, so the use of the earlier vote as a control tends to understate campaign effects, even though it provides a very considerable goodness of fit.

One way to illustrate this is to assume that model D is dynamic, and from this to estimate the long-run effects of spending on the vote, by taking into account feedback within the model. If this is done, the 'elasticity' of the change in the vote in response to a change in spending is approximately 1. This means that a 1 per

---

[15] Model D is essentially a multiplicative version of the regression model. This can be seen as follows: $Con92 = (Consp92)^a(Labsp92)^b(Libdsp92)^c(Natsp92)^d (Con87)^e$ is the same as: $\ln(Con92) = a(\ln(Consp92)) + b(\ln(Labsp92)) + c(\ln(Libdsp92)) + d(\ln(Natsp92)) + e(\ln(Con87))$, where the variables are defined (later) in the text. Note also that when a variable scores 0, the logarithm is undefined; in this case we add 0.01 to the variable before the logarithmic transformation.

cent change in Conservative spending produces approximately a 1 per cent increase in the Conservative share of the vote.[16]

One other interesting feature of model D is that the nationalist spending variable is much less significant than in the other models, and the coefficient is negative. This means that in a multiplicative model of the influence of campaign spending on the vote, nationalist campaigning reduces, rather than increases, the Conservative share of the vote.

The standardized coefficients in Table 8.5 make it possible to compare the magnitudes of the different effects with each other, but they are hard to interpret in terms of the quantitative impact of campaign spending on the vote. This is much easier to do with the unstandardized coefficients.[17] Model C is the best version for accurately estimating the impact of campaigning, and it can be written in unstandardized form as follows:

$$\text{Con92} = 17.17 + 0.133 \text{ Consp92} - 0.079 \text{ Labsp92} - 0.061$$
$$(9.1) \quad (8.7) \qquad\qquad (6.9) \qquad\qquad (6.3)$$
$$\text{Libdsp92} + 0.076 \text{ Natsp92} + 11.31 \text{ Incumbency} +$$
$$(11.6) \qquad\qquad (14.7)$$
$$0.536 \text{ Professional} - 0.713 \text{ Unemployment}$$
$$(9.6) \qquad\qquad (5.2)$$

$$R^2 = 0.83 \qquad\qquad F = 420.9 \qquad N = 633$$

where Con92 is the Conservative percentage share of the vote in 1992; Consp92, Labsp92, Libdsp92, and Natsp92 are the Conservative, Labour, Liberal Democrat, and nationalist spending percentages; 'Incumbency' refers to Conservative incumbency; 'Professional' is the percentage of professionals and managers; and 'Unemployment' is the number of unemployed expressed as

---

[16] Equation D can be written in unstandardized form as follows: LCon92 = 0.20 + 0.09LCons92 − 0.04Llabsp92 − 0.04Llibsp92 − 0.02Lnatsp92 + 0.92LCon87. The definition of these variables is given in the text. If we assume that in the steady state LCon92 = LCon87 = LCon*, this can be written as follows: LCon* (1 − 0.91) = 0.20 + 0.09LCons92 − 0.04Llabsp92 − 0.04Llibsp92 − 0.02Lnatsp92, and the long-run effect of spending on the Conservative vote is therefore: 0.09/(1 − 0.91) LConsp92 = 1.00LConsp92. Since the coefficients of the model in logarithmic form are elasticity coefficients, this implies an elasticity of one.

[17] The standardized coefficients measure the impact of a change of one standard deviation in the independent variable on the standard deviation of the dependent variable. By contrast, the unstandardized coefficients measure the impact of a % change in, e.g., Conservative spending, on the Conservative share of the vote. The latter are much easier to interpret.

a percentage of the electorate. The numbers in parentheses are *t* statistics, and they indicate that all the variables are statistically significant predictors.

The interpretation of these coefficients is straightforward; a 1 per cent increase in Conservative party spending, expressed as a percentage of the maximum, produces an increase of 0.133 per cent in the Conservative share of the vote in the 1992 general election. The same increase in Labour party spending decreases the Conservative share of the vote by 0.079 per cent; the equivalent figure for Liberal Democrat spending reduces the Conservative vote share by 0.061 per cent; and so forth.

To put these effects in focus, they imply that if the Conservatives had increased their average spending on the campaign in 1992 from approximately 79 per cent of the legal maximum to 89 per cent, then their share of the vote would have increased from approximately 42 per cent to 43.3 per cent of the poll. While modest in size, these effects can make the difference between winning and losing in a number of close marginal constituencies.

One of the reasons why the effects are not of the same magnitude as those found by Seyd and Whiteley for the Labour party (1992: 197–8) is because a direct measure of local campaigning was used for the latter.[18] We suggest that spending data provide a useful indicator of campaigning, but are none the less imperfect by comparison with more direct measures. Consequently, it is particularly interesting to repeat the analysis with 1987 election data, but this time incorporating the canvassing data from the British Election Study referred to earlier. The authors of the election study decided to drop any questions relating to local campaigns from the 1992 study; otherwise this could have been done for the later election as well.

Model A in Table 8.6 shows that in the 1987 election the canvassing variables for both Labour and the Conservatives are statistically significant predictors of the Conservative vote, in addition to the spending variables. This supports the point that the spending variable does not fully measure all aspects of campaigning, since if it did, canvassing effects would be negligible.

The most interesting model in Table 8.6 is model B, which shows

---

[18] However, the Seyd and Whiteley results are likely to overstate the effects, because they did not control for the campaigns of other parties.

TABLE 8.6. *The Relationship between Campaign Spending, Canvassing, and the Conservative Vote in 1987, Controlling for other Variables* (N = 250)

Predictor variables	A	B
Conservative spending	0.53**	0.16**
Labour spending	−0.38**	−0.15**
Liberal Democrat spending	−0.03	−0.08**
Nationalist spending	−0.20**	−0.14**
Conservative canvassing	0.21**	0.11**
Labour canvassing	−0.10*	−0.06*
Liberal Democrat canvassing	−0.08	−0.07*
Nationalist canvassing	−0.06	−0.05*
Professionals and managers (%)	——	0.17**
Unemployed in 1987 (%)	——	−0.22**
Conservative incumbency	——	0.41**
Marginality of seat	——	−0.10**
R^2	0.67	0.89

* denotes significant at the $p < 0.05$ level, ** at the $p < 0.01$ level.

that all the canvassing variables are significant predictors of the Conservative vote when social background and political controls are introduced into the equation. It is also the case that the signs of these variables accord with expectations. Both canvassing and campaign spending by the Conservatives increased the Conservative vote in 1987, and these activities by the other parties reduced it.

The unstandardized version of model B in Table 8.6 can be written as follows:

$$\text{Con87} = 39.64 + 0.101 \text{ Consp87} - 0.086 \text{ Labsp87} - 0.039$$
$$(13.2) \quad (5.0) \qquad\qquad (4.8) \qquad\qquad (2.9)$$
$$\text{Libdsp87} - 0.150 \text{ Natsp87} + 0.077 \text{ CanvCon} -$$
$$(5.9) \qquad\qquad (3.6)$$
$$0.041 \text{ CanvLab} - 0.053 \text{ CanvLD} - 0.240 \text{ CanvNat}$$
$$(2.0) \qquad\qquad (2.3) \qquad\qquad (2.1)$$
$$+ 11.829 \text{ Incumbency} + 0.313 \text{ Professional} - 0.982$$
$$(12.1) \qquad\qquad (4.1) \qquad\qquad (6.0)$$
$$\text{Unemployment} - 0.101 \text{ Marginality}$$
$$(3.5)$$

$$R^2 = 0.89 \qquad\qquad F = 163.39 \qquad\qquad N = 250$$

where CanvCon, CanvLab, CanvLD, and CanvNat are the percentages of the electorate canvassed by the Conservatives, Labour, the Liberal Democrats, and nationalist parties respectively. In this version of the model, an average increase of 10 per cent in Conservative spending would have increased the Conservative share of the vote by just over 1 per cent in 1987, and an average increase in canvassing of 10 per cent would have increased it by just under 1 per cent. The canvassing effect is independent of the spending effect; thus an increase in the overall campaign 'effort' in 1987, combining spending and canvassing, would have increased the Conservative share of the vote by approximately 2 per cent in that election. In other words, the Conservatives would have won just over 44 per cent of the popular vote, instead of the just over 42 per cent which they actually received.

Clearly, if the same relationships applied in the 1992 election and the Conservatives had improved their local campaigns during that election, they could have saved a number of the seats which they lost to Labour and the Liberal Democrats. Information from the models about changes in the share of the vote is interesting, but it is more important to assess the effects of campaigning on changes in seats. This is done in the next section, which explores the effects of different levels of campaigning on the overall election results.

SIMULATING THE 1987 GENERAL ELECTION

The results in Tables 8.5 and 8.6 indicate that it is important to take into account canvassing as well as spending when evaluating the effects of campaigning on the vote. Thus the 1987 model, which is an excellent fit, can be used to simulate the 1987 election, assessing the impact of changes in the campaign variables on the number of seats gained or lost by the Conservatives in that election. Thus, within limits, we can 'rerun' the 1987 election, making different assumptions about the level of campaigning, in order to see more clearly how campaign spending and canvassing influence the vote.

One requirement for this exercise is to have predictor models for the Labour and Liberal Democrat votes as well, since changes in Conservative campaigning will influence the votes for their major rivals, and this will ultimately affect the number of seats won by the Conservatives. Accordingly, predictor models for these two

TABLE 8.7. *Predictions from Simulations of the 1987 Election*

Assumption that Conservatives:	Conservative seats gained (+) or lost (−)
Spent 10% more	+3
Spent 25% more	+10
Canvassed 10% more	+3
Canvassed and spent 10% more	+8
Canvassed and spent 25% more	+16
Spent 50% less	−16
Canvassed and spent 50% less	−23
Canvassed and spent 29% of actual 1987 level	−52

Note: It is here assumed that other parties campaign at their actual 1987 rates.

parties were calculated, using the same set of variables as those used in model B of Table 8.6. In the event, the Labour model explained 91 per cent of the variance in voting, and the Liberal Democrat model 68 per cent.[19]

The simulation proceeds by predicting the vote for the three parties in each constituency, and from that the number of seats won by the Conservatives, using the regression model B specified in Table 8.6. The changes in seats in the 250 constituencies which occur under different assumptions about campaigning are then scaled up to predict what would have happened in all 633 constituencies in Great Britain.

Table 8.7 contains various predictions from the simulation models about the number of seats that would have been gained or lost as a result of changes in the levels of campaign spending and canvassing by the Conservatives in that election. The assumption in this table is that the other parties campaigned at the same rates as they did in the actual election; so it describes changes that would be brought about exclusively by the Conservatives.

There are some interesting features in this table. First, it appears that small changes in campaigning have rather modest

[19] The simulation could be done only for the 250 constituencies used in the 1987 election study, since these are the only ones in which it is possible to calculate the canvassing variables. The nationalist parties did not win any seats, so the predictive models are confined to the three major parties.

effects. Thus a 10 per cent increase in spending, assuming no change in canvassing, would have gained another three seats;[20] the same is true of a 10 per cent increase in canvassing with no increase in spending. Interestingly enough, a 10 per cent increase in both spending and canvassing would bring a seat gain of eight rather than just six, the sum of the individual effects. Thus canvassing and spending interact to bring gains that are bigger than the sum of the two activities considered separately.

A second interesting point is that a drastic reduction in the local Conservative campaigns to levels just under 30 per cent of their actual level would have lost the party fifty-two seats and their overall majority in Parliament. Of course, it is important to stress that this simulation assumes that everything else remains un-changed, a hard assumption to make if the departure from the actual experience of the 1987 campaign is very great.

But setting this aside, the prediction is interesting, since it shows that the Conservatives could have lost what was for them a very successful election in 1987 if they had decided to substantially abandon campaigning at the local level. It demonstrates, if nothing else, how important local campaigning is during a general election.

Figure 8.2 plots the relationship between campaigning (that is, campaign spending and canvassing) and seats gained or lost to the Conservatives during the 1987 election, using different assump-tions about rates of campaigning by the party at the local level. Thus the horizontal axis measures varying campaign rates expressed as percentages of the actual campaign rate in 1987, and the ver-tical axis the number of seats gained or lost. The break-even point in this figure, where the Conservatives neither gain nor lose seats, is where they campaign at 100 per cent of the 1987 rate (that is, the rate at which they actually did campaign). Below that rate they would lose seats, and above it they would gain seats. For example, if they had campaigned at 150 per cent of the actual rate, or 50 per cent more than they did, they would have gained twenty-three seats.

Figure 8.2 is interesting, since it demonstrates a clear asymmetry with respect to campaigning; the party is punished more for weak local campaigning than it is rewarded for strong local campaigning.

---

[20] Note that a 10% increase in spending would exceed the legal limits for some constituency parties. For the purposes of the simulations this fact is ignored.

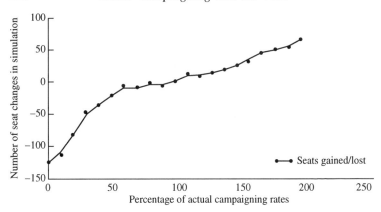

F IG. 8.2 The relationship between campaigning and seat changes in 1987: other parties campaign at 1987 rates

Thus, if campaigning had been 170 per cent (that is, plus 70 per cent) greater than it actually was, the Conservatives would have won forty-four seats; but if it had been only 30 per cent (that is, minus 70 per cent) of the actual rate, they would have lost forty-nine seats.

Up to this point, we have assumed that the campaigns of the other parties remained the same as in 1987. But it is interesting to relax that assumption, and examine the trade-offs in the Conservative campaign resulting from different rates of campaigning by the other parties. Figure 8.3 describes this trade-off for the Conservatives on the assumption that the other parties campaigned at 125 per cent of the 1987 rate. Thus the assumption is that Labour, the Liberal Democrats, and the nationalist parties all did 25 per cent more canvassing and spent 25 per cent more money on their campaigns than they actually did.

The relationship in Figure 8.3 is particularly interesting, since it demonstrates that the asymmetry referred to earlier becomes much greater when the other parties campaign more. In this scenario the Conservatives do not break even in terms of seats until they campaign at 140 per cent of the 1987 rate; they have to work much harder to catch up. Furthermore, they begin to lose substantial numbers of seats once their campaigning falls below 90 per cent of the 1987 rate. For example, if they had campaigned at 70 per

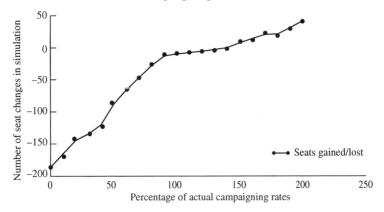

FIG. 8.3 The relationship between campaigning and seat changes in 1987: other parties campaign at 125 per cent of 1987 rates

cent of the 1987 rate, they would have lost forty-seven seats, and put them close to losing their overall majority.

Figure 8.4 illustrates the opposite scenario to that depicted in Figure 8.3. It depicts the trade-off for the Conservatives in a situation where the other parties campaigned at only 75 per cent of their 1987 rates. In this case the asymmetry shifts in favour of the Conservatives. In this simulation they can break even if they campaign at only 70 per cent of the 1987 rate; and if they campaign at the actual 1987 rate, they capture thirteen seats.

While the asymmetry shifts in Figure 8.4, it still remains, to a limited extent, something which can be illustrated by examining the extreme cases in the two simulations of Figures 8.3 and 8.4. In Figure 8.3, when the other parties are campaigning at above actual rates, the 'worst case' scenario has the Conservatives losing 185 seats, when they do no campaigning at all. In Figure 8.4, when the other parties are campaigning at below actual rates, the 'best case' scenario has the Conservatives winning ninety-four seats when they campaign at twice the actual 1987 rate. In the language of the stock-market, the 'downside' is worse than the 'upside'.

Once again, it is important to stress the fact that these are simulations, and as such are likely to be increasingly inaccurate the further one moves away from the data used to estimate them in the first place. But notwithstanding, they convey an important

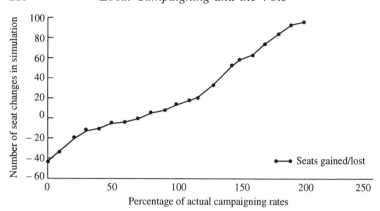

F IG. 8.4 The relationship between campaigning and seat changes in 1987: other parties campaign at 75 per cent of 1987 rates

message to all parties in British politics, including the Conservative party. The message is that a party which allows its grass roots to wither and decline is likely to run into serious electoral problems. Moreover, if the decline in grass-roots campaigning goes beyond a certain point, the electoral consequences rapidly become quite severe, particularly if rival parties are building up their local organizations at the same time.

This completes the discussion of the influence of local campaigning on the vote. In the last chapter, we examine the prospects for the Conservative party in the future, drawing together different threads of the earlier discussion.

9

Conclusions—the Future of the Party

The spectre of bankruptcy faces the Conservative Party as its
financial affairs plunge further into the red with personal,
company and constituency donations all down in the current
financial year.

Brown, 1993

This quote from the journalist Paul Brown captured the magnitude of the problems facing the Conservative party in 1993. Brown
pointed out that personal donations to the party fell from £14
million in 1992 to £3 million in the financial year ending in April
1993. Income tends to fall after an election year anyway, but
this precipitous decline was the worst since Conservative party
records began. Overall, Conservative Central Office income fell
from £22 million in 1992 to £8.3 million in 1993. The financial
situation of the party has however recovered in 1994 to a modest
£2m surplus.

In the past, Conservatives have claimed, with some justification,
that their party is one of the most successful political organizations to be found in any democratic political system. Yet at the
end of nearly fifteen years in power, the party has never faced
such formidable financial and political problems as it does at the
present time.

The aim of this chapter is to try to examine recent trends in the
grass-roots membership of the party, examining prospects for the
future if these trends continue. The evidence is limited, but it
suggests that the Conservative party is going through a precipitous
decline in membership. We consider the reasons for this decline as
well as the implications for the future, if it is allowed to continue.

We started out in Chapter 2 by asking the question: why should
the Conservative party want to recruit members? We suggested
that the two key reasons for this were first, the need to raise

money for the national party; and secondly, the need for a grass-roots organization to help fight and win elections. Clearly, if members are very important for both tasks, a decline in grass roots has serious implications for the future of the party.

We saw in Chapter 2 that local members are much more important in raising funds for the national party organization than conventional wisdom suggests. The same point could also be made about election campaigning; the evidence in Chapter 8 shows that grass-roots campaigns are much more important for winning elections than has been generally recognized in the past.

Given this, if the Conservative party is to revitalize itself, dealing with the problems of fund-raising and sustaining the electoral success it has achieved over the last fifteen years, it needs to revive the grass-roots party as a matter of urgency. A few large donations from well-wishers might alleviate the crisis in finances in the short run, but there are long-term trends at work to make these problems recur, which derive from a withering of the grass-roots party. In the absence of action to renew the party at the local level, it could rapidly slide into a vicious circle of declining membership, mounting debt, and electoral failure.

Political opponents of the Conservative party might well applaud this situation. But our evidence from the earlier study of the Labour party (Seyd and Whiteley, 1992), and our ongoing studies of trends in party membership for both Labour and the Conservatives over time, suggest that the whole British party system is in serious decline at the grass-roots level.[1] Since the uncodified British Constitution relies heavily on parties to recruit and sustain the executive, an unravelling of the party system in this way could create a serious long-term problem of 'ungovernability' for Britain. Thus any prospects for short-term party advantage should be set against this serious longer term erosion of support for the party system as a whole.[2]

---

[1] Panel surveys, in which members are reinterviewed over time for both Labour and the Conservatives, are currently being administered and analysed by the authors. Preliminary evidence from these surveys suggests that there is a steep decline in membership and in levels of activism in both parties. A full analysis of the results of these longitudinal studies will be published in a subsequent volume on the dynamics of the British party system.

[2] We do not have any evidence relating to the Liberal Democrats or Nationalist parties, but published studies of these parties do not suggest that they are exempt from these trends. For example, Denver (1993) points out that only 78,000 people

The discussion in this chapter is divided into three parts. First, there is an analysis of recent trends in Conservative party membership over time. This is derived from very limited time-series data on party membership, but it shows that a sharp decline has occurred in membership since the 1960s. A second trend, which is apparent from the survey data analysed by the year in which members joined the party, shows a decline in both activism and the members' expressive attachment to the party in recent years. Thus the evidence suggests that the party has both shrunk in size and become less active over time.

The second section discusses the causes of these trends, some of which derive from social and cultural developments, which are not amenable to political action; other causal factors, however, are a product of political decisions made by the Conservative leadership while in office. Thus the third section of the chapter considers different courses of action that the party leadership might take to try to halt the decline, and possibly reverse it in the long run.

TRENDS IN PARTY MEMBERSHIP OVER TIME

An accurate assessment of trends in the membership of the Conservative party can only be obtained by tracking the membership over time. Thus cross-section data of the type obtained in the survey are of limited use in this respect. On the other hand, as we point out in Chapter 2, the records of Conservative party membership at the national level are very fragmentary, which makes it hard to get an accurate picture of trends in membership over time.

The most accurate and up-to-date information on trends in party memberships throughout the advanced industrial democracies is to be found in Katz and Mair's (1992) handbook on party organizations. This volume is the product of an extensive collaboration between political scientists in a number of advanced industrial democracies. In the section on Britain, they provide five separate observations for the national membership of the Conservative party between the years 1960 and 1989 (1992: 847).[3] If we add to these

joined the Liberal Democrats when they were first established in 1988, a far smaller total than the previous joint total memberships of the Liberals and SDP.

[3] The section on Britain in the handbook is written by P. D. Webb who acknowledges the help of Conservative Central Office and National Union staff in compiling the data.

the estimates of membership for 1991 obtained from the present survey, and then regress the membership data against time, the resulting model is:

$$\text{Membership} = 6486.8 - 63.89 \,(\text{Year})$$
$$\qquad\qquad\qquad (12.3) \quad (9.9)$$

Adjusted $R^2 = 0.95$ (Membership is measured in thousands).

This model should be interpreted with care, since it is estimated from only six observations, but the adjusted R^2 shows that it fits the data very closely, and the t statistic (in parenthesis) shows that time is statistically a very significant negative predictor of membership. The model suggests that on average the Conservative party has been losing some 64,000 members each year since 1960. On the assumption that the model is a good predictor of future trends, it implies that if nothing is done to change this, the party membership will fall below 100,000 by the end of the century.

These estimates may be crude, but it is interesting that they are consistent with the recent financial difficulties of the party, referred to earlier. Clearly, a party which is haemorrhaging members at that rate, and which at the same time is very dependent upon the membership for a large portion of its funds, is sooner or later bound to face a severe financial crisis.

The survey evidence shows that the party appears to be able to recruit new members, since, as we pointed out in Chapter 2, some 45 per cent of the respondents joined the party since 1979. Since the trend model measures the net loss of support—the number of 'exitors' minus the number of 'joiners'—this means that the average number of people leaving the party annually must be well above the net figure of 64,000 a year.

The frequency plot of the years that existing members joined the party, taken back to 1945, appears in Figure 9.1. Figure 9.1 has some interesting features; for one thing, it shows that the party tends to recruit at an above average rate in election years. The 'spikes' in the series all coincide with election years, so an election campaign acts as an excellent recruiting ground for new members. It also shows that more members joined the party in recent years than joined prior to the mid-1970s.

However, it would be misleading to interpret Figure 9.1 as an accurate record of the numbers who have joined the party over

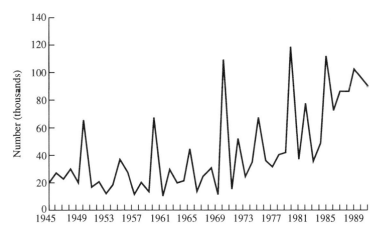

FIG. 9.1 Year respondents joined party

time, since it excludes individuals who have joined and then subsequently left the party prior to the survey. By definition, Figure
9.1 provides a record only of the current members. Without the
additional information on the 'exitors'—the members who have
left the party—it is impossible to determine trends in the membership over time purely from the survey.

Another important aspect of recruitment relates to rates of
activism of the most recent members, in comparison with members who were recruited in earlier periods. Figure 9.2 provides
information about the levels of activism of existing members broken
down by the year they were recruited, again going back to 1945.[4]
Starting from about 1977, it can be seen that there has been a
trend decline in the average levels of activism of party members.
It might be tempting to explain this in terms of new members
going through a 'probationary' period of inactivity before they get
fully involved. In the language of longitudinal analysis this would
be a 'life-cycle' effect, or a change which occurs as a result of
existing members growing older and more experienced. A second
alternative explanation of the trends in Figure 9.2 is that the party
is currently recruiting members who are significantly less active
than those it recruited a generation ago. If this is true, then a

[4] The activism scale is the same one as that used in Chapter 5, and so Figure 9.2
measures the activism rate of the average member.

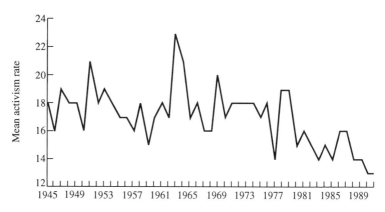

F IG. 9.2 Activism rates for different year cohorts

change clearly occurred in the type of member who joined the party during the Thatcher years. Again, in the language of longitudinal analysis this is a 'generational' or 'cohort' effect—a change which comes about because of the recruitment of a new cohort of members into the party. If this is true, the party is both shrinking in size and becoming more inactive over time.

Another type of life-cycle explanation of the decline relates to the flow of new members into the party compared with existing members. It might be argued that recent recruits include a number of people who are not very committed to political activism, and so after a while they tend to drop out, leaving the more committed members behind. This could have been true of all new cohorts of members recruited since the party began to enrol individual members in the nineteenth century.

If this is true, the frequency plots of the existing members displayed in Figures 9.1 and 9.2 show a decline in activism and commitment in recent years because the weakly attached, inactive, recruits have not yet left the party. Thus these 'temporary' members tend to dilute the levels of activism and commitment of the most recent recruits. If so, it is possible that eventually those recruits who remain in the party will be just as active as their predecessors from the earlier cohorts.

The fact that our survey is a cross-sectional study makes it impossible to determine which of these alternative interpretations is the most accurate. In general with cross-section data, it is impossible to distinguish between cohort and life-cycle effects.

But an additional piece of information, relating to the age of new recruits, is more consistent with a cohort rather than a life-cycle interpretation of the changes in the party in the 1980s. As we saw in Chapter 3, the average age of the members as a whole is 62. But the average age of new members recruited since 1979 is 54. Thus the party has been recruiting people who are not that much younger than the existing members, many of whom are retired.

For life-cycle effects to be important there has to be a significant difference between the ages of existing members and new recruits. This is because such effects are caused by the changing experiences of individuals over their time. Obviously, if the age of new recruits is similar to that of existing members, it is unlikely that their experiences are all that different, which weakens the life-cycle interpretation.

Another problem for a life-cycle interpretation of these trends relates to the point about new recruits taking time to become fully active. If members who joined in the early 1980s were going to become more active as they got older, one would have expected this to happen by now, thereby offsetting the trends observed in Figure 9.2. In other words, it appears that this decline in activism has been going on too long for it to be simply a matter of social-izing new recruits.

Figure 9.3 shows another piece of evidence which supports the interpretation that a change has occurred in the cohort of members being recruited into the party since the mid-1970s: a frequency plot of the number of weakly attached party members analysed by the year in which they joined the party. A weakly attached individual is defined as a member who assigns a very low score to the Conservative party on the thermometer scale for the party in the survey; in other words, it is a member who does not feel at all warm and sympathetic to the party in comparison with most other members.[5]

It can be seen in Figure 9.3 that there has been a significant increase in the number of weakly attached individuals who have

---

[5] The mean score for all members on the Conservative party thermometer scale was 80.9 (see question 36 of Appendix II), and the standard deviation of scores was 14.34. A weakly attached member in Figure 9.3 is defined as someone who gives the party a thermometer score which is two standard deviations, or 28.64, below the mean. Thus it includes anyone with a thermometer score of 52.24 or less.

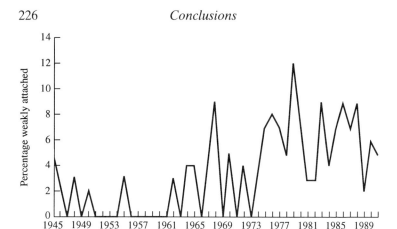

F IG. 9.3 Percentage of weakly attached party members by year they joined

joined the party since the mid-1970s. Again, this trend has been going on for too long for it to be consistent with life-cycle effects. If it were just a matter of socializing new recruits, or of waiting for weakly attached individuals to leave the party, it is unlikely to have been going on for such a long period of time.

To summarize the discussion to this point, there has been a rapid decline in the size of the grass-roots Conservative party, and there is clear evidence of a decline in both activism and the strength of attachment to the party among the remaining party members. Cross-sectional evidence makes it impossible to decide if the latter is a life-cycle or cohort effect, but circumstantial evidence, particularly the timing of these trends, points to a change occurring in the recruitment of new members in the mid-to-late 1970s. In the light of these conclusions we examine factors which explain these trends in the next section.

EXPLAINING THE DECLINE

A dominant theme in much of contemporary literature on political parties is that parties are increasingly being marginalized in the political process (Flanagan and Dalton, 1984; Lawson and Merkl, 1988). It is argued that the growth of the media, particularly the electronic media, has marginalized the parties in the processes of communication between élites and the electorate. Another aspect of this is the growing reliance of parties on experts for policy advice, which has reduced the role of the amateur members in this arena. A third is the growth of direct mail, which enables parties to bypass members in fund-raising and campaigning. Finally, in some systems growing State subsidies to political parties threaten to co-opt or capture them, ultimately transforming them into agents of the State.

On the other hand, parties are particularly important in the British political system, with its uncodified constitution and ill-defined institutional responsibilities. Parties provide the cohesion that makes government possible; the executive could not be re-cruited and sustained in the House of Commons without party discipline. If parties were as weak in Parliament as they are, for example, in the United States Congress, then Britain would face a severe problem of 'ungovernability'.

Of course, it might be argued that parties can remain strong without having significant numbers of grass-roots members. But we would challenge that interpretation; weak local parties are likely to produce an increasingly non-partisan local politics, which will eventually spill over into national politics. Again, the extreme example is the United States Congress, where it is often argued that there are 535 members of Congress, and 535 parties (Arnold, 1990). In the United States, the weakness of party cohesion is one of the causes of policy 'gridlock', or the inability of the system to deal with major problems like the budget deficit (see Cox and Kernell, 1991). In Britain, where the executive is not elected inde-pendently of the legislature, it would make government very dif-ficult, if not impossible.

Given this debate, it is interesting to look at the issue of party membership in the light of the general-incentives theory devel-oped in Chapter 4. If party membership can be explained by in-dividuals responding to various incentives, we might reverse the logic and ask what can have happened to these incentives in recent years to explain the decline. It will be recalled that the general-incentives theory postulates that five distinct factors are at work in explaining why people join a political party, or why they become active once they have joined. These are selective and collective incentives, altruistic motives, affective or expressive attachments to the party, and social norms, or a desire to conform to the wishes of other people.

Selective incentives can be subdivided into process, outcome, and ideological incentives for political action. With regard to process incentives, or the incentive to be involved in politics for its own sake, there are many non-political leisure pursuits which provide an attractive alternative to party activity. The leisure industry has grown in importance over time, and so the growth of attractive alternatives to party activity is one possible explanation of declining membership. This includes everything from watching TV to sports and home improvement.

In the political arena, there are also other competing organizations which provide process incentives such as interest groups and new social movements—the women's movement, the environmental movement, and the peace movement. These are attractive alternatives for an individual who enjoys being involved in politics for its own sake. Conservatives are more likely to be involved in environmental groups than they are in peace or women's movements, as can be seen by the fact that some 27 per cent of party members are also members of the National Trust.[6] If many party members are attracted by conservation groups, it seems plausible that many members of these groups will find them an attractive alternative to Conservative party membership.

A third problem facing the party in relation to process incentives for participation derives from the average age of members, which, as we saw earlier, is 62. It seems likely that many young people will think of the party as essentially a retired persons' club. The survey shows that the Young Conservatives have declined dramatically in numbers since their heyday of the 1950s, and this image of the party is likely to deter many young people who might otherwise be attracted into politics.

A fourth problem, which also influences other types of selective incentives, is the growth in female participation in the work-force over the last quarter of a century. With some 64 per cent of females now in the work-force in full- or part-time occupations, the opportunity costs of being involved in party activity have risen

---

[6] It is noteworthy that some 12% of party members are also members of the World Wildlife Fund, the second most popular membership group after the National Trust (see the list of sixteen different types of interest groups in question 16 of Appendix II).

significantly for working women who in the past were homemakers, and who might have participated primarily for social reasons.

Selective-outcome incentives relate to private incentives for participating in politics such as the desire to achieve elected office in local government, or the goal of developing a full-time career in party politics. In the early 1960s the party employed some 677 individuals at the central or subnational levels. By the late 1980s this had shrunk to 391, the reduction being entirely explained by the decline in the number of professional agents at the constituency level (Katz and Mair, 1992: 850). Thus the incentive to become involved with the aim of working for the party has clearly declined.

However, this is a small change in comparison with the decline in local government, which affects many more thousands of party members. Since the late 1970s there has been a dramatic decline in the powers and prestige of local government (Jones and Stewart, 1983; Stewart and Stoker, 1989). Rhodes points out that 'During the 1980s there were some 40 Acts affecting local government in general and local government finances in particular' (1992: 50), most of which placed new restrictions on local government of various types.

Of course, restrictions on local government spending and political activities predate the period of Conservative government. In 1975, for example, the Labour government established the Consultative Council on Local Government Finance to act as a forum for curbing rapidly growing local expenditure (Bailey and Paddison, 1988). But there can be little doubt that central government restrictions on local government have become very much greater over the last fifteen years.

If the importance and prestige of local government has declined, this will reduce selective-outcome incentives for participation in local politics and in the Conservative party. Individuals who might otherwise have valued a career in local government as a Conservative councillor will be inclined to decide that it is not worth getting involved, and this in turn will inhibit their participation in local Conservative party politics.

It is particularly noteworthy that the decline in the powers of local government in the 1980s coincides with the decline of activism in the Conservative party shown in Figure 9.2. This provides strong circumstantial evidence that a change in the incentives for participation is influencing the commitment of grass-roots party members.

The third type of selective incentives are ideological incentives which were discussed most fully in Chapters 5 and 6. We observed in Chapter 5 that members who coded themselves on the left of the ideological spectrum were rather more active than members who coded themselves on the right. Again, this has implications for the recruitment and retention of party members during the 1980s. As we pointed out in Chapter 6, Mrs Thatcher shifted the centre of gravity of the Conservative party to the right. Clearly, if left-wing Tories are more active than right-wing Conservatives, this shift will very likely have produced a decline in activism over time, as many active members find themselves out of sympathy with ideological trends within the party.

At first sight this conclusion seems paradoxical, because Mrs Thatcher appeared to be very popular among grass-roots members in the survey. Her mean thermometer score was 78 out of a possible 100. But the range of scores on this scale was high too, the standard deviation being 18.9, which means that even though many Conservatives thought highly of her, a significant group did not like her at all. Thus a shift to the right in the ideological centre of gravity of the Conservative party during Mrs Thatcher's leadership very likely produced a decline among some members both in activism and in affective attachments to the party.

Up to this point we have focused on the effects of changes in selective incentives on the recruitment and retention of party members. But collective incentives, associated with policy goals, also play a role in influencing the commitment of grass-roots party members. Again, in Chapter 6 we observed that Mrs Thatcher had a strong base of support among both individualists and traditionalists in the grass-roots party. But we also saw that many grass-roots members are 'One Nation', or progressive Tories.

Supporters of poverty programmes, advocates of the National Health Service, and sympathizers with the idea of generous unemployment benefits, will have found themselves increasingly at odds with the party during the Thatcher era. Many of them will have remembered the Macmillan years, when 'One Nation' Toryism was at its height, and the changes in party programmes since that time will have discouraged them. To be fair, many grass-roots members are clearly strong supporters of Thatcherite policies, but the fact that many progressives exist in the grass-roots party is likely to have created problems during the Thatcher era. Moreover, if they followed the Conservative tradition of avoiding criticism of the leadership in public and quietly withdrawing from the party, their departure would have been relatively unnoticed.

A decline in expressive or affective attachments to the party, which we observed in Figure 9.3, is an additional factor in explaining the decline in membership. Among the electorate there has been a long-term decline in party identification, or the strength of psychological attachment of the voters to the political parties. According to the British Election Study, some 93 per cent of the electorate identified with a political party, and some 48 per cent of these were very strongly attached to that party, at the time of the 1964 survey. By 1987 some 85 per cent of respondents identified with a party, but only 23 per cent of them were strongly attached (Heath *et al.*, 1991: 12–13).

This long-term decline in the strength of party identification in Britain is very likely to have affected recruitment to the political parties. If party identification has weakened, the pool of individuals who are potential recruits for the parties is going to shrink. Fewer people will be motivated to join, or become active if they do join.

This process of partisan 'dealignment' has been linked to changes in the social structure, particularly the decline of class voting (Sarlvik and Crewe, 1983). But some researchers have suggested that party identification is ultimately a product of policy outcomes (see Fiorina, 1981). Thus an incumbent party with a successful record of policy achievement can foster expressive attachments to itself among the beneficiaries of these policies in the electorate. If so, then partisan dealignment in Britain might be explained, at least in part, by policy failure. Applying this idea to the expressive attachments of party members, these may have declined because of the failure of the Conservative government to achieve policy success, particularly in relation to the management of the economy.

Yet another factor in the decline of party membership relates to the influence of social norms on political participation. Integrated, stable communities with a strong tradition of Conservative party support will sustain the party over time by a set of social norms which promote party membership. Rural villages in the South of England come to mind as clear examples of this type of party membership. However, social and geographical mobility over the years, and the 'gentrification' of rural communities in places like the Cotswolds, will change this picture.

Such places will remain fairly Conservative in their voting behaviour—although this is increasingly no longer true in the rural South-West—but they will be less likely to sustain an active local party. Affluent, educated, middle-class commuters or weekenders have too many other leisure pursuits or activities to occupy their time to become involved in the routine tasks of running the local Conservative party. They will not be so integrated into the local communities, and this weakening of social and community ties will tend to weaken the local parties for reasons quite separate from policy concerns or expressive attachments to the party.

In what is likely to become a classic study of the origins of successful democracy, Putnam (1993) shows that democracy requires a substantial stock of 'social capital' to succeed. He defines social capital as 'features of social organization, such as trust, norms, and networks, that can improve the efficiency of society by facilitating co-ordinated actions' (Putnam, 1993: 167). He shows that networks of civic engagement, or extensive patterns of participation in voluntary organizations of all kinds, are crucial to the development of social capital. His analysis goes well beyond analysing the roots of successful democratic politics, since he shows that high levels of social capital promote economic growth and development as well.

His concept of social capital is broader than Almond and Verba's (1963) notion of 'civic culture' but the latter is clearly an important component of social capital. In their classic study, Almond and Verba defined the civic culture as a set of 'attitudes towards the political system and its various parts, and attitudes to the role of the self in the system' (Almond and Verba, 1963: 13). They argued that Britain had a political culture which encouraged participation, although this was mediated by a widespread sense of deference to authority. Some 39 per cent of the respondents in their 1959 survey of the UK electorate, for example, thought that the ordinary person should be active in his or her community (Almond and Verba, 1963: 171).

We have suggested that a strong civic culture promotes political participation and high levels of trust in government and support for the political system. Moreover, if Putnam is correct, this brings with it successful policy implementation over a wide field of government activities, as well as high rates of economic growth.

Writing some thirty years later, Kavanagh (1989) argued that there had been a significant decline in this civic culture, much of it related to voter dissatisfaction with policy outcomes, and disillusionment with the performance of governments in power. Indicative of this development is the fact that some 46 per cent of respondents in the 1992 British Election Study survey agreed or strongly agreed with the statement: 'People like me have no say in what the government does.' Obviously a decline in the civic culture is likely to produce greater apathy among the electors, and fewer people who believe that it is the duty of the citizen to participate in politics. This in turn will contribute to the decline in local party membership and activism.

To summarize the discussion up to this point, a number of cultural and sociological factors are at work which have produced a long-term decline in the membership and in levels of political activism within the Conservative party. These predominantly influence altruistic motives and social norms as determinants of participation. The decline in the civic culture, increased social and geographical mobility, and the changing character of the rural Tory heartlands, will have served to weaken the motives for participation in local parties.

However, this decline seems to have accelerated during the leadership of Mrs Thatcher, and this can be explained by changes in various incentives for participation which occurred during this period. Selective incentives associated with building a political career have been reduced by the decline in the powers and prestige of local government, and to a lesser extent by the decline in the party organization itself. In addition, policy failures, such as the serious economic recessions of the early 1980s and 1990s, may have weakened expressive attachments to the party, as well as the civic culture which underpins the party system.

These processes have been reinforced by changes in the ideological composition of the party leadership. The shift to the right during the leadership of Mrs Thatcher alienated many progressive Conservatives who are more heavily represented in the grass-roots party than conventional wisdom suggests. Since many progressives are also quite active, this development partly accounts for the decline in activism as well.

In the light of this discussion, in the next section we examine steps which the party leadership might take to try to revive the grass-roots party.

REVIVING THE GRASS ROOTS?

A long-standing paternalistic tradition in the Conservative party tends to prevent it from taking a very close interest in the health of the grass-roots membership. But as indicated by the figures on party finance and the evidence on the relationship between local campaigning and the vote, the party is unlikely to recover from its present problems without developing a strategy for reviving the grass roots.

It is true that the party has been phenomenally successful in the past, but that is no guarantee of success in the future. Indeed, one very plausible scenario for the future could put the party into permanent opposition—the scenario in which a minority Labour government is elected and governs with the support of the Liberal Democrats. This centre-left coalition then changes the electoral system to some form of proportional representation, and entrenches itself in power. Since Labour and the Liberals combined have taken a majority of the votes cast in every general election since 1959, this entrenchment could be a semi-permanent phenomenon.

Thus the leadership needs to take seriously the state of the local party membership, and consider initiatives that might help to revive the grass roots. The first point to make about such initiatives is that the state of the local membership needs to be made into a high profile concern. The party leader should consider setting up a high-level commission to include senior Parliamentarians, representatives of the National Union and Central Office, as well as local party members, to examine strategies for change. If this issue is not highlighted, the present slide in membership and in local activism is likely to continue.

The second point to make is that a party in government is in a position to change some of the perverse incentives for participation which currently exist. With regard to policies or collective incentives, we can get some idea of the preoccupations of grass-roots members from their responses to an open-ended question asked at the end of the survey. This asked: 'Finally, what in your opinion are the main issues (policy and/or organizational) which the Conservative party needs to face up to either at the present time or in the future?' A list of these concerns appears in Table 9.1.

It can be seen that members are principally concerned with the same kind of policy issues as the wider electorate. These include

TABLE 9.1. *Perceptions of Issues Facing the Party*
(First Issue Mentioned) (percentages)

Issue or Problem	
The National Health Service	10
The Economy	10
Unemployment	10
The European Community	9
Crime	8
Education	6
Inflation	4
Poll-tax	4
Tory party publicity	3
Immigration	3
Defence	2
Taxation	2
Housing	2
Manufacturing industry	2
MPs' accountability	1
Pensions	1
State of the nation	1
General party policies	1
Other party-related concerns	4
Other policy-related concerns	8
Other institutional-reform concerns	2

the National Health Service, the economy, unemployment, and the European Community. It is an obvious point, but still important, that if the government were more successful in managing the economy and its relationships with the European Community, grass-roots members would be much happier with the state of the party. As mentioned earlier, policy success, particularly in relation to the management of the economy, is a key factor in reviving the grass roots.

In addition, the survey shows that there is a small but important number of party members who are concerned about the state of the party itself. Clearly, most concerns are about policies, but a significant group of members are concerned about party-related matters. Items under this heading include perceptions of party disunity, the problem of declining membership, concerns about election campaigns, and the need to rethink Conservative principles. Thus a commission of inquiry into the state of the party would address the concerns of a significant group of people in the grass-roots party.

The leadership is not really in a position to do much about the cultural and social changes discussed earlier, but it is in a position to address some of the perverse selective incentives for participation which now exist in Britain. The single most important reform would be to do something about the state of local government. If the importance and prestige of local government were restored, that would be the single most positive step that the government could make towards the task of reviving incentives for participation.

Compared with many of our competitor nations such as Germany, Italy, and the United States, Britain has a grossly over-centralized political system. A comparison of the powers and functions of state and local governments in the United States with those in Britain, for example, reveals just how marginalized the latter have become in the political process.

Decentralization and diversity create incentives for participation, allow policy innovation, and when working well, help to legitimize policies in the eyes of local communities. In contrast, centralization can produce bureaucratic rent-seeking, insensitive and inefficient policy-making, which becomes remote from the local communities it is supposed to serve. In addition, it often subordinates efficiency to capricious and shifting political goals, which can in turn produce severe problems of implementation.

This is not the place to examine fully the reform of local government, or of the British political system, except to make the point that reforms made over the last fifteen years have continually subordinated the goals of pluralistic democracy to managerialist ideologies of centralized control. It is perhaps ironic that bureaucratic centralization is now largely rejected by management theorists as a model for efficiency in the private sector (see, for example, Drucker, 1992).[7] Moreover, if Putnam's (1993) findings in his study of democracy are to be believed, political changes which

---

[7] Of course, it could be argued that privatization programmes are designed to eliminate bureaucracy by handing over allocation decisions to the market. But privatization under Mrs Thatcher has seen a very marked increase in regulation. Some would argue that the newly privatized industries are more regulated than the nationalized industries they have replaced (see Johnson, 1991: 216).

undermine democratic participation will ultimately inhibit economic performance. In other words, managerialism promotes inefficiency and slows growth.

The most disturbing part of this trend is that it clearly serves to undermine the party system upon which pluralist democracy is built. The paradox is that a Conservative government, which is rooted in a tradition largely hostile to an over-bearing centralized state, is undermining its own grass roots with policies that promote excessive centralization. Clearly, none of the ministers who drafted the various Acts restricting local government paid any attention to the incentives for participation in their own party. Had they done so, the legislative outcomes in this area may well have been different.

In fact, a perverse dynamic may now be at work, whereby the State seeks to subordinate all independent sources of power and authority in society, whether they be in local government, the universities, the BBC, or the quangos that are an increasing feature of the policy-making process.[8] This is done in the name of greater efficiency and uniformity of standards. However, the net result is to debase the efficiency of policy-making by imposing shifting goalposts, arbitrary restrictions, confused regulations, and perverse incentives. Eventually, these institutions start to fail, which prompts the government to impose further centralization, giving the cycle of centralization and failure a further twist.

A third change which would promote greater participation would be to engage in dialogue with the grass-roots party to a greater extent. We have seen that the Conservative party-conference system, discussed by Kelly (1989), gives the leadership ample opportunity to listen to the grass roots. But the party does little to try to bring members, many of whom have valuable expertise, directly into the policy-making process. If it ran a series of policy-making forums in which ordinary members could participate and give their views, as a direct input into the processes of policy formulation and agenda setting, that would promote incentives for participation.

In other words, merely listening to the grass roots is not enough; the party should try to give members influence in policy formulation. This would, of course, be a break with a long tradition of paternalism within the party, and it can bring its own problems,

---

[8] Quasi non-governmental organizations.

but reviving the grass roots means giving members meaningful influence in all aspects of party life.

The evidence of this chapter suggests that, though it appeared very successful at the time, Mrs Thatcher's premiership damaged the grass-roots Conservative party. What were held to be the strengths of Thatcherism—the refusal-to-seek consensus, the commitment to ideological politics, and wilfulness in the face of reasoned opposition—have served to undermine the party in ways not apparent to the day-to-day observer of British politics.

The Conservative party's long and successful history can be largely explained by the ability of the party leaders to adapt to changing circumstances and times; to embrace pragmatism and to try to build consensus around policies which the leaders felt were in the national interest. Mrs Thatcher consciously strove to abandon this long tradition of pragmatic Conservative leadership, and the party is now paying the price for this abandonment.

It is perhaps appropriate to give the last word to Benjamin Disraeli, the founder of the modern Conservative party and the man who saved it from becoming a minority rump of landowning aristocrats, a real prospect facing it in the mid-nineteenth century. In a speech delivered in Edinburgh in November 1867, just prior to a key turning-point in the fortunes of the party, he told his audience:

In a progressive country change is constant; and the great question is, not whether you should resist change which is inevitable, but whether the change should be carried out in deference to the manners, the customs, the laws, and the traditions of a people, or whether it should be carried out in deference to abstract principles, and arbitrary and general doctrines. (Bradford, 1982: 273)

APPENDIX I

The Design of the Survey

The first stage of the project involved the development of the survey instrument itself. Prior to commencing the project, contact had been established with senior officials at Conservative Central Office to elicit general support for the survey. Through this channel, we contacted party agents in three constituencies—Manchester Hazel Grove, Eastleigh, and Glasgow Cathcart—and obtained their permission to approach members of the local Conservative Associations for a series of pilot interviews.

Over a period of six weeks in autumn 1990 we interviewed fifty party members in these constituencies with various versions of the draft questionnaire. This face-to-face contact with party members proved to be an invaluable means of testing the survey instrument, both in terms of the insights it gave into the validity and reliability of particular questions, but also in terms of achieving the optimum length and layout for the final version of the questionnaire.

Following the successful completion of the piloting stage, we began the task of drawing the national sample of members. A two-stage sampling design was used. First, a 5 per cent sample of constituencies was drawn at random from the regional lists contained in the 1990 Conservative Party Conference Handbook. The use of a sampling frame stratified by Conservative party regions ensured that a representative regional distribution of constituency associations was obtained. Because Conservative Central Office does not hold a database of the names and addresses of the party members, the research team was obliged to make individual contact with the agents and party chairmen in each selected constituency in order to secure access to the full membership lists.

Local Conservative constituency associations are completely autonomous and negotiations with them proved to be rather more protracted than we had originally envisaged. Even though letters had been sent out to all party agents and chairmen in the selected constituencies from the Chairman of the National Union of Conservative and Unionist Associations recommending them to collaborate with the project, we experienced some degree of resistance from local party officers on occasions. We think this was due, first, to suspicions about the role of Conservative Central Office in the research; local associations jealously guard their autonomy. But, secondly, some of them were reluctant to hand over personal membership records to outsiders.

In a few cases local associations refused to collaborate, which meant that in some regions alternative constituency associations had to be randomly selected. Eventually a representative sample of thirty-four constituency associations was drawn whose officers agreed to participate, and from which membership records were obtained. From these a one in ten systematic random sample of party members was selected. In one constituency, membership records for only nine of the fifteen wards were provided, and so in this case a 10 per cent sample of the membership in these nine wards was selected. A one in seven sample of the members was selected in the West Midlands region, to compensate for a reduced number of constituencies agreeing to participate in the survey from this region.

Uncertainties over the date of the general election caused us problems, because once the survey commenced we needed at least three months for completion. During the early spring and summer months of 1991 an election was often mooted; only when it was clear that the election would not be called until the spring of 1992 did we commence the survey. The first questionnaires were dispatched in January 1992 and the cut-off date for final respondents was immediately before the general election in April.

We stressed in our dealings with Conservative Central Office, the constituency associations, and the individual respondents that we undertook to protect the individual anonymity of respondents. We believe that this guarantee considerably assisted us, first, in gaining access to the original membership records and, secondly, in achieving our eventual response rate.

In all, 3,919 questionnaires were sent out and we received back a total of 2,466 usable replies: a response rate of 63 per cent. This figure is almost identical to that achieved in the 1989 survey of the Labour party membership (Seyd and Whiteley, 1992). In addition, we received back a further 600 blank or partially filled-in questionnaires: the main reason given for their return in such a form was the sickness or old age of the respondents. Overall, a total of 3,066 Conservatives (78 per cent) responded in some form to our survey. This is an excellent response rate for this kind of survey.

The first stage of the survey itself involved mailing a copy of a letter signed by the Conservative party chairman giving his personal support to the project and stressing the bona fide academic nature of the research. This also emphasized the guarantee of personal anonymity promised to each respondent. This mailing had the additional advantage of identifying those members of the sampling frame who, for whatever reason, no longer lived at the given address. Approximately one week after this we sent out the questionnaire, together with a letter from ourselves explaining who we were and the purpose of the research. We included a telephone number for individual respondents to call if they required any further information. A large number of party members in the sample did indeed use this facility to ask for further information. There is little doubt that this telephone 'hotline' convinced a number of people to participate who otherwise might not have done so.

Two weeks after the second mailing we sent a reminder letter to nonrespondents, and two weeks after that a further reminder letter together with a second copy of the questionnaire. Each of these stimulated responses from significant numbers of sample members.

Having done all we could to maximize the response rate, we designed a one-page questionnaire covering basic social background variables and sent it to a random sample of 150 non-respondents some three months after the initial mailing. This group was pursued vigorously by telephone and by post in order to maximize their responses. The aim of this follow-up survey was to identify any significant differences between the non-respondents and respondents to the full survey. Almost two-thirds replied to the follow-up survey, and the information from this suggested that weak partisans and males were both under-represented in the main survey, although the discrepancies were not large. Accordingly, interlocking weights for strength of partisanship and gender were calculated and applied to the original sample of respondents, to correct for the lower response rates among these groups. All the analysis in this book uses the weighted file, which consists of 2,467 respondents. The weighting and the statistical analysis were all performed using SPSS (Statistical Package for the Social Sciences).

The majority of questions were closed-ended and we trained a group of undergraduate students at the University of Sheffield to code the questionnaires. The quality of the coding was monitored by the research officer who ran a number of reliability checks on the data as they were being processed.

Overall, we feel that the methodological aspects of the research were carried out as efficiently as possible in the light of the resource limitations. As a consequence we believe that the data are fully representative of the entire membership of the Conservative party. As always, the interpretation of the results is solely that of the authors, and does not represent the views of the ESRC or the Conservative party.

APPENDIX II

The Questionnaire

INTRODUCTION

The questions inside cover a wide range of subjects, but each one can be answered simply by placing a tick (√) or writing in a number in one or more of the boxes provided. In some cases you are asked to write in answers. No special knowledge is needed to fill in the questionnaire, and we are sure that everyone will be able to give an opinion on all questions.

We want all people to take part, not just those with strong views about a particular issue. The questionnaire should not take too long to complete and we think you will find it interesting and enjoyable. It should be completed only by the person to whom it was sent, so that responses will reflect all shades of opinion within the Conservative Party.

When you have filled it in, please place it in the enclosed postage paid envelope and post it back as soon as you possibly can.

THANK YOU FOR YOUR HELP

1. Would you call yourself a very strong Conservative, fairly strong, not very strong, or not at all strong?

PLEASE TICK ONE BOX ONLY

Very strong	33
Fairly strong	50
Not very strong	14
Not at all strong	4

2. Thinking back to the time you first joined the Conservative party, did you approach the party to apply for membership, or did they approach you?

PLEASE TICK ONE BOX ONLY

I approached the local party	34
The local party approached me	50
Don't remember	16

2a. IF YOU APPROACHED THE LOCAL PARTY
Did you find it easy or difficult to make contact with them?

PLEASE TICK ONE BOX ONLY

Very easy	47
Easy	48
Difficult	4
Very difficult	1

3. In which year did you first join the Conservative party?

PLEASE WRITE IN THE YEAR _____

4. Have you been a member continuously since that time?

PLEASE TICK ONE BOX ONLY

Yes	92
No	8

4a. If No, how many years have you been a member altogether?

PLEASE WRITE IN _____ Years

---

5. What was your MOST important reason for joining the Conservative party? (feel free to explain in detail)

PLEASE WRITE IN

5a. Did you become a member of the Conservative party as a result of:

PLEASE TICK AS MANY BOXES AS APPLY

Doorstep canvasser	11
Social contacts	22
Church contacts	0.4
Conservative club	7
Work contacts	2
Family contacts	22
As a result of a party political broadcast	0.7
Constituency association 'book scheme'	0.8
None of these	7
Other (please specify)	28

---

6. Thinking back over the LAST 12 MONTHS, how often have you had contact with people active in your local ward or constituency Conservative association?

6. (*Continued*)

PLEASE TICK ONE BOX ONLY

Not at all	22
Rarely (once or twice)	30
Occasionally (three to five times)	21
Frequently (more than five times)	27

---

7. Thinking back over the LAST 12 MONTHS, how often have you attended a LOCAL (e.g., ward or constituency) Conservative party meeting?

PLEASE TICK ONE BOX ONLY

Not at all	66
Rarely (once or twice)	14
Occasionally (three to five times)	8
Frequently (more than five times)	12

7a. If you attended AT LEAST ONE LOCAL party meeting within the LAST 12 MONTHS, please indicate your reactions to it using the following scales.

If, for example, you found the meeting very interesting, you would mark the box on the left-hand side. If you found it very boring, you would mark the box on the right-hand side. If you found it neither boring nor interesting, you would tick the middle box. Then continue the same process for the next six scales.

If you attended more than one meeting, think about the LAST meeting you attended.

IF YOU DID NOT ATTEND A MEETING WITHIN THE LAST 12 MONTHS, GO TO QUESTION 8.

PLEASE TICK ONE BOX ONLY
FOR EACH DESCRIPTION

	Very	Fairly	Neither	Fairly	Very	
Interesting	33	49	9	7	2	Boring
Unfriendly	3	7	9	26	56	Friendly

7a. (*Continued*)

	Very	Fairly	Neither	Fairly	Very	
Efficiently run	42	43	7	7	2	Badly run
United	42	39	10	6	3	Divided
Hard to understand	1	4	12	23	60	Easy to understand
Left-wing	0.4	0.4	42	40	17	Right-wing
Old-fashioned	6	17	37	28	13	Modern

7b. Thinking about the LAST LOCAL meeting, how much time at the meeting was spent on:

	None of the time	Some of the time	Most of the time	All of the time
Internal party organizational matters	14	63	20	3
Fund-raising	10	67	20	3
Local politics	11	70	17	2
National politics	15	69	13	3

7c. If you discussed local or national politics at this LOCAL meeting, did you discuss any of the following?:

PLEASE TICK AS MANY AS APPLY

Housing	7		Education	10
Local government	18		Law and order	10
Defence	3		Taxation	7
Health	11		The economy	15

If you discussed any other issues, please tell us what they were:

8. How active do you consider yourself to be in the Conservative party?

PLEASE TICK ONE BOX ONLY

Very active	6
Fairly active	14
Not very active	36
Not at all active	45

IF FAIRLY OR VERY ACTIVE, what is your MOST important reason for being active?

PLEASE WRITE IN

8a. Are you more active, or less active within the party than you were five years ago, or about the same?

PLEASE TICK ONE BOX ONLY

More active	8
Less active	25
About the same	57
Not applicable (recently joined member)	9

IF MORE OR LESS ACTIVE

8b. What is the single MOST important reason why you are more or less active than five years ago?

PLEASE WRITE IN

8c. Over the last five years, have you found that you tend to get actively involved in the party only at election times?

PLEASE TICK ONE BOX ONLY

Election times only	49
Other times	36
Not applicable (recently joined member)	15

---

9. Do you at present hold any office(s) within the Conservative party? (e.g., ward party secretary or constituency treasurer)

PLEASE TICK ONE BOX ONLY

Yes	8
No	92

9a. If YES, which ones?

PLEASE WRITE IN   Since when

_____   _____

_____   _____

_____   _____

---

10. How much time do you devote to party activities in the average MONTH?

PLEASE TICK ONE BOX ONLY

None	76
Up to 5 hours	15
From 5 to 10 hours	5
From 10 to 20 hours	2
From 20 to 30 hours	0.8
From 30 to 40 hours	0.4
More than 40 hours	0.7

11. What annual membership contribution do you pay to the party?

PLEASE WRITE IN THE AMOUNT _____

11a. Generally speaking, do you think that the annual membership contribution to the party made by a member like yourself is too little, too much, or about right?

PLEASE TICK ONE BOX ONLY

Too little ☐ 17

Too much ☐ 1

About right ☐ 76

11b. What is your estimate of the *total* overall financial contribution which you make to the party each YEAR? (e.g., fund-raising events, jumble sales, parties, etc.)

PLEASE WRITE IN THE AMOUNT _____

11c. What do you think the total overall annual contribution to the party should be for someone like yourself?

PLEASE WRITE IN THE AMOUNT _____

12. Before you joined the party, were either your father or mother a Conservative party member?

PLEASE TICK ONE BOX ONLY

Both father and mother were members ☐ 32

Father was a member ☐ 6

Mother was a member ☐ 6

Neither were members ☐ 44

Don't know ☐ 13

13. Are you currently a local Conservative councillor?

PLEASE TICK ONE BOX ONLY

Yes	2
No	98

13a. Are you currently on any official bodies? (e.g., school governor/ Scottish school board, member of a health authority, Scottish community council)

PLEASE TICK ONE BOX ONLY

Yes	7
No	93

If YES, please write in which one(s):

_____

_____

_____

13b. Are you currently a magistrate/JP?

PLEASE TICK ONE BOX ONLY

Yes	1
No	99

13c. Are you currently a Special Constable?

PLEASE TICK ONE BOX ONLY

Yes	0.1
No	99.9

14. Are you currently a member of any group(s) within the party? (e.g., Conservative Teachers, Conservative Political Centre, Young Conservatives, Bow Group, etc.)

PLEASE TICK ONE BOX ONLY

Yes	3
No	97

14. (*Continued*)

If YES, please write in the name(s) of these groups.

_____

_____

_____

_____

_____

15. Next here is a set of statements about important political issues. We would like to know if you agree or disagree with them.

PLEASE TICK ONE BOX FOR EACH STATEMENT

	Strongly agree	Agree	Neither	Disagree	Strongly disagree
The Conservative party should adjust its policies to capture the middle ground of politics	16	54	13	15	2
The right to strike should not exist for public sector workers	28	41	7	20	4
The public enterprises privatized by the Conservative government should be subject to stricter regulation	24	48	12	14	1
Contracting out local government services to private firms has not improved the quality of local services	8	24	19	42	7
The next Conservative government should establish a prices and incomes policy as a means of controlling inflation	12	31	12	32	14

15. (*Continued*)

	Strongly agree	Agree	Neither	Disagree	Strongly disagree
A future Conservative government should privatize British Coal	12	44	17	22	5
Modern methods of farming have caused great damage to the countryside	22	41	15	18	4
The Conservative government should introduce a system of educational vouchers in the state school system	8	29	31	27	6
Further legal curbs on trade unions are necessary	16	41	21	21	2
Income and wealth should be redistributed towards ordinary working people	5	21	20	42	12
Privatization of public enterprises has resulted in private monopoly rather than public monopoly	12	43	19	24	2
A future Conservative government should not agree to a single European currency	25	33	12	24	6
Workers should be directly involved in the management of their companies	10	46	13	27	4
A future Conservative government should encourage repatriation of immigrants	32	38	12	15	4

15. (*Continued*)

	Strongly agree	Agree	Neither	Disagree	Strongly disagree
Introducing market forces into the NHS means that the quality of our health service will improve	16	54	15	13	3
Further nuclear energy development is essential for the future prosperity of Britain	12	48	17	19	4
A future Conservative government should not privatize British Rail	9	27	12	43	9
High income tax makes people less willing to work hard	33	49	6	11	2
The Conservative party should always stick by its principles even if this should lose it an election	24	58	8	9	1
All shops should be allowed to open on Sundays	16	30	10	24	20
A future Conservative government should make abortions more difficult to obtain	12	22	19	35	13
Charging motorists for their use of roads is the means by which Britain's traffic congestion can be alleviated	7	26	11	42	14

15. (*Continued*)

	Strongly agree	Agree	Neither	Disagree	Strongly disagree
Elected local government should be protected from central government interference	7	34	13	38	8
The welfare state undermines individual self-reliance and enterprise	16	46	14	21	3
Britain should stay in the European Exchange Rate Mechanism	8	59	17	13	4
Schools should not be encouraged to opt out of local education authority control	5	20	13	49	13
Her Majesty the Queen should pay income tax	16	27	12	28	17
The consumer needs much stronger protection from the effects of the free market	13	43	18	22	3
Unemployment benefit should ensure people a reasonable standard of living	14	60	13	11	2

16. Are you currently a member of any of the following groups or organizations:

PLEASE TICK AS MANY AS APPLY

National Trust/National Trust for Scotland   27   OXFAM   3

16. (*Continued*)

World Wildlife Fund	12	RSPCA	6	
Red Cross	4	NSPCC/RSPCC	6	
British Legion	8	Christian Aid	5	
Women's Institute	7	Consumers' Association	7	
National Viewers' and Listeners' Association	0.6	Society for the Protection of Unborn Children	1	
Chamber of Commerce	3	Chamber of Trade	1	
Rotarians	3	Age Concern	5	

Please write in any other groups, both national and local, of which you are a member:

16a. Do you do any voluntary work for any of these groups or organizations?

PLEASE TICK ONE BOX ONLY

Yes [34]

No [66]

If YES, which one(s) do you do voluntary work for?

PLEASE WRITE IN

16a. (*Continued*)

If YES, how much time do you devote to such voluntary work in the average month?

PLEASE WRITE IN

_____

_____

_____

17. Are you currently a member of a trade union, staff association, or professional association?

| Trade union | Yes | 10 |
| | No | 90 |

If YES, what is the name of your trade union?

_____

| Staff association | Yes | 4 |
| | No | 96 |

If YES, what is the name of your staff association?

_____

| Professional association | Yes | 18 |
| | No | 82 |

If YES, what is the name of your professional association?

_____

_____

18. Are you

PLEASE TICK ONE BOX ONLY

| Female | 52 |
| Male | 48 |

_____

19. We would like to ask you about political activities you may have taken part in during the last *FIVE* years

ACTIVITY   How often have you done this?

	Not at all	Rarely	Occasionally	Frequently
Displayed an election poster in a window	49	8	24	19
Signed a petition supported by the party	52	13	27	9
Donated money to Conservative party funds	15	10	45	30
Delivered party leaflets during an election	61	4	13	22
Attended a party meeting	51	13	20	17
Helped at a Conservative party function (e.g., jumble sale)	56	9	18	17
Canvassed voters on behalf of the party	75	6	9	10
Stood for office within the party organization	88	2	5	4
Stood for elected office in a local government or national parliamentary election	94	1	2	3
Other (please specify)				

20. How old were you when you finished continuous FULL-TIME education?

PLEASE WRITE IN _____ Years

21. Which of these descriptions applies to what you were doing last week, that is, in the seven days ending last Sunday?

PLEASE TICK ONE BOX ONLY

In full-time work	27
In full-time education	0.4
On a government training/employment scheme (e.g., Youth Training Scheme)	0
In part-time paid work	9
Waiting to take up paid work already accepted	0.2
Unemployed and registered at benefit office	1
Unemployed and NOT registered	0.5
Permanently sick and disabled	2
Wholly retired from work	40
Looking after the home full-time	16
Other (please specify)	3

22. Which type of organization do you work for? (If you are not working now, please answer in terms of your LAST job)

PLEASE TICK ONE BOX ONLY

A private company or firm	59
Nationalized industry/Public corporation	5
Local Authority/Local Education Authority	14
Health Authority/Hospital	7
Central Government/Civil Service	6
Other (please specify)	10

22a. Are you self-employed, or do you work for someone else as an employee? (If you are not working please answer in terms of your LAST job)

22a. (*Continued*)

PLEASE TICK ONE BOX ONLY

Self-employed	27
Employee	69
Never had a job	3

22b. In your job do you supervise any other people? (If you are not working, please answer in terms of your LAST job)

PLEASE TICK ONE BOX ONLY

Yes	60
No	40

22c. If YES, how many adult people do you supervise?

PLEASE WRITE IN THE NUMBER

22d. What is the title of your present job? (If you are not working, please answer in terms of your LAST job)

PLEASE WRITE IN

22e. Would you describe in detail the type of work you do, being as specific as you can? (If you are not working please answer in terms of your LAST job)

PLEASE WRITE IN

23. Do you ever think of yourself as belonging to any particular social class?

23. (*Continued*)

PLEASE TICK ONE BOX ONLY

	Yes	62
	No	38

If YES, which class is that?

PLEASE TICK ONE BOX ONLY

Upper class	4
Middle class	76
Working class	18
Other (please specify)	2

23a. When you were young (i.e., a teenager), would you say that your family belonged to a social class?

PLEASE TICK ONE BOX ONLY

	Yes	80
	No	20

If YES, which class was that?

PLEASE TICK ONE BOX ONLY

Upper class	5
Middle class	56
Working class	40
Other (please specify)	1

---

24. Thinking back to the time you were a teenager, was your father self-employed, or did he work for someone else as an employee?

24. (*Continued*)

PLEASE TICK ONE BOX ONLY

Self-employed	30
Employee	64
Not applicable	6

IF NOT APPLICABLE, PLEASE GO ON TO QUESTION 25

24a. Again thinking back to the time you were a teenager, what was the title of your father's job?

PLEASE WRITE IN

24b. Again thinking back to the time you were a teenager, would you describe in detail the type of work your father did, being as specific as you can?

PLEASE WRITE IN

25. What was your age last birthday?

PLEASE WRITE IN _____ Years

26. Which of these types of school did you LAST attend, FULL-time?

PLEASE TICK ONE BOX ONLY

None—never attended any school	0.1
Primary or elementary school	12

SECONDARY SCHOOL IN ENGLAND AND WALES:

Secondary or secondary modern	19
Comprehensive (including sixth-form college)	3

26. (*Continued*)

Grammar school	25
Direct grant school	1
Independent fee-paying (i e , private or public)	22
Technical school	6
Other (please specify)	4

SECONDARY SCHOOL IN SCOTLAND:

Junior secondary	1
Comprehensive (including sixth-form college)	1
Senior secondary (6-year selective) or 'Omnibus' school (pre-1960)	4
Grant-aided	0.2
Independent fee-paying (private)	1
Other (please specify)	1

27. Have you obtained any of the following qualifications?

PLEASE TICK AS MANY AS APPROPRIATE

None	31
CSE Grades 2 to 5	1
CSE Grade 1, GCE 'O' level, GCSE's, School Certificate	16
Scottish Ordinary/Lower Certificate	2
GCE 'A'/'S' level or Higher Certificate	6
Scottish Higher Certificate	1
Technical qualification (e.g., City and Guilds, ONC/HNC, B.TECH Ordinary/Higher)	11
Teachers' training qualification	5

27. (*Continued*)

University or CNAA degree or diploma ☐ 12

Other British qualification (please specify) ☐ 15

---

28. Have you ever served in the Armed Forces?

PLEASE TICK ONE BOX ONLY

Yes ☐ 33

No ☐ 67

If YES, what is your rank, or what was your rank on leaving?

PLEASE WRITE IN

28a. Are you a service reserve volunteer?

PLEASE TICK ONE BOX ONLY

Yes ☐ 2

No ☐ 99

If YES, with which service are you a volunteer?

PLEASE TICK ONE BOX ONLY

Army ☐ 39

Navy ☐ 30

Air Force ☐ 25

Marines ☐ 7

---

29. Next, here is another set of statements about various political issues. We would like to know if you agree or disagree with them.

29. (*Continued*)

PLEASE TICK ONE BOX FOR EACH STATEMENT

	Strongly agree	Agree	Neither	Disagree	Strongly disagree
The death penalty should be reintroduced for murder	36	33	7	17	7
Britain's national sovereignty is being lost to Europe	22	46	10	20	2
Britain's present electoral system should be replaced by a system of proportional representation	5	17	12	43	24
It is best to leave government to people from the upper class	3	7	11	50	29
When it comes to raising a family, a woman's place is in the home	15	41	14	20	11
Restrictions on immigration into Britain are too loose and should be tightened	54	37	5	3	1
Conservatives should resist further moves to integrate the European Community	20	34	16	27	3
Conservative Central Office should have a more influential role in the selection of parliamentary candidates	6	26	27	35	6

29. (*Continued*)

	Strongly agree	Agree	Neither	Disagree	Strongly disagree
A Conservative Chancellor of the Exchequer should introduce additional tax concessions for child care	9	39	20	28	5
A future Conservative government should introduce a directly elected Scottish assembly with taxing powers	3	20	26	38	13
There is no need for a Bill of Rights in this country	6	34	27	28	6
Child Benefit should be abolished	8	13	12	53	15
The Conservative party leader should be elected by a system of one party member, one vote	11	39	14	29	6
When somebody is unemployed, it is usually their fault	2	5	15	56	22
The government should give more aid to poor countries	2	21	25	41	11
Generally, people with money are better at running the country	4	29	16	40	11
The reduction in East–West tension means that Britain can make significant cutbacks in defence spending	5	41	8	39	8

29. (*Continued*)

	Strongly agree	Agree	Neither	Disagree	Strongly disagree
Coalition governments are the best form of government for Britain	2	8	10	53	27
Divorce has become too easy these days, and the divorce laws should be tightened up	18	42	13	23	4
A Conservative government should aim to make Britain part of a federal Europe	3	18	15	40	24

---

30. In Conservative party politics people often talk about the 'left' and the 'right'. *Compared with other Conservative party members*, where would you place your views on this scale below?

PLEASE TICK ONE BOX ONLY

LEFT   RIGHT

2	2	4	7	26	17	22	9	13

30a. And where would you place your views in relation to British politics as a whole (not just the Conservative party)?

PLEASE TICK ONE BOX ONLY

LEFT   RIGHT

0.3	0.2	1	2	18	18	28	16	17

---

31. At the last general election in 1987 some people didn't manage to vote. How about you? Did you manage to vote in the general election?

PLEASE TICK ONE BOX ONLY

Yes   98

No   2

31a. If YES, which party did you vote for in the 1987 general election?

PLEASE TICK ONE BOX ONLY

Conservative	98
Labour	0.2
Alliance (SDP or Liberals)	1
The Scottish National party	–
Plaid Cymru	–
The Green party	0.1
Other (please specify)	0.1

32. Have you always voted for the same party in general elections?

PLEASE TICK ONE BOX ONLY

Yes	82
No	17

32a. If NO, which party or parties did you vote for previously?

PLEASE TICK AS MANY BOXES AS APPLY

Did not vote	6
Conservative	18
Labour	33
Alliance (SDP or Liberals)	26
The Scottish National party	1
Plaid Cymru	0.2
The Green party	1
Other (please specify)	1

33. Next, here are some statements about political activity in Britain. We would like to know if you agree or disagree with them.

PLEASE TICK ONE BOX FOR EACH STATEMENT

	Strongly agree	Agree	Neither	Disagree	Strongly disagree
People like me can have a real influence on politics if they are prepared to get involved	7	50	20	22	2
Attending party meetings can be pretty tiring after a hard day's work	7	62	20	11	0.3
When Conservative party members work together they can really change Britain	11	64	18	7	0.4
A person like me could do a good job of being a local Conservative councillor	4	23	24	39	9
Working for the party can be pretty boring at times	4	39	37	18	2
The local Conservative party has really made a difference to the way in which our community has developed	5	36	36	21	3
Voting is the only way people like me can have any say about how the government runs things	18	58	5	17	2

33. (*Continued*)

	Strongly agree	Agree	Neither	Disagree	Strongly disagree
Being an active party member is a good way to meet interesting people	6	53	30	9	1
The only way to be really educated about politics is to be a party activist	4	32	17	42	5
If a citizen is dissatisfied with the policies of the government he or she has a duty to do something about it	11	71	12	6	0.4
People like me have a real say in what the Government does	2	17	26	49	6
Getting involved in party activities during an election can be fun	5	40	36	16	2
Every citizen should get involved in politics if democracy is to work properly	8	48	21	22	1
Being a Conservative party member can help people like me in their business careers	2	16	37	39	7
The party leadership doesn't pay a lot of attention to the views of ordinary party members	7	36	24	31	2
Party activity often takes time away from one's family	6	62	26	7	0.2

33. (*Continued*)

	Strongly agree	Agree	Neither	Disagree	Strongly disagree
The Conservative party would be more successful if more people like me were elected to Parliament	4	17	32	41	6
For the Conservative party to have a reasonable chance of success, every party member must contribute as much as they can	9	61	16	13	1

---

34. Please indicate whether you think the government should or should not do the following things, or doesn't it matter either way?

PLEASE TICK ONE BOX ONLY FOR EACH STATEMENT

	Definitely should	Probably should	Doesn't matter	Probably should not	Definitely should not
Encourage private education	29	36	20	12	3
Spend more money to get rid of poverty	29	52	8	9	2
Encourage the growth of private medicine	17	35	16	25	7
Put more money into the NHS	31	49	8	11	2
Reduce government spending generally	14	46	9	27	4
Introduce stricter laws to regulate the trade unions	28	38	12	19	3

34. (*Continued*)

	Definitely should	Probably should	Doesn't matter	Probably should not	Definitely should not
Give workers more say in the places where they work	16	48	13	19	4
Spend less on defence	9	35	5	34	17
Cut income tax	21	41	13	22	4

35. Think about those people whose opinions are especially important to you, for example, your spouse, friends, or colleagues. Consider the person whose opinions you most respect: would you say that they agree or disagree with the following statements?

PLEASE TICK ONE BOX FOR EACH STATEMENT

	Strongly agree	Agree	Neither	Disagree	Strongly disagree
On the whole, members of the local Conservative association are respected figures in the community	8	61	22	8	1
Many Conservative party activists are extremists	2	15	25	51	7
People can have a real influence on politics if they are prepared to get involved	10	66	15	9	1

36. Please think for a moment of a thermometer scale that runs from zero to 100 degrees, where 50 is the neutral point.

If your feelings are warm and sympathetic towards something or someone, give them a score higher than 50; the warmer the feelings the higher the score.

36. (*Continued*)

If your feelings are cold and unsympathetic, give them a score less than 50; the colder your feelings, the lower the score.

A score of 50 means that your feelings are neither warm nor cold.

PLEASE WRITE IN

First give a rating to each of the party leaders.

RATING OUT OF 100

John Major	80
Neil Kinnock	20
Paddy Ashdown	37

Next, please give a rating to some Conservative party politicians. (Leave a blank if you feel you don't know enough about that person to rate them.)

RATING OUT OF 100

Margaret Thatcher	78
Norman Lamont	59
Chris Patten	64
Norman Tebbit	67
Douglas Hurd	70
Kenneth Baker	59
Kenneth Clarke	62
William Waldegrave	61
Edward Heath	40
Lynda Chalker	59
Geoffrey Howe	53
Nigel Lawson	47
Teresa Gorman	50
Malcolm Rifkind	56
Michael Heseltine	63
Virginia Bottomley	64

36. (*Continued*)

David Hunt	55
Ian Lang	55
Michael Forsyth	52
Edwina Currie	58

Next, please give a rating to the political parties:

	RATING OUT OF 100
The Conservative party	80
The Labour party	26
The Liberal Democrat party	36
Scottish Nationalist party	19
The Green party	19
Plaid Cymru	13

Finally, please give a rating to the following people and organizations. (Again leave a blank if you feel you don't know enough about them to give a rating).

	RATING OUT OF 100
George Bush	68
Mikhail Gorbachev	71
Enoch Powell	63
Jacques Delors	30
Boris Yeltsin	54
The BBC	59
ITV	59
The Stock Exchange	59
The European Community	50
The *Sun* newspaper	19
The Trades Union Congress/ Scottish Trade Union Congress	26

36. (*Continued*)

The Police	73
The House of Commons	68
The House of Lords	62
The Confederation of British Industry/Scottish Confederation of Industry	59
Her Majesty the Queen	86
Prince Charles	74
Prince Edward	46
The Armed Forces	82
The Church of England/Scotland	58
Doctors	75
Teachers	60
Judges	60
Lawyers	54
Social workers	46

37. Describe in your own words the most important qualities needed by the leader of the Conservative party.

PLEASE WRITE IN

37a. If John Major resigned the leadership of the Conservative party, whom would you like to see elected as leader?

PLEASE WRITE IN

38. Suppose the Government had to choose between the following three
options. Which do you think it should choose?

PLEASE TICK ONE BOX ONLY

Reduce taxes and spend less on health,   ☐ 7
education, and social benefits

Keep taxes and spending on these services   ☐ 67
at the same levels as now

Increase taxes and spend more on health,   ☐ 26
education, and social benefits

---

39. Think of the accommodation where you live now. Do you:

PLEASE TICK ONE BOX ONLY

Own the property   ☐ 91

Rent it from the council   ☐ 3

Rent it from a private landlord   ☐ 3

Rent it from a housing association   ☐ 1

Or are you living with family or friends   ☐ 2

Other (please specify)   ☐ 1

---

40. IF YOU OWN YOUR PROPERTY, were you a council tenant in
your PRESENT accommodation before you purchased it?

PLEASE TICK ONE BOX ONLY

Was previously a council tenant   ☐ 4

Was not previously a council tenant   ☐ 96

---

41. Do you regard yourself as belonging to any particular religion?

PLEASE TICK ONE BOX ONLY

No   ☐ 10

41. (*Continued*)

IF YES AND CHRISTIAN:

Roman Catholic	7
Church of England/Wales, Anglican, Episcopalian	63
Church of Scotland/Presbyterian	7
Methodist	4
Baptist	2
United Reform Church, Congregational	1
Christian, but no denomination	4
Other Christian (please specify)	1

IF YES AND NON-CHRISTIAN:

Jewish	1
Hindu	0.3
Islamic/Muslim	0.4
Sikh	0
Buddhist	0.1
Other non-Christian (please specify)	0

42. Please indicate your ethnic origins

PLEASE TICK ONE BOX ONLY

White (British, Irish, or other)	99
Asian (Indian, Pakistani, Chinese, or other)	1
Black (African, Caribbean, or other)	0
Other (please specify)	0.3

43. Which of the following categories represents the present total annual income of your household from ALL sources before tax?

43. (*Continued*)

PLEASE TICK ONE BOX ONLY

Under £5,000	8
£5,000 up to £10,000	19
£10,000 up to £15,000	18
£15,000 up to £20,000	14
£20,000 up to £30,000	19
£30,000 up to £40,000	10
£40,000 up to £50,000	5
£50,000 up to £60,000	3
£60,000 up to £70,000	1
£70,000 up to £80,000	1
£80,000 plus	3

---

44. Do you (or your husband/wife/partner) own any shares quoted on the Stock Exchange, including Unit Trusts?

PLEASE TICK ONE BOX ONLY

Yes	70
No	30

If YES, were any of these shares purchased from the public enterprises sold off as a result of the government's privatization programme? (e.g., British Gas, British Telecom, etc.)

PLEASE TICK ONE BOX ONLY

Yes	71
No	29

If YES, did you (or your husband/wife/partner) own any shares BEFORE you purchased these shares in the public enterprises sold off as a result of the government's privatization programme?

PLEASE TICK ONE BOX ONLY

Yes	62
No	38

---

45. Which daily morning paper do you read MOST?

PLEASE TICK ONE BOX ONLY

I don't read a daily paper	11
Daily Express/Scottish Daily Express	14
Daily Mail	17
Daily Mirror/Daily Record	1
Daily Star	0.2
The Sun	3
Today	1
The Scotsman	1
The Glasgow Herald	1
Daily Telegraph	28
Financial Times	1
The Guardian	0.4
The Independent	2
The Times	6
Other (please specify)	6

46. We would like to ask you the *extent* to which you think you can personally influence politics, if you participate in the following activities:

PLEASE TICK ONE BOX FOR EACH ACTIVITY

	A large extent	Some extent	Small extent	Not at all
Displaying an election poster in a window	4	19	37	40
Signing a petition supported by the party	9	36	40	16
Donating money to Conservative party funds	13	43	35	9

46. (*Continued*)

	A large extent	Some extent	Small extent	Not at all
Organizing fund-raising events (e.g., jumble sales)	7	33	32	29
Delivering party leaflets during an election campaign	11	34	30	25
Attending a party meeting	5	26	37	32
Canvassing voters on behalf of the party	11	30	26	33
Standing for elective office within the party organization	8	24	19	49
Standing for elective office at a national parliamentary or local government election	13	22	13	52

47. Finally, what in your opinion are the main issues (policy and/or organizational) which the Conservative party needs to face up to either at the present time or in the future?

END OF THE QUESTIONNAIRE

PLEASE CHECK THAT YOU HAVE ANSWERED ALL THE QUESTIONS

THANK YOU VERY MUCH FOR YOUR HELP

REFERENCES

ADDISON, PAUL (1977), *The Road to 1945*, London: Quartet Books.

All England Law Reports (1982), London: Butterworth.

ALMOND, GABRIEL, and VERBA, SIDNEY (1963), *The Civic Culture*, Princeton, NJ: Princeton University Press.

ARNOLD, R. DOUGLAS (1990), *The Logic of Congressional Action*, New Haven, Conn.: Yale University Press.

AXELROD, ROBERT (1984), *The Evolution of Co-operation*, New York: Basic Books.

BAILEY, S. J., and PADDISON, R. (1988), *The Reform of Local Government Finance in Britain*, London: Routledge.

BALL, ALAN (1981), *British Political Parties*, Basingstoke: Macmillan.

BARNES, SAMUEL H., and KAASE, MAX (1979), *Political Action: Mass Participation in Five Western Democracies*, Beverly Hills, Calif. and London: Sage.

BARRY, BRIAN (1970), *Sociologists, Economists and Democracy*, London: Collier-Macmillan.

BEALEY, FRANK, BLONDEL, JEAN, and MCCANN, W. P. (1965), *Constituency Politics*, London: Faber.

BEER, SAMUEL H. (1965), *Modern British Politics*, London: Faber and Faber.

BERELSON, BERNARD R., LAZARSFELD, PAUL F., and MCPHEE, WILLIAM N. (1954), *Voting*, Chicago: University of Chicago Press.

BIRCH, ANTHONY (1964), *Representative and Responsible Government*, London: Allen and Unwin.

BLAKE, ROBERT (1955), *The Unknown Prime Minister: The Life and Times of Andrew Bonar Law, 1858–1923*, London: Eyre and Spottiswoode.

—— (1966), *Disraeli*, London: Eyre and Spottiswoode.

—— (1970), *The Conservative Party from Peel to Churchill*, London: Eyre and Spottiswoode.

—— (1985), *The Conservative Party from Peel to Thatcher*, London: Methuen.

BLONDEL, JEAN (1973), *Voters, Parties and Leaders*, rev. edn., Harmondsworth: Penguin.

BOCHEL, JOHN M., and DENVER, DAVID D. (1972), 'The Impact of the Campaign on the Results of Local Government Elections', *British Journal of Political Science*, 2: 239–43.

BOGDANOR, VERNON (1993), 'A New Leadership By the People and For the People', *The Times*, 27 Sept.

BRADFORD, SARAH (1982), *Disraeli*, London: Weidenfeld and Nicolson.

BRADSHAW, JONATHAN (1992), 'Social Security', in David Marsh and R. A. W. Rhodes (eds.), *Implementing Thatcherite Policies*, Buckingham: Open University Press, 81–99.

BRENNAN, GEOFFREY, and BUCHANAN, JAMES (1984), 'Voter Choice: Evaluating Political Alternatives', *American Behavioral Scientist*, 28: 185–201.

BROWN, PAUL (1993), 'Tories Face Crisis over Party Debt', *Guardian Weekly*, 19 Sept.

BULPITT, JIM (1986), 'The Discipline of the New Democracy: Mrs Thatcher's Domestic Statecraft', *Political Studies*, 34: 19–39.

——(1991), 'The Conservative Party in Britain: A Preliminary Paradoxical Portrait', Paper presented to the annual meeting of the Political Studies Association.

BUTLER, DAVID, and KAVANAGH, DENNIS (1992), *The British General Election of 1987*, London: Macmillan.

—— and PINTO-DUSCHINSKY, M. (1980), 'The Conservative Élite 1918–78: Does Unrepresentativeness Matter?', in Z. Layton-Henry (ed.), *Conservative Party Politics*, London, Macmillan, 186–209.

—— and STOKES, DONALD (1974), *Political Change in Britain*, London: Macmillan.

BUTLER, RICHARD A. (1971), *The Art of the Possible*, London: Hamish Hamilton.

CAIN, BRUCE, FEREJOHN, JOHN, and FIORINA, MORRIS (1986), *The Personal Vote: Constituency Service and Electoral Independence*, Cambridge, Mass.: Harvard University Press.

CAMPBELL, ANGUS, CONVERSE, PHILIP E., MILLER, WARREN E., and STOKES, DONALD (1960), *The American Voter*, Chicago: University of Chicago Press.

CARTER, JOHN R., and GUERETTE, STEPHEN D. (1992), 'An Experimental Study of Voting', *Public Choice*, 73: 251–60.

Charter Movement (1981), *A Charter to Set the Party Free*, Richmond: The Charter Movement.

—— (1991), *Charter News*, Swanley: The Charter Movement.

CONOVER, PAMELA JOHNSTON, and FELDMAN, STANLEY (1986), 'Emotional Reactions to the Economy: I'm Mad as Hell and I'm Not Going to Take it Anymore', *American Journal of Political Science*, 30: 50–78.

Conservative Party (1990), *Model Rules*, London: The Conservative Party.

—— (1992), *109th Conservative Conference Handbook*, London: The Conservative Party.

—— (1993a), *Working Together: To Build a Strong Voluntary Party*, London: The Conservative Party.

—— (1993b), *One Party: Reforming the Conservative Party Organisation*, London: The Conservative Party.

—— (1993c), *Welcome to the Conservative Party*, London: The Conservative Party.

CONVERSE, PHILIP (1964), 'The Nature of Belief Systems in Mass Politics', in David Apter (ed.), *Ideology and Discontent*, New York: Free Press, 206–61.

Cox, Gary W., and Kernell, Samuel (1991), *The Politics of Divided Government*, Boulder, Colo.: Westview Press.

Crewe, Ivor, and Fox, Anthony (1984), *British Parliamentary Constituencies: A Statistical Compendium*, London: Faber and Faber.

—— and Harrop, Martin (1986), *Political Communications: The General Election Campaign of 1983*, Cambridge: Cambridge University Press.

—— —— (1989), *Political Communications: The General Election Campaign of 1987*, Cambridge: Cambridge University Press.

—— and Searing, Donald (1988), 'Ideological Change in the British Conservative Party', *American Political Science Review*, 82: 361–84.

Critchley, Julian (1985), *Westminster Blues*, London: Elm Tree.

Crossman, Richard (1961), *New Statesman*, 23 June, 7, 21 July.

Crotty, William J. (1971), 'Party Effort and its Impact on the Vote', *American Political Science Review*, 65: 439–50.

Crouch, Colin (1990), 'Industrial Relations', in Patrick Dunleavy, Andrew Gamble, and Gillian Peele (eds.), *Developments in British Politics*, iii, New York: St Martin's Press, 322–30.

Cutright, Phillip (1963), 'Measuring the Impact of Local Party Activity on the General Election Vote', *Public Opinion Quarterly*, 27: 372–85.

—— and Rossi, Peter H. (1958), 'Grass Roots Politicians and the Vote', *American Sociological Review*, 23: 171–9.

Denver, David D. (1993), 'The Centre', in Anthony King (ed.), *Britain at the Polls 1992*, Chatham, NJ: Chatham House Publishers, 101–28.

—— and Hands, Gordon (1974), 'Marginality and Turnout in British General Elections', *British Journal of Political Science*, 4: 17–35.

—— —— (1985), 'Marginality and Turnout in General Elections in the 1970s', *British Journal of Political Science*, 15: 381–98.

—— —— (1992), 'Constituency Campaigning', *Parliamentary Affairs*, 45: 528–44.

—— —— (1993), 'Measuring the Intensity and Effectiveness of Constituency Campaigning in the 1992 British General Election', Paper presented at the European Consortium for Political Research, Joint Sessions, Leiden University, Netherlands, Apr. 1993.

Dowse, Robert, and Hughes, J. (1977), 'Sporadic Interventionists', *Political Studies*, 25: 84–92.

Drucker, Peter (1992), *Managing for the Future: The 1990s and Beyond*, New York: Dutton.

Duverger, Maurice (1954), *Political Parties*, London: Methuen.

Eccleshall, Robert (1990), *English Conservatism since the Reformation*, London: Unwin Hyman.

Elster, Jon (1989), *The Cement of Society*, Cambridge: Cambridge University Press.

Ewing, Keith (1987), *The Funding of Political Parties in Britain*, Cambridge: Cambridge University Press.

FEILING, KEITH (1946), *The Life of Neville Chamberlain*, London: Macmillan.

FEUCHTWANGER, EDWIN (1968), *Disraeli, Democracy and the Tory Party*, Oxford: Clarendon Press.

FINKEL, STEVEN E., MULLER, EDWARD N., OPP, KARL-DIETER (1989), 'Personal Influence, Collective Rationality, and Mass Political Action', *American Political Science Review*, 83: 885–903.

FIORINA, MORRIS (1981), *Retrospective Voting in American National Elections*, New Haven, Conn.: Yale University Press.

FLANAGAN, SCOTT C., and DALTON, RUSSELL J. (1984), 'Parties under Stress: Realignment and Dealignment in Advanced Industrial Democracies', *Western European Politics*, 7: 7–23.

FRENDREIS, JOHN P., GIBSON, JAMES L., and VERTZ, LAURA L. (1990), 'The Electoral Relevance of Local Party Organisations', *American Political Science Review*, 84: 225–35.

GALLUP POLLS (1992), *Gallup Political Index, Report No. 379*, London: Gallup Polls.

GAMBLE, ANDREW (1974), *The Conservative Nation*, London: Routledge and Kegan Paul.

—— (1988), *The Free Economy and the Strong State*, Basingstoke: Macmillan.

—— (1990), 'The Thatcher Decade in Perspective', in Patrick Dunleavy, Andrew Gamble, and Gillian Peele (eds.), *Developments in British Politics*, iii, London: Macmillan.

GIBSON, JAMES L., and SMITH, GREGG (1984), 'Local Party Organizations and Electoral Outcomes: Linkages between Parties and Elections', Paper presented at the annual meeting of the American Political Science Association.

GILBERT, MARTIN (1991), *Churchill: A Life*, London: Heinemann.

GILMOUR, IAN (1971), *The Body Politic*, London: Hutchinson.

—— (1977), *The Right Approach*, London: Hutchinson.

—— (1983), *Britain Can Work*, Oxford: Martin Robertson.

GORDON, IAN, and WHITELEY, PAUL F. (1980), 'A Comment on "Campaign Expenditure and the Efficacy of Advertising in the 1974 General Election in England" by R. J. Johnston', *Political Studies*, 28: 293–4.

Greater London Young Conservatives (1969), *Set the Party Free*, London: Greater London Young Conservatives.

GREENLEAF, W. H. (1983), *The British Political Tradition*, ii, London: Methuen.

GUTTSMAN, W. L. (1963), *The British Political Élite*, London: MacGibbon and Kee.

Hansard Society (1991), *Agenda for Change*, London: the Hansard Society.

HARDIN, RUSSELL (1971), 'Collective Action as an Agreeable N-Prisoner's Dilemma', *Behavioral Science*, 16: 472–81.

HARMAN, H. (1967), *Modern Factor Analysis*, Chicago: University of Chicago Press.

HARRIS, NIGEL (1972), *Competition and the Corporate Society*, London: Methuen.

HARROP, MARTIN, HEATH, ANTHONY, and OPENSHAW, STAN (1992), 'Does Neighbourhood Influence Voting Behaviour—and Why?', in Ivor Crewe, Pippa Norris, David Denver, and David Broughton (eds.), *British Elections and Parties Yearbook 1991*, London: Harvester Wheatsheaf, 103–20.

HEATH, ANTHONY, JOWELL, ROGER, and CURTICE, JOHN (1985), *How Britain Votes*, Oxford: Pergamon Press.

—— —— —— EVANS, GEOFF, FIELD, JULIA, and WITHERSPOON, SHARON (1991), *Understanding Political Change*, Oxford: Pergamon Press.

HEATH, ANTHONY, JOWELL, ROGER, and CURTICE, JOHN (1994), *Labour's Last Chance?*, London: Dartmouth Press.

HERRNSON, PAUL (1986), 'Do Parties Make a Difference? The Role of Party Organisation in Congressional Elections', *Journal of Politics*, 48: 589–615.

HILDE, HIMMELWEIT, HUMPHRIES, PATRICK, JAEGER, MARIANNE, and KATZ, MICHAEL (1981), *How Voters Decide*, London and New York: Academic Press.

HMSO (1974), *Report of the Committee on Financial Aid to Political Parties*, Cmnd. 6601, London: HMSO.

—— (1987), *Employment Gazette*, London: HMSO.

—— (1992), *Employment Gazette*, London: HMSO.

—— (1993), *Election Expenses*, London: HMSO.

HOGWOOD, BRIAN (1992), *Trends in British Public Policy*, Buckingham: Open University Press.

HOLMES, MARTIN (1985), *The First Thatcher Government 1979–1983*, Brighton: Wheatsheaf.

—— (1989), *Thatcherism: Scope and Limits 1983–7*, London: Macmillan.

HOLT, R., and TURNER, J. (1968), *Political Parties in Action: The Battle for Barons Court*, New York: Free Press.

HORNE, ALISTAIR (1988), *Macmillan*, i, London: Macmillan.

—— (1989), *Macmillan*, ii, London: Macmillan.

HUCKFELDT, ROBERT, and SPRAGUE, JOHN (1992), 'Political Parties and Electoral Mobilization: Political Structure, Social Structure, and the Party Canvass', *American Political Science Review*, 86: 70–86.

INGLE, STEPHEN (1987), *The British Party System*, Oxford: Blackwell.

INGLEHART, RONALD (1990), *Culture Shift in Advanced Industrial Society*, Princeton, NJ: Princeton University Press.

JAY, RICHARD (1981), *Joseph Chamberlain: A Political Study*, Oxford: Clarendon Press.

JENKINS, PETER (1987), *Mrs Thatcher's Revolution*, London: Cape.

JENKINS, PETER (1989), *Mrs Thatcher's Revolution*, London: Pan Books.

JESSOP, BOB (1974), *Traditionalism, Conservatism and British Political Culture*, London: Allen and Unwin.

—— BONNETT, KEVIN, BROMLEY, SIMON, and LING, TOM (1988), *Thatcherism: A Tale of Two Nations*, Cambridge: Polity Press.

JOHNSON, CHRISTOPHER (1991), *The Economy under Mrs Thatcher 1979–1990*, Harmondsworth: Penguin.

JOHNSTON, R. J. (1987), *Money and Votes: Constituency Campaign Spending and Election Results*, London: Croom Helm.

—— and PATTIE, C. J. (1993), 'The Effectiveness of Constituency Campaign Spending at Recent General Elections', in *Funding of Political Parties*, House of Commons Home Affairs Committee, 177–88.

—— —— and ALLSOP, J. G. (1988), *A Nation Dividing?*, London: Longman.

—— —— and JOHNSTON, L. C. (1989), 'The Impact of Constituency Spending on the Result of the 1987 British General Election', *Electoral Studies*, 8: 143–55.

JONES, G., and STEWART, J. (1983), *The Case for Local Government*, London: Allen and Unwin.

KATZ, DANIEL, and ELDERSVELD, SAMUEL (1961), 'The Impact of Local Party Activity upon the Electorate', *Public Opinion Quarterly*, 25: 1–24.

KATZ, RICHARD S., and MAIR, PETER (1992) (eds.), *Party Organizations: A Data Handbook*, London: Sage.

KAVANAGH, DENNIS (1976), 'The Deferential English: A Comparative Critique', in Richard Rose (ed.), *Studies in British Politics*, 3rd edn., London: Macmillan, 58–83.

—— (1987), *Thatcherism and British Politics*, Oxford: Clarendon Press.

—— (1989), 'Political Culture in Great Britain: The Decline of the Civic Culture', in Gabriel Almond and Sidney Verba (eds.), *The Civic Culture Revisited*, Newbury Park, Calif.: Sage.

—— (1990), *Thatcherism and British Politics*, Oxford: Oxford University Press.

KEEGAN, WILLIAM (1984), *Mrs Thatcher's Economic Experiment*, Harmondsworth: Penguin.

KELLY, RICHARD (1989), *Conservative Party Conferences*, Manchester: Manchester University Press.

—— (1991a), 'Party Organisation', *Contemporary Record*, 4/4: 6–8.

—— (1991b), 'The Tories and the Poll Tax', unpublished paper.

—— (1992), 'Power in the Conservative Party', *Politics Review*, 1/4: 26–9.

KITSCHELT, HERBERT (1989), 'The Internal Politics of Parties: The Law of Curvilinear Disparity Revisited', *Political Studies*, 37: 400–21.

KRAMER, GERALD H. (1970), 'The Effects of Precinct-Level Canvassing on Voter Behavior', *Public Opinion Quarterly*, 34: 560–72.

Labour Party (1983), *Labour's Programme 1983*, London: The Labour Party.

Lawson, Kay, and Merkl, Peter (1988) (eds.), *When Parties Fail*, Princeton, NJ: Princeton University Press.

Layton-Henry, Zig (1973), 'The Young Conservatives 1945–70', *Contemporary History*, 8/2: 143–56.

—— (1980), *Conservative Party Politics*, London: Macmillan.

Lindsay, T. F., and Harrington, Michael (1974), *The Conservative Party 1918–1970*, London: Macmillan.

Mackintosh, John (1982), *The Government and Politics of Britain*, London: Hutchinson.

Marcus, George (1988), 'The Structure of Emotional Responses: 1984 Presidential Candidates', *American Political Science Review*, 82: 737–62.

Margolis, Howard (1982), *Selfishness, Altruism and Rationality*, Chicago: University of Chicago Press.

Marquand, David (1988), *The Unprincipled Society*, London: Fontana.

Marsh, Alan (1977), *Protest and Political Consciousness*, Beverly Hills, Calif., and London: Sage.

Maxwell-Fyfe, David (1949), *The Final Report of the Committee on Party Organization*, London: The Conservative Party.

May, John D. (1973), 'Opinion Structure of Political Parties: The Special Law of Curvilinear Disparity', *Political Studies*, 21: 135–51.

McKenzie, Robert (1961), *New Statesman*, 30 June, 14, 28 July.

—— (1964), *British Political Parties*, 2nd rev. edn., London: Mercury Books.

—— and Silver, Alan (1968), *Angels in Marble*, London: Heinemann.

Mellors, Colin (1978), *The British MP*, Farnborough: Saxon House.

Middlemass, Keith, and Barnes, John (1969), *Baldwin*, London: Weidenfeld and Nicolson.

Miller, William L. (1977), *Electoral Dynamics*, 2nd edn., London: Macmillan.

Minkin, Lewis (1978), *The Labour Party Conference*, London: Allen Lane.

—— (1992), *The Contentious Alliance*, Edinburgh: Edinburgh University Press.

Minogue, Kenneth, and Biddis, Michael (1987), *Thatcherism*, Basingstoke: Macmillan.

Moran, Michael (1985), *Politics and Society in Britain*, Basingstoke: Macmillan.

—— (1989), *Politics and Society in Britain*, 2nd edn., Basingstoke: Macmillan.

Morris, Rupert (1991), *Tories*, Edinburgh: Mainstream.

Mueller, Denis C. (1989), *Public Choice II*, Cambridge: Cambridge University Press.

Muller, Edward N. (1979), *Aggressive Political Participation*, Princeton, NJ: Princeton University Press.

—— and Opp, Karl-Dieter (1986), 'Rational Choice and Rebellious Collective Action', *American Political Science Review*, 80: 471–89.

MULLER, EDWARD N., and OPP, KARL-DIETER (1987), 'Rebellious Political Action Revisited', *American Political Science Review*, 81: 561–4.

—— DIETZ, HENRY A., and FINKEL, STEPHEN E. (1991), 'Discontent and the Expected Utility of Rebellion: The Case of Peru', *American Political Science Review*, 85: 1261–82.

NIEMI, RICHARD G. (1976), 'Costs of Voting and Non-Voting', *Public Choice*, 27: 115–19.

NORRIS, PIPPA, and LOVENDUSKI, JONI (1992), 'If Only More Candidates Came Forward: Supply-Side Explanations of Political Representation in Britain', Paper presented to the American Political Science Association, Chicago.

NORTON, PHILIP (1978), *Conservative Dissidents*, London: Temple Smith.

—— (1990), ' "The Lady's Not for Turning" but What about the Rest? Margaret Thatcher and the Conservative Party 1979–89', *Parliamentary Affairs*, 43: 41–58.

—— (1992), 'The Conservative Party from Thatcher to Major', in Anthony King (ed.), *Britain at the Polls*, Chatham, NJ: Chatham House, 29–62.

—— and ARTHUR AUGHEY (1981), *Conservatives and Conservatism*, London: Temple Smith.

OLSON, MANCUR (1965), *The Logic of Collective Action*. New York: Schocken Books.

OPP, KARL-DIETER (1990), 'Postmaterialism, Collective Action, and Political Protest', *American Journal of Political Science*, 34: 212–35.

PANEBIANCO, ANGELO (1988), *Political Parties: Organization and Power*, Cambridge: Cambridge University Press.

PARKIN, FRANK (1967), 'Working Class Conservatives: A Theory of Political Deviance', *British Journal of Sociology*, 18: 278–90.

PARRY, GERAINT, MOYSER, GEORGE, and DAY, NEIL (1992), *Political Participation and Democracy in Britain*, Cambridge: Cambridge University Press.

PATTERSON, SAMUEL C., and CALDEIRA, GREGORY (1984), 'The Etiology of Partisan Competition', *American Political Science Review*, 78: 691–707.

PATTIE, CHARLES, WHITELEY, PAUL F., JOHNSTON, RON, and SEYD, PATRICK (1994), 'Measuring Local Campaign Effects: Labour Party Constituency Campaigning at the 1987 General Election', *Political Studies*, 42: (forthcoming).

PELLING, HENRY (1961), *New Statesman*, 7, 21 July.

PIMLOTT, BEN (1972), 'Does Local Party Organization Matter?', *British Journal of Political Science*, 2: 381–3.

—— (1973), 'Local Party Organization, Turnout, and Marginality', *British Journal of Political Science*, 3: 252–5.

PINDYCK, ROBERT S., and RUBINFELD, DANIEL (1991), *Econometric Models and Economic Forecasts*, New York: McGraw-Hill.

PINTO-DUSCHINSKY, MICHAEL (1981), *British Political Finance 1830–1980*, Washington, DC: American Enterprise Institute.

POMPER, GERALD, MOAKLEY, MAUREEN, and FORTH, R. (1980), 'The Conditions of Political Parties: Testing Organizational Conditions of Political Party Success', Paper presented at the annual meeting of the American Political Science Association.

PUTNAM, ROBERT (1993), *Making Democracy Work*, Princeton, NJ: Princeton University Press.

RAMSDEN, JOHN (1978), *A History of the Conservative Party: The Age of Balfour and Baldwin 1902–1940*, London: Longman.

RANNEY, AUSTIN (1965), *Pathways to Parliament*, London: Macmillan.

REIF, KARLHEINZ, CAYROL, ROLAND, and NIEDERMAYER, OSKAR (1980), 'National Political Parties: Middle Level Elites and European Integration', *European Journal of Political Research*, 8: 91–112.

RHODES JAMES, ROBERT (1970), *Churchill: A Study in Failure, 1900–1939*, London: Weidenfeld and Nicolson.

RHODES, R. A. W. (1992), 'Local Government Finance', in David Marsh and R. A. W. Rhodes (eds.), *Implementing Thatcherite Policies*, Buckingham: Open University Press, 50–64.

RIDDELL, PETER (1985), *The Thatcher Government*, Oxford: Blackwell.

—— (1989), *The Thatcher Decade*, Oxford: Blackwell.

RIKER, WILLIAM, and ORDESHOOK, PETER (1968), 'A Theory of the Calculus of Voting', *American Political Science Review*, 62: 25–42.

ROSE, RICHARD (1964), 'Parties, Factions and Tendencies in Britain', *Political Studies*, 12: 33–46.

—— (1976), *The Problem of Party Government*, Harmondsworth: Penguin.

—— and MCALLISTER, IAN (1990), *The Loyalties of Voters*, London: Sage.

SAMUELSON, PAUL (1954), 'The Pure Theory of Public Expenditure', *Review of Economics and Statistics*, 36: 387–9.

SARLVIK, BO, and CREWE, IVOR (1983), *Decade of Dealignment*, Cambridge: Cambridge University Press.

SCARROW, SUSAN (1990), 'The Decline of Party Organization? Mass Membership Parties in Great Britain and West Germany', Paper presented to the American Political Science Association, San Francisco.

SEYD, PATRICK (1975), 'Democracy within the Conservative Party', *Government and Opposition*, 10: 219–37.

—— and WHITELEY, PAUL F. (1992), *Labour's Grass Roots: The Politics of Party Membership*, Oxford: Clarendon Press.

SEYMOUR-URE, COLIN (1974), *The Political Impact of Mass Media*, London: Constable.

SKIDELSKY, ROBERT (1988) (ed.), *Thatcherism*, London: Chatto and Windus.

SMITH, STEVE (1990), 'Foreign and Defence Policy', in Patrick Dunleavy,

290   *References*

Andrew Gamble, and Gillian Peele (eds.), *Developments in British Politics*, iii, New York: St Martin's Press, 246–68.

STEWART, J., and STOKER, G. (1989), *The Future of Local Government*, London: Macmillan.

SWADDLE, KEVIN, and HEATH, ANTHONY (1989), 'Official and Reported Turnout in the British General Election of 1987', *British Journal of Political Science*, 19: 537–50.

TAYLOR, MICHAEL (1976), *Anarchy and Co-operation*, London: Wiley.

TETHER, PHILIP (1991), 'Recruiting Conservative Party Members', *Parliamentary Affairs*, 44/1: 20–32.

TRUMAN, DAVID B. (1951), *The Governmental Process: Political Interests and Public Opinion*, New York: Knopf.

TULLOCH, GORDON (1971), 'The Paradox of Revolution', *Public Choice*, 11: 89–99.

VERBA, SIDNEY, and NIE, NORMAN (1972), *Participation in America: Political Democracy and Social Equality*, New York: Harper and Row.

—— —— and KIM, JAE-ON (1978), *Participation and Political Equality: A Seven Nation Comparison*, Cambridge: Cambridge University Press.

VON BEYME, KLAUS (1985), *Political Parties in Western Democracies*, Aldershot: Gower.

WEALE, ALBERT (1990), 'Social Policy', in Patrick Dunleavy, Andrew Gamble, and Gillian Peele (eds.), *Developments in British Politics*, iii, New York: St Martin's Press, 197–217.

WHITELEY, PAUL F., and SEYD, PATRICK (1992), 'The Labour Vote and Local Activism: The Impact of Local Constituency Campaigns', *Parliamentary Affairs*, 45: 582–95.

—— —— (1994), 'Local Party Campaigning and Electoral Mobilization in Britain', *Journal of Politics*, 56/1: 242–52.

WILSON, M. (1977), 'Grass Roots Conservatism: Motions to the Party Conference', in N. Nugent and R. King (eds.), *The British Right*, Farnborough: Saxon House, 64–98.

WISTOW, GERALD (1992), 'The National Health Service', in David Marsh and R. A. W. Rhodes (eds.), *Implementing Thatcherite Policies*, Buckingham: Open University Press, 100–16.

YOUNG, HUGO (1987), *The Guardian*, 6 Oct.

—— (1989), *One of Us*, London: Macmillan.

INDEX

Index compiled by Ann Barham

TIMBERFRAME

The Art and Craft of the Post-and-Beam Home

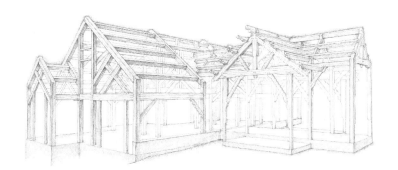

TIMBERFRAME

The Art and Craft of the Post-and-Beam Home

TEDD BENSON

Foreword by Norm Abram

The Taunton Press

Publisher
Jim Childs

Acquisitions Editor
Steve Culpepper

Editorial Assistant
Carol Kasper

Copy Editor
Peter Chapman

Jacket and Interior Design
Carol Singer

Photographer (except where noted)
James R. Salomon

Illustrator
Kathy Bray

The Taunton Press
Inspiration for hands-on living™

Printed in the United States of America
10 9 8 7 6 5 4 3 2 1

Timberframe was originally published in hardcover in 1999 by The Taunton Press, Inc.

The Taunton Press, 63 South Main Street, PO Box 5506, Newtown, CT 06470-5506
e-mail: tp@taunton.com

Distributed by Publishers Group West

FRONTISPIECE PHOTO
Tedd Benson

DEDICATION PHOTO
Bill Holtz

Library of Congress Cataloging-in Publication Data

Benson, Tedd.
    Timberframe : the art and craft of the post-and-beam
home / Tedd Benson; foreword by Norm Abram.
      p. cm.
   ISBN 1-56158-281-6 (hardcover)
   ISBN 1-56158-608-0 (paperback)
   1. Wooden-frame houses—Design and construction.   I. Title.
TH4818.W6B46523   2001
728'.37—dc21
                                          99-31212
                                           CIP

In memory of my father,
Ted M. Benson
(1910–1997)

Contents

Foreword 2
NORM ABRAM

*Prologue: The Art and Craft
of the Timberframe* 4

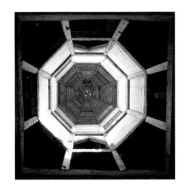

Ah, to build, to build! That is the noblest of all the arts.

—Henry Wadsworth Longfellow

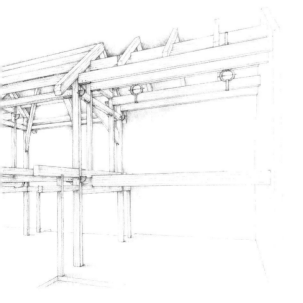

Foreword

Nothing in homebuilding is more dramatic than raising a timberframe. I've watched Tedd Benson oversee the process done the old-fashioned way with lots of people pulling on ropes and pushing with poles as a timberframe that had been assembled on the deck was raised into place section by section, and fastened with joints cut into the wood.

When Tedd and a crew from his shop in New Hampshire erected the timberframe of the ell in my own new house almost five years ago, however, the process didn't look very much like the Amish do it. True, Tedd's crew of five, joined by two carpenters I brought along to assist us, completed the structure in one day. But there were no ropes to be pulled, no crowd watching. The frame was literally more lowered than raised, as a large portable crane lifted great trusses and other members of the frame from a huge logging truck, swung them through the cold November air, and lowered them gently into place. The trusses looked like huge birds gliding through space toward a landing. I still have a photograph of Kurt Doolittle, the lead framer for the project, balancing on one leg on the ridge beam, arms extended like a gymnast, a happy grin plastered on his face.

The frame itself was a fascinating medley of things old and new. The concept of the frame and the nature of the joinery were old. Dimitri Gerakaris had heated the metal for the stirrup braces holding the bottom chords to the king posts on a traditional coal-fired forge and shaped them by hand on an anvil with a 1916-vintage power hammer, but if the job had called for it, he would have cut steel with a plasma cutter. The computer engineering used to design the frame and calculate its weightbearing capacity was new, as were the power tools used to shape and finish the various members and the high-tech glues used to bond the laminated layers of the bottom chords together.

I had selected a truss design in which the horizontal member is slightly arched. The best way to make such an arch is to cut a large beam (Sitka spruce in this case) lengthwise into inch-thick slices, slather epoxy on all the surfaces to be laminated, and then clamp the laminated chord against a curved form until the epoxy is fully set. The spruce was springy enough in its thin slices that it didn't need to be steamed to be flexible enough to bend to the form. Tedd invited me to help laminate one of the bottom chords, so I drove up to New Hampshire just before Halloween that year and joined the crew. I've done a lot of gluing and clamping in my woodworking, but nothing on that scale before!

Almost all of the framing I've done myself has been the construction of skeletons that, however well crafted, were destined to be covered over with exterior siding and roofing and interior finishes. But timberframes are those wonderful exceptions in which the frame is meant to be seen and admired as a finished surface and an architectural element.

In the five years that the timberframe ell has sheltered the open kitchen, family room, and family dining room in my house, the Sitka spruce of the trusses and the Port Orford cedar of the posts and plate beams have darkened slightly under their citrus-based oil finish to a honey brown. The oak pegs and cherry splines make a pleasing variation of color in the woods. The joinery fully deserves the accolade the designer, Bill Holtz, gave it: "a celebration." I gravitate to that part of the house whenever I can because I take so much pleasure in studying the frame. I look at its sturdiness and know it will be standing for many decades, maybe a century or two. In our part of the country, that's what one wants in a home: a sense of durability.

Norm Abram
Boston, Massachusetts
May, 1999

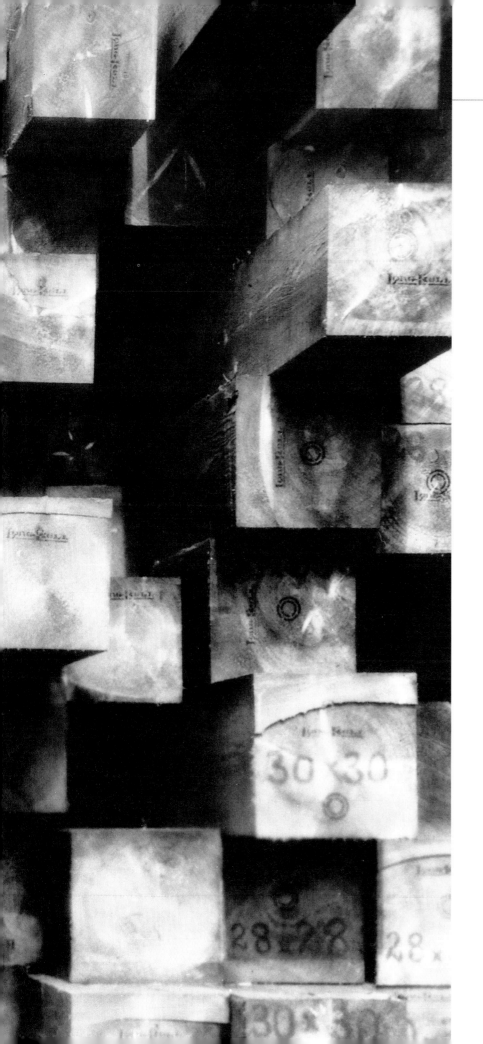

Prologue:
The Art and Craft
of the Timberframe

The strength of a nation

is derived from the

integrity of its homes.

—Confucius

left The Long-Bell mill produced these incredible lumber cants
in the early 1900s, but it was the salvaged timbers
from the dismantled mill itself that contributed to many
modern timberframe homes.

Today's timberframe homes are historical and contemporary, relevant and vigorous. Flexible in design and inherently beautiful, they give evidence to the fact that the centuries-old craft of timberframing has returned as a practical and environmentally sensitive building technique.

The timberframe renaissance in North America began with a small group of New England craftsmen in the early 1970s and spread rapidly throughout the continent. Today, timberframing is practiced in nearly every part of North America, and there are hundreds of professional companies making thousands of homes annually. It has been a fortuitous confluence of awakened desires: builders who want work that is more interesting, challenging, and rewarding and owners who aspire to have homes that truly enrich their lives through the structure's art and craft.

A modern timberframe is like a large piece of furniture, intended to be both visible and appreciated. One of the most appealing aspects of the modern timberframe home is the quality and variety of its spaces. Because all of the space within is opened to the living area, timberframes tend to provide more volume per square foot, which makes small spaces feel larger and large spaces more dramatic.

Timberframe homes easily adapt to different regional requirements, climates, and architectural influences. Unlike log buildings, timberframe homes don't all look alike. From coast to coast, from mountains to lakes to prairies, regional and stylistic differences are clear. Timberframing does not dictate the building shape or design and imposes no limitations regarding exterior finishes. Timberframing can be used to build a shingle-style seaside retreat or a rugged stone-and-wood, high-mountain lodge. The design style can be elaborate and formal or simple and rustic. What is constant is the crafted integrity of the timberframe.

While the exterior can be designed to fit public requirements or expectations, the interior is always a unique and personalized work of art. Interior spaces can be open, airy, and light-filled or cozy interior chambers made more comfortable by the warmth of the timbers. The timbers themselves can be highly polished or

The Guildhall of Corpus Christi in Lavenham, England, was built in 1520. Some of the most sophisticated timberframes of all time were produced during this era.

Salvaged fir timbers join to a huge cedar log in a recently built timberframe home.

left with a rough-textured, natural finish. With timberframing, there is always a rich palette of design and decoration possibilities, depending on the finishes, the species, and the sculptural arrangement of the framework.

Like the frame itself, today's timberframe home encompasses influences from around the world. You won't see reproductions of homes from Japan, Germany, or England in this book, but you will see the clear influence of these international forms. For the most part, however, the homes featured here evolved most directly from the English medieval building form. This is the dominant tradition in North American timberframe design, and you'll see the "great hall" look—in a variety of styles, shapes, and finishes—repeated throughout.

But the timberframe halls of today are far from medieval. Besides their extremely effective insulation, the biggest difference is light. Unlike other forms of residential construction, timberframing

automatically provides openings between the widely spaced posts and beams that make the installation of doors, windows, or fixed glass a simple proposition. In timberframe building, the spaces between the timbers are literally framed openings, which can be used in a variety of ways without compromising the strength of the structure.

Timberframe homes are sustainable. They use forest resources wisely. In fact, most of the timberframes featured here were built with timbers salvaged from dismantled buildings, and all have the potential to last 300 to 600 years, or the time it takes trees to reach full maturity. Timberframe structures survive because of their rugged strength, but also because the frames are open skeletons that allow extensive flexibility and long-term adaptability. Additionally, because the timberframe is separated from its insulating skin, timberframe homes are among the most energy-efficient available. For these reasons and more, though it is an ancient building form, timberframing is now thoroughly progressive and has carved a solid niche in mainstream home-building.

A LOOK BACK

Timberframing is as old as our concept of home. A self-supporting framework of timbers fastened with wooden connections, timberframing began with the first mortise-and-tenon joint, somewhere between 500 B.C. and 200 B.C. Shaping and joining timbers proved to be a building system so primal and basic that it found its way into forest cultures all around the world.

These 17th-century German buildings show characteristics of style and technique that are similar to timberframes in the rest of Europe and the Far East at the same period. (PHOTO BY TEDD BENSON)

In the earliest days, posts for the structures were driven into the ground, where they quickly rotted. So, bringing the timber structure entirely above ground was a huge innovation, which was achieved in several parts of the world at about the same time. With this advance, timberframe buildings could survive for generations. The frames also became more sophisticated because all of its strength was derived from the network of timbers and joinery rather than from the in-ground anchoring. These realities accelerated the development of timberframing, and it came to a full flowering by the end of the Middle Ages. From the 15th through the 18th centuries, timberframing was the dominant wood frame building method in much of the world. As evidence, there are thousands of magnificent timberframe buildings—houses, barns, temples, churches, and public halls—that survive from that period.

As good-quality buildings became more available to the general populace, the buildings became less elaborate and the frames more utilitarian. Over time, the timbers were less often fully revealed to the interior and the timberframe, while still the preferred method of building, lost its decorative value as the posts and beams became encased in plaster and other

In this 15th-century Japanese building, the open timber hall allows smoke from an open fire to escape through vents in the roof. (PHOTO BY TEDD BENSON)

The simple and elegant beauty of Japanese architecture influenced the Arts and Crafts movement and modern North American timberframe design and construction.

(PHOTO BY TEDD BENSON)

finish materials. Japan is one of the few places where the appreciation for the beauty of the exposed timbers was never lost.

In North America, timberframing fell out of use in the second half of the 19th century in favor of stud framing, which allowed quicker construction using less-skilled labor. The transition was so rapid that by the 1920s timberframing was a forgotten craft in this part of the world. But North America is unique in this regard. Most of the world stuck with timberframing and still uses it today. Stud framing, now known as "platform framing," has only recently made inroads into Europe and Japan.

THE TIMBERFRAME REVIVAL

Despite the long hiatus in the North American construction environment, the quality of the modern era timberframe is consistently excellent. Because of the passion and perseverance of the many men and women of the timberframe industry, the revival has been swift and the standards set high.

The contemporary timberframe renaissance has much in common with the turn-of-the-century Arts and Crafts movement. In both eras, there is a celebration of craft in basic building materials and an emphasis on honesty in material function and architectural design. There is also a tendency to avoid unnecessary ornamentation and design affectation in favor of the practical and simple.

The Arts and Crafts movement was first inspired by the architecture and craftsmanship of the English Middle Ages, which was a premier timberframe building culture, and later was greatly influenced by the Japanese style, another timberframe culture. These two influences are also probably the most significant in timberframe design and craftsmanship today.

Timberframe buildings are durable, and the timbers are reusable. This 16th-century Japanese building was dismantled and re-erected.

(PHOTO BY TEDD BENSON)

There is no doubt about the durability of timberframe buildings. On the eastern side of North America, thousands of timberframe houses, barns, churches, and town halls are still in use after 250 to 350 years. But in Europe and the Far East, 500- to 600-year-old buildings are common. Many are older.

This recently built southwest Colorado timberframe was constructed primarily with timbers from dismantled mill buildings.

Even when the useful life of a timberframe building is over, it is still possible to salvage and reuse the timbers. In timberframing, the very best material available is often that which can be salvaged from old timber buildings. Using recycled timbers has the inherent benefit of preserving living trees, but the wood is also generally better than that cut from the faster-growing trees of today.

Most of the timberframe homes featured in this book were built with timbers salvaged from other timber structures. And when these houses are dismantled—hopefully at least 500 years in the future—there is no reason the same timbers can't be used again. This unique attribute is satisfying to the owners' ecological conscience, while it also gives the homes added character and an interesting history from the outset.

Whether from old factories, defunct mill buildings, or old barns, the beauty of the wood is enhanced by its history. In this book, some of these histories derive from a Great Salt Lake railroad trestle, a Royal typewriter factory, a Vlasic Pickle factory, an old Massachusetts bridge, and 200-year-old barns. In at least one case, the recycled timbers were from a 19th-century structure that had recycled some of its timbers from an even earlier building.

LONG-BELL'S GIFT

One particular recycling story deserves to be told in full. Nearly two-thirds of the timberframe homes presented in this book share a unique history: Many or all of the timbers in their frames were salvaged from the demolition of a single facility—the Long-Bell Lumber mill complex in Longview, Washington.

In 1918, Robert A. Long, President of the Long-Bell Lumber Company, had a problem: His southern timber holdings were nearly depleted. He would

Located in farm country north of Baltimore, this home's timberframe was built with Douglas fir timbers salvaged from the demolition of the Long-Bell mill buildings in Longview, Washington.

Southern pine timbers salvaged from mill buildings and factories on the East Coast live on in this Nebraska home.

When the Long-Bell mill buildings were built, they were harvesting timbers from the virgin forests in the Longview, Washington, area. Wood from those magnificent trees was also used to build the huge industrial facility. (LONGVIEW PUBLIC LIBRARY, LONGVIEW ROOM COLLECTION)

either have to liquidate his sizeable logging operations and concentrate on his line of hardware stores and retail lumberyards or find another source of timber. Less than a year later, Long and a small crew went on a horseback exploration of the virgin forests in the foothills of the Cascade Mountains in southwestern Washington (where it is estimated that the trees averaged 9 ft. in diameter and 150 ft. in height!).

What Long saw on that expedition must have been breathtaking, even for a man who had spent a lifetime logging the ancient forests. These forests inspired a massive plan that included the design and construction of a city to house the people who would cut the forest down. In the next few years, the Long-

Bell Lumber Company purchased 70,000 acres that contained approximately 3.8 billion board feet of virgin northwestern timber.

As Long's plans for his new Long-Bell mill grew, it became apparent that he would need more than 14,000 workers at the site. He realized it would take a mighty appealing hook to bring that many people to the yet-unsettled outpost. So he hired George Kessler, who was already known for his plans of Kansas City, Dallas, Oklahoma City, Mexico City and the 1904 St. Louis Exposition, to help design a city for 50,000.

Construction of the mill complex and the town began in 1922 and was substantially completed in four to five years. The mill itself was in production by 1924, but didn't reach full capacity until 1926. The first wood to be gleaned from the mammoth trees was used for town and mill buildings. No mill like Long-Bell had ever before been constructed. It wasn't so much different from other Northwest mills, simply bigger, more mechanized, and better planned to produce lumber in vast quantities. It had 30 mill buildings that averaged 700 ft. in length, with some well over 1,000 ft.

In full production, Long-Bell was milling 2 million board feet of lumber a day, making it, briefly, the largest lumber producer in the nation. But in 1927, a decline in construction activity was making it more difficult for Long to sell his lumber. Capital assets had to be sold to keep the company alive. To make matters much worse, the market crash of 1929 brought the economy to a halt. Somehow, Long-Bell limped along until the war effort required increased production and the postwar housing boom further

To maximize production, the Long-Bell mill was huge, with 72 acres of building under roof. Many individual sawmills operated simultaneously, and for a time it had the greatest output of any mill in the world.

(PHOTO COURTESY LONGVIEW PUBLIC LIBRARY, LONGVIEW ROOM COLLECTION)

As Long-Bell is dismantled, the immense size of the individual buildings is revealed. The mill's sad story became a boon to many timberframe homeowners.

(PHOTO BY TEDD BENSON)

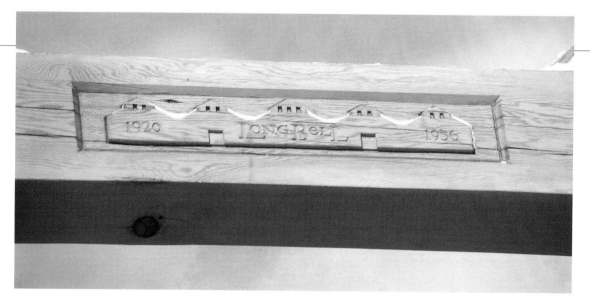

In homage to the Long-Bell mill, a relief of some of its buildings was carved into one of the timbers for a central Colorado home.

(PHOTO BY BILL HOLTZ)

revived the mill for a few years. But it was too little, too late. In 1956, the mills fell silent. New sawmill technology had made the whole Long-Bell facility and its equipment obsolete.

The Long-Bell mill buildings had been entirely constructed with large, old-growth timbers. In the years when they were built, clear, straight-grained fir flowed like manna from the ancient forests. When it was determined that the buildings would be dismantled, word quickly spread among timberframers, who knew that wood of that size and quality might never be seen again. But when the bids for the salvage rights began climbing, the timberframers began to wonder who else could want dirty, old timbers more than they would. (Bill Gates, for one, who wanted Long-Bell timbers for his home compound in Seattle.) It was estimated that more than 7 million board feet of timbers would be salvaged from the many buildings scheduled for dismantling, so any serious bidder would need deep pockets. It wasn't long before the prices escalated beyond the meager means of the average timberframer.

Still, Bill Gates couldn't use it all. So, over the next few years about 5 million board feet became available to timberframers around the country. It should therefore not be surprising that this magnifi-cent wood made its way into quite a few of the homes featured in this book.

INTO THE FUTURE

I hope that someday in the far distant future (say around the turn of the 26th century) people will tell stories about some of the homes in this book. They would admire their durability and beauty (enhanced with age), and there would be much to say about their history. It is my dream that the houses would have survived both because they are inherently durable and because the occupants thought them worthy of maintenance and preservation. It is also my dream that at that future time they won't be historical relics but rather would have adapted to the needs of the inhabitants and the technology and style of the time.

Some of the buildings would perhaps no longer be homes, and that would be fine. For those that don't survive intact, it is realistic to think that their frames will be dismantled and re-erected or that the individual timbers will be used again. I don't believe we'll have to wait long before it is well understood that timbers such as you see in this book are precious. And when they move on to new buildings, they will come with stories, including the one from Long-Bell.

This central Montana timberframe was built entirely with timbers from the Long-Bell facility. There's every reason to believe that the building will last for hundreds of years, but if it must come down, its timbers can be used again. (PHOTO BY TEDD BENSON)

In

Architecture is the handwriting of man.... When you enter his domain you know his dreams.
—Bernard Maybeck, architect

the Country

Whether people are fully conscious of this or not, they...derive countenance and sustenance from the "atmosphere" of the things they live in or with.
—Frank Lloyd Wright

Prairie Prospect

"The home you design for us will be our dream home, the one in which we raise our children, celebrate holidays, and grow old." So said the owners in a questionnaire submitted early in the design process. The designers took the message to have a wider meaning: That home design is not really about physical matter—the concrete, bricks, stone, and wood—but about the people who

will inhabit the home, how it functions for them, and how it might enrich their lives. Designing homes to reach this higher goal requires humility and listening skills.

The building sits on a windswept grassy slope with beautiful views in three directions. The owners felt that a horizontal, multilevel, cantilever-roofed Prairie-style home would fit nicely into the surroundings.

A confluence of connections is both an engineering event and a sculpture. Diagonal struts deliver building loads to this interior post on each of its four faces, while the laminated arch is connected with a complex joint at the post corner. A cherry spline provides additional joint strength.

left Celebrating the horizon views, grand space, and light, this room reflects the "big sky" landscape themes of central Nebraska. If the wall color seems bold, it is but a pale imitation of the stunning sunsets that inspired its hue.

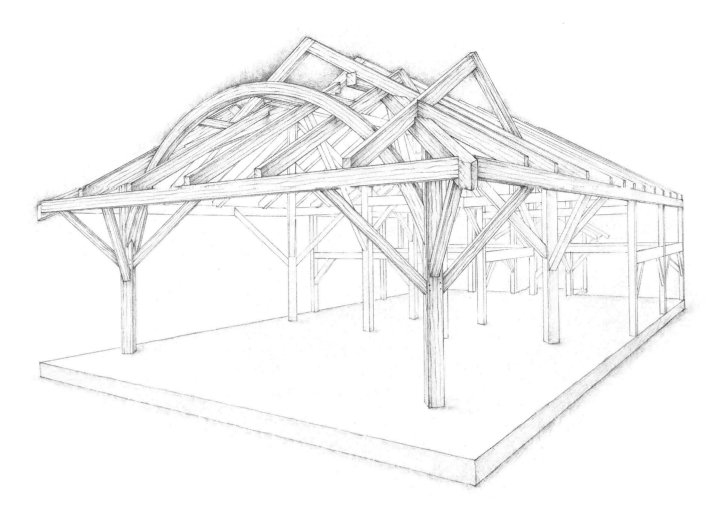

size
3,200 sq. ft.

completed
1997

location
Central Nebraska

The owners wanted a home that
was a celebration of the timberframe
space. "One of the many reasons
we like timberframed homes is the
expansive arched ceilings where you
can admire the wood and joinery."
The frame mixes salvaged Douglas
fir from a western mill, salvaged
southern yellow pine from an eastern
bridge, and new eastern white pine.
A laminated pine beam frames the
eyebrow dormer. In the great room,
all exterior wall loads are directed
toward interior posts through
diagonal struts.

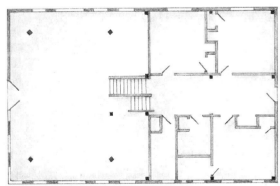

In the kitchen, a commercial stove, laboratory countertops, brushed stainless-steel hardware, and salvaged industrial lights were chosen for utility and durability, not for "show"—utility and durability *are* the show in this house.

below Industrial details give the house a feeling of spare functionality. Stainless-steel cables, steel grating, and painted steel combined with cherry form the stair. Red oak Mission-style cabinets define and separate the kitchen but also, because they are built to furniture standards, are in keeping with the rest of the great-room spaces.

Directly inside the front entry, the first glimpse of the house gives evidence of the grand spaces and the interplay of steel and wood.

below A third-floor loft is actually a "monitor," which rises above the timberframed roof. The loft serves several purposes. In the heat of summer, it ventilates the building, aiding draft and exhausting heat. Year round, it provides extra sleeping space or a quiet place to read.

As a way of expressing to the designers their own passion for the Prairie landscape, the owners quoted Willa Cather, from *O Pioneers!* "For the first time…a human face was set toward [the land] with love and yearning. It seemed beautiful to her, rich and strong and glorious. Her eyes drank in the breadth of it, until her tears blinded her." The house had to rise from the land and connect the owners to it.

One of the most prominent features of the Nebraska landscape is the wide-open sky with views from one horizon to the next. The owners wanted to incorporate as much of this sky as possible into their home. A low band of windows, including corner windows, opens the house to the horizons, while the higher windows reveal the changing sky and allow light to penetrate deep into the space.

Home Spirit

It isn't always possible to capture the true essence of a home with photography. For the owners of this house, the real "spirit of the house" has to do with the many things that have happened there. Their children grew up in the house, which has been the setting for countless gatherings, celebrations, and all the joys and sorrows that make up family life. "The timberframe spaces are

When you spend your days working in the nation's capital, the ideal home is a refuge of authenticity and integrity. Hidden in a deep, old forest of beech and oak, this home, like its occupants, exudes honest values.

'people friendly' and wonderfully comforting," said one of the owners, as if speaking of another member of the family. Many of a home's most important attributes accrue over time through the lives of its inhabitants.

"There isn't a warmer house in northern Virginia," said one of the owners, referring to the quality of light. She attributes the cast of light to the tone and texture of the impeccable Douglas fir in the frame.

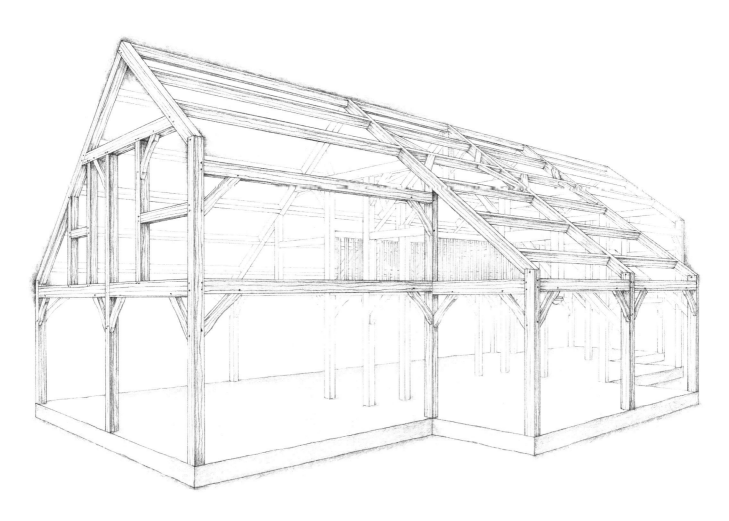

size
2,500 sq. ft.

completed
1987

location
Northeast Virginia

Arching over the bridge and the stairway in the great room is a hammerbeam truss. An ingenious structural device used to span large spaces, it transfers roof loads through post and beam brackets to the outer walls. The hammer-beam concept was developed during the Middle Ages by timberframers who were, by all evidence, the best of all time.

left The owners spend most of their time in this part of the house. The dining and kitchen areas are open to each other in a traditional country-kitchen arrangement. Because most families tend to congregate where food is prepared and eaten, dining is often the only time when the whole family is together in the course of a day. The open kitchen is the hearth of our times and should be designed to be special, spacious, and comfortable.

below A peaceful, light-filled solarium off the front entry is one of those special places that beckons use and is easily changed to suit. It is variously the family game center, a second dining area, a tea-room, and a private reading nook.

The bridge is real. It passes under the central hammer-beam truss and spans between second-floor bedrooms, which are separated by the two timber bays of the great room. Oversize handrails are structural upper chords, tied to the lower chords through several balusters.

We have from the first planned houses that are based on the big fundamental principles of honesty, simplicity, and usefulness.
—Gustav Stickley

Craftsman's Way

Around the turn of the century, the Arts and Crafts movement—with its emphasis on hand craftsmanship and the simple display of natural materials—began to have a strong influence on American architecture. Its most recognized masters were the Greene brothers and Bernard Maybeck of California, but it was primarily popularized by Gustav Stickley. The timberframe revival, which began in the 1970s, springs from the same philosophical roots. In this Washington state home, the two strands merge in a wonderful display of their respective attributes.

A rail detail on the stair landing uses a joint common in Mission furniture (note the chair arms, facing page), which also arose from the Arts and Craft movement. Exposing joint elements and celebrating the beauty of wood is also a central theme of timberframing.

Deep overhangs and carved beam and rafter ends are typical Arts and Crafts details. The recessed window adds dimension to the lines of the otherwise basic building shape and gives emphasis to one of its simple, delightful features.

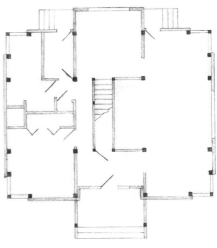

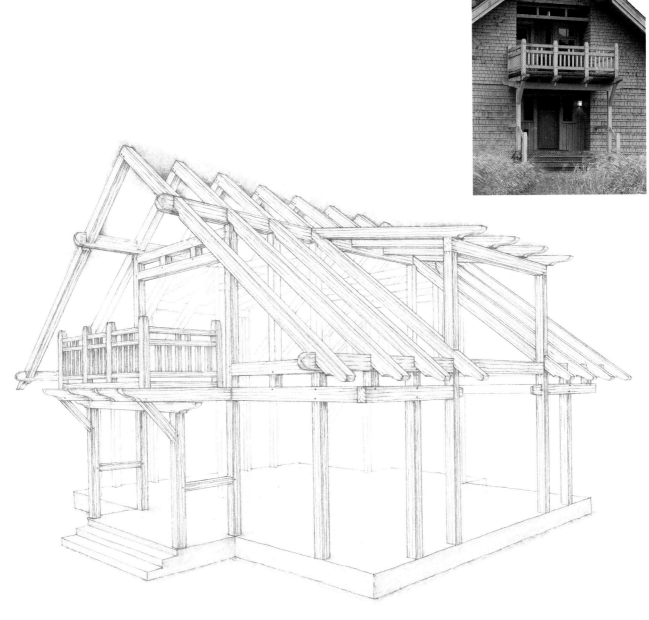

size
1,600 sq. ft.

completed
1994

location
Western Washington

Originating in Europe, the Arts and Crafts architectural style reveals the influence of the Swiss chalet, with its balconies and exposed timberframing in extended gable overhangs. Built with timber salvaged from the Long-Bell mill (see pp. 10-14), the frame has a sense of heritage in accord with the owner's collection of Mission furniture and handmade Arts and Crafts objects. Parallel beams were used on the exterior walls, substituting for typical diagonal bracing.

"We try to plan and build houses which will simplify the work of home life and add to its wholesome joy and comfort....We have paid particular attention to the convenient arrangement of the kitchen." (Gustav Stickley)

below As evidenced by this home's small size but expressive character, trading quantity of space for the best qualities of design, craftsmanship, and materials is a basic tenet of the Craftsman style.

left In the words of Gustav Stickley, "We like to have pleasant nooks and corners which give a comfortable sense of semi-privacy and yet are not in any way shut off from the larger life of the room." The doubled beams—or plates—above the windows provide the strength that allows each of the corners to be opened to a wrap-around window.

Have nothing in your home that
you do not know to be useful or believe to be beautiful.
—William Morris

England West

There was never any doubt about the architectural style. Although the house is located near Denver, it was to have a decidedly English country influence. One of the owners had spent some time in England and had become enthusiastic about the casual formality of this style. Also,

English immigrants heavily affected Colorado's Front Range architectural heritage, especially in the 40 years bridging the turn of the 20th century. So, the design was a fit both of taste and context. The interior takes on the feeling of a manor house and recalls the elaborate open halls that were common in the Middle Ages.

A poorly built, run-down bungalow was torn down to make room for the new house. Because the site contained mature landscaping, pains were taken during construction to preserve the setting. The covered entry is weather protection for visitors and for the cherry-wood entrance door.

Tall patio doors surround the dining room, giving it the feeling of a porch and connecting it to the terrace and the parklike landscaped acreage. The timbers are salvaged Douglas fir, recovered from the Long-Bell mill (see pp. 10-14). When the owners toured the timber yard to look at the various options, the mention of Long-Bell sparked a distant memory in one of the owners: Her grandfather had been the treasurer of the Long-Bell mills. The choice was made.

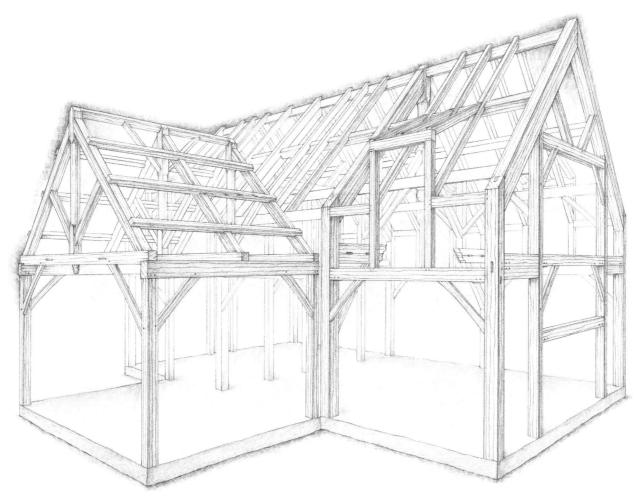

size
5,000 sq. ft.

completed
1993

location
Central Colorado

The house is specifically zoned. Private bedrooms and utility spaces are standard stud-frame, while the public spaces are timberframed. In this type of hybrid, it is important to keep the ties between the two framing types nonstructural, due to different patterns of settling. The principal-purlin and common rafter roof-framing configuration is common in traditional English-style construction. The frame is elaborated with chamfering, carved timber ends, and the use of cherry for joint details.

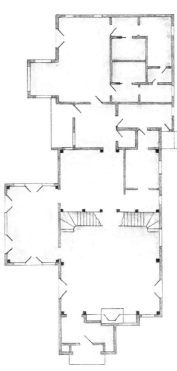

left The open-timber-roofed space is made up of three "bays," which are spaces between the structural cross sections, or "bents." Two bays form the vaulted great-room space, while the third bay is floored over to create a loft. The loft has two study nooks and serves as the home's library. It also provides passage to the second-floor bedrooms.

Although there is little head-room at the low side of the roof slope, no space is wasted. With a shed dormer to provide light, ventilation, and a spatial lift, the result is an intimate, inviting space, efficiently used.

A king post terminates many of the structural members in the center of the great room. The post features inset cherry panels and a carved pendant. Spaces on the top side of the central roof purlin and the ridge beam are used for indirect lighting.

Master woodworking skills were needed for the curved cornice-like treatment of this range hood. Diamond-shaped pegs are end-grain cherry. And what's the least expensive way to get a copper detail on the cabinet pulls? Polished pennies.

left For color and grain consistency, salvaged fir used for the kitchen-cabinet panels came from the same stock of wood as the timberframe. The cabinet drawer and door frames are cherry. Granite and copper complete the palette of materials. The kitchen is chock-full of custom design details for serious gourmet cooking.

The spiral stair is the main access to the upstairs bedrooms and to the recreation room on the ground floor. Looking from the master bedroom into the kitchen, it's evident that the private spaces are not timberframed.

below Primary exterior materials—limestone, brick, stucco, and slate—were chosen for low maintenance and longevity. The half-timber accents were gleaned from piles of wood salvaged from the original timber surfaces. Roofing is Vermont slate. The house is roughly halved, with the public timberframe spaces on the right and private bedrooms and bathrooms in the stud-framed part of the building on the left.

What constitutes charm to the eye of the old-fashioned country barn but its immense roof—a slope of gray shingle exposed to the weather like the side of a hill...
—John Burroughs, naturalist

Concord Barn

For several weeks in 1989, twenty million people watched a real drama unfold on PBS's *This Old House.* As the series opened, plans developed to renovate a Concord, Massachusetts, barn into a new home.

However, it was discovered that the apparently sound timbers had rotted out due to a leaking roof early in the barn's history. It was a major setback: The frame had to be razed and replaced. The Timber Framers Guild of North America was quickly enlisted to build a new timberframe, demonstrate the trade skills to the viewing audience, and still keep the show on schedule. It was a tall order but good TV.

The original barn was built in 1845—not so long ago by timberframe standards—but the roof was allowed to leak for many years, which rotted the timbers and led to its razing.

Engineer Ben Brungraber sifted through the rubble of the razed barn to find any remaining structurally sound timbers. He found only a few diagonal braces, which became a vital link to the barn's history and so were used in the main living area.

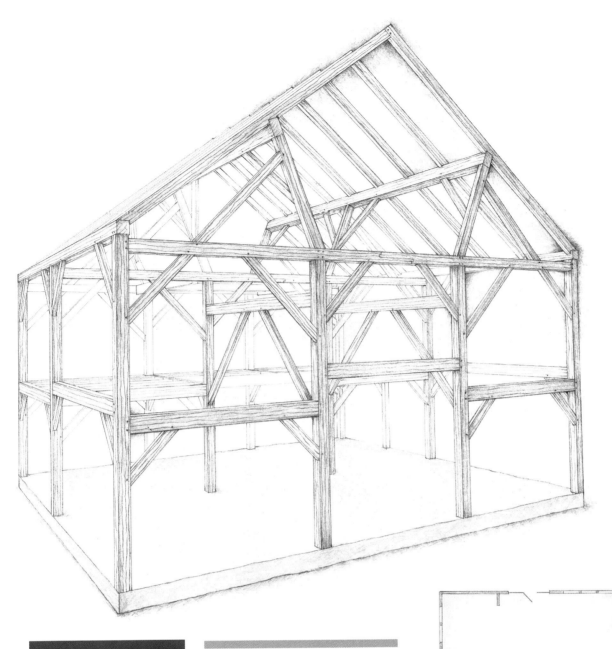

size
3,000 sq. ft.

completed
1989

location
Eastern Massachusetts

The shape of the new barn and the arrangement of timbers closely followed the original. Canted purlins with common rafters are typical of Early American barn framing. The entire frame was built by a class of 35 students, overseen by 6 professionals and aided by 30 volunteers. Making such a complex frame so quickly was an enormous feat.

below Except for the plates on which the rafters sit and a few salvaged knee braces, the timberframe is built with eastern white pine. Steel stair railings are reminiscent of cow stalls and the building's agricultural roots.

Due to time and money constraints, only two timberframe bays were rebuilt. The third, containing kitchen and bedrooms, was built using structural insulated panels. A turned structural column also serves as a newel-post termination for the stair.

right Rustic sliding doors help maintain the barn's basic aesthetics, closing off a small, intimate study when privacy is desired. A barn is a barn, and less interior decorating is better. A hot water radiant-heating system is encased in lightweight concrete beneath the handmade clay-tile flooring.

The space within a building is the reality of that building.
—Frank Lloyd Wright

Vaulted Dwelling

This deceptively modest house was designed with minimal complexity, ornamentation, or architectural pretense. Its grand presentation was intended to be the interior, not the exterior. With their children grown, the owners wanted a single-floor living arrangement for themselves and ample room for visiting family and friends. The design takes advantage of the sloping site and places the secondary living areas on the ground floor. This decision saved money and allowed the owners to make the living level more dramatic, with open timber roofs throughout.

What's dramatic here is not the building, but the woodland setting. Located in the Greater Boston area, the natural beauty and privacy of the site are almost startling. The house is in thrall to its environment.

In timberframe design, the principal columns and beams of the frame naturally delineate and define the rooms. Here, the kitchen is separated from the dining area not by a wall but by structural members. Less is more. East-oriented roof windows allow the morning sun into the kitchen area. A network of floor joists forms a trellised ceiling, which creates a sense of lower enclosure while still allowing the light to spill through from above.

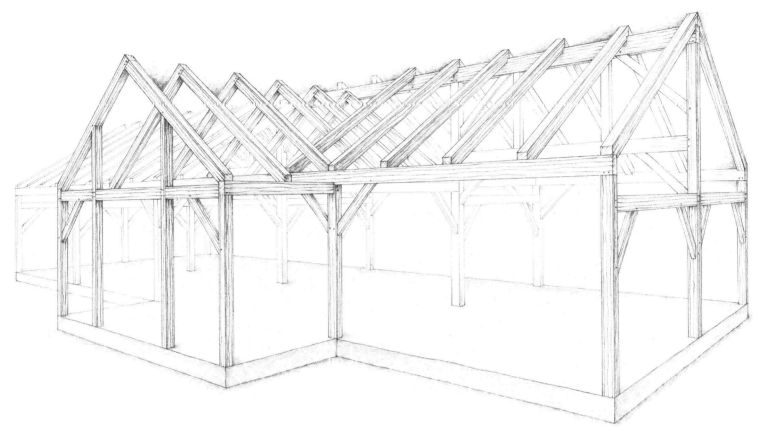

size
3,500 sq. ft.

completed
1994

location
Eastern Massachusetts

Resembling a Native American long house, the exterior simplicity of this building belies the intention and majesty of its interior. Salvage Douglas fir from a western mill building was used for the frame. Three 65-ft. timbers used as outside plates and ridge beam define the building's longitudinal orientation, and woven rafters are a feature at the cross-gable.

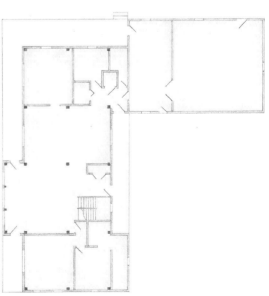

below Where gables cross, rafters interweave, and the sense of tension between the opposing gables is enhanced. The masonry chimney falls outside the structure of the living room, which helps maintain the unbroken space.

From the kitchen, the top of the living room "roof" is visible, which suggests an additional building form within the larger building and further defines the living area. The last pair of rafters are actually braces projecting from the central wall posts to the ridge.

Wood, stone, and tile are basic building materials and almost always work well together. Cherry is used here for the cabinets. Its reddish tones and natural elegance mate well with the other materials, especially the fir, which is complementary but has a rustic appearance.

A subtle alcove gives a little more room for the bed, while also creating a lighting soffit and breaking up a rather tall wall. The blackened notch in the post is a remnant of the timber's former life in the Long-Bell mill building.

*A striking building stands before us
as an individual every bit as soulful as we are.*
—Thomas Moore, author of *Care of the Soul*

Time Crafted

The 18th-century saltbox home needed no amendment. Its proportions were right, and its historical authenticity deserved preservation. Still, the owners required additional space if the property was to function well for their family. The wise solution was to build a complementary

new building rather than compromise the old one. What grew out of this decision is a traditional carriage-style barn that blends new and old. Amenities and functionality are modern, but the building features an old tower clock and 200-year-old reclaimed barn timbers.

Encircled with windows, the cupola is a kaleidoscope in wood: a play of symmetry, convergence, and light. And though its space is inaccessible for use, the barn and the living areas within seem bound to its axis.

If protected from decay, there's no reason the timbers should not last indefinitely. Most of the timbers in this frame are at least 200 years old and being put to use here for the second time. Remarkably, some of the timbers are clearly in their third structural use, having been salvaged from a previous building before being used for the barn that was dismantled to make this building. Old barn boards were used for the ceiling.

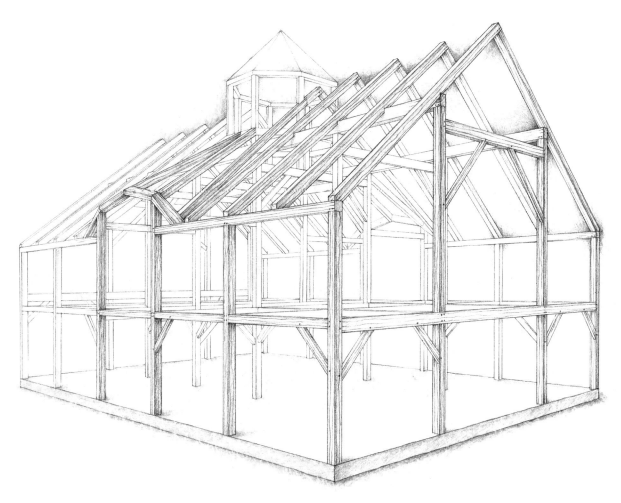

size
3,500 sq. ft.

completed
1997

location
Eastern Massachusetts

Salvaged timbers come from dilapidated barns with leaking roofs, failed foundations, or worse. Therefore, every timber has to be inspected for rot or structural defects. In addition, most barns were under-built by today's standards, making it difficult to find timbers of adequate size for some of the modern loads they must carry. The timbers for this frame were winnowed from the salvage piles of four barns.

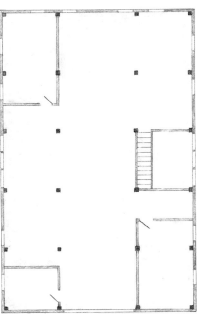

left Spline joinery and short sections of barn timbers were used to create the eyebrow lift to the roofline. Changing roof angles made the rafter-joint geometry complex. As is the case here, posts and beams, not walls, often define timberframe spaces.

right The cupola's spin of light and towering volume has a powerful effect on everything below.

below The barn—a short distance from the family's 18th-century home—is simply a detached addition. The lower level holds a three-car garage and a study, while the upper level has two guest bedrooms and a place for social gatherings and recreation. A natural oak log supports the post at the enclosed entry.

An 1870s tower clock is both whimsical and functional: The turning gears and oscillating pendulum provide fascination and inspire appreciation, while the 8-ft. translucent clock face is a primary source of daylight. Whitewashed boards reflect the natural light to brighten the space despite the predominance of darkly aged salvaged barn wood used for the roof boards and timbers.

With a turn of the eave and an oversize octagonal cupola topping the ridge, an otherwise simple structure of barn proportions appears much more complex, elegant, and sophisticated. But here function trumps ornamentation: These exterior features provide critical space and light to the interior.

The owners wanted two guest bedrooms, but closing them in was a problem. If their partitions extended to the roof, the great space of the barn's second floor would have been disrupted. The solution was to put the rooms at opposite corners for privacy and retain the open space.

A board meeting in the barn? Why not. The unusual, heavily chamfered hewn post in the foreground was discovered in the basement of a gristmill in East Berne, New York. Each timber brings its own unique history to this new building.

left A carved limestone fireplace, painted paneling, and leather furniture transform this corner of the barn into a baronial lounge. The deep, charcoal blue paint is particularly inspired, bringing more effect than color and recalling the feeling of pub more than parlor.

*How the eye loves a genuine thing;
how it delights in the nude beauty of the wood!*
—John Burroughs, naturalist

Horse Haven

In beautiful rolling hills north of Baltimore, horses reign. The land is given over to grazing pastures, riding rings, prim barns, and orderly white fences. It's a landscape of formal utility, a place that recalls its productive agricultural past and is still habit-bent to feed with its fertile soil. When the owners of this home and horse farm decided to build on a knoll overlooking their acreage, they knew they wanted to honor the area's traditional architecture by complement rather than reproduction. In the end, the design became a barn home overlooking pastureland.

A grand, open-timber-roofed great room looks in three directions. It has enchanting views, near, far, and inward. The big space is a solitary retreat or an accommodation for large gatherings.

Elegant timberframe engineering is revealed from this loft. Structural solutions in timberframe home building are also meant to be pleasing to the eye, even emotionally gratifying. Because most timberframe buildings are insulated with foam-core panels, the usual assumptions about heat layers in tall spaces such as this do not apply. In fact, the insulating method yields such a high R-value and low air-exchange rate that large spaces help keep the air fresh.

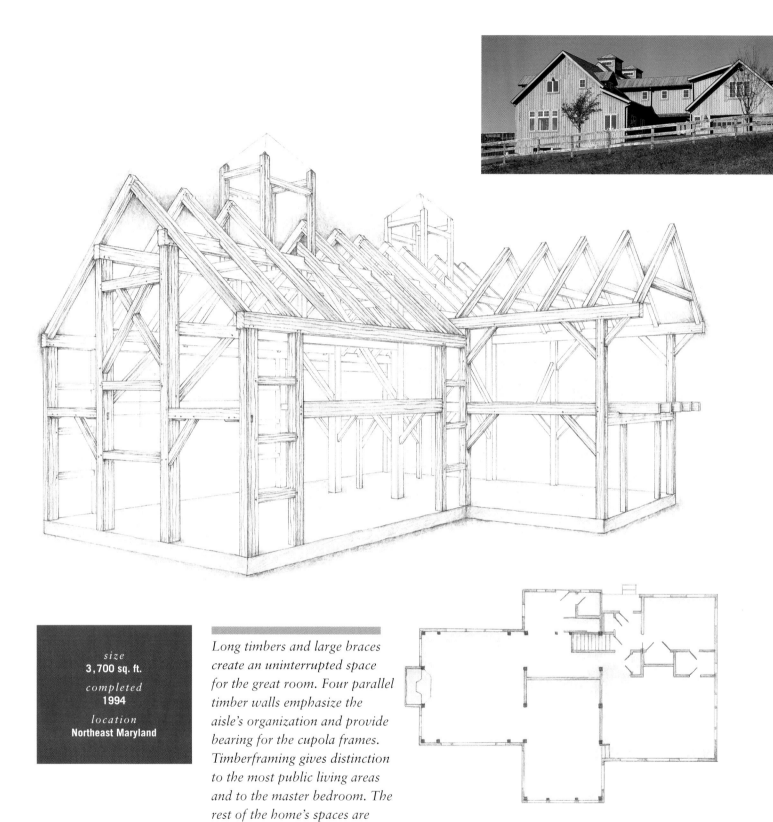

size
3,700 sq. ft.

completed
1994

location
Northeast Maryland

Long timbers and large braces create an uninterrupted space for the great room. Four parallel timber walls emphasize the aisle's organization and provide bearing for the cupola frames. Timberframing gives distinction to the most public living areas and to the master bedroom. The rest of the home's spaces are framed conventionally.

left Country furniture, an old woodworking bench, and salvaged fir timbers make the dining room casual and comfortable. This is the center of domestic activities and the place where the family is most likely to linger in conversation. With so many distractions to pull children and adults into isolation—television, stereo, computer games, telephone—the dining room has replaced the hearth as the place where this family is most likely to gather each day.

Located over the kitchen/dining area in the cross-gabled ell, the master-bedroom suite looks out over the pastoral landscape. Surrounded by light and views, the room is further enhanced by the open timbered ceiling, while the ceiling-height collar ties give a defining break to the volume.

Located at the crossroads of the family room, dining room, and great room, a wormy chestnut island, built with reclaimed barn wood, forms the home's hub. The post-and-beam arrangement distinguishes the spaces and keeps the plan open.

below An architectural synthesis gives the home and barn a strong relationship. Plain lines, vertical siding, metal roofing, and a pair of cupolas help to lean the home's design toward an agricultural motif.

A timberframe

creates (and is created by)

a more settled landscape

than a balloon frame.

—Michael Pollan,
A Place of My Own

On the Water

There is an undiscovered beauty, a divine excellence, just beyond us.
Let us stand on tiptoe, forgetting the nearer things, and grasp what we may.
—Bernard Maybeck, architect

Timber Bonded

Underlying the design of this pair of buildings—a house and a library—was a lofty and elusive idea the owners wanted to see reflected in their home, an idea they described to the designers as "The Circle and The Bond." The circle symbolizes family, community, seasons, and

the owners' day-to-day lives in their inner-island sanctum. This ideal is manifest in the house's circular traffic pattern. Commitment and responsibility are "the bond," represented by the timberframe, with its structural integrity, strength, and legendary endurance.

Appearing to float in the glade, the library was positioned so that one would feel free of moorings, in a place where thought and imagination might sail away.

top and left "Simplicity and integrity are the hardest things to achieve," according to the owners, who acknowledged that their intangible desires were the most elusive. Stripped of artifice and ornament, the home's design is all about scale, symmetry, and proportion.

When you have a home on a quiet and beautiful spot on an island, life is not spent indoors: The wraparound porch gets a lot of use.

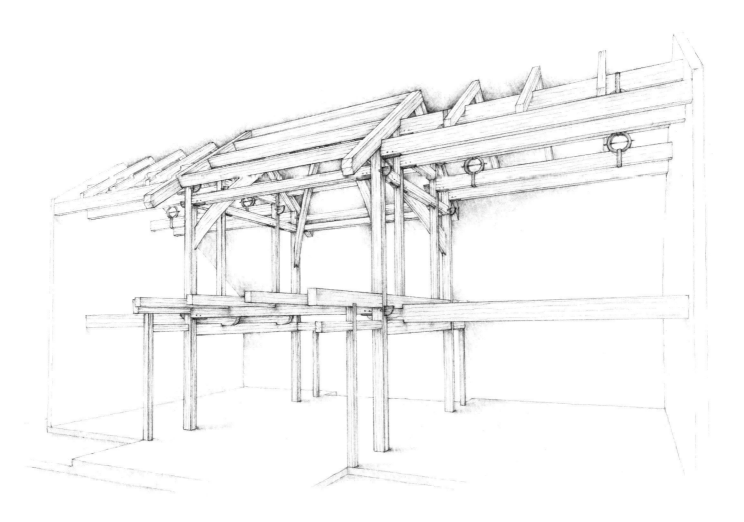

size
3,500 sq. ft.

completed
1993

location
**Nantucket Island,
Massachusetts**

A typical stud frame and timber-frame coexist in the house. The "livable sculpture" (the owner's reference to the timberframe) is entirely inside the exterior walls. With the exception of a couple of notable features, the timber structure is spare and straight-forward. In the central bay, laminated curved timbers create a vaulted feeling under the ridge, while also serving as bracing for the whole structure. In the outer bays, rafters bear on parallel beams that are tied together by iron rings to make the long span.

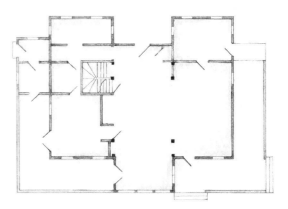

"Ornament is the adoration of the joint," declared architect Louis Kahn, suggesting that it is the connections and transitions between elements and materials that are the natural embellishments of a building. Cherry splines and wedges interplay with fir timbers and a blackened iron bracket to achieve both structure and decoration.

below Contemporary timberframe design and construction is a present-day Arts and Crafts movement, combining good design, traditional building materials, and skilled work. Here, a black slate proscenium celebrates the hearth, and an opening atrium lifts the space beyond its confines.

The master bedroom is open to the bathing area of the bathroom, which enlarges the space while expressing the owners' sense of intimacy. Evidence of the timbers' former life in the Long-Bell mill can be seen in the plugged bolt holes and nail stains. The load-transfer mechanism between the beams is an iron ring with a rod through it, which symbolizes the project's philosophical theme—The Circle and The Bond.

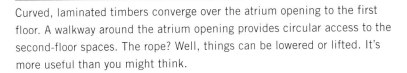

Curved, laminated timbers converge over the atrium opening to the first floor. A walkway around the atrium opening provides circular access to the second-floor spaces. The rope? Well, things can be lowered or lifted. It's more useful than you might think.

below Restraint and simplicity were design and construction watchwords. The design team and building crew were often reminded that less is usually harder to achieve than more. It helped to keep the variety of wood species restricted. Salvaged fir was used for the timberframe; cherry for interior doors, trim, and exposed joint parts; ash for the floors and stairs. The timberframe rests on conventional exterior walls.

Seen from the far side of a bordering cranberry bog, the house rises up and looks outward, toward the horizon, while the library hunkers down, looking inward.

below For the frame timbers, it's a long way from the industrial setting of the Long-Bell mill to the sophisticated and scholarly ambience of this library.

Welcome to the "bog room," the gabled room that overlooks the cranberry bog. From this vantage point, you can see the distant ocean as well as the interior island, with its wildlife, vegetation, gnarled forest, and unique landscape.

Light Hall

In the decades following the Civil War, as industry blossomed along the East Coast and in the Midwest, great factories and mill complexes were constructed at a furious pace. Until the early part of the 20th century, when it was nearly harvested out (and eventually replaced by

steel beams), longleaf southern pine provided the framework for these vast buildings. This lakeside home utilizes the salvage from one of those 19th-century factories. It seems fitting that after 100 years of service the timbers have come to "retire" in a warm, well-lit space where they are cherished by the inhabitants.

Inspired by Japanese timberframe construction, a single natural-form timber, called a taiko beam, is featured in an otherwise rectilinear framework. The beam is intended to give tribute to the trees from which the timbers came.

The timberframe raising, usually accomplished in a single day, is always a dramatic event. At the end of the day, the sculptural form of a timberframe structure stands against the evening sky, almost always inspiring a celebration. During the course of that celebration, someone will inevitably stare wistfully at the frame and say, "It's a shame to cover it up. We should just enclose it in glass." These homeowners weren't kidding.

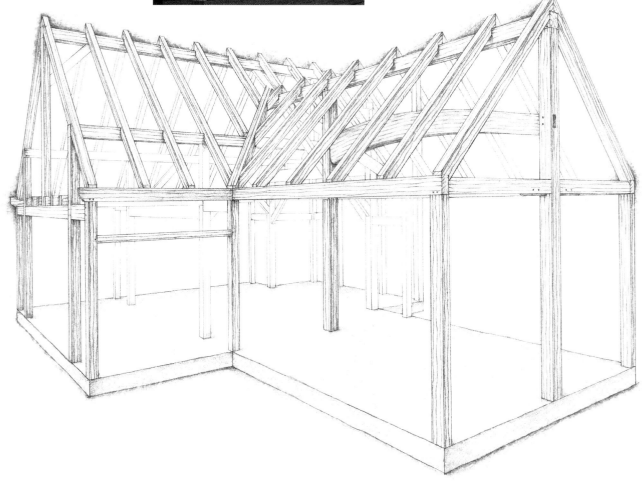

size
6,000 sq. ft.

completed
1995

location
South Carolina

In the medieval tradition, this home is essentially an open timberframe hall, flanked by secondary living spaces. In the entry foyer and adjacent kitchen, a hybrid structure with interior timber posts and ceiling joists connects to stud-framed exterior walls, thereby extending the timberframed look to all the public areas. The two timberframed structures intersect at the roof in valley timbers, where complex joinery is required.

Overlooking the great room, a balcony study enjoys a special perch. The study receives light from the high windows and has a view to the lake. The compound-angle roof connections, visible in the background, require strong timberframe skills.

below In the kitchen, only the ceiling is timbered, but it's enough to give continuity to the space, which overlooks the dining room and the "glass hall." Like the timbers, the pine flooring is also salvaged from an industrial building, this one with a tasty history—the Hershey chocolate factory.

left Although the dining area is open to the great room, a sense of intimacy is achieved by locating it under the balcony. As is common in timberframe design, spatial definitions tend to correspond to zones defined by post and beam placement.

Island Sentinel

A hand-painted sign down by the Nantucket ferry dock used to read: "Boat to America." Nantucket is far enough out in the ocean that it almost feels like foreign territory—a place with its own unique culture and its own way of doing things. In the old days, the island's wealth came from whaling. Seafaring men were pragmatic about design but demanding about construction quality. When the going got rough, they knew what mattered. Today, land values are the real wealth on Nantucket, yet the houses being built there clearly grow out of the whaling heritage. Drawing from that history, this house was built to ship standards, prepared to face the open ocean with integrity and respect.

The "barn" contains spaces for recreation and exercise, as well as a complete guest apartment. Another guestroom is in the pool house, at left. On Nantucket, choosing the exterior siding is easy: shingles are mandatory.

below Carved Douglas fir columns and curved beams define a central arcade through the barn guest quarters. Warmed by the many wooden surfaces, light from the cupola and dormers gives the space a luxurious glow.

One of the first things you discover when you build a nice home in a spectacular setting is that you have more friends than you thought. Guestrooms are needed everywhere. The pool-house guestroom features diamond-oriented Port Orford cedar frame members.

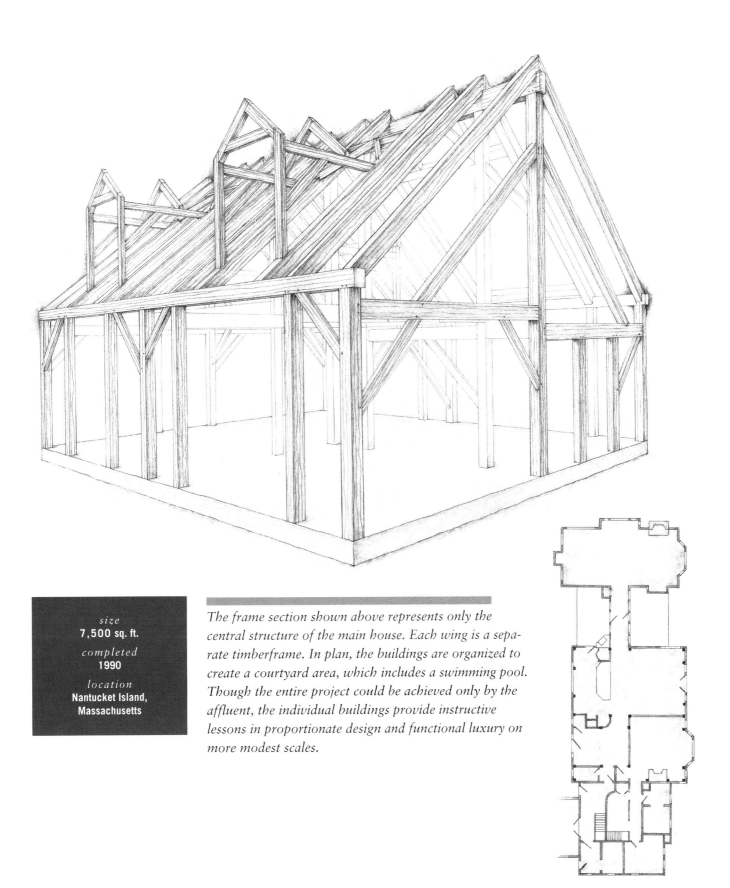

size
7,500 sq. ft.

completed
1990

location
**Nantucket Island,
Massachusetts**

The frame section shown above represents only the central structure of the main house. Each wing is a separate timberframe. In plan, the buildings are organized to create a courtyard area, which includes a swimming pool. Though the entire project could be achieved only by the affluent, the individual buildings provide instructive lessons in proportionate design and functional luxury on more modest scales.

above According to legend, the wives of Nantucket's seafaring men had rooftop decks built so they could look out to sea and watch for the ships to come home. The men didn't always return, and the roof decks came to be known as "widow's walks." Today, the roof deck is simply a place with a great view.

right The grand size of this home is reduced architecturally to cottage scale by connecting a series of small structures. Viewed from the dining area, a timber colonnade leads to the living room (seen at left, above), revealing the unity of the interior spaces despite the apparent exterior separation.

left A paneled, movable wall was built between the kitchen and the dining area. The idea was to allow the kitchen to be closed from the dining room on an occasional basis, dictated by the formality of the function and the mess in the kitchen. Here, the attractive closed panels have won out over the open kitchen.

below A cozy corner by the fireplace in the living room is inspired by the style common to timberframe buildings of the 17th and 18th centuries. Discreet chamfers with decorative stops soften the timber edges. The planed and oiled finish and the high ceilings are qualities more common to contemporary timberframed homes.

Framed with Port Orford cedar timbers, the study has the integrated, crafted feel of a ship captain's galley. One of the truly unique wood species in the world, Port Orford cedar is strong, light, and moisture resistant. It is also reputed to be one of the few woods from which one cannot get a splinter (which is why it has commonly been used for stadium seats).

right A shed dormer lifts a sloping roof enough to make a second-floor bedroom spacious and light-filled. Keeping the rooflines low gives the large home a more modest appearance.

Yellow wallpaper and fabrics heighten the bright outlook of this bedroom, while Port Orford timbers and roof boards lend a warm and elegant rusticity. In conventional framing, opening the space to the rafters would have little aesthetic benefit; in timberframing, roof space is always too compelling to hide.

The stone and wood in construction bear the same relation to architecture as the piano does to the music played upon it.
—Bernard Maybeck, architect

World Apart

Imagine what it would be like to live on your own small island. You get there by boat, which makes living there a real commitment of time and effort. Your 15-acre island is too small to warrant its own vehicle, so walking is the primary mode of transportation, and provisions have to be carried to and from the boat dock. However, such inconveniences are also an advantage. Although the

home is not far from the bustle of southern Connecticut, your island (your world) is a world away. With that seclusion in mind, the owners of this island timberframe built a relaxing home for family and friends that is dedicated to the enjoyment of life at a quieter pace.

Attached firmly to the island rock and built stoutly with stone and timber, the house is resolutely prepared for the tough weather it will surely endure.

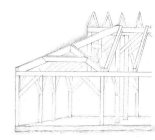

Parallel-chord timber trusses are used to span the length of the great room. The framework adds textured layers to the space and thereby brings the perceived ceiling level down. Spectacular stonework maintains the quality and craft of the timberframe and is the focus of the great room. Porthole windows continue the nautical theme.

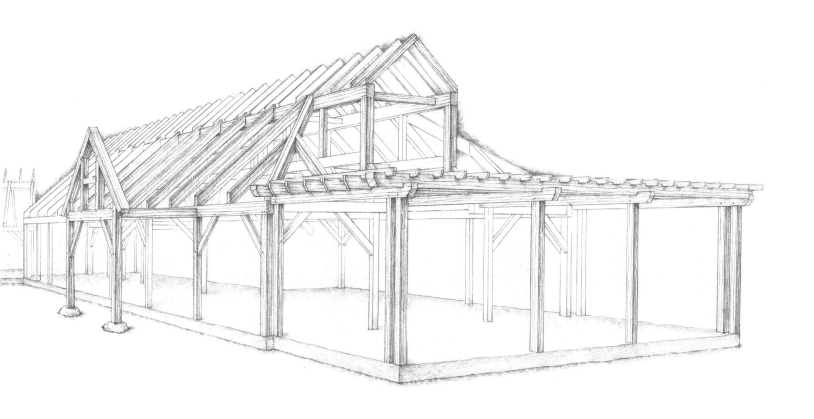

size
3,900 sq. ft.

completed
1996

location
Connecticut

The two upper mid-plates in the main timberframe are 70 ft. long (see p. 99 for a view of one of the continuous plates). They came from the Long-Bell mill, where they were lower chords of 72-ft. trusses. The Port Orford trellis covering makes a semiprotected outdoor space in the pergola and shades the south-facing glass of the great room. In plan, the house is configured to create a wind-buffered courtyard on the entry side.

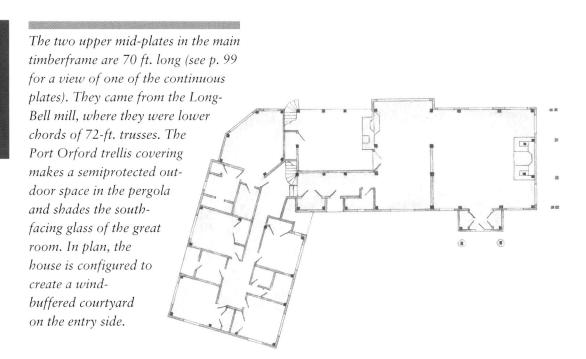

Nestled into the natural terrain and lying low on the horizon, the home is designed to deflect the wind. You can't go wrong with natural building materials and basic building forms.

right Wood species traditional to boat building were used for exterior applications: Port Orford cedar for the timberframing of the entry and pergola, mahogany for the entrance and trim boards. A terrace of stone and the rubble-stone base wall ground the house to its rocky setting.

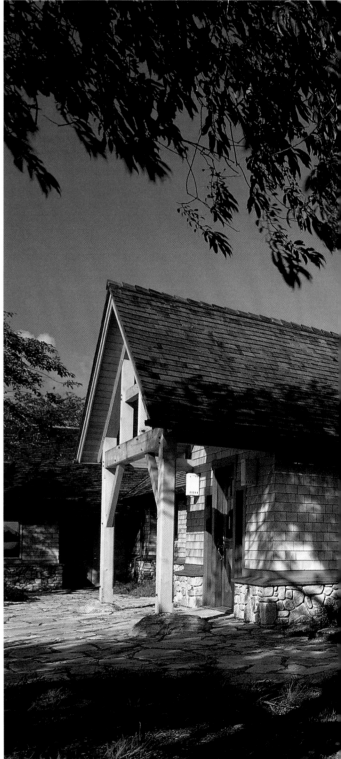

Right Cherry splines and wedges help to make rugged connections in the salvaged fir frame. A huge timber, which had long been waiting a proper use, found a home with owners who welcomed the bold and unusual. The carved date ensures that their wedding anniversary won't easily be forgotten.

Port Orford "staves" wrap the base of the stair and are contrasted by the cherry treads and railing. Salvaged fir balusters and newel post are from the same lot of wood as the timberframe. The glass-lined corridor connects the "dormitory" wing to the great room.

right Located at the crook of the building, the master bedroom has an unusual shape. But whatever might be different about the bedroom pales in comparison to what's different about the bed. Feeling the need for a touch of whimsy, the owners chose a bed that looks like something right out of a Disney movie.

left It's a child's dream space: a loft over the bedroom nearly as large as the bedroom itself. Painted the color of the evening sky, the loft is a perfect place for a pajama party or for a private getaway—an in-home tree fort.

Tree House

Early in the design process, when the owners had only a basic notion of where their house would be built, a large white pine tree stood where the house would go. That's when they came up with the idea of building the house around the tree. The location of the house was later

changed and the tree didn't have to be cut down, but the designers and the owners held onto the idea of using a tree as a central column in the house frame. With some help, a 5-ft.-diameter red-cedar log was found moldering on the forest floor in Oregon and was "transplanted" on the lakeside New Hampshire site.

On the second level, a bridgelike connection ties the outer wings to the octagonal central hall. Diagonal struts to the roof structure are the tree's grafted branches.

right All the timberframe material came from the Long-Bell mill: Nothing else can substitute for the authentic character and patina of time. Three knee braces project to respective beams at one of the corners of the octagon.

It's entirely fitting that Stickley furniture would be used in a timberframe environment. Gustav Stickley was the leading popularizer of the early-20th-century Arts and Crafts movement. Its proponents advocated that the elements of craftsmanship should be made visible in furniture and building—also a central tenet of contemporary timberframe design.

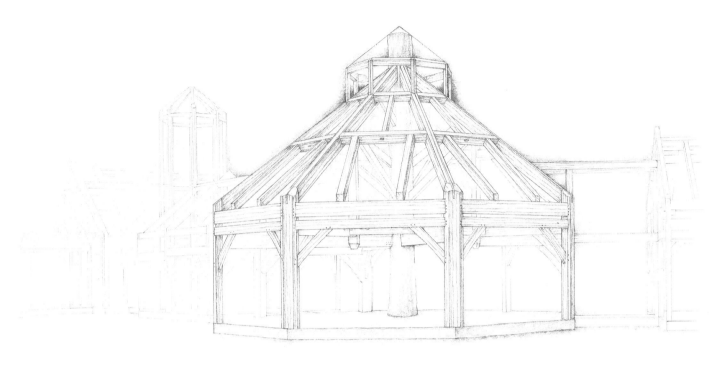

size
5,000 sq. ft.

completed
1993

location
Northern New Hampshire

The basic organization of this home is logical and simple, but it took a great deal of work to draw out the simplicity. An octagon core, which serves as the central public hall, is flanked by gabled wings, which house bedrooms and the kitchen. Only at the garage end does the home become more complicated. A stairway tower leads to the second-floor space, to the basement, and to a guest suite over the garage. It also leads to a great view.

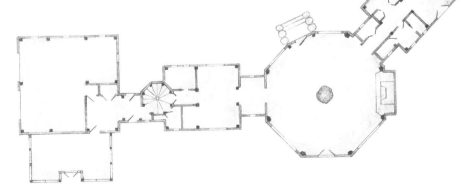

above The lakeside solarium is an elegant transitional space—the place to be on a chilly morning or to take refuge in during New Hampshire's spring bug season. Timberframing and glass is a natural marriage.

right Every effort was made to give the home a low profile to reduce its visibility from the lake. The siding color was chosen to blend with the surrounding tree bark and the roof color with the tree needles and leaves. A perimeter stone base grounds the house to the site. (PHOTO BY BRIAN SMELTZ)

left Fir framing, cherry treads, and Port Orford cedar planking are the wood medley for the stair tower. There's a great view from the top of the tower; the view of the workmanship inside isn't bad either.

below With naturally compatible colors, cherry cabinet frames and cherry flooring are combined with salvaged fir panels and timbers in a partnership of the refined and the rustic. A "ribbing" of arched floor joists accentuates the colonnade leading to the stair tower and the back entry. The carved detail at the post reduction is repeated in the beam and in the oak spline that connects them.

Though the home is large, the scale of individual spaces throughout is reduced to make them more personal and cozy. In timberframe design, there are typically no attics. The area under the roofline is simply too useful and beautiful to be relegated to storage.

right Throughout the home, a limited palette of wood species is used. Salvaged Douglas fir, cherry, and Port Orford cedar interplay in the bathroom but are used in a consistent manner. The granite slabs in the kitchen and bathrooms were cut from the same stone.

above Custom-made doors combine cherry frames with salvaged Douglas fir panels. Leaving the pegs proud of the door surface is a detail derived from the timberframe.

right On the balcony overlooking the great room, the wide dormers create delightful alcove sitting areas where the roofline is otherwise low. Since timberframes are generally enclosed by attaching materials to the outside timber surfaces, the finish work is nearly done when the building has been enclosed.

Three things are to be looked to in a building: that it stand on the right spot; that it be securely founded; that it be successfully executed.
—Goethe

On Rocks

You cannot live by the ocean and not be affected by it. For those who know the ocean well, its majesty and mystery can inspire a lifetime love affair. The owners of this house grew up on this rocky coastal site, and the home's design had as much to do with connecting them to the ocean as it did with protecting them from its elements. They knew this "bony" coast, knew where to put the house and how to capture the best views in the morning and in the evening. They also knew that any structure built by the sea needs to be firmly anchored. So they pinned the foundation to bedrock and built a timberframe.

Winding under a collar beam and king post, the stairway is tightly integrated into the home's design.

Since the owners had spent much of their lives on the land before deciding to build, they had an intimate knowledge about where best to site the house and how to organize the plan to take full advantage of the sun and views.

right Integrated into the main body of the home, the all-season porch is located in one of the corner quadrants as defined by the timberframe. Redwood window and panel units, made from decommissioned wine tanks, fit snugly into the post-and-beam framework.

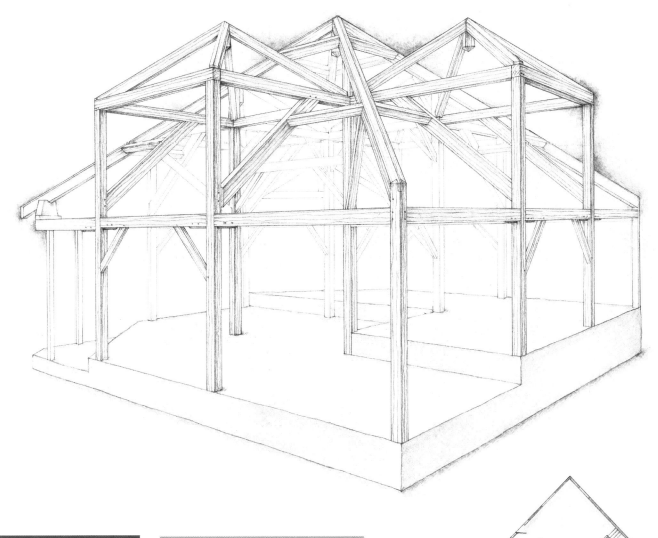

size
3,500 sq. ft.

completed
1993

location
Connecticut

The arrangement of the timberframe logically divides the footprint of the building into nine sections. By combining or separating the spaces as design needs suggested, there were numerous room-layout possibilities in this simple grid. From the interior, the hipped dormers create interesting timberframe pyramidal shapes, but the most important effect of the roof lift is that the dormers increase the second-floor living space.

With 100-year-old salvaged fir timbers locked together with wooden splines and pegs, living in this timberframe space is like living in heirloom furniture. Here, one is surrounded by the elemental effect of wood and stone, in a lofty space where natural light is carried to the core. In such a place, one becomes convinced that the quality of life can be improved by the quality of the space one lives in.

below Loosely defined by the post-and-beam grid, an efficient kitchen space is opened to the other public living areas. Whitewashed ceiling boards maintain the wooden texture of the timber joists and brighten up the area.

right In an unusual orientation, one of the corners of the house is directed toward the owners' favorite view of the open ocean and a distant lighthouse. To allow a corner window placement, a large laminated timber directs building loads into cantilevered beams. The carving honors the Indian chief who "owned" the land before the English came.

It is the nature of any organic building
to grow from its site, come out of the ground into light.
—Frank L. Wright

Glass Bunker

In British Columbia, on the Gulf of Georgia island where this home is built, there is evidence of aboriginal settlement going back 3,000 years. The owners had lived in an old cottage on their land periodically for 20 years before deciding to build a permanent home. They took great interest in the discovery that there had been an ancient settlement on their land, but only when they discovered a 1,000-year-old skeleton not far from the house site did they come to appreciate that their location was sacred. Together with their architect, they determined that, in respect to the ancients who preceded them, they would design their new home to honor the land.

It's almost as if the house footprint was cut from the land with a giant knife so that a surface section could be lifted high enough to fit living spaces beneath. With its sod roof and transparent walls, the house is well camouflaged on its site.

A view through the central corridor shows how the home's spaces cascade downward from the entry, following the slope of the land. Acting like the home's spine, the corridor is the structural and spatial link to the two serpentine outer wings. Custom-laminated curved roof joists, topped by clear panels, light the passageway and extend the connection to the outdoors.

A wooden scarf joint is used to connect timbers to make up one of the two continuous beams that pass through the middle of the house. A central key and interlocking geometry keep the scarf joint tight.

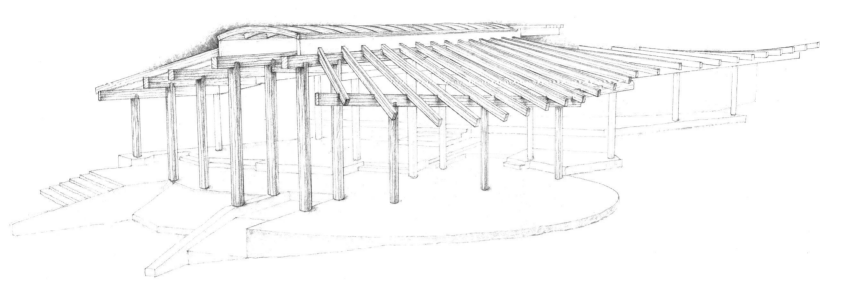

size
3,500 sq. ft.

completed
1994

location
**Gulf of Georgia,
British Columbia, Canada**

Made of salvaged Douglas fir, the timberframe structure posed special challenges because the shape and slope of the building meant that each rafter had to be a different length and pitch. The important design feat was to support the building loads inboard from the free-form glass panels, allowing the building's exterior walls to be liberated from typical configurations and so transparent as to be barely existent.

left The sandstone for the fireplace and chimney was quarried on the island and brought to the site by barge. A master mason custom-cut each stone and created a unique sculptural interplay of color and shape. Light-colored maple flooring helps brighten the interior.

above Looking through the kitchen space and the small study beyond, you can see how the interior plates, supported by peeled logs, allow the rafters to cantilever to the non-load-bearing glass curtain walls.

left To be inside a building designed in a natural form and built with natural materials and to be surrounded by walls of glass panels is essentially to be outside at the same time.

A heavy, wide entrance door is hinged away from the outside edge for better weight control and balance. The door's framework is part of the timberframe. Ingenious wooden hardware does all the work of its metal counterpart except allow the door to be locked. But then, why lock the door in a house of glass?

Privacy is not an issue in a secluded corner of an island, so why not be open to a great view of the gardens even while bathing or showering?

In an ancient time, the Saanich people built a longhouse not far from where this house sits. Part of the inspiration for the home came from that traditional form: The long, linear central corridor is the backbone of the design. A forest of peeled columns is an appropriate reflection of the home's natural setting.

Bras d'Or Ark

At the northeastern end of Nova Scotia lies Cape Breton Island, a remote and beautiful place with a rich heritage and fabulous landscape. The island is nearly cut in half by a large saltwater lagoon, known as Bras d'Or Lake. Before deciding to build a permanent home overlooking the lake, the owner of this house had lived seasonally in a small cabin on the land for many years. Torn between Cape Breton's majesty and the friends and culture of her former cosmopolitan home, she determined to a build a place that would support art and music and draw her many friends for visits.

As if steaming toward the horizon, this home is a "ship" with a mission. Part of the year, the house is given over to music and art education for young people, and occasional professional concerts are open to the community, turning the home into a music hall.

A view down through the dramatic central atrium reveals the home's three levels. Bedrooms are located on the ground level, along with the entry and utility rooms. The primary living spaces are on the second floor, and a loft with the highest outlook to the lake is on the third level. A handmade German kacheloven, or masonry stove, is capable of heating the entire open space.

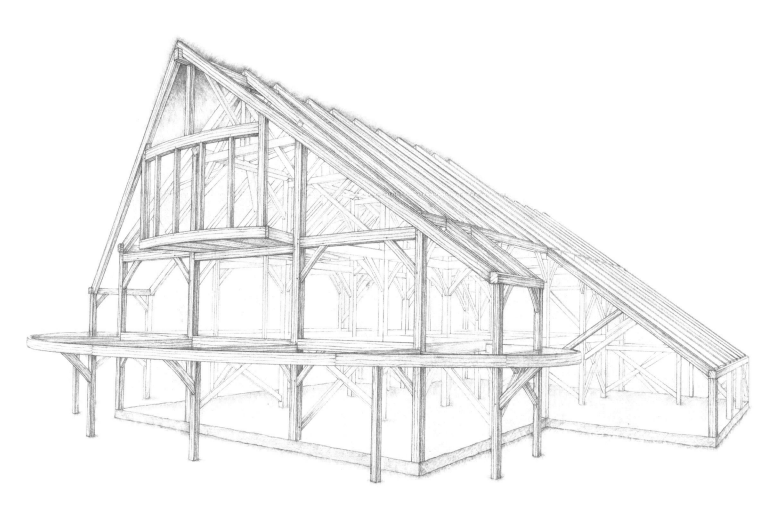

size
6,000 sq. ft.

completed
1990

location
Cape Breton, Nova Scotia, Canada

Because the home is perched on a windy location high above the lake, the timber-frame was heavily braced in preparation for the worst of storms. Cross-bracing was used to bring about the necessary rigidity and was featured in the exposed structure. Double cross-braces in a timber truss span over the atrium (see the photo on the facing page). Laminated timbers give the curved shape to the upper cantilevered balcony and the outside deck.

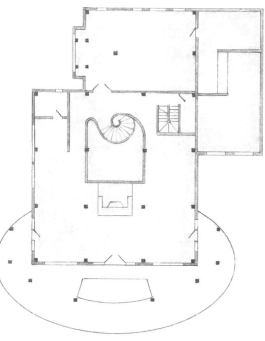

Douglas fir joists radiate outward to support the curved third-floor balcony in the living area. Wooden furniture was made from the same lot of wood as the timberframe to ensure compatibility of color and texture. The tiled corner fireplace is also a very efficient masonry heater and can radiate heat into the space for many hours after the fire is out.

above Redwood light fixtures and the fir timberframe have a harmonious relationship in their celebration of wood and craftsmanship. The beam is secured to the post with a hidden hardwood spline.

right Massive braces high in the roof system help to prepare the building for very high wind conditions, which are common to the building site overlooking the Bras d'Or Lake. Typical of modern timberframe design, the timber configuration is intended to be both structural and sculptural.

left The custom-made walnut dining table is crafted in a style popularized by George Nakashima, which celebrates the natural characteristics of the wood. Owners of timberframe homes find that the crafted quality of the frame tends to set a standard for finishes and furniture.

above Fabric and carpets bring rich colors and textures to this bedroom. Though most of the home's spaces are more restrained, the lavish decorating creates a place with a more luxurious and sensuous feeling. In this case, direct sunlight was not desired, so the bedroom is under the overhung exterior deck.

In the

A house is in many

ways a microcosm

of the landscape;

the landscape explains

the house.

—J. B. Jackson,
landscape theorist

Mountains

Reveal the nature of wood, plaster, brick or stone in your designs.
—Frank Lloyd Wright

High Plains Salvage

It was the perfect place for the owner's new ranch—a lush piece of land on the High Plains, sandwiched between mountain ranges and watered by runoff streams. The challenge was to build a house that wouldn't mar the beautiful landscape. Good ranch buildings are humble and pragmatic, worn by weather and use, rugged and persevering. The owner wanted his ranch to be that way, so it was designed to be simple and low-lying and built mostly with salvaged materials. Using peeled logs, old timbers, rocks from the land, and junk materials gathered from here and there, he built a sturdy, unique, and unaffected house.

If this building is a celebration of stone and wood, the two materials come together at the stairway in a joyous dance. Intermingling in the stair parts are juniper, lodgepole pine, willow, river birch, and heart pine. (PHOTO BY WILL BREWSTER/MERLE ADAMS)

Between 1901 and 1904, a remarkable 12-mile wooden railroad trestle, known as the Lucin Cut-Off, was constructed across the Great Salt Lake. The rafters and posts of this entry cover are salvaged pilings from that hard-worked trestle. The long immersion in salt water preserved the wood, some of which was cut into thin slabs and used to pave the entranceway—where the salt-impregnated slabs actually melt snow.

Were it not for the funky old building materials, the architecture might evoke a more contemporary intention. As it is, with so many construction treasures rescued from the maw of a landfill, the ranch's derivation and age are nicely unsettled.

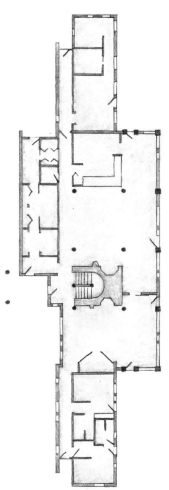

size
4,800 sq. ft.

completed
1997

location
Central Montana

Pretense is not in the vocabulary of ranchers. Function and resource efficiency are more to the point. The frame is constructed with materials "harvested from the industrial forest" and gleaned from loggers' rejects. The structure is a testament to the sustainability of timberframing: The material for framing can come from old buildings and young trees and can live numerous useful lives.

In the soft light of the late-afternoon sun, the home's low profile and natural materials seem very appropriate for the site.

(PHOTO BY WILL BREWSTER/MERLE ADAMS)

left Because the pieces of this timberframe are so natural, crooked, and unique, there had to be trust between the owner, architect, and builder. Many critical decisions were made not on paper, but in the timberframe shop or up in the air, where the pieces were joined.

right Salvaged: The rusted vent hood comes direct from a salvage yard; the door and cabinets are from beer and wine tanks; window frames and other beams are fir from old mill buildings; and the rafters are pilings from the Great Salt Lake railroad trestle.

It's all backwards on the garage. Siding is on the inside, structure on the outside; skeleton and skin are reversed, as they would be on an industrial building used to store bulk material. Salt Lake trestle pilings, mill timbers, and logs too-small-to-saw make up the frame.

left Vlasic pickles used to be made in tanks of cypress and redwood, but the modern tanks are stainless steel. All the siding here once knew pickles well.

Built in the late 1800s, the barn was an anchor for the new house. It defined the place and influenced the style. The barn's construction is a combination of stacked logs and conventional stud framing. Timberframing was not used much in the rapid westward expansion because of the skill and time required.

(PHOTO BY WILL BREWSTER/MERLE ADAMS)

The eye craves lines of strength, evidence of weight and stability…. Hence the lively pleasure we feel…in every architectural device by which the real framework of the structure, inside or out, is allowed to show, or made to serve as ornament.
—John Burroughs, naturalist

Mountain Manor

Not since the Middle Ages have timberframe structures been so expressive. Now, as then, the organization of the timbers within the frame may have additional design intent and structural members may double as carved ornamentation. Compare this home's frame with that

of Little Hall (pp. 210-214) and with the elaborate frames in the town of Lavenham (pp. 215-217) and you'll see more similarities than differences, despite the 600-year age gap. The kind of space created in the modern timberframe, with its soaring volumes and the interplay of parts, is an old idea. The new ideas are light and comfort.

The frame extends from inside the entrance-hall (see photo, right) to the exposed porch section. In this dry, western environment, wood can be exposed to the weather without much risk of decay.

Hammer-beam roof trusses, such as the one in the foreground, were developed in the Middle Ages to make large spans without supporting columns or long timbers. One probable reason for their development was the lack of long timbers—most of Europe's virgin forests had been harvested by the 12th century. Hammer beams were usually ornately carved and molded, making this one a subtle echo of its medieval archetype.

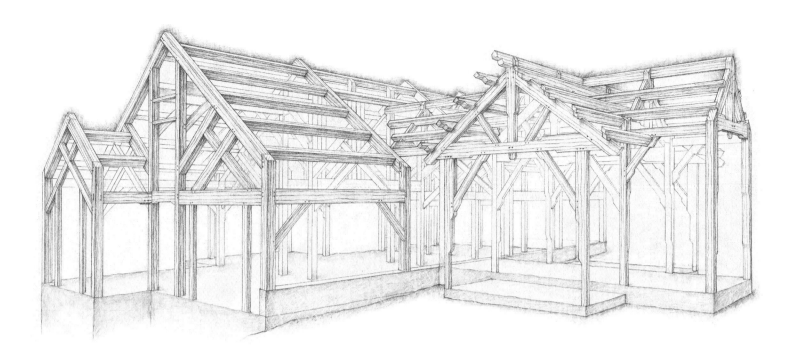

size
5,200 sq. ft.

completed
1992

location
Central Montana

Banked into the side of a hill, the house cascades down with the terrain, from the garage to the main living level. To keep the first-floor level open, the ground floor is used for additional bedrooms and a recreation area. The cross-gabled entry roof timbers do not join at the intersection but rather weave by one another.

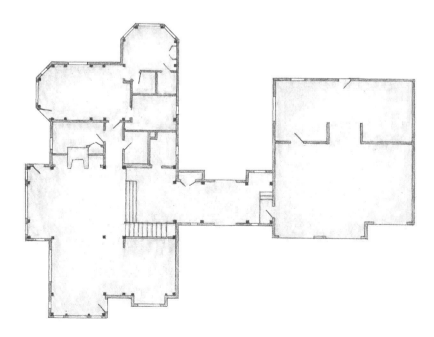

left Built with timber salvaged from the Long-Bell mill, the frame was rich with quality and character from the beginning. Molding and carving details enhance the elegance, while large timbers, extra bracing, and rugged joinery make the structure sturdy enough to withstand the region's snow and wind loads.

Cross-bracing, or scissors bracing, has the effect of bringing the high ceiling down in the dining area, while still leaving the space vaulted. The braces also bring great lateral strength to the structure. The fir roof boards got a light whitewash to brighten their color.

High ceilings do more than enlarge spaces; combined with tall windows, they allow light to penetrate more deeply into the living spaces and open up views of the sky, trees, and mountains. The owner can check out skiing conditions while still in bed. The frame not only holds up the house but also defines zones and frames interior spaces. Even the bed's headboard is directly attached to the posts.

Western Chateau

Tops of buildings are "peaks," the continuous crest is a "ridge," and the low-lying creases between roof slopes are "valleys." Much of the language of architecture grew out of nature, and it follows that good design "learns" from its natural context. In a mountain setting, the appropriate building geometry mimics the terrain. This home is hunkered into a mountainside at nearly 10,000 ft. For many years the site was a pastureland for sheep, and it is still visited more by elk than by people. Though of grand quality, the architectural intent was to blend, because the most magnificent thing about this home is its spectacular setting.

Height restrictions forced second-floor spaces to fit snugly under the roofline, but adding dormers to the individual rooms solved the problem, bringing in light, ventilation, headroom, and emergency egress.

A projecting gable bay extends the great room just enough to allow traffic flow around the furniture, while interior posts anchor and loosely define spatial boundaries. Large interior braces give the lateral strength needed for this wall of glass. The window wall is specifically organized so that each unit fits tightly between the posts and beams of the framework. It's not as simple to achieve as it looks. Either frame-opening dimensions determine custom window sizes or standard window sizes determine opening dimensions—either way there's no room for error.

size
5,600 sq. ft.

completed
1996

location
Southern Colorado

Though the frame encloses a considerable volume, its configuration is straightforward: Common rafters bear on a central wall, extending to exterior plates. Cross-gables and dormers break up the roofline and extend the interior spaces. Rooms and living areas tend to follow the patterns articulated by the frame, but there are no strict rules. The timber positions are fixed, but the defined boundaries are elastic.

In this open arrangement, the kitchen is the command post and a common gathering place. A raised counter provides visual separation and serves as an informal eating bar. The "formal" dining room is directly to the right; the small breakfast table (photo at left) is in the next bay, and the great room is in the bay beyond, defined by the interior posts. From the kitchen, one can survey it all.

Salvaged fir timbers and southern pine flooring are remnants of the early industrial revolution. Recycling wooden building materials is not only responsible but also brings a level of quality not readily available from today's forests. Generally, there is more heartwood in the slow-growing virgin timber, which enhances color, texture, and strength.

Frame details are simply expressed, and the timber edges are only lightly chamfered. This restraint helps to retain the utilitarian heritage of the timbers' earlier industrial life in mill buildings. Metal stains, nail holes, and other "defects" are evidence of this former life.

Exterior decks, typically of poor design and minimal structure, have ruined the appearance of many a fine building. With large limestone pillars and heavily built railings, this home doesn't fall into that trap.

To anyone who has lived in a timberframe home, the typical American bedroom has the look and feel of a shoebox. In this room, by contrast, exposed timbers lend an air of natural beauty and add texture to surfaces and edges. Framed without timbers, the dormer is a spatial counterpoint and this room's lightwell.

left The home's insulating system wraps the timberframe in a thick blanket of unbroken, rigid insulation, so lofty spaces don't lose heat to the upper regions. Iron grilles for the railing came from a dismantled New Orleans building, and an old, refurbished iron light fixture of a similar style continues the period influence. But enough iron and wood: A beautifully crafted, pure white cast fireplace is a bold and contrasting feature.

No space is wasted in good timberframe design. The most interesting areas are often those tucked under sloping rooflines. By organizing storage and counters at the low eaves, it's possible to use all floor space productively and still have full headroom where necessary.

Light and space are the hallmarks of modern timberframe design. This solarium is actually a hallway, which allows natural light and heat to spill into the master bedroom to the left. Windows and doors are simply trimmed with wood at their head and sill, but the sides are trimless with rounded plaster corners.

There is nothing lavish about this space, except that the entire built volume is visible. If exposing it all seems an extravagance, losing it would be a waste. Here, the window and door openings are framed only with plaster, which serves to accentuate the timberframe.

The house is more than a box within which to live; it is a soul activity to be retrieved from the numbness of the world of modern objects.
—Robert Sardello, *Facing the World with Soul*

Chalet West

The archetype of mountain architecture is the chalet. In the alpine regions of Switzerland, Germany, and Austria, broad-gabled buildings with huge sheltering roofs have been the vernacular style for hundreds of years, suggesting that the proper design in the mountains is mountainlike. The owners of this home had traveled extensively in Switzerland and were unequivocal about their desire to bring the chalet style to their mountain site in Montana. But the traditional influence only prevailed on the exterior; the interior was opened to space and light in the manner of contemporary timberframe homes.

The big, overhanging roof protecting an exterior balcony, the carved newels and balusters, and the course-textured siding all add to the chalet's authenticity. What is most authentic, though, is the timberframe, which was the structural system historically used for this type of building.

Structural timbers frame the tiled chimney. While the upper beam doubles as the loft railing, cherry splines pass through the braces and give support to the loft floor where it wraps around the chimney. The ruddy tones of the tile complement the natural color of the salvaged fir timbers and emphasize the pleasingly simple lines of the chimney.

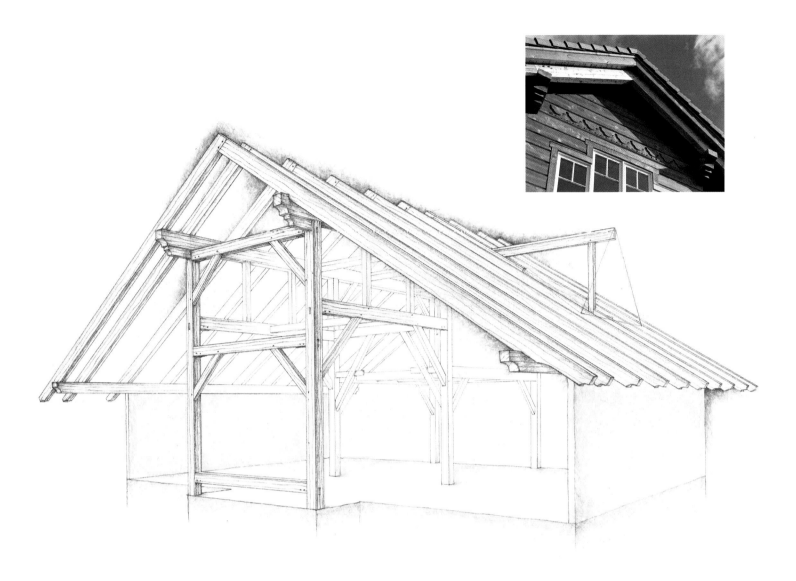

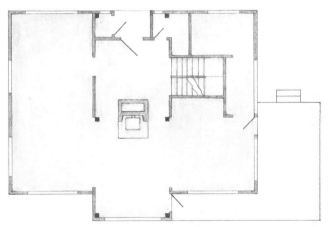

size
3,200 sq. ft.

completed
1995

location
Central Montana

Parallel with the ridgeline, the frame forms three aisle spaces and two perpendicular bays. Within such basic grids, there are numerous organizational possibilities. In this plan, primary areas face the south-side views, a work center is in the second-floor loft, and secondary spaces and bedrooms are on the north side and in a ground-floor level. Exterior walls below the eaves are conventionally framed.

From the loft level, you can see through the upper gable windows to the southern view. Though there isn't a great deal of south-facing glass, there's enough to provide passive solar heating on sunny days.

below The gable's broad face and the projecting roof define the chalet style. Upper timbers extend to support the outermost rafters. Chinked horizontal planks, with an occasional carved layer, make a unique siding with an old-world appearance.

left Because the primary living areas are open, the cherry cabinets and granite countertops play an important interior design role as partitions. Exterior posts and braces can be difficult to work around in a kitchen (upper cabinets and shelving tend to get in the way), so the timber-frame does not extend to the side walls, which are conventional construction.

*Isn't it true that a pleasant house makes winter
more poetic, and doesn't winter add to the poetry of a house?*
—Thomas De Quincey

Snow Barn

Timeless integrity in architecture can be elusive. Passing fancies often prevail, and there's usually an attempt by the designer to achieve too much. As naturalist John Burroughs suggested, the biggest pitfall of all is lack of humility: "Pride, when it is conscious of itself, is death to the nobly beautiful, whether in dress, manners, equipage,

or house-building." The owners of this home wanted a solid, comfortable, low-maintenance dwelling, with an uncomplicated design. Timberframe barns are a significant part of Vermont's farming heritage, so a timberframe barn home was a simple and appropriate solution.

Classic New England barns have consistent shapes for a simple reason: Farmers aren't big on pretense. Make a house like a barn and the style is practical and frugal.

(PHOTOS BY TEDD BENSON/BRIAN SMELTZ)

Kitchen and dining areas are defined by their open timber spaces. The timberframe is constructed with Port Orford cedar, a wood revered by Japanese temple builders for its beauty, strength, weather resistance, and workability. Hardwood splines, used to strengthen the connections, are left exposed to celebrate the joints.

size
2,500 sq. ft.

completed
1993

location
Northwest Vermont

"*The lesson for the ages from three-aisled structures is that columns articulate space in a way that makes people feel comfortable making and remaking walls and rooms anchored to the columns*" (Stewart Brand, How Buildings Learn). *Four simple bents, or frame cross sections, divide the interior spaces into a series of defined spaces with more potentials than restraints. This elementary grid has been the basis for countless unique homes throughout the world. Inspired by barn interiors, there are several ceiling heights.*

Sunlight streams through the space from tall doors and high windows on the opposite wall. In the background, expressive through-tenon joints for joists double as support shelves for laminated stair stringers.

above right A loft over the high-ceilinged living room serves as a home office and study area. The master bedroom is on a lower level at the far end.

left The craft of timberframing is all about strong, tight-fitting joints. Here, walnut wedges secure a tenon (and add contrast to the light-colored, soft-textured Port Orford cedar).

right Although barnlike from the outside, the interior is rich with timber details and a variety of spaces. In the entryway, the ceiling height drops to the lowest of its three levels. Wedged stair treads echo the timberframe joinery.

Light, God's eldest daughter, is a principal beauty in a building.
—Thomas Fuller, English cleric

Sun Lodge

In the mountains of southern Colorado, there is little precedent for residential architecture. For the Native Americans, the elevation was too high for settlement. And when the miners came for gold and silver, all their energy was directed into the earth; little is left of what they built above ground. Those who design and build in this region must therefore be aware that the building archetypes for the future are being created today. With the ever-present sun, the magnificent views, and the rugged terrain as inspiration, and a timberframe at its core, this home's design is a bold and appropriate stride in the right direction.

Cutting into a hillside site created a protected area for the building, which is oriented to capture the panoramic views to the south. The north-side entry faces onto an interior courtyard.

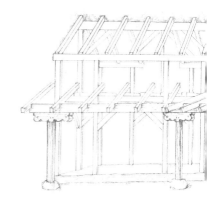

More than just a vaulted space, the great room is a stunning hall of light. High windows and lofty spaces allow the light to penetrate deep into the home. Roof extensions and conventionally framed bays not only make cozy alcoves, but their projected sides also bring morning and evening sunlight into the great room space.

size
4,950 sq. ft.

completed
1992

location
Southwest Colorado

Three independent frames, with conventionally framed connections and bay extensions, make up the building's primary structure. Salvaged fir timbers were used in the central frame, while the outer wings are made with new fir. The porch timbers were sandblasted to make them look older. The round columns, which once were pillars in the Boston College ice arena, are longleaf southern pine. Porch plates, rafters, and column capitals are salvaged fir.

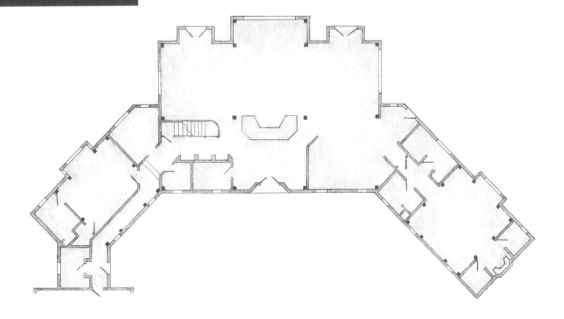

An oak spline, connecting to a beam on the opposite side, is extended to add strength to the joint. Its carved end is both decorative and structural.

left A well-built stone chimney brings with it the rugged textures and mottled coloration that are the real stuff of the earth; as with natural timber, imitation always fails.

The Southwest design influence is evident in the extended log joists, the arched cavities between them, the rounded corners, the geometric pattern on the balusters, and the rustic post and capital detail on the porch. Timberframing is an elemental and adaptable building system. It doesn't dictate design style.

Soft-textured timbers and the planked ceiling create an elaborate wooden canopy over the white plaster walls and the light-filled space of the master bedroom. It's hard to imagine the proportions of the room working without the timbers, which add texture and lower the volume to a comfortable level.

Timbers anchor and frame an extended bay, which is this bedroom's natural light and ventilation source. It's also an inviting window seat for reading, soaking in a little sunlight, or just enjoying the view.

left A second-floor bedroom fits snugly under the sloping roof. There is a both a sense of enclosure and spaciousness as the room rises from the low eaves to the ridge beam. A gable dormer lifts the exterior wall high enough for full-height windows and creates added headroom.

(PHOTO BY TEDD BENSON)

right Twig shutters and a bentwood sink base are fine examples of the owners' inspired decorating abilities. While an interior decorator can help, interior design is one area where homeowners can really make a difference. It's what makes the home personal.

Mining Hall

You don't have to go far up into the mountains west of Denver before you come upon the last built vestiges of the region's mining era. The first mining-town homes were often nothing more than canvas tents; most of those made of wood were temporary shacks, little better than

wooden tents. The best-quality construction was reserved for the mine buildings themselves, which were rugged structures built with heavy timbers and logs. This Colorado home was inspired by that sturdy and hopeful mining architecture, not by the houses that went up during the gold rush. Its other significant influence is the modern timberframe hall.

Among its many functions, an entryway needs to serve as a transition, to give a sense of the home and its organization without revealing it all.

(PHOTOS BY TEDD BENSON)

A successful home design has small nooks and alcoves to augment the larger living spaces. If convenient to the kitchen, a cozy eating corner is likely to see more use than a large dining room, simply because its intimate scale is appealing for small groups or for solo dining. Salvaged fir ceiling timbers extend to conventionally framed walls.

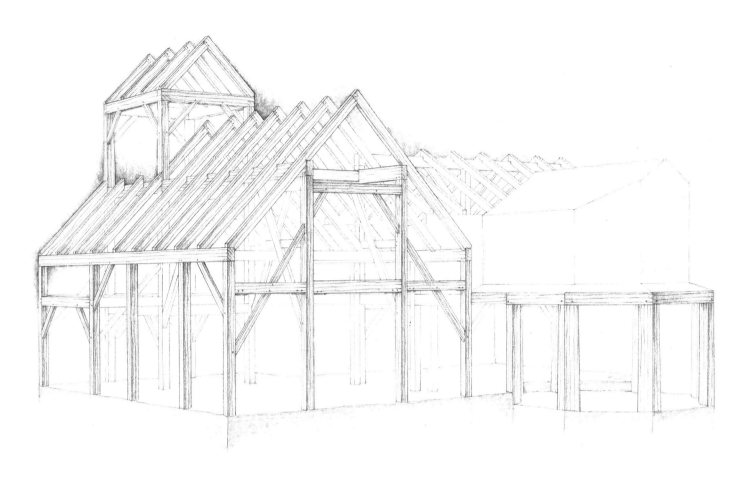

size
4,400 sq. ft.

completed
1994

location
Colorado

Employing several hybrid construction techniques and anchored by the open-timber-roofed great room, this home uses timberframing to good advantage. One wing of the house has roof and floor construction tied into conventionally framed walls, and the room over the octagon dining room has no timberframing. Salvaged fir timbers, mostly from the Long-Bell mill, are used in the primary living areas and left exposed.

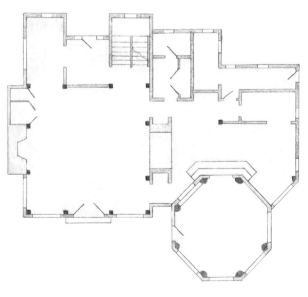

Large salvaged timbers support the elevated bridge, which also creates a convenient port cochere for unloading people or groceries before parking the car. A heavy oak door and thick, natural-edged siding express the rugged simplicity of the design.

left Clearly inspired by the design of mine buildings common to this region, the home has a utilitarian appearance and delightful features. The tower room is designed after a mine building element called a "tipple." The bridge connects the main house to guest bedrooms above the garage.

right Dining can be both rustic and luxurious, when the room is spacious and the view is glorious. Pine log posts encircle the room, echoing the forest setting. Two large, recycled beams orient the room and define a space for the table. The south-facing room receives sunlight throughout the day.

In Addition

A comfortable house is a great source of happiness. It ranks immediately after health and a good conscience.

—Sydney Smith, English cleric

Architecture is the reaching out for the truth.
—Louis Kahn, architect

Master's Wing

Norm Abram has had a significant influence on the shaping of our homes. Through his many years as the featured master builder on PBS's *This Old House*, he has become "America's carpenter." In this age of television hype and spin, what is most unusual about Norm is that he is the genuine article: a talented wood craftsman, a knowledgeable builder, and a good spokesman for the woodworking and building trades. It was therefore an honor and a special challenge to be asked to build the timberframe ell for his home. The resulting structure fused fine woodworking with frame carpentry, just as Norm does.

Details: Hand-wrought ironwork and cherry wedges fasten together a confluence of post and truss.

right Sitka spruce was used for the trusses, rafters, ridge, and purlins; Port Orford cedar for the wall plates and posts. Scale and proportion are enhanced by the arched trusses, which seem to pull the ceiling down toward earth.

below Between two television shows and numerous public appearances, Norm's a busy guy. That he still attempts to complete his own finish work is remarkable; that he isn't finished yet should be gratifying to other professional builders with unfinished houses.

The timberframe ell lies between the main house and the garage. It encloses the kitchen and the family room. A wall of south-facing glass, topped by small transom windows, brings light deep into the open space. (PHOTO BY TEDD BENSON)

Abundant Farm

For more than 30 years, the owner lived in the original
1773 timberframe home known locally as "Poor Farm"
(see pp. 224-229). She always loved
the old house, but it wasn't perfect.
Spaces were small and dark, which
accentuated winter's dreary effect.
Also, the house is located at the
dead end of a miles-long dirt road.
It gets lonely out there. So the
owner decided to build an addition
that would do three things: maintain the architectural and structural standards of the old house;
give her a spacious, sunlit room to
brighten her days; and create a
place for large and frequent parties.

Carved posts at either end of the space
help formalize the timberframe's effect
on the room.

above Adding to a stately old colonial home risked harming the building's architectural beauty and integrity. This addition successfully honors the traditional design without disturbing its classic lines. The cutaway corner subtracts space but adds light and interest.

right A truss spans the large, open room. To match the color and texture of the exposed timbers in the old home, the timberframe was built with salvaged Douglas fir, left with a rough-sawn surface, and stained with a brew of vinegar and rusty nails.

One must remember that there is a difference between a house, a place of shelter, and a home, a place where all your affections are centered.
—Lucy Maynard Simon, *The Domestic Service*

Trumpet Haven

Lives lived large sometimes need large spaces. Overlooking a private pond on a wooded site in northern South Carolina, this country home, unpretentious on the exterior, opens to a large central hall that gives evidence

of big passions and varied interests. The owners are both well-known physicians, people with much experience and accomplishment but with nothing to prove. Their home tells stories of their love of plants, art, and books; of an outdoorsman and many travels; and especially of a love of music and brass musical instruments. It also tells of their love of timber and wood.

The timberframe is built with a mix of species: Salvaged southern pine is predominant, but there is also Douglas fir, Sitka spruce, salvaged chestnut, and incense cedar from the site.

below A 200-year-old hand-hewn chestnut beam still works hard here, supporting a major roof load from the two posts, while throughout the space a world-class collection of trumpets and other brass instruments makes the room a veritable museum.

Valley timbers and a ridge beam converge. Because of the compound angles involved, cutting and laying out joints like these is demanding.

Only the central hall is timber-framed in this Southern "Up Country" style home. The outer service and bedroom wings are framed conventionally. As is often the case in timberframe building, the exterior gives no clue to the dramatic interior.

*...buildings give us a way to leave
a lasting mark, to conduct a conversation across the generations.*
—Michael Pollan, *A Place of My Own*

Barn Anew

The owners had lived comfortably in their 18th-century home for many years, but they knew it was not quite complete. A barn had once been connected to the house in the classic New England style, and it had always seemed to the owners that without it the house was missing a piece of essential architecture. When they sold their business and retired, they found themselves in a position to build a new home of their dreams. But after much soul-searching, they decided to stay in the old house, replace the missing barn, and build into it the additional spaces they wanted.

It couldn't be simpler—a thick oak beam, a glass bowl, and a faucet against a black backdrop of counter and floor—but it's an artistic touch that turns this utility/bath room into something special.

right Antique Italian furniture has been renovated to become a part of the guest quarters' galley kitchen. The loft provides an additional sitting or sleeping area and connects to the owners' workshop. The shaped pattern of the railing boards is in the Swedish Gustavian style.

The table and "eckbank" (corner bench) were custom-made in Switzerland out of old wood (built-in corners like these are common in Swiss homes). The timberframe is oak, roof boards are white pine, and the floorboards are salvaged southern pine.

The barn banks into a natural slope. Seen from the back side, its upper level is used as an exercise area that contains an outside spa; the guest quarters are to the left.

*Should not every apartment in which man dwells be lofty enough
to create some obscurity overhead, where
flickering shadows may play at evening above the rafters?*
—Henry David Thoreau

Timber Sanctum

It was inevitable: A timber engineer who spends his days designing timberframes wanted more than vicarious pleasure from his work. He would build a timberframe building for himself and his family. Before the situation got dangerous, a class was organized to teach timberframing lessons to paying students, who at the same time would

build a new great-room addition to the engineer's existing home. More than 30 students from around the country spent a week cutting and shaping a variety of unique joints on numerous kinds of timber to bring a long-held dream to reality.

Projecting beams at the gables give a hint of what lies behind the unassuming facade. Master stonework is a feature of both the exterior and interior.

above Sitka spruce and laminated fir braces connect to a salvaged fir post. Timber joinery was precisely cut by a group of first-time timber-framing students.

left It's only one room, but it contains salvaged Douglas fir, southern pine, and spruce; redwood rafters reclaimed from wine-tank staves; laminated fir cutoffs from a church truss project; fresh-sawn Port Orford cedar and eastern spruce from the site; oak pegs and splines; and wooden nuts and bolts.

A home is not a mere transient shelter; its essence lies in its permanence, in its capacity of accretion and solidification, in its quality of representing, in all its details, the personalities of the people who live in it.
—H. L. Mencken

Thatched Nest

The timberframe tradition in North America has its roots in England, so it seems fitting that this book should end in that country with this 20th-century barn addition. After more than 300 years of development and a modern timberframe resurgence, we return to Suffolk, East Anglia, the area of England the first colonists came from, with a sample of modern American timberframing.

Though the finish on the timbers is more polished, the timberframe still reveals its English roots and appears quite at home under a traditional thatched roof.

Adding the thatched barn to the property took some doing. The beauty of the English countryside reflects good taste, but it is also carefully controlled. The pink cottage is 18th century; the thatched barn is new.

Thatch, coupled with modern waterproofing techniques, is an effective roofing material, and in England thatching is still a relevant craft. The barn was designed to give the owners a larger space for parties and family gatherings, while also serving as guest quarters and as a service building for the in-ground pool.

right Bedrooms are located at either end of the second floor, tucked under the gabled roof. In modern timberframe design, it is typical to incorporate all the enclosed volume into the living area. White plastered wall and ceiling surfaces help to make the smaller spaces feel light and airy.

left A spacious living room is located in the end of the barn. Douglas fir timbers and a simple, pine-planked ceiling bring warmth to the room. A bridge connects the two second-floor bedrooms.

Epilogue:
In the Past

We shape our

buildings; thereafter

they shape us.

—Winston Churchill

left By the time the virgin forests of the West Coast
were set upon by ax and saw, timberframing had already been replaced
by balloon framing throughout North America.

This soaring room was originally open to the lower level, and smoke from a firepit escaped through exposed roof tiles and gable openings, blackening the timberframe, including its meticulously carved crownpost. The floor and chimney were added in the 1500s.

The timberframe homes featured in this book reflect the technology and taste of our times. Their design and decoration arose from a general evolution of lifestyle and our expectations of comfort as much as from the effect of their geographic setting, climate, and the building system itself. It has always been so. The story of timberframe building is intertwined with the development of the many societies in which it was practiced.

Continuously occupied for over 600 years, Little Hall absorbed numerous renovations and additions but never lost its medieval essence. It has witnessed a good portion of England's history and weathered vast changes in technology and taste. The yellow ochre paint color is a naturally occurring pigment found in the East Anglia area.

Timberframing dates back several thousand years and has played a major role in the history of residential construction throughout the world. By the Middle Ages, timberframing had become the predominant method of wood frame building. The whole history from prehistoric beginnings to the fabulous luxuries we live with today is too broad and diverse to tell here, so we'll narrow our focus to the roots of the modern timberframe home in North America. We'll trace its evolution from England to North America by visiting three homes—all still in use—whose dates of construction span from the late Middle Ages to the pre-Revolutionary War years in the United States. The newest of the three is 225 years old.

Little Hall

The early history of the home called "Little Hall" is sketchy. It was built in the late Middle Ages in the town of Lavenham, in southwest Suffolk County, England. At the time, few public records were kept, but there is some evidence that the first wing of Little Hall was built in the late 1300s for William Causton, a clothmaker, and that the central hall and the opposite wing were added in the mid-15th century. To give this time period some perspective, recall that Europe was still reeling from the loss of a third of the population inflicted by the Black Death; the Bible had just been translated into English (1382) but wouldn't be in circulation for another 150 years; England's Hundred Years' War with France still raged; the Wars of the Roses were about to get

In the 15th century, this room was an open hall, with no flooring, fireplace, glazed windows, or second floor level. There was a dirt floor and, approximately where the table is now placed, a firepit for cooking and heat. Because many people probably lived and worked in this single room, neither privacy nor comfort were considerations.

under way (1455-1485), which would establish the House of Tudor; England was still Catholic; Christopher Columbus had not yet sailed to America; and Chaucer, not Shakespeare, was the bard of England. Little Hall, like many timberframe buildings from that period, has been continuously occupied for over 600 years.

From around 1350 to 1550, Lavenham was a thriving market town and an important center of the cloth industry in England. Even the Wars of the Roses did not dampen its surging prosperity. There was an enormous demand for the blue woolen cloth ("Lavenham Blues") for which Lavenham had become renowned throughout Europe, causing a building boom of homes large and small, several guildhalls, inns, pubs, and a magnificent parish church (see the photos on pp. 216-217). Over the centuries, Lavenham's wealth waned, but its ties to the cloth industry held fast, even during several hundred years of deep recession. As a result, there was little building in Lavenham from the late-17th century through the 19th century, making it one of the most unspoiled medieval towns in Europe. Centuries of prosperity built a village full of magnificent timber-framed buildings and centuries of poverty kept them from being ruined by changing fashion.

By the time Little Hall was built, timberframing was highly evolved. Not only were the craftsmen able to mold and shape large timbers into structures of furniture quality and beauty, but they also had developed sophisticated knowledge of timber engineering. Medieval timberframers were responsible for the magnificent open timber roofs of numerous cathedrals and manor halls, in which grand spanning roof systems were also highly decorated with intricate carvings on the timber surfaces. One of the more

Hall houses of the 15th century had standardized layouts. This room is called the "solar" and was located above the buttery and store in one of the cross wings. It was the bedroom for the master's family.

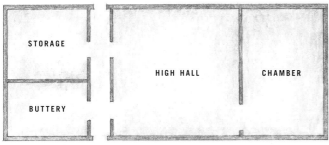

Little Hall's timberframe space was rather majestic, with its high roof, gothic arched braces, and carved crown post. The closely spaced timbers are all oak, but the trees from which most of the timbers were hewn were small and gnarled since England's forests were quite depleted by that time. Hall house plans of the period rarely varied much from the typical plan of two cross-wings sandwiching the central "high hall."

notable examples is London's Westminster Hall, built in the mid-1300s, which has multibracketed roof trusses that span 68 ft. and remains today as a marvel of timber engineering.

A "HALL HOUSE" OF OAK, WATTLE, AND DAUB

The materials used for construction were few and basic. Timberframes were made of oak. Nothing else was considered suitable. Ironically, although the timberframers were at a pinnacle of accomplishment, the wood they had available was of relatively poor quality. England's forest resources had been significantly depleted by the time of Little Hall's construction, which meant that suitable timbers often had to be shipped from distant places and framers had to use pieces that were twisted and crooked. The spaces between the timbers of the frame were filled with either bricks or "wattle and daub." Wattle was a woven lattice of withes, which was covered by layers of daub, consisting of clay, lime, horsehair and cow dung. Roofing was thatch or tile. And in the early 15th century, that's all there was to the building.

Until the end of the 16th century, the "hall house" was a standard for domestic dwellings. The hall itself was just a large open room with exposed rafters. Typically, but not always, two wings flanked the hall. On one side were two utility rooms adjacent to an entry and through-passage; on the other was a chamber used for sleeping. Before later modifications and additions, Little Hall was a slight variation of this basic layout.

The difference between the wealthy and the poor was in the size and height of the halls. We can assume that the Causton family, at least initially, had only modest means. At approximately 18 ft. by 22 ft., "Little Hall" is definitely small. More substantial halls are often 24 ft. by 40 ft., or larger. Still, Little

Hall's timberframe structure is of good quality. The elaborate work on the crown post, tie beam, and arched brackets reveals the work of excellent timber-framers.

But the quality of the craftsmanship belies the kind of life people would have lived in Little Hall. The reason the hall was originally open is that there

The oldest wing of Little Hall is the exposed-timber building to the left, dating from the 1380s. The central hall and the far wing were built early in the 1400s, probably replacing earlier construction.

Both of these Lavenham buildings reveal typical medieval timberframe building style, with the overhung jetties and the "wattle and daub" infill between limewashed oak timbers. The upper building is a guildhall, built in the early 1500s and showing the skill of the craftsmen who added intricate sculptural carvings to the timberframe structure.

wasn't a chimney. Smoke from an open fire on a dirt floor had to find escape through crevices in the roof tiles or openings in the high gables. Despite this natural ventilation, the small Little Hall must have been terribly smoky. Even today, the roof timbers are black with soot (see the photo on p. 211), or "full sooty" as Chaucer described the poor widow's hall in the Nun's Priest Tale.

In such conditions, comfort and privacy, as we think of them today, were not even considered. Life in the hall was like camping out in an open barn. It was the place for all things—cooking, eating, working, socializing, and sleeping—and was often the home of an entire extended family along with "hirelings," often 25 people or more. In the winter, the room would have been ghastly cold and very dark, since the windows were usually small and unglazed. A simple table and a couple of benches may have been the only furniture. Beds were usually just crude sacks stuffed with straw. During the daylight hours, the same room was used as a workplace. No doubt, handlooms were brought out in Little Hall and the other furniture was moved aside.

The rough and crude lifestyle seems now to mix oddly with the sophistication and beauty of the buildings. The open timberframe hall was as elegant as a chapel, yet the meticulously carved timbers became rimed with soot and the inhabitants lived like animals on its floor. With the great amount of ingenuity that was clearly available, we have to believe that, although a greater physical comfort was attainable, it just wasn't considered necessary. Author Witold Rybczynski concludes that the medieval person had a much less developed sense of self-consciousness than we do today. What was important in life was external and public, not internal and personal. Or as Sir Walter Scott said, "Magnificence there was, with some rude attempt at taste; but of comfort there was little, and, being unknown, it was unmissed."

A PLACE FOR THE SMOKE TO GO OUT

During the 16th century, this smoky, dirty lifestyle changed. With the advent of the brick chimney, the open hall began to disappear and Little Hall was no exception. Around 1550 a chimney was installed, and, because the open condition was no longer necessary, a floor was inserted. With less volume and fewer drafts, the fireplace probably provided reasonable heat and the added floor surely eased life. At about the same time, the floor was paved with brick and glazing was installed in the windows. By the beginning of the 17th century, the hearth had become the center of domestic life and furniture became more stationary, plentiful, and comfortable.

Constructed in the late 1500s, these Lavenham buildings were built with chimneys, which ended the era of the open hall. Buildings such as these were probably the prototypes for the early colonists.

Around 1650, an addition was extended from the backside of the north wing of Little Hall, greatly increasing the living area and suggesting improved economics for the Causton family. But only 100 years later, the cloth industry in Lavenham collapsed and Little Hall was divided into six tenements. During the next 150 years, like most buildings in Lavenham, Little Hall's framed overhangs were filled in and its exposed timbers were covered with plaster as a part of Georgian modernization. It remained in that condition until the Gayer-Anderson twin brothers purchased it in 1924. The brothers brought modern services to the building while also restoring Little Hall to its medieval appearance. After their deaths, it was left as a hostel for Art Students and later purchased by its current owners, the Suffolk Preservation Society.

Alden Spoke

Quite forgetful of self, and full of the praise of his rival / Archly the maiden smiled, and, with eyes overrunning with laughter / Said, in a tremulous voice, "Why don't you speak for yourself, John?" Thus, according to Longfellow's poetic fable, Priscilla Mullins gave John Alden a clue that she was more interested in the messenger than the message he felt obliged to deliver on behalf of Captain Miles Standish. There is more myth than reality in "The Courtship of Miles Standish," but it is fact that Priscilla and John's romance was true and legend-worthy, if only for its context. They met on the Mayflower in 1620 during its voyage from England to America and were the first newlyweds in Plymouth Colony.

John and Priscilla had long and successful lives together. While John was a lifelong leader in colony government, Priscilla managed their household and bore 11 children. Together they built a house and developed property that was destined to be home to generations of Aldens into the 20th century. John and Priscilla were fortunate just to survive. Due to inadequate housing during the first brutal New England winter, fully one-half of the 102 Mayflower passengers died, including Priscilla Mullins' parents and brother. If anybody came with illusions of Utopia, that first winter surely stripped those dreams to the bone. Because decent housing was an essential element in the society they hoped to create, timber-framing played a leading role in the building of early America.

Until the early 20th century, this home was continuously occupied by the Alden family. Over the years, they made few alterations to the original construction, but they did add the paneling and plaster.

Built in 1653, the Alden house is the only remaining house built by a Mayflower Pilgrim. By that time, the hearth was the heart of the home and a modicum of thermal comfort was expected. Clapboards replaced wattle and daub infill due to the harsh New England climate. (PHOTO BY TEDD BENSON)

Most of the colonists came from the southeastern counties of England, where timberframing was by far the predominant building system for residential dwellings. John Alden himself presumably came from the town of Harwich, which is about 30 miles from Lavenham. Clearly, the building traditions and evolutions that built and changed Little Hall were essentially the knowledge that informed America's first house builders. In fact, what the colonists built in early America was nearly identical in structure and style to those they left in England. Little Hall of the early 17th century, with its recent renovation of a hearth and second floor, was basically the dream home in the New World.

One great advantage the Colonial timber-framers had over their peers in England was the abundant virgin forests. Tall, straight trees allowed them to hew timbers to the building's length and height, making the timberframes stiffer and stronger. For example, this nicely shaped and chamfered gunstock post passes from the roof to the foundation.

John and Priscilla's first home in Plymouth was a one-room, windowless timberframed hut, probably with thatched roof and wattle-and-daub chimney. This home may have had wattle-and-daub infilling like those of England, but it was soon discovered that the climate was too harsh for that system. Governor Bradford reported after a winter storm that it "caused much daubing of our houses to fall down." Soon it was the norm to cover the timber-frame with lapped "weatherboards," which we now refer to as clapboards.

ADAPTING TO THE NEW WORLD

In 1627, the Aldens were granted land "on the other side of the bay," which they farmed seasonally before moving there permanently in 1632 along with many other settlers. This was the beginning of Duxborrough town, now known as Duxbury. It was also the beginning of a new era of independence for the colonists. Life in the Plymouth Colony was rigidly communal. It was basically an enclosed fort, with small building lots within and an acre for each family to garden outside of the palisaded village. In Duxbury the Aldens had 100 acres and were free to build a family estate and to prosper by dint of their own "severe effort."

As John and Priscilla contemplated building on their new land in Duxbury, they had been in New England for 12 years. Even by that time, some distinct differences between timberframe homebuilding in England and Early America had begun to emerge.

First, there were the climactic differences that had all but eliminated the wattle-and-daub infilling between timbers. It wasn't just that the winters were far colder and stormier than in England, the summers were also hotter. In Plymouth, England, the average yearly temperature variation between high and

By the late 17th century, there was a higher standard for personal comfort and a greater sensitivity regarding privacy. Alden's 1653 house almost certainly had a private bedchamber for John and Priscilla, which was rare only a century earlier.

The second-floor workroom, located above the kitchen in the rear of the house, reveals how the entire house was originally finished. Vertical pine planking was attached to the outside of the timberframe, serving as a nailbase for the exterior clapboards and as interior finish.

low is 63°F, while in Plymouth, Massachusetts, it is 110°F. Along with the temperature variance comes a significant change in relative humidity, which causes wood and other materials to shrink and swell and also induces rot more quickly. It wasn't long before John Alden and the other colonists learned that it was more practical to cover the timberframe with a protective, weatherproof skin of overlapped boards and to refrain from exposing frame members to the weather at eave and gable roof overhangs. They

were also learning that the shallow foundations (1-ft. to 2-ft. depth) common in England did not suffice when the soil freezes as far down as 4 ft.

BUILDING WITH BETTER MATERIALS AND METHODS

Two significant differences in the New World allowed carpenters to make some structural improvements over the Old World timberframes. Oak was still the wood of choice, as it had been in England, but the trees of the virgin New England forests grew tall and straight, while English carpenters struggled to make decent buildings out of depleted and scraggly forest resources.

In the New World, designs began to include timbers that spanned the entire length, width, and height of the building, rather than short timbers punctuated by beams and posts. In New England, although professionals were hired to design and prepare the timbers, raisings were generally accomplished by community work parties.

Early colonial homes were direct derivatives of the late medieval architecture in England—but stripped of ornamentation. Puritan settlers, in fact, disdained distinctions of class and strove for homes that were merely "faire and pleasant." "Faire" implied durable and well ordered, which was manifest in massive timberframes with little elaboration and exteriors that were honest expressions of the interior layout and the structural requirements. A building such as Lavenham's Guildhall would not have been appreciated in the colonies.

The first home built by the Aldens in Duxbury was a significant improvement over the primitive hut they left at Plymouth, but it was still small—only 10½ ft. by 38 ft.—and of a fairly typical "long house" configuration. It is easy to imagine that shelter was only one of the pressing matters facing the Aldens on their new land. Beside the necessities of farming and putting up food, John Alden also had to help others in the building of their homes, and because he was the assistant to the governor, he had to travel frequently. His house had three rooms in the main floor: a large central kitchen and work room, a "buttery" at one end, and a small bedroom on the other. The second floor might have had an open loft

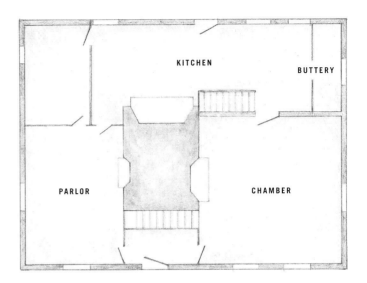

The floor plan has two parts. The back section is actually the Alden's 1628 house moved to the new foundation and added to the new (1653) hall and parlor layout. This two room configuration, with the added rear kitchen, is very common in early colonial building.

or a couple of bedrooms. For John, Priscilla, and as many as nine children, this was home.

BUILDING ON A NEW FOUNDATION

The Aldens prospered on their farm and eventually were able to build a larger home. It was usual to add to the original house as needs and means increased, but John Alden did it differently. He found a new site and constructed a proper foundation there. Then he moved the old house to that location and incorporated it into the construction of the larger home. The first home had been built on a thin stone foundation, which inevitably led to a freezing cold, constantly undulating floor and rapidly rotting sills. This was a practical move. He salvaged the earlier construction, while also building an enduring home that he could pass on to future generations. The new home was completed in 1653.

Like most 17th-century American homes, the Alden house timberframe was intended to be visible to the home's interior. The timbers were carefully finished, with chamfered edges and elegant shaping of gunstocked posts. The frame was enclosed with vertical pine planking, which served as both exterior sheathing and interior finish. Flooring was wide pine boards. In the middle of the home was a huge brick masonry mass that housed four fireplaces, three on the first floor and one on the second.

The room layout of the new house was simple. Four rooms were added to the home, two up and two down. The primary room downstairs was the hall, which was the most important room in the home, as it had been before the advent of the chimney in medieval England. This was the center of family activities. The parlor, on the side of the chimney, was reserved for more formal occasions, was used less frequently, and therefore was smaller. Upstairs were bedrooms, referred to as "chambers," and designated as hall chamber and parlor chamber. When John Alden's family was there, these chambers were packed with beds and children. John and Priscilla lived out their lives in that house and were married for 60 years. The home he built has been owned only by generations of Aldens since. Along the way, the interior of the house was plastered, painted, and paneled, but the house is otherwise much the same as it was when it was built by a man and a woman who arrived on the Mayflower to an unknown world with hopes, dreams, and young love.

Poor Farm

When Nathaniel Sleeper built his central New Hampshire home in 1773, the landscape of colonial America had changed considerably from the time John Alden's house was built a century earlier. The population had swelled to nearly 1.5 million, and the land was being quickly carved up as the settlers pushed north, south, and west. As the land was settled, the dense forests were cleared for farmland. Nature was being tamed and the "errand into the wilderness" seemed less forbidding. Homes were no longer seen as a fortress against a hostile environment.

Although the English were still predominant, there were now immigrants from nearly all the European countries. This great amalgamation was bringing with it changes in architecture and construction methodology. Especially influential were the Dutch in the New York area and the Germans in Pennsylvania, both of whom came to America with long histories of timberframing and who brought advanced skills and unique perspectives.

There was also a war brewing. In Sleeper's neighborhood, there had been a revolt against the "Pine Tree Law" just a year before his house was built. This law, which had been in effect for 50 years, decreed that all pine trees over 12 in. in diameter were reserved for the Royal Navy. There were severe penalties for owners who cut pine trees on their own land. This insidious law was particularly irksome in

When the Revolutionary War began, this home was three years old. One imagines the owners, gathered with neighbors and kin around this very fireplace, planning their participation in the raging battles in Massachusetts. (PHOTO BY TEDD BENSON/BRIAN SMELTZ)

In the 18th century, the most important room in the house was still called the "hall," long after it had lost its medieval appearance and purpose. In this hall, the timber-frame has been completely covered with plaster and paneling and its low ceiling makes it easier to heat, despite the lack of insulation. (PHOTO BY TEDD BENSON/BRIAN SMELTZ)

places where pine was the most abundant species and was needed for construction. When sheriffs tried to enforce the law by arresting and jailing a flagrant violator, 30 men with blackened faces arrived to free the prisoner and the hapless law officers were tarred, feathered, and "ridden on a rail."

There doesn't appear to be any pine in the Sleeper timberframe, but plenty was used for the paneling, sheathing, and flooring, much of it well over 12 in. wide. Perhaps Sleeper thought he was safe from scrutiny in his remote location or perhaps he was flaunting his offense. Whichever the case, his sympathies were not with the British. The New Hampshire Minutemen were among the first to join the fight at Concord and Lexington, and it is likely that Nathaniel and his brother Benjamin were among them. They both fought through the war, even though the battles never came to New Hampshire soil, and Nathaniel's wartime rifle still hangs above the fireplace in his home.

LOOKING OUT ON A NEW WORLD

Sleeper's home is remarkably similar to the John Alden house. This is not just coincidence. Home designs were quite vernacular in a time when security was in the land. Barns were more important than houses and often were built first. The house was a practical necessity and not a place to squander excessive time and resources. Like the Alden house, Sleeper built a three-bay timberframe structure with

a huge central chimney flanked by a hall and parlor in the front and a kitchen in the rear. Also like the Alden house, an ell was added later, expanding the kitchen, pantry, and storage. The fireplaces were shallower than the Aldens' and provided more heat. People now expected their homes to provide warmth and more physical comfort.

The later improvements of the Alden house had become common expectations during construction of the Sleeper home and were built into it. Walls were plastered, and there was elegant raised paneling at the hearths. Good-quality glass was more widely available, and the Sleeper house incorporated as much as possible. Large windows had become very popular not only because they let in light, but also because it was now possible to see through the glass (as a result of developments in the glass manufacturing process). It appears that Sleeper even positioned the house to capture a 180° panoramic view of lakes and hills, an idea that would not have meant much in the earlier era when houses typically had only a few panes of distorted blown glass.

Like many early homes, Poor Farm faces south for passive solar benefits. It also captures a 180° panoramic view. By the time this home was built, visibility through glass had been greatly improved, and glass had also become much less expensive, which led to more and larger windows.

(PHOTO BY TEDD BENSON/BRIAN SMELTZ)

In the back room of the house, the timbers are still exposed but the rough finish and minimal shaping suggest that the timberframe was not intended to have aesthetic value in the home. With that attitude prevailing, timberframing was doomed to be replaced by any method that would be quicker and cheaper.

(PHOTO BY TEDD BENSON/BRIAN SMELTZ)

When the Sleeper house was built, "house-joiners," or timberframers, were very much in demand. It is likely that it was difficult to find an experienced carpenter in the far reaches of New Hampshire. Still, the Sleeper timberframe shows professional skill, with excellent hewing of the major timbers and tight joinery throughout. Most of the smaller timbers were sawn, giving evidence that there must have been a sawmill nearby. But the overall appearance of the frame suggests that much of it was not intended to be visible, but rather covered with plaster. This subtle change in the function of the timberframe was the beginning of the end of the dominance of timberframing. When the timberframe was no longer appreciated for its aesthetic value, it was doomed to be replaced by any system that required less time and skill.

After Nathaniel Sleeper's death in 1821, the house received almost no maintenance or attention for more than 100 years. That it survived is remarkable. It is yet another story of impoverishment as the basis for preservation. In the middle 1800s, there was a mass exodus from New England with the discovery of the flat, rich, rockless soil of the Midwest. In 1849, the Sleeper homestead was sold to the town to be used as the Poor Farm. It served that purpose for nearly 40 years and subsequently received little attention from its owners until after World War II. It exists now with its original construction and finishes nearly perfectly preserved—yet another testament to the durability of well-crafted timberframe construction.

It is truly remarkable how close the Sleeper floor plan is to the Alden plan. Many variations were possible, but function was what really mattered, not innovation.

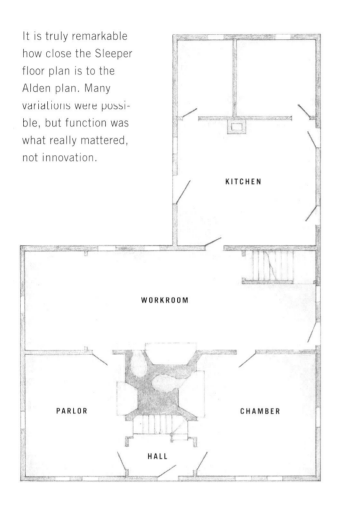

The second-floor parlor chamber is finished in very much the same style as the original Alden house. When the home was built, using these wide pine paneling boards was illegal.
(PHOTO BY TEDD BENSON/BRIAN SMELTZ)

In Conclusion

In the Victorian era, most of the old timberframe homes were renovated to remove evidence of the structure. Gunstock corner posts were chopped away; massive summer beams were encased in plaster; the building's bones were deemed unsightly. This decorative "cleansing" was coincident with the development of the wire nail, the circular saw mill, and the rapid expansion westward. Homes needed to be built quickly and timberframing was simply an obstacle to progress. Stud framing soon took over and by the late 1800s had totally displaced timberframing in residential construction. Aside from a few isolated religious communities, timberframing was discarded in North America until its resurgence in the early 1970s.

Acknowledgments

I express my deepest gratitude to the people whose hard work, patient assistance, encouragement, and tolerance made this book possible: Jamie Salomon and Norm Hersom for the excellent photography and the good times we had traveling together; Sheila Albere, for her diligent and professional assistance and her good cheer throughout the project; Randall Walter, for producing the three-dimensional frame drawings from inadequate information; Kathy Bray for turning these drawings into works of art; Brian Smeltz, for his good advice on many matters and for helping with photography; Marilyn Taggart (one of three wonderful sisters), for helping with the research about the Long-Bell mill; John Baker, of Beeton and Lennard, Ltd., for guiding me around England and leading me to Lavenham; and Renée Attew, for her hospitality during our visit to Little Hall.

I am also very thankful to the staff at Taunton Press. They are a fine team of talented people who are capable of wresting a good book from even the most bullheaded author. I am in their debt: Peter Chapman, Steve Culpepper, Carol Kasper, Carol Singer, and Paula Schlosser.

The true heroes of this book are the people who built the wonderful houses and additions that are featured in these pages. I thank all of them for their faith and vision and for allowing us to appreciate their creations. They are: Norm Abram, Connie and Kurt Bierkan, Hope Birsh and Stephen Plakatoris, Dr. Andrea Branch and David Elliman, Ben Brungraber, P. E. and Joel Feldman, Kevin and Mary Grace Burke, Charles and Peggy Carswell, Harriet T. Cope, Lucy and Stewart Evans, Marla Felcher and Max Bazerman, Austin and Leslie Furst, Robert and Sally Gillespie, Dennis and Eunice Guentzel, Sandra and John Hedlund, Rob and Scottie Held, Dr. Rusty and Kim Hilliard, Michael and Lisa Kittredge, Dr. and Mrs. Steven Leyland, Chuck and Marcia Raches, Michael and Maureen Ruettgers, Tom and Lucy Rutherford, Peter and Carol Sellon, Drew and Lynn Thorburn, Trailsend Ranch, Drs. Joe and Joella Utley, Thomas H. Wake, Angelika Weller, Lynn and Barbara Wickwire, and Gregory Whitehead and Lillian Lennox Whitehead.

I want to extend special thanks to the people in my company, affectionately known as the Beam Team. They spoil me every day with their dedication to the highest standards of product, service, and teamwork. I just cheer. I especially need to acknowledge and thank our design and engineering team for their splendid creations: Ben Brungraber, Tom Goldschmid, Bill Holtz, Brian Smeltz, and Randall Walter. The alumni designers who worked on some of these homes are Tafi Brown, Liz Calabrese, Paul Irwin, AnnMarie Rizzuto, and Andrea Warchaizer.

And finally, my wife, Christine, for her support, encouragement, tolerance, and love. You have my love too, and I will now stop using the dining room table as my office.

Credits

In the Country

Prairie Prospect
(pp. 18-25)
ARCHITECT/DESIGNER
Bensonwood Homes
224 Pratt Road
Alstead, NH 03602
(603) 835-6391
www.bensonwood.com
BUILDER
Johnson & Assoc., Inc.
Lanny Johnson
612 W. 25th Street
Kearney, NE 68847
(308) 234-5983
TIMBERFRAMER
Benson Woodworking Co., Inc.
224 Pratt Road
Alstead, NH 03602
(603) 835-6391

Home Spirit *(pp. 26-31)*
ARCHITECT/DESIGNER
Bensonwood Homes
BUILDER
Owner
TIMBERFRAMER
Benson Woodworking

Craftsman's Way
(pp. 32-37)
ARCHITECT/DESIGNER
The Johnson Partnership
P.O. Box 51133
Seattle, WA 98115
(206) 523-1618
BUILDER
Cascade Joinery
1330 E. Hemmi Road
Everson, WA 98247
(360) 398-8013
TIMBERFRAMER
Cascade Joinery

England West *(pp. 38-45)*
ARCHITECT/DESIGNER
Bensonwood Homes
BUILDER
Benson Woodworking
TIMBERFRAMER
Benson Woodworking

Concord Barn *(pp. 46-51)*
ARCHITECT/DESIGNER
Design Associates
432 Columbia Street
Cambridge, MA 02141
(617) 661-9082
BUILDER
Silva Brothers Construction
41 Locust Street
Reading, MA 01867
(781) 944-3462
TIMBERFRAMER
Timber Framers Guild
of North America
P.O. Box 60, Becket, MA 01223
(888) 453-0879
www.tfguild.org

Vaulted Dwelling
(pp. 52-57)
ARCHITECT/DESIGNER
Bensonwood Homes
BUILDER
Murphy & Furman, Inc.
P.O. Box 2483,
Framingham, MA 01703
(508) 879-5534
TIMBERFRAMER
Benson Woodworking

Time Crafted *(pp. 58-67)*
ARCHITECT/DESIGNER
Dewing and Schmid
146 Mount Auburn Street
Cambridge, MA 02138
(617) 876-0066
BUILDER
J. W. Adams Construction, Inc.
142 Farmers Cliff Road
Concord, MA 01742
(508) 371-0007
TIMBERFRAMER
Benson Woodworking

Horse Haven *(pp. 68-73)*
ARCHITECT/DESIGNER
Bensonwood Homes
BUILDER
Blackhorse Construction
4402 Crompton Court
White Hall, MD 21161
(410) 557-9319
TIMBERFRAMER
Benson Woodworking

On the Water

Timber Bonded
(pp. 76-83)
ARCHITECT/DESIGNER
Scott Wood, in association with
Bensonwood Homes
BUILDER
Benson Woodworking
TIMBERFRAMER
Benson Woodworking

Light Hall *(pp. 84-89)*
ARCHITECT/DESIGNER
Hollis-Crocker Architects, P.C.
1855 E. Main Street, Suite 400
Spartanburg, GA 29307
(864) 583-5296
BUILDER
Foys Construction, Denton Foy
138 Glen Eagles Road
Campobella, SC 29322
(864) 468-5460
TIMBERFRAMER
Benson Woodworking

Island Sentinel
(pp. 90-97)
ARCHITECT/DESIGNER
Milton Rowland and Associates
15 Commercial Wharf
Nantucket, MA 02554
(508) 228-2044

BUILDER
Hill Construction Co., Inc.
4 South Mill Street
Nantucket, MA 02554
(508) 228-3360
TIMBERFRAMER
Benson Woodworking

World Apart *(pp. 98-107)*
ARCHITECT/DESIGNER
Bensonwood Homes
BUILDER
Benson Woodworking,
in association with Sound
Builders, Andy Drakos
517 High Street
Mystic, CT 06355
(860) 536-8276
TIMBERFRAMER
Benson Woodworking

Tree House *(pp. 108-115)*
ARCHITECT/DESIGNER
Bensonwood Homes
BUILDER
Benson Woodworking, in associa-
tion with John McLean, Builder
P.O. Box 1285
Ashland, NH 03217
(603)968-3254; and Richard
Benton, Jr., Builder
154 Schoolhouse Road
Center Sandwich, NH 03227
(603)284-6860
TIMBERFRAMER
Benson Woodworking

On Rocks *(pp. 116-121)*
ARCHITECT/DESIGNER
Bensonwood Homes
BUILDER
Blaise Donnelly
46 Lakeside Road
Lakeside, CT 06758
(860) 567-3716
TIMBERFRAMER
Benson Woodworking

Glass Bunker
(pp. 122-129)
ARCHITECT/DESIGNER
Blue Sky Design
Hornby Island, British Columbia
Canada V0R 1Z0
(250) 335-0115
BUILDER
Pacific Wind Construction,
Alan Fletcher, Victoria, B.C.
(250) 388-9143
Tony Meek (interior)
Saltspring Island, B.C.
(250) 746-7257
TIMBERFRAMER
Cascade Joinery

Bras d'Or Ark
(pp. 130-137)
ARCHITECT/DESIGNER
Bensonwood Homes, in associa-
tion with Ron LeLievre, AIA
28 Prospect Street
New Glasgow, Nova Scotia
Canada B2H 4B6
BUILDER
Kavic Construction Co., Ltd.
Gary Wilneff
28 Gordon Avenue
Sydney, Nova Scotia
Canada B1M 1A6
TIMBERFRAMER
Benson Woodworking

In the Mountains

High Plains Salvage
(pp. 140-147)
ARCHITECT/DESIGNER
Big Timberworks
216 N. Church Street
Bozeman, MT 59715
(406) 763-4639
BUILDER
Big Timberworks
TIMBERFRAMER
Big Timberworks

Mountain Manor
(pp. 148-153)
ARCHITECT/DESIGNER
Bensonwood Homes
BUILDER
Tolefson Builders
624 S. 3rd Street
Bozeman, MT 59715
(406) 582-8952
TIMBERFRAMER
Benson Woodworking

Western Chateau
(pp. 154-163)
ARCHITECT/DESIGNER
Bensonwood Homes
BUILDER
Kent Building Co.
307 Society Drive, Suite B
Telluride, CO 81435
(970) 728-3381
TIMBERFRAMER
Benson Woodworking

Chalet West
(pp. 164-169)
ARCHITECT/DESIGNER
Bensonwood Homes
BUILDER
Tolefson Builders
TIMBERFRAMER
Benson Woodworking

Snow Barn *(pp. 170-175)*
ARCHITECT/DESIGNER
Bensonwood Homes
BUILDER
Sisler Builders, Inc.
1885 Barnes Hill Road
Waterbury, VT 05677
(802) 244-5672
TIMBERFRAMER
Benson Woodworking

Sun Lodge *(pp. 176-185)*
ARCHITECT/DESIGNER
Bensonwood Homes
BUILDER
Kent Building Co.
TIMBERFRAMER
Benson Woodworking, in associa-
tion with Timbercraft Homes
85 Martin Road
Port Townsend, WA 98368
(360) 385-3051

Mining Hall
(pp. 186-191)
ARCHITECT/DESIGNER
Bensonwood Homes
BUILDER
RCK Builders, Inc.
P.O. Box 3192
Evergreen, CO 80439
(303) 674-0350
TIMBERFRAMER
Benson Woodworking

In Addition

Master's Wing
(pp. 194-195)
ARCHITECT/DESIGNER
Design Associates
BUILDER
Norm Abram
TIMBERFRAMER
Benson Woodworking

Abundant Farm
(pp. 196-197)
ARCHITECT/DESIGNER
Steven Hale Associates
12 Everett Road
Jamaica Plains, MA 02130
(617) 522-9999
BUILDER
Robert Kennedy
New Boston, MA
TIMBERFRAMER
Benson Woodworking

Trumpet Haven
(pp. 198-199)
ARCHITECT/DESIGNER
Hollis-Crocker Architects P.C.
BUILDER
Daniel Owens Construction
25 Dug Hill Road
Landrum, SC 29356
(864) 457-4305
TIMBERFRAMER
Benson Woodworking

Barn Anew
(pp. 200-201)
ARCHITECT/DESIGNER
Durrant Design
P.O. Box 278
Harvard, MA 01451
(978) 456-3695
BUILDER
T. H. Smith Building and
Remodeling
4 Squareshire Road
Sterling, MA 01564
(978) 365-3611
TIMBERFRAMER
Benson Woodworking

Timber Sanctum
(pp. 202-203)
ARCHITECT/DESIGNER
Bensonwood Homes
BUILDER
Michael Nerrie
RR1, Box 545
Walpole, NH 03608
(603) 756-4179
TIMBERFRAMER
Benson Woodworking

Thatched Nest
(pp. 204-207)
ARCHITECT/DESIGNER
Bensonwood Homes
BUILDER
Beeton and Lennard Ltd.
Shottisham, Woodbridge
Suffolk 1P12 3ET, England
TIMBERFRAMER
Benson Woodworking

*The historical photos on
pp. 16-17, 74-75, 138-139, 192-
193, and 208-209 are courtesy
the Darius Kinsey Collection,
Whatcom Museum of History &
Art, Bellingham, Washington.*

Visit the author's website at:
www.bensonwood.com.